ARTHURIAN STUDIES XXIII

Publications of the Institute of Germanic Studies
Volume 44

GOTTFRIED VON STRASSBURG
AND THE MEDIEVAL TRISTAN LEGEND

ARTHURIAN STUDIES
ISSN 0261–9814

Publications of the Institute of Germanic Studies
ISSN 0076–0811

GOTTFRIED VON STRASSBURG AND THE MEDIEVAL TRISTAN LEGEND

PAPERS FROM
AN ANGLO-NORTH AMERICAN SYMPOSIUM

EDITED WITH AN INTRODUCTION BY

Adrian Stevens and Roy Wisbey

D. S. BREWER
THE INSTITUTE OF GERMANIC STUDIES

First published 1990 by
D.S. Brewer, Cambridge, and by
The Institute of Germanic Studies, University of London

D.S. Brewer is an imprint of Boydell & Brewer Ltd
PO Box 9, Woodbridge, Suffolk IP12 3DF
and of Boydell & Brewer Inc.
PO Box 41026, Rochester, NY 14604, USA

D.S. Brewer ISBN 0 85991 294 9
The Institute of Germanic Studies ISBN 0 85457 146 9

British Library Cataloguing in Publication Data

Gottfried von Strassburg and the medieval Tristan legend : papers from an
Anglo-North American symposium. – (Arthurian studies, ISSN 0261-9814;23).
– (Publications of the Institute of Germanic Studies, ISSN 0076-0811;v.44).
1. Poetry in German. Gottfried, von Strassburg I. Stevens, Adrian II. Wisbey, Roy
III. University of London *Institute of Germanic Studies* IV. Series
831.21
ISBN 0-85991-294-9   D. S. Brewer
ISBN 0-85457-146-9   Institute of Germanic Studies

Library of Congress Cataloging-in-Publication Data

Gottfried von Strassburg and the medieval Tristan legend : papers from an Anglo-North
American symposium / edited with an introduction by Adrian Stevens and Roy
Wisbey.
        p.   cm. – (Arthurian studies, ISSN 0261-9814 ; 23)
(Publications of the Institute of Germanic Studies, ISSN 0076-0811 ; v. 44)
    Symposium held at the Institute of Germanic Studies, London, Mar. 24-26, 1986.
    ISBN 0-85991-294-9 (Brewer) – ISBN 0-85457-146-9 (IGS)
    1. Gottfried, von Strassburg, 13th cent. Tristan – Congresses.
2. Tristan (Legendary character) – Romances – History and criticism – Congresses.
3. Arthurian romances – History and criticism – Congresses. I. Stevens, Adrian.
II. Wisbey, R. A. (Roy Albert), 1929– . III. University of London. Institute of
Germanic Studies. IV. Series. V. Series: Publications (University of London.
Institute of Germanic Studies) ; 44.
PT1526.G68 1990
831'.2-dc20   90-36411

This publication is printed on acid-free paper

Printed in Great Britain by
St Edmundsbury Press, Bury St Edmunds, Suffolk

Contents

Illustrations

Abbreviations

ADA	Anzeiger für Deutsches Altertum und Deutsche Literatur
BGDSLT	Beiträge zur Geschichte der deutschen Sprache und Literatur, Tübingen
DVLG	Deutsche Vierteljahresschrift für Literaturwissenschaft und Geistesgeschichte
GLL	German Life and Letters
GRM	Germanisch-Romanische Monatsschrift
JEGP	Journal of English and Germanic Philology
MAe	Medium Aevum
MGH	Monumenta Germaniae Historica
MLN	Modern Language Notes
MP	Modern Philology
PMLA	Publications of the Modern Language Association of America
RES	Review of English Studies
RPh	Romance Philology
SN	Studia Neophilologica
THES	The Times Higher Education Supplement
ZDA	Zeitschrift für deutsches Altertum und deutsche Literatur
ZDP	Zeitschrift für deutsche Philologie

Introduction

The Tristan symposium held at the Institute of Germanic Studies in London on 24–26 March 1986 was conceived by the organisers as an experiment in transatlantic co-operation. Papers were read by scholars from a variety of North American and British universities, and there was a lively but notably friendly and civilised exchange of views. Representatives of the New World and of the Old discovered, sometimes to their mutual surprise, that they were not too much divided by their common language, and were cheered to realise that Tristan studies in their respective parts of the English-speaking community were in an exciting and challenging state of flux. Gottfried's *Tristan* emerged, by an unforced consensus, as the main focus of attention. The questioning of familiar assumptions about the text and the desire to find fresh perspectives from which to approach contentious issues inform the papers collected in this volume. On many basic questions there is disagreement, but the disagreements are themselves a reflection of the complexity of the problems of interpretation posed by Gottfried's masterpiece. Public and private debate led to extensive revisions by a number of contributors, some of whom here record second and even third thoughts, but no last words. Two of the papers printed here – those by Margaret Brown and C. Stephen Jaeger, and by George Gillespie – augment the number of those formally delivered at the symposium.

On a general level, Michael Curschmann considers the relationship between the Tristan story and the pictorial tradition which it generated, and argues that artists worked largely independently of authors. He suggests that even in the earliest surviving illuminated Tristan manuscript, the Munich copy of Gottfried's text and Ulrich von Türheim's continuation, the picture sequences are quasi-autonomous, and offer an interpretation of the story that is very different from Gottfried's. And when it comes to artefacts such as mirror cases, combs and caskets, the gap between written narrative and visual representation is even wider. W.J. McCann offers a sceptical re-examination of recent research by Celtic scholars into the question of the origins of the Tristan legend, and outlines some of the major developments that have occurred since the publication of Gertrude Schoepperle's monumental source study.

Of the detailed studies of Gottfried's text which follow, several empha-

sise its indebtedness to clerical modes of writing. Starting from an analysis of the procession of the hunters, Margaret Brown and C. Stephen
Jaeger examine Gottfried's presentation of court ceremony. Their point is
not only that Gottfried's depiction of pageantry has counterparts in historical writing, but that both fictional and non-fictional texts make apparent the social and political functions of the aesthetic of court ceremony.
Martin Jones addresses the question of whether Gottfried's accounts of
armed conflict are intended, as is often claimed, as a critique of the model
of chivalry embodied in Arthurian romance. He concludes that Gottfried
stands in a tradition of clerical historical writing which antedates the
works of Chrétien and Hartmann, and that *Tristan* should not be read as
an attempt to subvert Arthurian concepts of chivalry. Rather, Gottfried
reflects the practice of contemporary warfare, and even proves to have a
keen eye for military strategy. Adrian Stevens also emphasises the clerical
nature of Gottfried's writing, its indebtedness to the Trivium, and the
extent to which it attempts to transpose into the vernacular the literary
norms associated with the composition of classical Latin texts. Arthur
Groos approaches the use of rhetoric from a different angle. In his study
of the relationship between Wagner's *Tristan* libretto and Gottfried's
work, he employs Harold Bloom's concept of the anxiety of influence to
argue that Wagner saw himself as appropriating and transforming what
he took to be an incompetent medieval narrative. Wagner's aim was to
subsume and complete Gottfried's *Tristan* fragment while at the same
time establishing his libretto as the culmination of a modern literary tradition having Goethe's *Faust* as its most important antecedent. His rhetoric,
and in particular his use of the figures of chiasmus and oxymoron as a
kind of intertext, reflects this grandiose aim.

A number of papers take up the topic of character and character portrayal. Thomas Kerth assesses Gottfried's presentation of the figure of
Marke and examines some of the ways in which his kingship appears
divorced from historical reality. Michael Batts suggests that Marke is
depicted as a relatively sympathetic character; in some ways a ruler par
excellence, Marke becomes culpable only after the grotto episode because
of the strength of his carnal passion for his wife. Gottfried's great achievement, according to Batts, is to have portrayed Marke both as a representative figure and as an intensely human individual. Marianne Wynn
shifts the spotlight from Marke to Isot. She argues that Isot should be
viewed as an individual who possesses a distinctive personality, and
finds that Gottfried has carefully plotted a development in her character.
Janet Wharton also turns her attention to Isot, and to the theme of love
and marriage. Her reading of the much-discussed 'huote' discourse is that
the ideal condition for lovers is marriage entered into freely and based on
affection; the fact that Isot is married to a man she does not love means

that she cannot achieve the kind of happiness which Gottfried posits as ideal. George Gillespie who, following the lead given by Hugo Kuhn, considers affinities between the Tristan and Siegfried stories, also makes a number of observations on character, and on the relationship between character and plot. In his view, Tristan and Siegfried are unlike the heroes of Arthurian romance in that they do not develop through experience.

Joan Ferrante offers a reading of Gottfried's text which shows one way in which it might be deconstructed. She argues that Gottfried's text betrays an ambivalence towards words and speech which extends to the mode of fiction itself and which obliges the reader to question both his authority as narrator and the truth of his story. Pointing to the ubiquity in *Tristan* of lies, broken promises, manipulation and deception, she finds in these a possible figure of Gottfried's relation to his audience. Leslie Seiffert also addresses the problem of lies and truth in Gottfried's text, but he does not find Gottfried as narrator either deceiving or self-deceiving: he sees him rather as a master of dialectical subtlety, exposing facets of truth and truthfulness for the benefit of those equipped with the mental agility to follow the twists and turns of his exposition.

Sidney Johnson considers the function of the dwarf Melot in Gottfried's poem, and compares and contrasts Melot with other dwarf figures who feature in historical sources and literary texts. Petrus Tax explores the latent sexual symbolism of wounds and healings in *Tristan*, and finds in the initial encounters between the hero and heroine in Ireland prefigurations of their subsequent love relationship. August Closs concurs with Tax in stressing the importance of the symbolic dimension of Gottfried's narrative, and argues that Tristan and Isolt are strongly but unconsciously drawn to each other before they come to drink the love-potion on the voyage to Cornwall. H.B. Willson, unlike Joan Ferrante, cannot entertain the idea that Gottfried may have left his poem intentionally unfinished. He argues that it is impossible to do justice to Gottfried's design by reading his *Tristan* in isolation from the 'conclusion' provided by the surviving fragments of Thomas's text. Roy Wisbey's paper, with which the present volume concludes, explores some of the ways in which Gottfried's work can be read as a sustained dialogue with Ovid and with the cautionary Ovidian diagnosis that illicit love goes hand in hand with ruin. In general, a key theme of the text is seen to be the evocation of the past and the overcoming of it in the present, a process from which Tristan and Isolt are not exempt. Once again, a clerical dimension of Gottfried's writing is revealed, and the question arises as to whether the true addressees of *Tristan* were not, like Gottfried himself, members of the educated minority: only men or women of considerable learning would have been in a position to identify the allusions to a classical Latin author who is never mentioned by name. Whatever conclusions are drawn, the papers col-

lected here bear eloquent testimony to the power, complexity and sophistication of Gottfried's narrative and to its capacity, undiminished by the
centuries that lie between its writing and its reading, to generate new
interpretations.

Editorial Note and Acknowledgements

In keeping with the international character of this volume, English and American preferences in usage and orthography have been largely – if not entirely – respected, so that forms like *manoeuvre* and *maneuver*, *armour* and *armor*, *fulfilment* and *fulfillment* may both be found, although not, it is hoped, within a single contribution. No attempt has been made to impose total uniformity on the names of personages in the Tristan legend, except where the lack of it might lead to confusion. Nor have the Editors tried to remedy the notorious lability of Straßburg / Strassburg, whether in references to Gottfried's name, or in citations of scholarly literature on his *Tristan*. Unless otherwise stated, the latter is quoted in the (eleventh) edition by Friedrich Ranke (Dublin/Zürich, 1967). The list of Abbreviations provided for periodical titles follows the practice of *The Year's Work in Modern Language Studies*. Series titles have, however, normally been printed in full. The editorial conventions followed are largely those of the *MHRA Style Book*, edited by A.S. Maney and R.L. Smallwood, third edition (London, 1984).

The Editors are grateful to Dr Janet Wharton for compiling the Index to this substantial volume, especially in view of the very short space of time available for the task. The book itself contains the contributions of nineteen scholars from two continents; in publishing terms it is also based on a collaborative effort, between Boydell & Brewer – chosen for their medieval and historical interests – and the Institute of Germanic Studies, University of London, which also provided the congenial setting for our symposium. We thank all those involved, whether in London or at Woodbridge, but above all Dr Richard Barber and the members of his production team.

As so often, financing the volume was not easy. The Editors were enabled to find their share of a considerable print-subvention from sources at King's College London and University College London (Fielden Fund). Their hapless fellow contributors were left, on the principle of *sauve qui peut*, to steer their own course between public patronage and private liberality. We are thus indebted for generous support to the individuals, and to many of the Institutions, named in the List of Contributors on p. xvi.

List of Contributors

MICHAEL BATTS	University of Vancouver
MARGARET BROWN	University of Washington, Seattle
AUGUST CLOSS	University of Bristol
MICHAEL CURSCHMANN	Princeton
JOAN M. FERRANTE	Columbia University
GEORGE GILLESPIE	University of Cardiff
ARTHUR GROOS	Cornell University
C. STEPHEN JAEGER	University of Washington, Seattle
SIDNEY M. JOHNSON	Indiana University
MARTIN H. JONES	King's College London
THOMAS KERTH	State University of New York
W. J. McCANN	University of Southampton
LESLIE SEIFFERT	Hertford College Oxford
ADRIAN STEVENS	University College London
PETRUS W. TAX	University of North Carolina
JANET WHARTON	Westfield College London
H. B. WILLSON	University of Leicester
ROY WISBEY	King's College London
MARIANNE WYNN	Westfield College London

Images of Tristan

MICHAEL CURSCHMANN

'Cest cunte est mult divers', – Thomas of Britain's words[1] might well serve
as the motto of the Tristan legend, and not least in the additional sense
that the diversity of verbal forms is matched by a rich and varied pictorial
tradition. That is well known, and a certain amount of serious thought has
already been given to the question of how the former relates to the latter.[2]
We have learned, for instance, not to try and align every one of those
artefacts, be they tapestries, frescos or misericords, with a specific written
version.[3] While it is true that forms of a vulgate version rather than spe-
cialized, esoteric remakes such as Gottfried's dominate general awareness
of the legend – what it consists of and what it is about – it is true also that
artists giving it visual expression rarely, if ever, translate from texts. The
relationship between the literary and the pictorial is much more complicated than that and probably changes quite a bit from case to case. If we as
literary historians wish to include this dimension of the medieval reading
process in our own picture of the past, we ought to understand that at
least in principle. So I would like to offer two examples which raise this
general issue in different individual ways and may help us explore it at

1 *Les fragments du Roman de Tristan. Poème du XIIe siècle par Thomas*, edited by Bartina
H. Wind (Leiden, 1950), fragment Douce, v. 835.
2 In addition to the classic collection of material by Roger S. Loomis, *Arthurian Leg-
ends in Medieval Art* (London, 1938), esp. pp. 42–69 and figs 19–136, the most important
studies and summaries are: Doris Fouquet, *Wort und Bild in der mittelalterlichen Tristan-
tradition* (Berlin, 1971). Hella Frühmorgen-Voss, 'Tristan und Isolde in mittelalterlichen
Bildzeugnissen', in H. F.-V., *Text und Illustration im Mittelalter. Aufsätze zu den Wechsel-
beziehungen zwischen Literatur und bildender Kunst*, edited by Norbert H. Ott (Munich,
1975), pp. 119–139. Norbert H. Ott, 'Katalog der Tristan-Bildzeugnisse', ibid., pp. 140–
171. Ott, 'Tristan auf Runkelstein und die übrigen zyklischen Darstellungen des
Tristanstoffes. Textrezeption oder medieninterne Eigengesetzlichkeit der Bild-
programme?', in *Runkelstein. Die Wandmalereien des Sommerhauses*, edited by Walter
Haug (Wiesbaden, 1982), pp. 194–238. Ott, 'Epische Stoffe in mittelalterlichen Bildzeugnissen', in *Epische Stoffe des Mittelalters*, edited by Volker Mertens and Ulrich
Müller (Stuttgart, 1984), pp. 449–474 (pp. 455–459).
3 The clearest statement to that effect can be found in Ott, 1984, pp. 459f.

least a little distance beyond the point where the discussion seems to have come to a halt, basically, a few years ago.

I

My first example comes from the earliest illuminated Tristan manuscript we possess, the Munich copy of Gottfried's version and Ulrich von Türheim's continuation (Cgm. 51), written in the second quarter of the thirteenth century and illustrated not very much later.[4] And this example needs a brief introduction.

Systematic illustration of assorted vernacular texts begins in Germany long before it does in France, but it remains sporadic well into the thirteenth century when the French and Norman west very quickly develops its own splendid tradition of romance illustration. In fact no such tradition ever developed in Germany. On the other hand, what romance illustration there is in thirteenth-century Germany displays a distinctly German format, quite unlike that used further west. French workshops produce relatively small, framed miniatures inserted here and there into the column of text, as we encounter them, for instance, in another illuminated copy of Gottfried's *Tristan*, dated 1323 and obviously done 'in French style'.[5] The few German illustrated romance manuscripts dating

[4]   It is manuscript M, the oldest: Bayerische Staatsbibliothek, Cgm. 51, now available in a good facsimile edition: Gottfried von Straßburg, *Tristan und Isolde. Mit der Fortsetzung Ulrichs von Türheim* (Stuttgart, 1979). A companion volume contains an excellent codicological introduction by Ulrich Montag and extensive descriptions of, and some commentary on the pictures by Paul Gichtel. The latter's contribution essentially repeats his earlier essay, 'Die Bilder der Münchener Tristan-Handschrift (Cod. germ. 51)', in *Buch und Welt. Festschrift für Gustav Hofmann* (Wiesbaden, 1965), pp. 391–457. Recent studies of the pictures: Jörg Hucklenbroich, 'Einige Bemerkungen zum *Münchener Tristan*', in *Diversarum artium studia . . . Festschrift H. Roosen-Runge*, edited by H. Engelhart and G. Kempter (Wiesbaden, 1982), pp. 55–73; Bettina Falkenberg, *Die Bilder der Münchener Tristan-Handschrift* (Frankfurt, 1986). Gottfried's text will be quoted from Ranke's edition: Gottfried von Straßburg, *Tristan und Isold*, edited by Friedrich Ranke (Dublin/Zurich, [14]1969).
[5]   It is manuscript B: Cologne, Historisches Archiv der Stadt, W 88*. Since Karl Menne, *Deutsche und niederländische Handschriften*, Mitteilungen aus dem Stadtarchiv von Köln. Sonderreihe: Die Handschriften des Archivs. H.X, Abt. 1, Teil 1 (Cologne, 1931), p. 25, mentions 'zahlreiche farbige . . . Federzeichnungen', it is worth stressing that the illustration is actually quite sparse, amounting to a total of nine pictures for all of Gottfried's text plus Ulrich's continuation. The text is written in two columns, and the pictures never take up more than one third of a column, usually less. They invariably show only two or three characters, without scenery, against ornamental background. Frühmorgen-Voss has published a total of four: figs 1–3 in *Text und Illustration*, and fig. 3 in the original version of the same essay, in *DVLG*, 43 (1969), but unfortunately without the context of the page as a whole. The others have never been published at all. For a list of subjects see Gichtel, 1965, p. 455 n. 118. Only brief reference can be made

from the thirteenth century, on the other hand, have full-page miniatures (or tinted pen drawings) on both sides of separately prepared leaves, with each side subdivided into two or three registers. These pictures do not accompany or punctuate the narrative; they gather it together, contracting and reorganizing episodes from the surrounding text into a separate, quasi-autonomous picture sequence. In the Berlin *Eneit*, a splendidly illuminated copy of Heinrich von Veldeke's poem,[6] double leaves with pictures alternate regularly with double leaves of text so that, except for the middle of every quire, every page of text faces a picture page. The two stories are never far apart, at least physically. But in the Munich *Tristan* such picture leaves are few and far between: after the loss of possibly one or two, fifteen remain today. They are distributed quite unevenly, and the density of illustration on the individual page is much higher: these fifteen leaves (thirty pages) contain no fewer than 118 different scenes. Obviously this format leaves a great deal of room for, even encourages, independence of the picture program, the overall concept or structure of the story as it unfolds before the reader's eyes as distinct from his ears.[7]

Uneven distribution means, among other things, that, while the story of Tristan's parents and of his own youth finds its visual equivalent in a fairly tight cluster of picture leaves (folios 7, 10, 11 and 15: twenty-four scenes) the following two major phases of Tristan's life, spanning *c*.8000 lines of text, are covered by no more than the same number of leaves, namely four (eight pages) distributed over seventy-four pages: folios 30, 37, 46 and 67. In terms of the emerging picture program, the first two of these comprise the story of Tristan's life as Mark's heir, while the other two depict his Irish adventures, and these two phases are loosely connected through the encounter with Morolt.[8] Thus we see, in the last scene of folio 37v (fig. 1), how Tristan returns after the successful pacification of

here to the exciting discovery of a set of eight full-page tinted drawings or sketches in a Latin theological miscellany from the turn of the fourteenth century: Tony Hunt, 'The Tristan Illustrations in MS London BL Add. 11619', in *Rewards and Punishments in the Arthurian Romances and Lyric Poetry of Medieval France*, ed. P. V. Davies and A. J. Kennedy (Cambridge, 1987), pp. 45–60. These pictures are entirely without text, and the question of their original purpose is one of several that await further investigation and discussion.

6   See the facsimile edition of the picture pages by Albert Boeckler, *Heinrich von Veldeke, Eneide. Die Bilder der Berliner Handschrift* (Leipzig, 1939). A recent study is by Jörg Hucklenbroich, *Text und Illustration in der Berliner Handschrift der 'Eneide' des Heinrich von Veldeke . . .*, Würzburg dissertation (Würzburg, 1985).

7   One can, of course, posit losses almost at will to obtain more even coverage, as does Gichtel (1979, pp. 83f, particularly also with regard to the unillustrated space between folios 46 and 67), but the only place where the manuscript itself gives reasonable ground for such an assumption is the space between folios 71 and 74, where a whole quire was lost even before the manuscript was re-bound in the fourteenth century.

8   Single leaves now, like all the other picture leaves, the two may originally have been joined as the outer double leaf of the fifth quire (Montag, p. 33).

Parmenie and discovers Morolt: a threat to the state, sitting next to Mark, larger than life, Morolt concludes a series of scenes that begins on folio 30r, with Rual's arrival at Mark's court and the revelation of Tristan's identity.

The actual fight with Morolt is shown as well, but not until 17 pages later, on folio 46r (fig. 2) and in a different context: Tristan's first voyage to Ireland, as will become apparent in a moment. And that context extends to a second leaf of very similar content and organization which features the main events of Tristan's second Irish voyage and occurs near the end of this whole narrative phase, as folio 67. And these two leaves, folios 46 and 67, with a total of eighteen scenes, I want to examine somewhat more closely now.

Folio 46r is devoted entirely to Tristan's fight with Morolt: arrival – combat on horseback – victory on foot – return of the victor. The presentation even includes some of the more significant details (bottom register right to left): Tristan wounded on the left thigh, leaving in Morolt's boat. When Tristan comes face to face with Morolt the first time it is in the context of his public role as redeemer and prospective heir of Cornwall. This here, the actual combat and tainted victory, is much more his own personal story, as the verso side makes clear. This page (fig. 3), traces Tristan's own path to salvation and cure, the (temporary) resolution of the problem exposed on the preceding page: sickbed (with King Mark and the doctor) – voyage to Ireland in two phases – Tristan/Tantris consulting with the local physician (wrongly titled 'Isoit') – and (right to left) in symmetrically arranged separate vaulted interiors – cured by the elder Isolde and harping with the younger. In sum, folio 46 as a whole sends a carefully composed message: there are two sides to this life: knightly combat and victory at arms on one, and healing, salvation, the redeeming presence of women on the other.

The second of these two leaves uses the events of Tristan's second voyage to Ireland for basically the same purpose, in a composition that parallels this one in considerable detail. First we see on folio 67r (fig. 4) again a battle scene. But in a surprising change of mood, the artist has portrayed the mock heroic aspect of the dragon episode, very likely taking his cue from Gottfried himself.[9] As expression and posture of the dead animal change from eagerly helpful to downright smug, Tristan cuts out its tongue, the steward attacks it ferociously, and carts off its head. But mock battle and mock victory only mask Tristan's earlier serious feat of arms for which, once again, he suffers grievously. We turn the page (fig. 5) to follow the sequence of actions on the part of the ladies that will once again save him: they find the headless dragon, discover the senseless

9   See vv. 9097ff. In that connection, it is interesting to note, though, that some of the most openly comic lines are not to be found in the text (of M): 9187–9210; 9221–9232.

Tristan in the water, and take him home. And then – bottom left to right – the ultimate discovery: two interior scenes again, as on folio 46v, but this time under one (vaulted) roof, depicting successive stages of one dramatic confrontation: the young Isolde threatens to kill the defenseless man in the bath, but her mother stops her; on the right Brangane counsels moderation and forgiveness.

Thus the pattern which informs the organization of the earlier leaf repeats itself, but with a difference. Folio 67 must go beyond folio 46 in what it implies about the relationship between the two central themes of chivalric life, honor (*aventiure*) and love.[10] The corresponding scenes in the third register on the verso of folio 46 reflect only a partial or temporary solution to the problems created in Tristan's victory over Morolt. The final resolution follows here, on the verso of folio 67, and it involves the complete submission of the hero. He must be put – or put himself – completely at the lady's mercy to win that kind of battle, to be victorious in love.

This deliberate juxtaposition cannot fail to remind one of the 'Iwein' frescos at Rodenegg Castle[11] – of how the painter of this first known cycle of wall paintings derived from vernacular romance thought of his own subject, most probably in the second decade of the thirteenth century.[12]

---

10 On these two themes as foci for the portrayal of courtly romance see esp. Norbert H. Ott, 'Geglückte Minne-Aventiure. . . Die Beispiele des Rodenecker *Iwein*, des Runkelsteiner *Tristan*, des Braunschweiger *Gawan*- und des Frankfurter *Wilhelm-von-Orlens*-Teppichs', *Jahrbuch der Oswald von Wolkenstein-Gesellschaft*, 2 (1982/83), 1–31. See also Ott and Walliczek on Rodenegg (below, note 11).

11 The literature on Rodenegg has grown rapidly, and I shall list only the most important recent contributions: Norbert H. Ott and Wolfgang Walliczek, 'Bildprogramm und Textstruktur. Anmerkungen zu den *Iwein*-Zyklen auf Rodenegg und in Schmalkalden', in *Deutsche Literatur im Mittelalter: Kontakte und Perspektiven*, edited by Christoph Cormeau (Stuttgart, 1979), pp. 473–500 (see also N. Ott, 1982/83). Volker Schupp, 'Die Ywain-Erzählung von Schloß Rodenegg', in *Literatur und bildende Kunst im Tiroler Mittelalter*, edited by Egon Kühebacher (Innsbruck, 1982), pp. 1–27. Achim Masser, 'Die *Iwein*-Fresken von Burg Rodenegg in Südtirol und der zeitgenössische Ritterhelm', *ZDA*, 112 (1983), 177–198. Anne Marie Birlauf-Bonnet, 'Überlegungen zur Brixener Malerei in den ersten Jahrzehnten des 13. Jahrhunderts', *Wiener Jahrbuch für Kunstgeschichte*, 37 (1984), 23–39 and 187–198. idem (as Anne-Marie Bonnet), *Rodenegg und Schmalkalden. Untersuchungen zur Illustration einer ritterlich-höfischen Erzählung und zur Entstehung profaner Epenillustration in den ersten Jahrzehnten des 13. Jahrhunderts* (Munich, 1986). This is the major part of a 1981 Heidelberg dissertation, essentially unchanged, and does not take into account any of the scholarly discussion since 1978. James Rushing, 'Adventures Beyond the Text: Iwain in the Visual Arts', Princeton dissertation, 1987.

12 On the basis of a comparative stylistic analysis, Bonnet has established the second or even third decade as by far the most likely period of composition: 'in den zwanziger bis dreißiger Jahren des 13. Jahrhunderts': 1984, p. 38; 'in den 20er Jahren des 13. Jh.': 1986, p. 62 (see also Schupp, esp. pp. 9 and 11). This effectively disposes of the earlier dating around 1200 that is not supported even by Masser's new arguments and has been the root cause of much confusion among literary historians. In opting for the

On one wall of this chamber at Rodenegg we see Iwein's encounter with Ascalon, successful demonstration of knightly prowess (fig. 6). On the opposite wall, this prototypical chivalric adventure ends with a gesture of total submission before Ascalon's widow: Iwein waiting to receive love as a gift not as a prize (fig. 7). I do not think that this dialectic of love and honour or adventure explains the Rodenegg program in its totality[13] – this is not a happy end in the conventional romance sense; the predominant mood of the final scene is sadness and grief, reminding the viewer that the centerpiece of the whole cycle is a lamentation scene.[14] Naturally, the general pattern that is being applied (or extracted) here will, in individual instances, undergo modification beyond that required by the individual plot in order to articulate more specific concerns that may be raised by the story itself or by its social environment. But that does not alter the fact that this pattern and this dialectic are fundamentally important to this composition, and they also dominate the picture program of the Munich *Tristan* in the particular phase I have discussed.

This configuration of scenes brackets that major part of the narrative which couples Tristan's premier feats of arms with the initial development of his relationship to Isolde and it constitutes an almost programmatic statement about Tristan as hero. While he clearly appreciates some of Gottfried's finer points, the artist has freely disregarded his larger design and meaning, to the point even of omitting the most important plot element of all: he has given no indication whatever that the events highlighted and connected visually in his own design take place on two different journeys dedicated to totally different goals.[15] Although he, like almost all Tristan illustrators, loves to draw ships to mark major caesuras

twenties rather than the thirties myself, I have in mind the close geographic proximity and potentially very close intellectual relation of this undertaking to Thomasin's lecture to the German nobility on how to derive spiritual benefit from vernacular romance: Thomasin von Zerclaere, *Der welsche Gast*, edited by F. W. von Kries, vol. 1 (Göppingen, 1984), vv. 1635ff. This is a point which requires much further discussion; for the time being see Rushing.

13 It is on this point that I disagree with Ott and Walliczek, whose essay has provided the foundation for all further discussion of these matters, and particularly with Ott's subsequent statement, 'die durchaus problematische Erringung der Dame . . . gerät nicht ins Bild' (1982/83, pp. 18f).

14 This has been pointed out by Bonnet, 1986, pp. 58 and 70. Her thesis that the cycle as a whole portrays 'eine reale ritterlich-höfische Problematik mittels Illustration eines Romans' (p. 71) is well worth discussing, although it, too, is not without its problems. See Rushing, pp. 58–61.

15 One recalls here particularly how Gottfried himself takes special care to provide proper motivation for the second voyage, including, vv. 8601ff, his most explicit invective against those who have failed to do so in the past. On this subject of motivation, see the recent article by James A. Schultz, 'Why do Tristan and Isolde Leave for the Woods? Narrative Motivation and Narrative Coherence in Eilhart von Oberg and Gottfried von Straßburg', *MLN*, 102 (1987), 586–607.

in the story, he has in this instance reduced epic narrative to emphasize structural parallels and he has used those parallels to create two self-contained but interrelated expository demonstrations of what is typical and paradigmatic in Tristan's life as knight and lover. He has not translated or even interpreted Gottfried's text; he has related it to the legend and, beyond that, to more general and typical patterns of romance. This does not happen everywhere, even in the same manuscript,[16] but it goes to show that, even in closest proximity to the text (a text) visual representation of the subject may reflect and articulate perceptions that are essentially non-textual, social perceptions.

II

My second example comes from the other end of the spectrum of pictorial response to a literary subject: visual representation entirely divorced, at least physically, from any text and essentially non-narrative, emblematic in character and function. Of all the images created by the Tristan legend, the one that had the firmest hold on the medieval imagination, coming to stand, *pars pro toto*, for the legend as a whole, visualizes the secret tryst by the spring in the garden or orchard under the eyes of King Mark, hiding in the tree above. Nearly half of the 57 Tristan monuments listed in Ott's catalogue[17] show this scene either by itself or in combination with similar-

---

16 Quite apart from that, the question of how many illustrators actually were at work (two or three?) and where one leaves off and the other begins is still a matter of debate.
17 Not to mention a dozen or so others in which it appears as part of a Tristan cycle. To Ott's catalogue (1975), which extends to the sixteenth century but does not include illuminated manuscripts, should be added the following: (1) another wooden comb, from the Museum of Fine Arts in Boston, an exact pendant to the one listed as no. 50 (which, incidentally, is not in London but in Bamberg: Ott, 'Epische Stoffe' (above, note 2), p. 458): cf. *The International Style. The Arts in Europe Around 1400* (Baltimore: The Walters Art Gallery, 1962), pp. 100f and pl. CII. (2) Five triangular pieces of leather excavated in the Netherlands (Dortrecht and Leiden) and Belgium (Mechelen) between 1969 and 1978 – remnants of slippers that were in all likelihood used as wedding gifts for brides: cf. Herbert Sarfatij, 'Tristan op vrijersvoeten?', in *Ad fontes. Opstellen aangeboden aan prof. dr. C. van de Kieft* (Amsterdam, 1984), pp. 371–400. (3) A relief carved on the lid of an ivory mirror case in the Museum Mayer van den Bergh in Antwerp: cf. Jozef de Coo, *Museum Mayer van den Bergh, Catalogus 2: Beeldhouwkunst . . .* (Antwerp, 1969), p. 133 (no. 2126). – Ott's catalogue continues with additional lists of objects known only from contemporary inventories (12) and of objects whose identification with the Tristan legend is questionable (14). To the latter should probably be added a second console from the town hall in Bruges. The one that shows the orchard scene is widely known (no. 8 in the catalogue; fig. 47 in Frühmorgen-Voss), but there is another one from the same facade and done by the same workshop that might very well represent Brangane and Tristan and Isolde moments after the couple have drunk the love potion. According to local experts, it definitely does, see Alin Janssens de Bist-

ly evocative motifs from related subjects. These combinations as well as
the preponderance, among those monuments, of objects associated with
female toiletry – mirror cases, combs, and the ubiquitous 'Minnekästchen'
– indicate that, from this even narrower social perspective, the message of
Tristan is the triumph of love and its deceitful energy.

All of these emblematic representations show the same basic iconographic configuration (fig. 8), organizing the scene around a tree by a well
or fountain, man-made successor to the little stream that flows through
the garden and by (or through) Isolde's chamber. In the tree, the face of
King Mark, and directly below its mirror image in the water to which
Tristan points. The dwarf (Frocin/Melot), Mark's companion, is rarely
seen at all, and in this as well as in other respects this French ivory mirror
case from the first half of the fourteenth century exemplifies the kind and
degree of formalization and stylization that typically occur – also, for
instance, in the introduction of lap-dog and falcon in the figures' arms,
unmistakable symbols of their respective sexuality. Frequently the couple
even sit, almost as if in casual conversation. The source of the water has
become an elaborate fountain: on a casket in the Metropolitan Museum in
New York (fig. 9), another well-known French ivory from the first half of
the fourteenth century, dramatic action in epic time has been converted
into a playfully suggestive courtly tableau, with a setting that is more
reminiscent almost of the Garden of Love in – mostly later – medieval art
than of its literary origins. The unicorn hunt to the right adds its share of
playful eroticism. No matter what medieval (and modern) clerks say, the
unicorn in the lady's lap is above all a symbol of human sexuality, even in
the *Physiologus* which proclaims it as Christian allegory of the incarna-
tion.[18]

And yet, we will not learn all we can from this example about the
formation and nature of medieval literary consciousness, if we do not
look beyond the obvious connections being made here. These connections
reveal a perception of the literary subject which is entirely devoid of
tragedy, conflict and so forth; the picture extracts and isolates that particular element of the subject that makes it fit into the same canon that also
produces – at an even higher level of abstraction – the well-known 'Minnesklaven' series. But at the same time it also reflects back on this subject
in a way which adds something from the outside, as it were. That something is the notion of the Fall of Man.

hoven, 'Het beeldhouwwerk van het Brugsche Stadhuis', *Gentsche Bijdragen tot de
Kunstgeschiedenis*, 10 (1944), 7–81 (pp. 57–61 and figs on pp. 58 and 60); Valentin Ver-
meersch, *Bruges: mille ans d'art* (Bruges, ²1986), p. 87 and fig. 88. The basic text on this
subject is by Doris Fouquet, 'Die Baumgartenszene des Tristan in der mittelalterlichen
Kunst und Literatur', *ZDP*, 92 (1973), 360–70.
18 See *Denkmäler deutscher Prosa des 11. und 12. Jahrhunderts*, edited by Friedrich Wilhelm (Munich, 1960), pp. 21f: 'De vnicorni'.

Fig. 1 Munich, Bayerische Staatsbibliothek, Cgm. 51, fol. 37v

Fig. 2 Munich, Bayerische Staatsbibliothek, Cgm. 51, fol. 46r

Fig. 3 Munich, Bayerische Staatsbibliothek, Cgm. 51, fol. 46v

Fig. 4 Munich, Bayerische Staatsbibliothek, Cgm. 51, fol. 67r

Fig. 5 Munich, Bayerische Staatsbibliothek, Cgm. 51, fol. 67v

Fig. 6   Rodenegg Castle, Iwein Frescoes, Detail

Fig. 7   Rodenegg Castle, Iwein Frescoes, Detail

Fig. 8 Paris, Musée de Cluny, Ivory Mirror Case

Fig. 9 New York, The Metropolitan Museum, Ivory Casket

Fig. 10   Orvieto Cathedral, West Facade, Relief Sculpture

Fig. 11   Milan, Biblioteca Trivulziana, Cod. 2139, fol. 4r

In order to pursue this trail further, we must digress briefly, back into literary history. With the notable, but in this case not very helpful, exception of the so-called Forrer casket,[19] none of the artefacts that show the tryst divorced from its context and are still available to us date from before 1300, and virtually all of the early examples come from France. As far as one can tell from the manuscript evidence and from the general course of literary history, the twelfth-century verse narratives which had created and promoted this particular image had faded into the background by then. And yet, the image was established firmly enough to maintain a comparatively traditional view of things while the more and more popular *Tristan en prose*, the Italian *Tavola ritonda*, and other such *rifacimenti* moved the literary episode into a marginal position in new contexts and settings or simply omitted it.[20] Established so firmly, in fact, that the fresco cycle of St Floret in the Auvergne, which was painted around 1350 and took its narrative from Rusticiano da Pisa's *Meliadus*, included a splendid and prominent rendering of the meeting in the garden in spite of the fact that Rusticiano does not report this episode at all.[21] How was this possible without the continued support of a firm literary base? It has been pointed out on occasion that yet later literary traditions in France and elsewhere also tend to lift the encounter in the garden out of its narrative romance context, thereby reducing it once more to the kind of anecdotal comic tale it must have been before it joined the Tristan legend in a common process of literarization during the twelfth century.[22] Some time the question should be discussed properly whether this could not in fact be due to the influence of its immensely popular visual representation rather than to intra-literary factors and forces.[23] This is not the place to do so, but I do want to bring up the one case in which the text in question does indeed seem to reflect such a picture as its source. That text is one of hundreds of moral and religious *exempla* contained in the anonymous prose work 'Ci nous dit' from the first half of the fourteenth century.[24]

---

[19] No. 35 in Ott's catalogue. It is usually dated in the very early decades of the thirteenth century, but the Tristan reminiscences are quite indistinct, particularly with regard to the orchard scene.

[20] Renée Curtis' critical edition of the prose Tristan has not reached that particular point even after three volumes. See instead E. Loseth, *Le Roman en Prose de Tristan, le Roman de Palamede et la compilation de Rusticien de Pise: Analyse critique* ... (1891; reprint New York, 1970), §282. *La Tavola Ritonda o L'Istoria di Tristano*, edited by Filippo-Luigi Polidori, vol. 1 (Bologna, 1894), ch. LXIII. The motif of the water under the tree (laurel and pine, respectively) has been omitted in both prose texts. In the French version, Tristan sees a man hidden in the tree, as he approaches, and in the Italian, Mark's shadow on the ground alerts both lovers at the same time.

[21] No. 1 in Ott's catalogue. Cf. Loomis (above, note 2), p. 59.

[22] Fouquet, 'Die Baumgartenszene', pp. 361f.

[23] Loomis (above, note 2) has already pointed in this direction: p. 66.

[24] 'Ci nous dit'. *Recueil d'exemples moraux*, edited by Gérard Blangez, vol. 1 (Paris, 1979),

A (nameless) queen and a (nameless) knight sit under a tree by a fountain to talk about 'folles amours'. In the tree sits the king, listening. However, the couple notice the king's image in the water, change their minds and converse upon proper courtly topics. The moral of this story, according to the author, is that we should always guard against evil thought for the love of God, who sees everything we do.

This religious contrafact of the scene does not accord very well with the literary narrative, although it clearly echoes it, of course. There the lovers do not *sit* under a tree; they do not talk of 'folles amours' before they discover Mark's shadow or reflection; and their subsequent conversation is about their own relationship and how it is being misunderstood or misrepresented by others at court, including Mark. But if one looks at the New York ivory casket once again, one realizes immediately that this text provides a quite accurate description of what is depicted there: a (nameless) couple seated in a semiformal courtly setting, relaxed, in conversation which is about to change its content, judging by the gesture of Tristan's hand. Whatever the author knew about the Tristan story clearly appears to be filtered through the visual experience of this typifying imagery with which so many in his audience had become thoroughly familiar in their daily lives. And when the illustrator of one of several illuminated manuscripts of the 'Ci nous dit' drew, in his turn, a picture to go with this *exemplum* it became yet another representative of the standard scene, primitive but unmistakable – and totally neutral with regard to its message.[25]

Thus the idea of a religious contrafact, a deliberate reinterpretation for spiritual purposes, brings us back to the question of religious connotations in the iconography of this Tristan picture-type. It has been noted and said before, of course, that there is a fairly close resemblance here to the standard iconography of the Fall of Man in what might be called its minimal form: a man and a woman standing on either side of a tree in which lurks danger.[26] But does this actually mean anything in particular, and if so, what does it mean? To answer this question we shall have to

ch. 293. See Loomis, p. 28; Fouquet, loc. cit. It will become apparent in a moment why I wholeheartedly disagree with Fouquet's conclusion, 'Die Fabel läßt, wie die Einzelheiten zeigen . . ., auf eine genaue Kenntnis der Tristangeschichte schließen' (p. 362).

25 Chantilly, Musée Condé, MS 1078 (26), fol. 189r – before 1330. Loomis, fig. 120.

26 Fouquet, 'Die Baumgartenszene', p. 363: 'Die Bildkomposition der Szene . . . zeigt einige Verwandtschaft mit den Darstellungen des Sündenfalls . . .'. Ott, commenting on the image as it occurs in an early fourteenth-century tapestry from Luneburg, has a somewhat more specific observation ('Tristan auf Runkelstein' (above, note 2), p. 216): 'eine Ableitung aus dem zweifigurigen Sündenfall-Bildtyp mit dem Baum in der Mitte: man könnte soweit gehen, in Marke und Melot die kompositorische Umsetzung der Schlange, die lange mit menschlichem Gesicht dargestellt wurde, zu sehen'. Cf. also Ott, 'Mittelalterliche Bildzeugnisse', p. 458.

consider a few additional details of the Fall-of-Man iconography,[27] among other things, and I would like to begin with an example that is contemporaneous with the earliest preserved examples of the orchard scene in secular art and at the same time comes as close to being a 'Tristan picture' as any I have been able to find (fig. 10).

This relief sculpture at Orvieto cathedral was done in the early fourteenth century as part of the Creation sequence on the left pilaster of the west facade, possibly by Lorenzo Maitani.[28] The characters are arranged in perfect symmetry under the canopy of the fig tree and united in common pursuit through the gesture with which Eve offers and Adam accepts the forbidden fruit. The substantial, expressive head of the serpent between them almost reaches into the foliage. Behind the tree is a large ornamental basin from which issue the four rivers of paradise. Looking back now at a Tristan picture like that on the French mirror cases we have already seen (fig. 8) – the carefully arranged symmetry under the tree; the face in the middle just above the couple's heads; gestures that forge a strong link of understanding across the central divide; and the water basin below, at the foot of the tree – one is struck by a resemblance that goes well beyond general structural likeness and into significant compositional detail. It suggests a kind of elective artistic affinity that could conceivably serve ulterior purposes, and could at any rate have considerable effect on the perception of the profane garden scene among viewers familiar, through everyday exposure, with the underlying iconographic convention.

It needs to be said at this point that, in substance, the basin in the Orvieto relief is of course not an iconographic requirement: it is as accidental to this picture-type as it is essential to the scene of the secret tryst. It goes to show, though, that the formal similarity between the profane image and its religious counterpart acts as a potential bridge-builder, at least in the fourteenth century, between that canonical example of courtly love and the idea of original sin. It also raises the question of original intent: could the evident adoption of Fall-of-Man imagery to visualize this meeting of adulterous lovers reflect more than simple workshop pragmatism?

The basic pattern – Adam and Eve flanking the Tree of Knowledge and the serpent coiled around its trunk – was established firmly in late antiquity by the early Christians.[29] Although never exclusive of other schemes,

---

27 There is, strangely enough, no comprehensive monograph on this popular subject. Apart from the usual handbooks, my own narrow survey is based primarily on the resources of the Princeton Index of Christian Art.

28 Cf. Enzo Carli, *Le sculture del Duomo di Orvieto* (Roma, 1947); Otto von Simson, *Propyläen Kunstgeschichte. Das Mittelalter*, vol. 2 (Berlin, 1972), pp. 355f and pl. 370.

29 See, for instance, the examples shown by Theodore Ehrenstein, *Das Alte Testament*

it became the standard for pictorial representation of the Fall, either by itself or as part of a creation series. Examples from the twelfth century abound.[30] For any artist in the position in which so many found themselves during this and the following century, having to change and adjust their repertoire of forms and formulas to the demands of new, secular, narrative texts, this simple pattern offered by far the most natural way to recast a key scene of the vulgate twelfth-century version of the Tristan legend in an already available mold and memorable visual form. And that in turn is no doubt what accounts for the visual stylization of that encounter and, consequently, its durability as a representative image.

Details that had to be incorporated as essential to the identity of the profane counterpart are the head in the tree and its reflection in water on the ground. The former may be said to have a given, approximate equivalent in the head of the serpent that is part of the Christian picture-type – a connection (or allusion) that was strengthened and articulated further in the course of the thirteenth century when, in the wake of Petrus Comestor's exegesis, the serpent came to be represented more and more frequently with a human (female) head.[31] That is a secondary development, though. The maiden-headed serpent does not appear in France and Spain before the second or third decade of the thirteenth century,[32] and its subsequent popularity in German-speaking regions is due mainly, I would assume, to its prominent and frequent display in copies of the *Biblia pauperum* that was put together about a generation later.[33]

im Bilde (Wien, 1923), pp. 37f. Cf. also Sigrid Esche, *Adam und Eva* (Düsseldorf, 1957), and *Lexikon der christlichen Ikonographie*, edited by E. Kirschbaum, vol. 1 (Freiburg, 1968), art. 'Adam und Eva', cols 41–70 (H. Schade), esp. 54–61.

30 Two examples from the monumental arts: Rome, S. Giovanni a Porta Latina, fresco in the nave (1191/98): *Die römischen Mosaiken und Malereien der kirchlichen Bauten vom IV.–XIII. Jahrhundert*, edited by Joseph Wilpert, vol. 4, 2 (Freiburg, 1916), figs 252–255. Hildesheim, St Michael, fresco on the nave ceiling (1186): Johannes Sommer, *Das Dekkenbild der Michaeliskirche zu Hildesheim* (Hildesheim, 1966), p. 70, fig. 68, and color pl. B66. Cf. ibid., p. 71, examples from the minor arts: a chalice made in Hildesheim *c.*1170 (fig. 72) and a manuscript in the cathedral treasury in Trier, MS 141, historiated initial on fol. 15r (*c.*1200).

31 See the study by Henry A. Kelly, 'The Metamorphoses of the Eden Serpent during the Middle Ages and Renaissance', *Viator*, 2 (1971), 301–327. Kelly's datings tend to be a little on the early side, as Nigel Morgan points out to me.

32 The 'Beatus' in New York, Pierpont Morgan Library, MS 429, fol. 6v (Kelly, fig. 4) or the relief panel in the west portal of Amiens cathedral (Kelly, fig. 6).

33 See the examples published, in another context, by Clausdieter Schott, 'Sachsenspiegel und Biblia Pauperum', in *Text – Bild – Interpretation. Untersuchungen zu den Bilderhandschriften des Sachsenspiegels*, edited by Ruth Schmidt-Wiegand, vol. 2 (Munich, 1986), plates XLIII–XLIV, figs 31–37. In this connection, it should be pointed out, though, that the image from the so-called Verdun Altar which Schott published as part of this series belongs to the fourteenth-century restoration of the altar and not to the twelfth-century original. There is a good possibility, however, that at least one

Genesis 2.9 places the Tree of Life and of Knowledge in the center of paradise, and in the very same sentence (2.10) it speaks of the river ('fluvius') that springs in paradise, irrigates it, and subsequently divides itself into four streams. To depict this river (or these rivers) in direct conjunction with the kind of highly formalized image of the Fall which we have discussed was apparently not very common, but there are several interesting examples. Most of them date from the fourteenth century, as does the relief at Orvieto, and one of these, in the Trivulzio Bible from the workshop of Pacino di Bonaguida, also displays the kind of courtliness of setting and style that is so reminiscent of the Tristan ivories (fig. 11): Adam and Eve sit (!) on either side of a stylishly ornamental tree from which a maiden-faced serpent addresses Eve, who takes the fruit and makes a gesture of eating. On the other side, Adam makes expressive gestures of apprehension. In front of the tree between the couple is a large hexagonal fountain from which flow rivulets of water in four directions.[34] The composition is as reminiscent of the New York ivory casket (fig. 9) as the Orvieto relief was of the ivory mirror case which shows the couple standing (fig. 8).

But in the case of this particular motif, it also pays to look much further into the past. One finds, for instance, that two related bibles from Leon, one from 960 and the other a copy of 1162, use it in their depiction of the Fall:[35] in the foreground flows the River of Paradise, through the whole width of the picture, and divides into four on the right-hand margin of the page. Of more direct interest, at least geographically, is perhaps the Josephus copy made at the abbey of Werden in 1159. In the first of its three historiated initials it shows a highly sophisticated and programmatic arrangement of several motifs normally treated in a narrative series by Genesis illustrators. Within the confines of this very large Initial 'I' ('In principio'), the artist tells the story of the whole creation in one composite image, an image that focuses on the Fall and combines the standard version with, among other motifs, the half-figure of Christ-Logos in the

---

monumental representation of the maiden-headed serpent predates the 'Biblia': the Fall fresco in the choir of Brunswick cathedral (not mentioned by Kelly). See p. 75, fig. 77 in Sommer.

[34] Milan, Biblioteca Trivulziana, cod. 2139, fol. 4r. See Richard Offner, *A Critical and Historical Corpus of Florentine Painting*, vol. 3, 6 (New York, 1956), pl. LXIIa and pp. 218–220. This scene is part of a garland of small scenes, figures, and ornaments that frames the text of the whole page and connects with the richly historiated initial 'I' of 'in principio' with which it forms an elaborate creation-scene program. Cf. also the picture bible in Rovigo, Biblioteca dell' Accademia dei Concordi, MS 212, fol. 2v: G. Folena and G. L. Mellini, *Bibbia istoriata Padovana della fine del trecento* (Venice, 1962), color pl. no. 4. Here there is in the foreground a natural well from which flow four rivers.

[35] León, S. Isidoro, MS 2, fol. 15v, and 3, fol. 12v. Photographs in the Index of Christian Art.

tree above and the River of Paradise as a broad band of water running through the foreground below.[36]

Of course, it does not follow from any of this that this relatively rare additional detail was in any way instrumental in causing the general application of the religious prototype to the portrayal of secular narrative. It may, however, have facilitated the transition in individual instances or made it even more attractive where it was available, and above all it provided one more substantial point of contact between the two traditions as they developed further side by side. It is during this further development, for instance, that the general tendency towards refinement and courtification of the imagery transformed both the river in the Garden of Eden and the brook in Isolde's garden into wells caught in man-made, architectural structures. In all likelihood early pictures of the garden scene showed a river under the tree and not a fountain.

How early were these pictures? All we can say with assurance as the result of the foregoing review is that they were considerably older than the ones that have survived. It may be significant that the Munich *Tristan* does not render the scene in this particular fashion, but I am inclined to think that that has more to do with the medium than with anything else. Even before the influence of the twelfth-century literary prototypes began to wane, traditional Christian iconography took over, selected and stabilized this particular episode as an emblematic visualization of the whole, and not the least of the many attractions of the resulting image became its built-in ambiguity. Seeing Tristan and Isolde meet in this delightfully deceitful way *could* also remind one that original sin came into the world because Adam could not resist the blandishments of Eve, who could not resist the temptation of the forbidden fruit. Thus Adam became the first of the 'Minnesklaven'.

It is this connotation – much more specific than any general idea of original sin – that must have constituted the strongest intellectual or philosophical link between these two situations as they were being visualized by means of a common iconographic denominator. Workshop pragmatism and practice, and intellectual history combined and reinforced each other to produce an image that was essentially ambiguous, at least for those who, by experience, training, temperament or inclination were sensitive to such ambiguities. This double-edged thought was constantly in the air, so to speak, and our best witness for that is none other than Gottfried von Strassburg as he relates what is in effect a second orchard scene in his *Tristan*.

Tristan and Isolde have returned from the solitude of the lovers' cave,

36 Berlin, Staatsbibliothek, Cod. lat. fol. 226, fol. 3r. See *Zimelien. Abendländische Handschriften des Mittelalters aus den Sammlungen der Stiftung Preußischer Kulturbesitz Berlin*, edited by Thilo Brandis (Wiesbaden, 1975), color pl. 73 and pp. 89f.

and the renewed social constraints soon arouse what the narrator describes as Isolde's instinctive desire for the forbidden fruit of the fig tree (17925ff). After all, she is a child of mother Eve, he continues, and his introduction and description of the following love scene on a bed 'in her orchard' ('in ir boumgarten', 18129), in the shade of a tree, abound in explicit references to paradise and the Fall, culminating in this comment on Tristan's response:

> nu tete er rehte als Adam tete:
> daz obez, daz ime sin Eve bot,
> daz nam er und az mit ir den tot.   (18162ff)

The specific Tristan concept behind these comments need not concern us here.[37] What is instructive for us is the ready availability of such metaphors and what that says about the intellectual climate in general. These metaphors reflect an intellectual climate in which the application of Fall-of-Man iconography to another 'Tristan' episode that was even better suited to accommodate it, namely that first orchard scene, would be a titillating thought, whatever the direction of such thinking. The primary theme of the first orchard scene is clever deception of the cuckold in his own presence, not love and its consequences *per se*. It can provide the actors and the scenery, but the sentiment or argument that would call forth an image of the Fall of Man as a means of ordering these elements for visual presentation has to be added from somewhere else. Not necessarily from a text such as Gottfried's, for instance – it is in fact more likely a way of thinking in moral terms and religious images.

After Gottfried's comments it will come as no great surprise that Adam does in fact head the list of 'Minnesklaven' which developed in thirteenth-century Germany, that canon of famous men from the Old Testament, antiquity, and eventually romance, who were deceived and weakened by love and female wiles. When finally that concept began to generate a pictorial tradition of its own, in the early fourteenth century, a wall painting (now destroyed) was done for a private dwelling in the city of Constance that consisted of twelve medallions arranged in rows of four:[38]

---

[37] See Franziska Wessel, *Probleme der Metaphorik und die Minnemetaphorik in Gottfrieds von Straßburg 'Tristan und Isolde'* (Munich, 1984), p. 363.

[38] Only a cardboard copy survives that shows eleven of the twelve original medallions. For a photograph of the relevant portion see *Das Bodenseebuch*, 27 (Ulm/Lindau, 1940), following p. 32. The painting was based directly on a contemporary 'Spruch' in the manner of Heinrich Frauenlob: *Heinrichs von Meißen des Frauenlobes Leiche, Sprüche, Streitgedichte und Lieder*, edited by Ludwig Ettmüller (1843. Reprinted Amsterdam, 1966), no. 141. Cf. Friedrich Maurer, 'Der Topos von den *Minnesklaven*: Zur Geschichte einer thematischen Gemeinschaft zwischen bildender Kunst und Dichtung im Mittelalter', *DVLG*, 27 (1953), pp. 182–206; reprinted in Fr. M., *Dichtung und Sprache des Mittelalters* (Bern/Munich, 1963), pp. 224–248.

here Adam appeared in the top row, between Samson and Solomon, and in order to portray his particular weakness and failing the artist had, of course, chosen a simple and straightforward rendering of the Fall of Man. In this composition, the religious image has moved into the foreground, so to speak. Rather than serve as a more or less remote and potential or incidental point of (artistic) reference in the intellectual background to the debate on secular love it serves as a direct and deliberate reminder of the religious dimension of that debate.

Thus this final example of the visual conjunction of deceitful love and original sin adds yet another aspect to, and demonstrates once again the complexity of, the phenomenon which I have attempted to describe. Simple, one-sided and one-dimensional explanations are certainly not in order, particularly when it comes to questions of cause and effect. Nevertheless a few general observations and reasonable assumptions have emerged that can be stated as follows. Albeit in ways we shall never be able to reconstruct in any detail, existing workshop practice in religious art and the intellectual climate of the times must have combined to single out the scene of the tryst as the pictorial emblem of the Tristan legend as a whole and to stabilize the evolving tradition of this profane image. At the same time, and for the same reasons, that image can never be seen as entirely divorced from that background. Of course I do not mean to plead for ham-fisted allegorical interpretation. Just as surely as Gottfried's literary reaction to the story he inherited from Thomas and probably knew from at least one other written (German) version amounts to something much more subtle and ambiguous than that, it would have been almost unnatural for anyone to 'read' one of those pictures as a condemnation of secular, or, more specifically, courtly love and its rituals. But it also seems clear, not least from Gottfried's example and what it says about his audience, that an educated, literate viewer may have found in such pictures the opportunity, the incentive even, to look beyond them and to engage in playful contemplation of the original sinfulness of the human condition. If and to what extent individual women and men who walked through these halls and used those objects in their daily lives actually availed themselves of this opportunity is of course another matter, just as it is impossible to determine – and irrelevant by and large – if and to what extent these connotations were being created intentionally in individual instances. Ultimately that depended not only on the individual viewer and her or his basic disposition, but also on the occasion, the social context of the moment.

And this brings us, finally, to the point to be made in conclusion. Be it in manuscripts and thus in close proximity of the text (a text) or through largely isolated, floating images, in the dimension of pictorial representation the literary subject leads a separate, basically autonomous kind of life, a life that is different from that which it leads in the texts, although there may be a high degree of interdependence in individual instances. The text is the ultimate authority in the sense that it fashions the minimal consensus necessary to establish an iconographic tradition at all. But that tradition touches on other such traditions, reaches into other corners of literary and social consciousness, and in that way it helps shape the broader consensus that determines the meaning of the story. It is a dimension of literature which we as literary historians ignore at our peril.

Tristan: The Celtic Material Re-examined

W. J. McCANN

I feel that it is necessary to begin this paper by pointing out that little, if anything, that is said in it is original in itself: what is being attempted is a synthesis of the most recent research by Celtic scholars into the problems of the origins of the Tristan legend in order to show scholars outside the field of Celtic studies that there have been some advances in this direction since the time of Schoepperle.[1] In presenting this material, I feel not so much like a dwarf standing on the shoulders of a giant, as a dwarf balancing precariously at the summit of a pyramid of dwarfs (no disrespect being intended to the scholars whose works will be cited hereafter). The nature of the relationship between Celtic and continental sources, particularly in the field of the Arthurian Romance and the Tristan legend, is a question which has given rise to fierce controversy, with some scholars both modern and not so modern representing extreme positions on both sides. I hope that this study, by eschewing both extremes, will achieve that *mâze* which is the aim of so many mediaeval authors.

One is supported in this sensible approach to the problem of sources by Bruford in his work on Gaelic folk-tales and mediaeval romances:[2]

> It is dangerous to be too dogmatic about the sources of episodes in mediaeval romances: so much of the relevant material must have been lost . . . that the mere fact of a motif first appearing in a French MS dated, say, about 1250, and then in an Irish one of the fifteenth century, cannot be taken as conclusive proof that the motif is of French origin or even was known in France before it was known in Ireland . . . The fact that motifs found in continental lays and romances also appear in Irish tales which, on linguistic grounds can be dated earlier, often centuries earlier, has led to a situation where

---

[1]   Gertrude Schoepperle, *Tristan and Isolt: A Study of the Sources of the Romance*, second edition (New York, 1960).
[2]   Alan Bruford, *Gaelic Folk-Tales and Mediaeval Romances: A study of the Early Modern Irish 'Romantic Tales' and their oral derivatives* (Dublin, 1969), p.12.

some Arthurian scholars seem to describe any motif whose source is
unknown as 'Celtic', and may even treat nineteenth-century Irish
folk-tales as accurate representatives of the source drawn on by a
twelfth-century *lai*.

As we shall see, that last remark is particularly pertinent when we
come to look at some of the Irish 'sources' of the Tristan material. This
study divides into two main parts: firstly, the question of the actual material concerning Tristan in the mediaeval Celtic languages (which basically means in Welsh); and secondly, the question of the Celtic nature of
the story itself. Since the majority of the surviving material in Welsh is
later than the period to which the origin of the legend must be ascribed,
we will start with the second question first.

Two studies which are of immense use in this respect are those of
Rachel Bromwich and Oliver Padel,[3] which in themselves represent both
original ideas and excellent syntheses of the available material. A good
deal of the evidence for the Celtic origin of the material is derived from
similarities, or supposed similarities, to episodes and motifs found in Old
Irish literature: what, then, are these, and how valid are they?

It would be difficult to deny that there are certain types of narrative as
listed in the Old Irish tale-lists[4] which do seem to be very close to the
major elements of the Tristan legend, particularly the *aitheda* (elope-
ments), *tochmarca* (wooings) and possibly (for Tristan's voyages to Ireland
or to Cornwall) the *immrama* (sea voyages). Also, given the consistently
Celtic background and location of the legend, it would seem foolish to
posit any other than a Celtic origin for the stories of Tristan. The question
is, however, which branch of the Celtic tradition is at the root of what we
have today? Is it Irish, North British, Pictish, Cornish, even Breton? Some
confusion no doubt also arises from the common habit of assuming that
where two texts dealing with a similar subject exist, one of them must be
based on the other, as if we were dealing with textual criticism based on a
presumed authorial archetype, so that if there is an Irish *aithed* with a
similar narrative pattern to that of *Tristan*, then there must be some kind
of direct connexion between them. This may be so, but it seems far more
likely that both are versions of common Celtic analogues (MacCana, for
example, sees the *aitheda* and *tochmarca* as 'the diversified reflex of myths,

3   Rachel Bromwich, 'Some Remarks on the Celtic Sources of "Tristan" ', *Transactions
of the Honourable Society of Cymmrodorion*, Session 1953 (1955), 32–60 (hereafter Bromwich, *THSC*). O. J. Padel, 'The Cornish Background of the Tristan Stories', *Cambridge
Medieval Celtic Studies*, 1 (1981), 53–81 (hereafter Padel).
4   The Old Irish Tale-Lists, their content, date and provenance, are discussed in detail
in: Proinsias MacCana, *The Learned Tales of Medieval Ireland* (Dublin, 1980), and Rudolf
Thurneysen, *Die irische Helden- und Königsage bis zum siebzehnten Jahrhundert* (Halle,
1921), pp. 21–24.

which are as old, and older, than the Celts', p. 75), since so much material has been lost in languages other than Irish. As will be seen below, we do know of Tristan material in Welsh from the Triads which does not exist in any surviving narrative. The Irish texts, then, may be useful, not as source material, but as providing analogues of the kind of narrative pattern which could lie at the base of the Tristan legend. Their usefulness does, however, depend on them presenting this material in an unadulterated form, and this is where the major problem lies for those attempting to analyse both them and the Tristan material.

The first text to concern us is The Wooing of Emer (*Tochmarc Emire*). One episode in this text, which is dated by Thurneysen to the eighth century *in its earliest form* (though he says (p. 382) that the composite form which we have at present dates from soon after the first half of the twelfth century), concerns an exploit of CuChulainn at the court of the 'King of the Islands'. As is well known,[5] this is a version of the Andromeda story, but it has links with the Tristan legend because it contains, firstly, the recognition motif, where CuChulainn is recognised because he has been bandaged with a piece of the princess's shift; secondly, a possible connexion with the name Morholt, since the oppressors who are demanding the maiden as tribute are the Fomori;[6] and also a character, otherwise inactive, named Drust mac Seirb. It has been suggested that this indicates that Drust was the original hero of the exploit who has been displaced by CuChulainn, and further that this indicates a Pictish origin for the story, since, as Thurneysen says, 'Drostan findet sich mehrfach als Piktenname in der irischen Literatur' (p. 392, n. 2). Carney (cf. note 5 above) sees these elements as an indication that 'the Irish story is obviously borrowed through the medium of the primitive British Tristan' which he earlier suggests 'was composed and written in N. Britain sometime before the year 800' (p.197). We will return to the question of the Pictish name below, though in view of the prevalence of the name Drostan in Irish literature, it could just be that this was the closest approximation to the name Trystan/Drystan available, and therefore not admissible as evidence of Pictish origins. While one might be prepared to see the influence actually being that of 'Britain' (and here one must ask oneself whether we are referring to North or South Britain, to Brittonic or Pictish speakers) on Ireland, the late dating of the version of *Tochmarc Emire* which is concerned (and Padel (p. 56) suggests that as a digression this episode may well be as late as the twelfth century) brings us no closer to a version of Tristan that precedes the earliest continental versions.

The story of Deirdre (found in the Irish text *Longes mac n-Uislenn*, dated

5   See James Carney, 'The Irish Affinities of Tristan', in *Studies in Irish Literature and History* (Dublin, 1979), pp.189–242 (p. 241); also Bromwich, THSC, pp. 38–42.
6   See Bromwich, THSC, 39–40.

to the eighth or ninth century[7]) has affinities with Tristan because of the elements of fatal love, and of the life of the lovers in the wilderness (though one could ask oneself if all tales of adultery between the young wife or betrothed of an older man and a more attractive young hero really need to be traced to literary antecedents; and the fact that people who act in this way are forced to live outside normal society also seems relatively logical). Nevertheless, in spite of its early dating compared with the earliest extant Tristan material, even this is relegated to a secondary status by Carney: 'I now, however, regard *Deirdre* as the earliest Irish borrowing of the British Tristan' (p.190, n.1). Whether one agrees with his detailed reasoning or not, this does cast some doubt on the question of primacy in the relationship between the texts.

Toruigheacht Dhiarmada agus Ghrainne (The Pursuit of Diarmaid and Grainne)[8] is the Irish narrative which, possibly rightly, has been seen as the closest analogue to the Tristan legend. It has been widely discussed in the literature, so there is little point in going into narrative detail here. What is important is how much this can be taken to represent a 'purely Celtic' version of the theme, and here again the question of dating comes into play. There can be no doubt that some narrative dealing with the love between Diarmaid, one of Finn's warriors, and Grainne, Finn's betrothed, existed by the tenth century. Mention of an *Aithed Grainne ingine Corbmaic le Diarmaid ua nDuibne* occurs in the tale-lists, and there is a poem, dated by Gerard Murphy to the ninth or tenth century,[9] telling of Grainne's love: 'There is one / on whom I would gladly gaze / for whom I would give the bright world / all of it, all of it, / though it be an unequal bargain.' There are other mentions and fragments, listed in Ni Sheaghda's introduction, but the main text occurs in Early Modern Irish MSS, the oldest of which dates from 1651 (p. xiv). This gap between earliest mention of the tale and earliest MS need not necessarily mean that the version we have is unreliable, the tenacity of oral folk tradition being what it is (or is supposed to be), but both Padel and Carney cast doubt on the virginal purity of this narrative. The latter, for example, points out that the use of *gessa* by Grainne to compel Diarmaid to run away with her, far from being the sign of antiquity which Schoepperle considers it to be,[10] is in fact a corruption of the original meaning of the *geis* and thus 'nothing more than an author's lazy method of motivating action . . . artistically, but hardly an-

---

7   *Longes mac n-Uislenn: The Exile of the Sons of Uisliu*, edited by Vernam Hull (New York, 1949).
8   *Toruigheacht Dhiarmada Agus Ghrainne. The Pursuit of Diarmaid and Grainne*, edited by Nessa Ni Sheaghda (Dublin, 1967).
9   Gerard Murphy, *Early Irish Lyrics, Eighth to Twelfth Century* (Oxford, 1956), p.160.
10   Schoepperle, op. cit., p. 402. She also claims here that Deirdre's treatment of Noisiu in compelling him to go with her is a *geis*, though the text does not mention the word at this point.

thropologically, primitive' (p.193). The same could obviously be said of the 'love-spot' of which Schoepperle also makes so much (pp. 401–03). Padel points out that the 'horse's ears' episode (which makes sense in the Tristan legend, since the name March means 'horse'), found in the *Toruigheacht*, is likely to be derived from the Tristan legend, so that the tale *as we have it* may well be influenced by the Tristan tradition and therefore cannot be used as evidence of possible source material. He concludes: 'One can only say that ultimately there may be some unknown early Irish *aithed* behind the Tristan stories, but that there need not be.' (p. 57)

One is thus thrown back on the evidence, such as it is, for the existence of 'Tristan' that is found in Celtic sources outside Ireland. The first category to be considered is that of the personal names. The material is discussed in detail by Padel, and can be summarised thus:

(a) Though there are occurrences of a Pictish DRUST, DROSTEN, etc., the name DRYSTAN 'is a perfectly good Brittonic name, and its earliest occurrence is not in Pictland but on a Dark Age inscribed stone in Cornwall' (p. 55). Padel points to the similarity between the patronymic TALLWCH found in Welsh and TALARGAN found in Pictish, but finally dismisses it as interesting, yet hardly constituting 'evidence for the origin of the Tristan legend' (p. 55). This similarity, though, does seem, as he himself admits, to be more than coincidence. Unfortunately, in the present state of the argument and the evidence, it has to remain as one of those awkward and inexplicable things which bedevil just this subject.

(b) The name ESELT (the Cornish form of the name found as ESSYLLT in Welsh, probably the origin of the name Isolt, Iseult) is found in an Anglo-Saxon charter-boundary dated A.D. 967, in the form *hryt eselt* ('Isolt's Ford'). The stream concerned is on the Lizard peninsula (pp. 66–67).

(c) The name MARCH (though difficult to distinguish in place-names from the common noun *march*, 'horse') is also found traditionally as that of an early king of Cornwall (pp. 72–73).

Other evidence about personal names is discussed in Dr Bromwich's edition of the Welsh 'Tristan' poems,[11] which will be mentioned below. The gist of this is that the names Tristan, March and Kyheic (a character in the poems) are found in early Wales only in witness lists in the Llandaf charters, a fact which may point to the popularity of the literary material in South Wales – and some of the charters containing precisely these names are dated by Wendy Davies to the late eighth and early tenth centuries.[12]

---

11 Rachel Bromwich, 'The "Tristan" Poem in the Black Book of Carmarthen', *Studia Celtica*, 14/15 (1979/80), 54–65.

12 Wendy Davies, *The Llandaff Charters* (Aberystwyth, 1979):
MARCH, f. Pepiau . . . 235a; c.900 (p.179).
MARCH, . . . 224; c.935 (ibid.)
CEHEIC, . . . 206, 211b (Coheic); c.775 (p.153)

Place-names are also discussed by Padel, and he points out in great detail the way in which Béroul's use of Cornish place-names fits the geography of the county quite accurately. He also shows how the assumption that the place-name *Lohnois* (sometimes mentioned as Tristan's homeland) is Lothian in Scotland does not support the hypothesis of Pictish origin, as 'Lothian was never a part of Pictland' (p. 56). All in all, his conclusion is that 'a case can be made out, though only a very tentative one, for the Tristan stories having originated in Cornwall' (p. 80).

Finally, we come to the actual literary material in Celtic, or rather in Welsh. The only even vaguely complete text is the tale, found first in sixteenth-century MSS, told in a mixture of prose and *englynion*, of how Trystan and Essyllt outwit March: given the choice by Arthur between having Essyllt when the leaves are on the trees or when the trees are bare, March chooses the time when they are bare (presumably thinking of the long winter nights). To this Essyllt's reply is:

There are three trees that are good of their kind, holly, ivy and yew, which keep their leaves as long as they live. I am Trystan's as long as he lives.[13]

Here Trystan and Essyllt are set in the context of the 'classical' Arthurian court, where the main hero is Gwalchmai (Gawain), which would point to a date later in the evolution of the Arthurian legend in Wales than at least one of the Triads discussed below.

Another source in *englyn* form, which may again link a character from the Tristan legend with the Arthurian legend is the *Englynion y Beddau* (Stanzas of the Graves) from the Black Book of Carmarthen.[14] Though the MS itself is of the thirteenth century, Thomas Jones suggests that various criteria 'point to their composition in a period considerably earlier than even the Black Book . . . probably as early as the ninth or tenth century' (p.100). Here March (though one cannot be absolutely sure that it is the Mark of the Tristan legend) is mentioned in the same stanza as the famous passage that describes Arthur's grave as *anoeth bit* (the world's wonder – or mystery) (p.127). Unfortunately no geographical location is given for

Another example from a charter in the Book of Llandaf not used in Prof. Davies's collection is: Auel mab TRISTAN, in: *The Text of the Book of Llan Dâv Reproduced from the Gwysane Manuscript* by J. Gwenogvryn Evans, . . . with the co-operation of John Rhys (Oxford, 1893), p. 279, 1. 26.

13 R. L. Thomson, 'The Welsh Fragment of Tristan (Trystan ac Esyllt)', in *The Tristan Legend*, edited by Joyce Hill (Leeds, 1977), pp.1–5, gives a convenient version for non-Welsh-readers.

14 Thomas Jones, 'The Black Book of Carmarthen "Stanzas of the Graves" ', *Proceedings of the British Academy*, 53 (1967), 97–137.

March's grave, as is done for some of the other heroes mentioned in the Stanzas, so this source is not very helpful in any study of origins.

Similar to the Irish tale-lists in that they provide a catalogue of narrative material available, this time to the Welsh story-teller, are the Triads. These are available in Dr Bromwich's masterly edition, *Trioedd Ynys Prydein*,[15] which also acts as an *index nominorum* to a great deal of Welsh literature. Those wishing to investigate the use made of the characters of Tristan, Isolt and Mark by the Welsh poets of the Middle Ages – unfortunately at a time when the influence of the continental tradition cannot be discounted – have only to consult this work. The earliest MS of the Triads, Peniarth 16, dates from the third quarter of the thirteenth century, but linguistic features suggest an earlier dating (p. xviii). In them Tristan is mentioned a number of times: he is one of the three Enemy-Subduers of the Island of Britain, one of the three Battle-Diademed Men, one of the three Lovers, one of the three Stubborn Men, and finally one of the three Powerful Swineherds. This last Triad contains an interesting narrative element:

> Drystan son of Tallwch, who guarded the swine of March son of Meirchiawn while the swineherd went to ask Essyllt to come to a meeting with him. And Arthur was seeking to obtain one pig from among them, either by deceit or by force, but he did not get it. (variant: Arthur and March and Cai and Bedwyr were [there] all four, but they did not succeed in getting so much as one pigling – neither by force, nor by deception, nor by stealth (pp. 46ff)).

Here the warriors of Arthur's whom we meet are Cai and Bedwyr, who belong to the earliest stratum of the Welsh Arthurian legend, and the spirit of the Triad does seem comparable to that of the earliest Welsh Arthurian prose narrative, *Culhwch ac Olwen*. This would seem to suggest two things: firstly, that there was an early Tristan narrative in Welsh which predates the texts we know to have been influenced by continental sources (e.g. *Geraint, Iarlles Y Ffynnawn, Peredur*), and secondly, that like many other originally independent heroes Tristan was drawn into the Arthurian orbit – again, however, at a relatively early stage (*Culhwch ac Olwen* has been dated 'in its latest redaction about 1050–1100'[16]). Fascinating too, is the connexion with pigs: apart from the fact that we seem to have here an example of Tristan visiting Isolde in disguise, the coat of arms of Gottfried's Tristan is a boar and Diarmaid dies as a result of

15 Rachel Bromwich, *Trioedd Ynys Prydein, The Welsh Triads*, edited with *Introduction, Translation and Commentary* (Cardiff, 1961).
16 Brynley F. Roberts, 'Tales and Romances', in *A Guide to Welsh Literature*, edited by A. O. H. Jarman and Gwilym Rees Hughes (Swansea, 1976), p. 214.

hunting a boar whose life is magically connected with his. This connexion led Edward Davies in his *The Mythology and Rites of the British Druids* to suggest 'that the legend allegorized that period of British history when the Phoenician rites of the sow were introduced into Cornish religions'.[17] Such amusing speculations aside (and one cannot help wondering what the rites of the sow actually were!), there may be something more to this. Apart from the obvious symbolism of the boar as an emblem of courage and virility, there may be a connexion with Cornwall: Arthur himself is called *aper Cornubiae* in the Prophecies of Merlin, and the story of his hunting Twrch Trwyth is also linked to Cornwall.[18] One might tentatively suggest, then, that there is some emblematic connexion between Cornwall and boars: a further aid to one's attempts to locate the origins of the Tristan legend.

The final text is one that has recently been re-edited by Dr Bromwich, though it has been known for some time. This is the series of Stanzas, again in the Black Book of Carmarthen, which are connected with the Tristan legend by the fact that the name *Diristan* (a form of Drystan) appears in the last of them. They actually seem from their metrical structure to belong to two separate poems, but these poems are further linked by the fact that the unusual name *Kyheic* (which apart from the Book of Llandaf charters is not found elsewhere in Welsh tradition, see above) occurs in both. It may even be that this occurrence of an unusual name is what caused the juxtaposition of the stanzas in the MS in the first place. Fragmentary as they are, it seems clear that they belong, as Dr Bromwich says, 'to speech-poems of a passionate and highly dramatic character' (p. 54).

The texts are dated by the editor 'before 1100' (p. 55), and a version of her suggested translation (with some possible emendations, where the context is not clear enough to indicate which of two homonyms is to be understood) follows:

> I. 1. Though I love the sea-shore, I hate the sea
> That [or: why] the wave should cover the hero's rock.
> Brave constant courteous generous ?strong branch?
> Mounting block of the poets of the world, a victorious protector
> The cup-bearer of fame has done a disastrous favour.
> Till Judgement will last its/his ?lamentation?
>
> 2. Though I love the sea-shore, I hate the wave
> The violence of the wave has made a cold separation between us.
> I shall lament as long as I live because of this,

---

17 See Rosemary Picozzi, *A History of Tristan Scholarship* (Berne, 1971), p.19.
18 O. J. Padel, 'Geoffrey of Monmouth and Cornwall', *Cambridge Medieval Celtic Studies*, 8 (1984), 8, 13.

A ?nimble? deed washing on my breast[s],
Though it fills the thoughts it does not heat the heart
And ?after / [in the track / ?manner? / of] Kyheic, reconciliation
                                                      between us.

3. I regret his expedition
   When the strong man rushed far to death.
   A strong constant company were we two
   In the place where the water carries the leaves.

II. 1. Drystan is enraged [?flees] at your coming [destruction, leaving]
       I will not accept from you my ?dismissal?
       For my part I betrayed March [or: sold a horse!] for your sake.

2. Vengeance on/for Kyheic would be my wish
   Because of his sweet speech [or: For his wealth, for his court].
   Alas, dwarf, your anger was hostile to me.

A number of elements important to the Tristan legend, and also typical of the Celtic tradition are present in these intriguing fragments: the betrayal of Mark, the hostile dwarf, the water carrying the leaves are all found elsewhere. The importance of the sea, which is also a factor in the Tristan legend, is found both in Old Irish elegy, often in poems attributed to women lamenting their lovers' deaths[19] and in early Welsh poetry.[20] In view of this tradition, and particularly of the existence in Welsh of a number of poems, many in *englyn* metre as is the second of these poems, attributed to female personae,[21] it is tempting to speculate that the character speaking here may be Isolt. Unfortunately, there is no evidence from the texts themselves to suggest even the sex of the speaker, let alone his/her identity. One possible clue in the word *dwyvron* (dual of *bron*, 'breast') is shown to be invalid, in that early examples in *Geiriadur Prifysgol Cymru* (the University of Wales Dictionary) refer to both male and female.

In conclusion, then, it seems possible to say that there are a number of connexions, which seem both strong and valid, between the Tristan legend and Celtic literary and historical traditions. The main problem is that texts which have earlier been seen as sources (or perhaps more correctly analogues) of the Tristan material may actually have been influenced by that very material, and so become inadmissible as evidence for the provenance of any particular detail, motif or narrative sequence. The

---

19 Murphy, op. cit., provides examples in poems 36 and 39.
20 e.g. Hywel ap Owein Gwynedd, 'Tonn wenn orewyn', in *The Myvyrian Archaiology of Wales* (Denbigh, 1870), p.198.
21 e.g. Heledd in the Cynddylan saga found in *Canu Llywarch Hen*, edited by Ifor Williams (Cardiff, 1935).

question of the geographical or linguistic provenance of the legend, too, is one that is still undecided (if such a decision is ever possible). The long accepted Pictish hypothesis seems to have been called very much into question, if not entirely demolished (and there is the unsolved mystery of the *Tallwch* patronymic in the Welsh tradition) by Oliver Padel's detailed researches (including the wading of the *gué aventuros*, though without carrying a young lady for total verisimilitude). The pendulum has swung back towards a Brittonic origin for the legend, at least in its present form – we now await the discovery of new evidence which will reverse this trend, or even set us looking in a totally new direction.

Pageantry and Court Aesthetic in Tristan: The Procession of the Hunters

MARGARET BROWN and C. STEPHEN JAEGER

The fourteen year old virtuoso of the hunt, Tristan, ends his instructions to the royal Cornish hunting party with a demonstration of the 'prisant':

> 'so wizzet ouch ir selbe wol,
> wie man den hirz prisanten sol:
> prisantet in ze rehte!' (3055–57)

Again, as so often in the scene, the flower of Cornish venerie is confronted with its ignorance of customs that appear to the boy wonder as a measure of courtly attainment, and this time, rather than repeat their admissions of ignorance, they fall into the equally unappealing alternative into which Tristan's captious rhetoric maneuvers them: they stand there like raw amateurs reduced to silence by true mastery. Ignoring his 'so wizzet ouch ir selbe wol . . .' they ask him to continue and to crown his 'wunderlichiu underbint' with his arrangements for the presentation of the game. When they come in sight of the castle Tintajel, Tristan picks two branches from a linden tree and bends them into wreaths, one for himself, the other, larger, for the hunting master. Then, just before the castle gate, he arranges the party into groups of two, apologizing for not being able to call each of the men by name. They are to reconstruct the dismembered stag and ride to court, presenting, or re-presenting the game as it appears in life:

> 'wan varn ie zwene und zwene samet
> und ritet rehte ein ander bi,
> alse der hirz geschaffen si.' (3172–74)

They are to ride slowly ('niht ze gach'). The measured gait projects ceremony, nobility, and fulfills the practical need of allowing the audience to view this staged event well and fully. Though Tristan strikes the stance of master, he is careful to preserve a sense of hierarchy: he cuts the Cornish master a larger wreath and maintains with his words the priority of the older man:

> 'ritet schone ein ander nach:
> min meister hie *und ich sin kneht*
> wir riten samet, dunk ez iuch reht
> und ob ez iu gevalle.'   (3186–89)

Finally he takes a horn and begins the entry procession, trumpeting as loudly as possible, the others 'following' in a cacophony that strikes amazement into the castle dwellers.

Whatever the procession is for the ears, it is a feast for the eyes. Its formality and symmetry, its staged, arranged spectacle, the crowned masters in the lead, the pairs supporting the re-formed stag following, produces so strange and new an effect that Gottfried virtually exhausts his vocabulary of astonishment in describing it:

> si erschraken unde erkamen
> vil innecliche sere,
> wan ez da vor nie mere
> da ze hove wart vernomen.   (3226–29)

> si nam groz wunder über al
> waz des geschelles wære.   (3234–35)

Tristan's 'niuwiu meisterschaft' is a 'wunderlicher list' which the master huntsman cannot praise too much.

In coming to terms with this scene, it is easy to overstress its origins in hunting practice. True, Gottfried refers to Tristan's instructions as *jagereht* (3062) and to his version of *prisant* as *rehtiu jegerie* (3184), but these terms accept new customs as a fait accompli; they do not reveal a customary connection between this scene and contemporary hunting practice. Neither the surviving sources on the art of hunting, nor similar scenes in romance, show us a comparable example where a courtly procession is combined with a hunting presentation.[1] Nor does the loan word, *prisant*, *preisant*, help us to locate the procession in contemporary customs of the hunt.[2]

---

[1]   See Herbert Kolb, 'Ars venandi im *Tristan*', in *Medium Aevum deutsch: Beiträge zur deutschen Literatur des hohen und späten Mittelalters: Festschrift für Kurt Ruh zum 65. Geburtstag*, edited by Dietrich Huschenbett *et al.* (Tübingen, 1979), pp. 175–197, on the procession, especially pp. 192ff. Kolb gives some convincing parallels to the presentation, but not to the ceremony and formality of the procession. These aspects are surely not specific to hunt customs, but more generally part of the aesthetics of court ceremony.

[2]   Kolb points out that *prisanten* occurs in Middle High German for the first time in *Tristan* ('Ars venandi', p. 192). Though it is clearly a loan word from Old French,

We are dealing with forms of the ceremonial court procession and entry. These are imposed in the courtly versions of the Tristan romance onto the events of the hunt. Gottfried stresses the courtliness of the procession; it is ceremony appropriate to the court:

> 'und bringet iuwern prisant
> ze hove nach hovelichem site.'   (3052–53)[3]

It is to be done as things are done at court, in the courtly way. The ceremony is commensurate with rules, laws, an etiquette of court behavior: 'als soltez sin' (3208). And it is accordingly 'beautiful', the word that, next to *hovelich*, attaches most closely to the scene: 'ritet *schone* ein ander nach' (3186); 'und hürneten *vil schone*' (3217); 'daz wart *schoner* unde baz / ze hove geprisantet nie' (3300–01). And inseparable from the aesthetics of the procession are the aesthetics of the performing human being: the beauty and courtliness of the ceremony renders the participant courtly and beautiful:

> 'und bringet iuwern prisant
> ze hove nach hovelichem site:
> da hovet ir iuch selben mite.'   (3052–54)

Mutual intensification of beauty or courtliness: this is the relationship between Tristan and the ceremony, the artist and his work of art. It is similar to the relationship between the armor and the man wearing it in Gottfried's description of the arming ceremony: each piece has the effect,

> daz iegeliches schonheit
> dem andern schœne bære
> und sin geschœnet wære . . .   (6630–32)

and, by comparison, the man within appears so much the more ingeniously and beautifully wrought. As if to show how the courtly and beautiful work of art renders the artist courtly and beautiful, Gottfried presses these qualities of Tristan into the foreground: 'a herre, ez ist ein Parmenois / so wunderlichen curtois . . .' (3277–78); 'ouch kunde er selbe schone gan' (3331); 'sine vüeze und siniu bein, / dar an sin schœne almeistic schein . . .' (3341–42); 'an gebærde unde an schœnen siten / was ime so

---

Gottfried's *Tristan* seems to provide the only surviving example. Tobler-Lommatzsch, *Altfranzösisches Wörterbuch*, VII (Wiesbaden, 1966–69), has only one reference in the context of the hunt. This is to Bédier's reconstruction of Thomas, which depends for the hunt scene on Gottfried (VII, col. 1798).

3   Kolb, p. 192, argues that 'nach hovelichem site' implies 'eine ältere Jagdsitte', though both 'hovelich' and 'hovelicher site' need suggest only that courtly style here is imposed on the practices of the hunt.

rehte wol geschehen . . .' (3348–49). The same conceptual syntax is in effect here as in the arming ceremony:

> swie so der uzer wære,
> der inner bildære
> der was baz betihtet,
> bemeistert unde berihtet . . .   (6643–46)

Before we go on, we should note that Gottfried is probably translating his source, Thomas, very closely at this point. At least the hunting procession is present in its essential details in the Old Norse adaptation of Thomas by Friar Robert: Tristan instructs the Cornish hunters, shows them the 'pole present', and admonishes them to take the stag to the king 'in a courtly manner'. The ceremony is called by name, 'the gift of the chase'. It sets the court and the king in astonishment, and the master huntsman rehearses to the king the entire scene of Tristan's instruction.[4] Many details of description and ceremonial arrangement are lacking in the Old Norse version, but they are the sort of detail that may well have appeared to the Norwegian prose writer as superfluous fluff. We must assume that Gottfried's version of the procession was virtually identical with that of Thomas.

But we should not make the mistake of assuming that this sort of ceremony is present in Gottfried's work because of inertia. The German poet shows a genuine interest in court ceremony. He clearly was an engaged and like-minded adapter. This interest in some cases appears to go beyond what Gottfried received from his source. Apart from the hunt scene, there are the festival at Mark's court, Tristan's knighting and arming ceremonies, the preparations for the duel with Morolt, the court day at Dublin and solemn entry of the participants, and the ceremonies surrounding Isolde's testing. Gottfried's representation of court ceremony deserves a monographic study.[5] It would certainly have to include the literary excursus, which has the character of pageant-like celebration of Tristan's knighting, and which itself includes reference to a ceremony of a different kind, the crowning of a poet with the laurel wreath.

---

[4]   See *The Saga of Tristram and Ísönd*, translated by Paul Schach (Lincoln, Nebraska, 1973), pp. 26–29 (chapters 21–22); *Tristrams Saga ok Ísondar*, edited and translated by Eugen Kölbing (Heilbronn, 1878), pp. 21ff. The Old Norse term corresponding to *prisant* is *stangarsending*, and Tristram calls the arrival ceremony and presentation (of the head alone, not the entire stag) *komandi veiðifórn*, a custom of huntsmen in his land. The scenes in *Ipomedon* cited by Kolb (p.194) confirm that the presenting of the game was an accepted custom, but not that solemn courtly ceremonial accompanied it.

[5]   Court ceremonial in courtly literature is virtually unstudied. For a good introduction, see Joachim Bumke, *Höfische Kultur: Literatur und Gesellschaft im hohen Mittelalter* (Munich, 1986), pp. 276–341. For earlier literature see ibid., pp. 825–26.

Some analogues from other sources will help us analyse the scene and interpret its underlying aesthetic. Two sorts of sources are available: courtly romance and historical writings. In stirring through contemporary representations of processions in chronicle and romance, we want to avoid the trap of assuming that we can infer the reality of court practice from any representation of it. What we infer from both kinds of sources is a court ideal. That ideal and its aesthetic premises are the object of our analysis.

Courtly processions abound in twelfth- and thirteenth-century narrative.[6] Here is a typical example, the entry of Eneas and his followers to his wedding celebration in Veldeke's *Eneide*:[7]

> Her hiez mit ime riten
> Vunfhundert ritter wol geborn . . .
> Wol geziert mit gewande
> Unde ritterleiche,
> Wan sie waren reiche
> Und heten state gute
> An der habe und an dem gemute . . .
>
> Michel zierde do was . . .
> Man horte mit hoen stymmen
> Die vordern hin riten.
> Do zu den ziten
> Reit der herre Eneas . . .
> Mit michelem gedrange,
> Mit phifen und mit gesange,
> Mit trumben und mit seiten spil.
> Grozer vrouden was do vil.   (12814 *et seq.*)

The scene has two basic elements that dominate in scores of similar ones: magnificence and noise. The procession did not not become an elaborate conventional form in courtly fiction, as did the festival or the description of a person or a magnificent building or creature. Processions generally receive fairly short shrift. The same is true of the great majority of chronicle descriptions.[8] We cannot find essential distinctions between the

---

6   For many good examples, see Bumke, *Höfische Kultur*, pp. 290–99.
7   Henric van Veldeken, *Eneide*, edited by G. Schieb and Th. Frings, Deutsche Texte des Mittelalters, 58 (Berlin, 1964).
8   On the royal entry see R. Withington, 'The Early "Royal-Entry" ', *PMLA*, 32 (1917), 616–23; esp. Roy Strong, *Art and Power: Renaissance Festivals, 1450–1650* (Woodbridge, Suffolk, 1984), pp. 7ff. Also B. Guenée and F. Lehoux, *Les entrées royales françaises de 1328 à 1515*, Sources d'histoire médiévale, 5 (Paris, 1968); W. Dotzauer, 'Die Ankunft des Herrschers: Der fürstliche Einzug in die Stadt', *Archiv für Kulturgeschichte*, 55 (1973), 245–88.

representation of processions in fiction and in historical writings. Here also splendid clothing and noisy singing or cheering dominate. The atmosphere was what counted for the poet or chronicler; the details tend to fall by the wayside. But there are some exceptions, and it is worth our while to single out two of them.

The first is the procession of King Philipp of Swabia and his wife, the Byzantine princess Irene, on Christmas day 1199 in Magdeburg. The description of this event in the *Gesta episcoporum Halberstadensium* has the elements of pomp and noisy turmoil ('cum ingenti magnificentia celebravit . . . regalibus indumentis, imperiali dyademate insignitus . . .'; 'coniux sua . . . regio cultu excellentissime simul ornata . . .'; 'omnesque qui aderant . . . corde gaudentes, animis exultantes, manibus applaudentes, vocibus perstrepentes . . . huic sollempnitati uniformiter arriserunt . . .').[9] But there is a good deal more. The chronicler stresses the solemnity of the king's gait and of the entire ceremony ('sollempniter incedebat'). Duke Bernard of Saxony precedes carrying the royal sword. The king follows, and just behind him the queen with Abbess Agnes of Quedlinburg, Lady Judith, wife of Duke Bernard, and a crowd of noble ladies, who follow 'tam decentissime quam venustissime.' On either side of the king and queen is a host of bishops, conducting them 'reverently and respectfully' ('tam reverenter quam honorabiliter'). We also learn from this source that the entire ceremony was devised by the imperial chancellor, Konrad of Querfurt, 'wisely and prudently so that all would be carried out faithfully, as ordained.'[10] We have another description of the event in a poem of Walther von der Vogelweide, and the combination of poetic and historical text makes this entry especially instructive.[11] Walther also observes the beauty and solemnity of the gait ('Ez gienc . . . der künec Philippes schône . . . er trat vil lîse, im was niht gâch'). It seemed that the sum of courtly decorum was convened there ('diu zuht was niener anderswâ'). But Walther also has a sharper eye for the religious symbolism of the event than the chronicler. He suggests the connection between the *maget* who gave birth to Christ on this day and the *Megdeburc* where the event takes place. He imposes a Trinitarian allusion on the figure of the emperor:

9 *Gesta episcoporum Halberstadensium*, edited by L. Weiland, Monumenta Germaniae Historica, Scriptores, 23, pp.113–14.
10 'Domnus autem Conradus, imperialis aule cancellarius, sagaciter cuncta disposuit et prudenter, et ut ordinate fierent omnia fideliter procuravit' (ibid., p.114).
11 *Die Gedichte Walthers von der Vogelweide*, edited by K. Lachmann and Hugo Kuhn, 13th edition (Berlin, 1965), 19, 5ff. See the commentary by Peter Wapnewski, 'Die Weisen aus dem Morgenland auf der Magdeburger Weihnacht: Zu Walther von der Vogelweide 19, 5', in his *Waz ist minne: Studien zur Mittelhochdeutschen Lyrik* (Munich, 1975), pp.155–80.

dâ gienc eins keisers bruoder und eins keisers kint
in einer wât, swie doch die namen drîge sint.   (19, 8–9)

The parallels to the hunt procession in *Tristan* are striking, into details
of wording. All three stress slowness and solemnity: *The Hunt*: 'lazet iu
niht sin ze gach'; *The Royal Procession*: 'er trat vil lîse, im was niht gâch';
'solempniter incedebat'. Both are beautiful and highly courtly events: *The
Hunt*: 'ritet schone ein ander nach'; 'hürneten vil schone'; 'daz wart
schoner unde baz / ze hove geprisantet nie'; 'nach hovelichem site:/ da
hovet ir iuch selben mite'; 'wunderlichen curtois'; 'höfsch[iu] jegerie'; *The
Royal Procession*: 'tam decentissime quam venustissime prosecuta'; 'tam
reverenter quam honorabiliter conduxerunt'; 'Ez gienc . . . der künec . . .
schône'; 'diu zuht was niener anderswâ'. Striking also is the fact that in
both cases there is a master of ceremonies. In the hunt he is a participant;
the chronicle places him outside the events. But both procession-masters
clearly had similar guiding principles of organization. Konrad of Querfurt
shows his 'sagacity' and 'prudence', which has a close equivalent in the
'bescheidenheit' the Cornish master recognizes in Tristan's instructions
(3061), and a more distant equivalent in the 'kunst' (3075) and 'list' (3293,
3296, 3305) of the arrangements. Both are concerned 'ut ordinate fierent
omnia', 'als solte ez sin'. Gottfried and the chronicle stress the artistic
conscientiousness of design: 'sagaciter cuncta disposuit et prudenter'; 'wa
wart ie list so wol bedaht?' (3296). And this no doubt registers in the kinds
of symbolism both employ, disparate though they may be. Konrad of
Querfurt has provided for the hierarchical structuring of the event typical
of royal/imperial *representatio*,[12] and if Walther is a reliable witness to
Konrad's design, the whole event is overlaid with a religious symbolism
showing the emperor as an earthly embodiment of the trinity, incorpora-
ting the location into the Christmas symbolism: virgin birth celebrated in
the city of the virgin(s), and conjuring the three wise men from the Orient
as approving observers (see Wapnewski, op. cit.). In the hunt scene the
hierarchic structuring is present in the linden wreaths, Tristan's cut smal-
ler than the master's, and in Tristan's self-subordination ('min meister hie
und ich sin kneht'). A form of symbolism is evident in the re-presentation
of the stag, a subject we will return to later. The details of the symbolism
are not comparable; only the presence of comparable techniques in both
cases.

Now we turn to a more extensive procession description. It is a passage
that deserves to be included in the discussion of the literature of courtly

---

12 cf. P. E. Schramm, *Kaiser, Könige und Päpste: Gesammelte Aufsätze zur Geschichte des
Mittelalters* (Stuttgart, 1968), I, 31 (the coronation banquet as 'politisches Schauspiel').
Also Strong, *Art and Power*, p. 7: '. . . in one mighty sweep the onlookers saw pass
before them [in the medieval royal entry], in microcosm, the whole of society as they
knew it . . .'

ceremony. Thomas Becket as chancellor of the English king led a wooing party to France to court Margaret, the daughter of the French King. The description is from Becket's biographer, William Fitzstephen. We quote it at some length, omitting much of Fitzstephen's inventory of the supplies:[13]

> And so the chancellor took charge of the matter at hand, the persons involved, and his own duty, and rising to this great occasion . . . he prepared to display and to pour forth the opulence of English luxury, so that in all ways and in the eyes of all men the person of the sender would gain honor through his emissary, and that of the emissary through his sender. He took with him approximately 200 members of his household mounted on horseback: knights, clerics, stewards, servants, squires, sons of nobles to fight for him in arms, all of them instructed. They and their entire following were refulgent in the new festive splendor of their clothing, each dressed in his own fashion. The chancellor had twenty-four changes of clothes . . . many silk garments, nearly all destined to remain in France as gifts; grise and vair and exotic pelts in elegant variety, robes and coverlets with which the bed and bedchamber of the bishop were ornamented wherever he was received as a guest. He had with him dogs and birds of every kind that kings and great lords use. He had in his train eight official chariots, each pulled by five horses like chargers in build and strength. Each horse had assigned to it a strong youth clad in a new tunic accompanying the carriage, and each carriage had its own messenger and warden . . . The chancellor's portable chapel had its own carriage, as did his treasury, his provisions, his kitchen. Some helped carry food and drink, others blankets, sacks for bed clothes and other supplies. He had twelve pack animals and eight chests with the gold and silver utensils of the chancellor . . . Each of the pack animals had its own groom appropriately instructed in its care. Also, each carriage had a dog tied either above or below, large, powerful and terrifying, a match for any bear or lion. But also on each pack animal was a long-tailed monkey or 'a simian model of the human form'.
>
> When entering villages and castles in France, the grooms came first on foot . . . They numbered nearly two hundred and fifty, and marched together in groups of six or ten or more, singing in their native languages some song in the manner of their homeland. After them followed at some interval the dogs on their chains and the

13   *Vita Sancti Thomae, auctore Willelmo filio Stephani,* sect. 19, in *Materials for the History of Thomas Becket, Archbishop of Canterbury,* edited by J. C. Robertson, Rolls Series, 67, III (London, 1877), pp. 29ff. Translations are those of the authors, unless otherwise noted.

greyhounds with their leashes and restraints, or whatever name they are called by, along with their trainers and staff. After a space there followed the wagons covered with great blankets of animal skins sewn together, the iron-tipped wheels rumbling along the cobble-stoned streets. At some distance there followed the pack animals, straddled by their grooms.

Often the French came out of their houses to ask who it was who was arriving with such a din, whose household this could be? They were told that the chancellor of the English King was on his way as an emissary to the court of the King of France. Whereupon the French replied, 'What a wonder that king of the English must be whose chancellor makes so great and grand an entrance!'

After the pack animals the squires followed at an interval, bearing the shields of the knights and guiding their destriers, then more squires followed by other young men, then those who carried the birds, then the stewards and masters and ministers of the chancellor's court, then the knights and clerics, all riding two by two, and finally the chancellor himself surrounded by his closest retinue.

We have those two obligatory features of an entry procession: noise and opulence. The songs of the two hundred and fifty and more grooms fill the air like heralds' trumpets. Note that harmony and unison play no role at all. They sing whatever song they like ('aliquid . . . cantantes') in whatever language they command.[14] In fact loud noise seems desirable from whatever source it derives. The clattering of the iron-rimmed wheels on cobblestones is credited as much as the grooms' song. As in other processions, the splendor of the clothing plays a large part in this entry, but the rare furs and animals, the greyhounds, hunting hawks and monkeys give an especially exotic air to Becket's procession. A distinct parallel to the hunt procession in *Tristan* is the arrangement of horsemen riding two by two. This would seem to be part of the protocol of such events.[15]

But this scene was worth quoting in detail because the narrator shows us so clearly the underlying motives and the means of accomplishing them: 'He prepared to display and pour forth the opulence of English luxury, so that in all ways and in the eyes of all men the person of the

---

14 A conventional feature of grand processions. Cf. Benzo of Alba, *Ad Heinricum IV. imperatorem*, Bk. I, ch. 9, on imperial processions: '. . . imperatore gressum movente, tollitus clamor omnium ad sydera . . . Singule quidem nationes *secundum ritum patriae* prorumpunt in suas vociferationes. Tot igitur innumerabilium vocum clamoribus ex-territa tellus tremuit . . .' (*MGH*, SS 11, p. 602, 39ff). And Veldeke, *Eneit*, 13199f (the wedding feast of Aeneas and Lavinia): '[the minstrels] . . . lob dem kuninge sungen / Ir ieglich an syner zungen.'
15 cf. Bumke, *Höfische Kultur*, p. 293.

sender would gain honor through his emissary and that of the emissary through his sender.' Becket *represents* the king, and that word must be read as re-joining its aesthetic and its diplomatic areas of reference. The parade is the representation of the king of England; it stands for, symbolizes, re-presents him. The onlookers read it like a text and its meaning is: such a man is the king of England, 'mirabilis est ipse rex'. The staging of this scenario, the realizing of this 'theme', requires *mirabilia*, and the stage director, Becket, provides them in the form of monkeys, greyhounds, hunting birds (presumably not a practical element of a wooing party), furs and luxuries. These are not randomly chosen. Superficially seen, they lend style to the procession, and by no coincidence it is the style of the 'merveilleux', a style destined to become popular in courtly romance, called in the poetic terminology of MHG romance, *vremed* or *wild*.[16] In other words, the *significatum*, the subtext of this drama – the message, 'mirabilis est rex' – has a visible counterpart in the marvelous elements of the procession. The sight of monkeys and leopard skins in parades may call forth in a modern audience nothing more than thoughts of the zoo or the animal trade in Africa, but it transported a medieval viewer into the realm of the fabulous, lent an aura of exotic and magical fantasy to the king who moved in such a realm. It probably did something else as well. Chained creatures in court pageantry are not just display pieces, are not only to be read literally. They also make visible the ruler's dominance over the realm symbolized by the animal. The huge dogs chained to the carriages may be the party's security guards, but they also stand for savagery and violence; hunting birds for a much more refined form of violence; monkeys for sloth, stupidity and lustfulness.[17] Their captivity expresses the ruler's victory over the particular form of savagery or vice for which that animal is the allegorical emblem. The chained animals in other words are symbols of civilization. They assert the king's claim that he has conquered bestiality; they dramatize the high state of moral education attained by the king and his court, and that is a message entirely appropriate to a wooing party. We can see the same kind of logic at work in the funeral effigies of noblemen and women, depicted as standing on a lion or giant or dwarf, as a sign of their victory over vice, their command of courage, etc. It is also visible in processions from the later Middle Ages and Renaissance, in which wild men are led on chains by a princess or nobleman mounted on horseback. It represents the

---

16   Walter Haug, *Literaturtheorie im deutschen Mittelalter von den Anfängen bis zum Ende des 13. Jahrhunderts* (Darmstadt, 1985), pp. 347–48.
17   See E. R. Curtius, *European Literature and the Latin Middle Ages*, translated by W. R. Trask (New York & Evanston, 1953), pp. 538–40 ('The Ape as Metaphor'); also D. W. Robertson, *A Preface to Chaucer: Studies in Medieval Perspectives* (Princeton, 1962), p. 265 and fig. 6.

court's victory over rusticity and barbarity; it symbolizes courtliness and refinement.[18]

Here again we feel the element of careful design as an ingredient in a procession. It becomes a symbolic drama expressing the glory, wealth, refinement and courtliness of the king. It is laid out hierarchically and symmetrically. The costuming and gestures of the actors are arranged to maximize astonishment and admiration. Fitzstephen told us early on that each member of the party from groom to court minister had been instructed: 'omnes instructos'. What he means by this is a problem. If he means that all had received a courtly education, then the upshot is staggering: here is an entire household from menial to master in possession of an attribute that would be the envy of many a duke and count. Probably that is not what he means. More likely is the reading, all of them had received their instructions, all of them knew their part in the pageant. If so, then we have here what we had in the Christmas procession in Magdeburg and in the hunting procession of *Tristan*: a reference to the ordering of the procession according to a pre-arranged scenario. Becket's 'instructions' have a counterpart in Tristan's 'wunderlichiu underbint', in the huntsman's exclamation, 'wa wart ie list so wol bedaht?' and in Konrad of Querfurt's concern 'ut ordinate fierent omnia'.

The message conveyed by all this ordering is control. Everybody and everything in the procession is in control. As the chains control the wild animals, the instructions control the marching men. And so the visible order of the procession becomes testimony to the king's authority. The well-ordered procession represents and reinforces the power structures of the English monarchy.

These comparisons give us a detailed look into the workshop of a courtly master of ceremonies, or rather of three such figures. That two of them are king's chancellors and the other an up-and-coming courtier with many ties to the figure of the educated court cleric,[19] gives us some assurance that we have located the figure socially. Gottfried von Strassburg clearly thinks of his hero's handiwork here as a form of art deriving from learning. His vocabulary shows it: 'sin[iu] kunst' (3075); 'dise niuwe meisterschaft' (3290); 'wunderliche[r] list' (3293); 'list' (3296), and his insistence on the beauty of the performance underscores it.

[18] See T. Husband, *The Wild Man: Medieval Myth and Symbolism* (New York, 1980), pp. 61, 91. Also R. Bernheimer, *Wild Men in the Middle Ages: A Study in Art, Sentiment and Demonology* (Cambridge, Mass., 1952), p.142 and pp.176–85.
[19] See Bumke, *Höfische Kultur*, pp. 446ff and C. Stephen Jaeger, *The Origins of Courtliness: Civilizing Trends and the Formation of Courtly Ideals, 939–1210* (Philadelphia, 1985), esp. pp.100–110.

What do we gain for understanding the hunters' procession in *Tristan* from this perspective? Certainly if we understand this essay as a source study pointing to the forms on which Gottfried drew, the gain is slim, though it takes us beyond the narrower view of the *prisant* as a custom of the hunt. Another minor gain is the more general insight that courtly pageantry in romance has counterparts in historical writing,[20] and the one can illuminate the other.

But more important is the underlying aesthetic of court ceremony. This registers in reality, in history and in fiction. In each area there are aesthetic laws at work, and these deserve to be placed in the foreground and analysed. The art we are dealing with is inseparable from a social/political function; its aesthetics is determined by that role. A socially determined aesthetic: it is a difficult principle to deal with in a post-Lessing, post-Goethean theoretical climate. It forces us to think our way out of the notion that modern aesthetics has inherited from Lessing's *Laokoon*: that the fundamental laws of representation are native to the modes of representation, that art and poetry are realms separable from reality and from each other, operating according to laws inherent in genre. These laws function independently of society, as the acorn functions independently of the ground it is placed in. It may die if placed in the wrong soil, but it will never produce anything but an oak tree, and no change of environment can change that inborn teleology. Against this, let us imagine a socially determined aesthetic, a climate in which the work of art stands in a relation to the social order comparable to that of the chameleon to its environment; the plants which grow gain their character from the soil they grow in. The work of art derives its *telos* from the environment which produces it.

To return to our subject, let us put forward the premise: monarchic government and court society generate forms of representation. The particular art forms that owe their origin to court society are well known: courtly love-lyric and romance, the court masque, from a later period the opera and the ballet. But the forms that bring us closest to the political order itself are what P. E. Schramm calls the symbolism and mythology of state.[21] Royal insignia, table arrangements, the fixed forms of ceremony symbolize the state, represent certain conceptions of rule. The king must surround himself with symbols, must project an idea of the state into the reality surrounding him, must shape that reality according to that idea.

---

20 cf. the studies by H. Bodensohn, *Die Festschilderungen in der mittelhochdeutschen Dichtung* (Münster, 1936); W. Mohr, 'Mittelalterliche Feste und ihre Dichtung', in *Festschrift für Klaus Ziegler*, edited by E. Catholy and W. Hellmann (Tübingen, 1968), pp. 37–60; R. Marquart, *Das Höfische Fest im Spiegel der Mittelhochdeutschen Dichtung* (Göppingen, 1985).

21 *Kaiser, Könige und Päpste* (see note 12 above), I, 30ff.

The reasons for these 'musts' do not concern us, but the lesson that fore-going grand *representatio* diminishes power and weakens rule was recently brought home to us by Jimmy Carter, as the reverse – that an impressive style and self-representation can compensate for weaknesses of rule – by Ronald Reagan. Let us just assert: some compulsion inherent in the nature of concentrated power makes the head of state surround himself with symbols of rule that 'represent' and make visible the structures of power.

Monarchs draw the symbolism and mythology of state from two sources: tradition and the cosmic order. Their scenarios put forward in general two ideas: that they rule by ancestral custom and by the will of God. The monarch structures his surroundings so as to make visible in every state and administrative event the historical and cosmic legitimation of his actions and his station. And in this way the act of governing becomes at the same time a political event and a drama of the state affirming the ruler's place in the order of things.

In the center of power of a monarchic state reality tends to become aestheticised. Events, acts and human beings tend towards the condition of a work of art.[22] A simple and clear example is the development of acclamations for a ruler. When the ruler is crowned or arrives at a city or in any way is received and greeted by his subjects, the receivers hail him, with shouts, with cheers, with ceremonies etc. Such acclamations develop from unarticulated jubilating into shaped scenarios. Kantorowicz shows the development of hymns from cheers: 'Hymns are, in many respects, transcendentalized acclamations. They take the place of the former spontaneous hails of the crowds . . .'[23] A comparable development is observable in the history of the royal entry.[24] It begins as an event determined by the conditions of itinerant kingship and tends towards the quality of a liturgical or dramatical event. The artistry of the early royal entries seems to have been exhausted with pomp and noise. Gradually the event tends ever more towards allegorical drama: the city is decorated, becomes a stage, the reception crowd becomes now audience, now performers, the members of the procession perform ritualized dramas that take over the duty of representing the king or prince. And as with the development of

22 cf. the studies by J. Mazzeo, 'Castiglione's *Courtier*: The Self as a Work of Art', in his *Renaissance and Revolution: The Remaking of European Thought* (New York, 1965), 131–60; Stephen Greenblatt, *Renaissance Self-Fashioning from More to Shakespeare* (Chicago, 1980); Daniel Javitch, *Poetry and Courtliness in Renaissance England* (Princeton, 1978); E. Kleinschmidt, 'Minnesang als höfisches Zeremonialhandeln', *Archiv für Kulturgeschichte*, 58 (1976), 35–76.

23 E. Kantorowicz, *Laudes regiae: A Study in Liturgical Acclamations and Medieval Ruler Worship*, University of California Publications in History, 33 (Berkeley & Los Angeles, 1946), p. 73.

24 For literature see note 8 above.

hymns, there is a tendency of the developing ceremony to break off from its social/political matrix and become an autonomous art form. This is evident in the history of the *triumphus*, triumphal procession, from a ceremonial state event[25] to a separate poetic genre, or subgenre, as represented in the triumph of Beatrice of the *Divine Comedy* (Purgatory, Canto 29), or the series of allegorical poems by Petrarch, *I Trionfi*.

But the fixed forms of ceremony were only our point of departure. They are symptoms of a more embracing conceptual framework which we describe in our title as 'court aesthetic'. The urge to represent and to aestheticize reality is not restricted to the king and his exercising of power. It is a strong principle which is very evident, viewed diachronically, in the development of chivalric pageants, masques and court theater, but which is also at work throughout the hierarchy of any given court. Its influence moves downward from the king through all the levels of the court (and the kingdom, though it weakens fast outside the ruler's court). In any historical setting we will observe the tendency of the ruler and of anyone in his presence to participate in the drama of the state and to contribute to its symbols by shaping and constructing reality, entering into the fictions of the king, creating personal fictions in harmony with the prince's. Everyone in the presence of concentrated power becomes an administrator of the court aesthetic and an artist of his own person, or he does not stay there long. The retinue not only participates in the king's dramas, it creates its own.

The force of this aesthetic creates a need for scenarios, myths, stories, on which the court can pattern its behavior. The advent of the Arthurian matter in the twelfth century satisfied that impulse in a dramatic way. The Arthurian model shaped court sensibilities and court aesthetic in many forms from the twelfth century to the eighteenth, and that mode of existence native to the Arthurian matter – chivalry, the chivalric ideal – is far and away the dominant scenario in the court aesthetic of European aristocracy from the Middle Ages until the collapse of that social order. It provided the basic image of the great historical king surrounded by noble knights. It gave the prince his big illusion, and it gave the retinue or the nobles their small ones.

Now it is time to look at a particular detail of the hunters' procession in *Tristan* that we only mentioned briefly earlier. Tristan orders the parade so that the hunters enter the castle carrying the reconstructed stag, the parts of its dead body rearranged to form an effigy of the living animal. This impresses the master huntsman perhaps more than any of Tristan's skills:

---

25 *Paulys Real-Encyclopädie der classischen Altertumswissenschaft*, edited by W. Kroll and K. Mittelhaus (Stuttgart, 1939), Ser. 2, vol. 7, part 1, cols 493–511.

> 'A herre, er ist so tugenthaft:
> seht, dise niuwe meisterschaft,
> als wir nu ze hove sin komen,
> die habe wir gar von ime genomen.
> und hœret wunderlichen list:
> reht alse der hirz geschaffen ist,
> als ist er her ze hove braht.
> wa wart ie list so wol bedaht?' (3289–96)

In the full swing of his enthusiasm he goes on to tell the king how the head comes first, then the breast, and so forth, and in another mood than that of high-serious romance, we might expect the king to cut him short and retort that he knows perfectly well how a stag is put together. But both Mark and Gottfried were far too impressed by Tristan's art to see the huntsman's exuberance as anything but appropriate. After all the *prisant* is the finest ever seen in Cornwall:

> daz wart schoner unde baz
> ze hove geprisantet nie. (3300–01)

The re-presented stag states, 'we are hunters', or 'such hunters are we'. But that is the first and simplest level of symbolic meaning. It is comparable to the fishmongers of London celebrating Edward I's victory in the battle of Falkirk in 1298 by solemnly parading through the city carrying four gilt sturgeons and four silvered salmons.[26] The mere act of representing does honor to the king by calling on a courtly/royal mode of depiction, and be the symbols themselves ever so humble. Likewise the stag carried by the hunting party in *Tristan* says at the same time 'we are *royal* hunters, and we command the aesthetic of royalty'. The presentation causes such a fuss because it operates in that artistic mode. It transforms a real object into a work of art and each member of the party into an artist, or at least into an accomplished courtly gentleman, just as Tristan had promised: 'da hovet ir iuch selben mite'. What Mark and his court were used to regarding as an everyday event is now a drama with form, music, symbolism and spectacle. Tristan and his art are for them a kind of threshold, and they can cross it into an aestheticised world where life itself is a work of art.

Our reading of this scene raises the question: to what extent is it justified to regard the aesthetics of courtly literature as a 'literary aesthetic'? The very term places us in a post-Lessing theoretical frame. It may be that that frame is not time-bound and that there is a certain validity in regarding

---

[26] Withington, 'The Early "Royal-Entry" ', (above, note 8), p. 621.

any art as separate from the real conditions in which it arose. But the limitations of that perspective are much more severe for medieval courtly literature than for the post-Enlightenment period. Since the second half of the eighteenth century, literature and art tended indeed to separate ever further from reality and society, and that historical development accommodated and echoed the development of aesthetic theory. For court society into the early eighteenth century, we can say at the very least that the literature bound to that society is the product of two aesthetics which in various ways compete and cooperate with each other: court and literary aesthetics.

It is important to test every element of form and symbolism in courtly literature for the participation of court aesthetic in its shaping. Topoi and their arrangement may be superficially explained by their membership in a learned tradition, or even by some 'self-referentially' functioning literary aesthetic. The poet's sense of style and structure in depicting landscape, the interactions among human beings, emotions, clandestine love and its secret codes of communication, is tutored by the aesthetics of court life far more than by a sense of obligation to classical antiquity or to any learned tradition. It is the foundation of depiction, while learning is merely the building material. We stress again the distinction between elements of court pageantry in courtly poetry ('das höfische Fest in . . .') and the aesthetic principles shared in common by court pageantry and court poetry. Scenes like the hunters' procession are of interest as fictionalized pageantry, but more so as revelations of that underlying socially determined aesthetic. Kleinschmidt has proposed for Minnesang the model of 'höfisches Zeremonialhandeln'. It is a feature of courtly love lyric that Helmut de Boor also had noticed. He observed in passing about Reinmar's role as Viennese court poet; 'Er war der anerkannte Hofsänger, und er faßte seine Stellung so auf, daß er ein Zeremonienmeister der einzig wahren Minnehaltung war.'[27] The relation of the poet to his work in courtly literature generally is in some sense that of master to ceremony, and we propose the figure of Tristan marshaling the hunting procession as an emblem of the courtly poet ordering his material.

---

[27] H. de Boor, *Die Höfische Literatur: Vorbereitung, Blüte, Ausklang, 1170–1250*, Geschichte der deutschen Literatur, 2 (Munich, 1964), p. 288.

The Depiction of Military Conflict in Gottfried's Tristan

MARTIN H. JONES

Compared with most secular narratives of its time Gottfried von Straßburg's *Tristan* contains few episodes of military conflict. In fact there is detailed description of only six such episodes in Gottfried's poem, all of which are indicated by his source, the *Tristan* of Thomas, though none of them figures in the surviving fragments of that work. Of these six episodes, three involve fighting on a large scale: Riwalin's attack on Duke Morgan, Tristan's incursion into Brittany with a force for the purpose of killing Morgan, and the warfare in Arundel towards the end of the text. The remaining three are individual encounters in which Tristan slays his adversary: Morholt, the dragon in Ireland, and the giant Urgan.[1]

Among those who hitherto have subjected the military scenes of Gottfried's work to close scrutiny the predominant point of interest appears to be the extent to which armed conflict, be it in the form of large-scale engagements or of individual encounters, differs from – to be precise, falls short of – the model of chivalry embodied in the Arthurian romance of the Chrétien-Hartmann variety. With respect to the manner in which military action is depicted, it is argued that Gottfried diverges from the Arthurian norms as a matter of deliberate policy. Petrus Tax is particularly insistent on this.[2] Discussing the Morholt-combat, Tax claims 'daß er (Gottfried) offenbar vollbewußt jedes echt ritterliche Ethos von Tristan fernhält und ihn ausdrücklich als den durchaus unritterlichen

---

1 Apart from the six named episodes, military conflict is alluded to on the following occasions in Gottfried's work: 1119–42: the invasion of Mark's lands, in helping to repulse which Riwalin is wounded; 1373–79 and 1656–93: Morgan's attack on Parmenie during Riwalin's absence in Cornwall, and Riwalin's death in the attempt to defend his lands; 5912–26: Gurmun's conquest of Ireland and neighbouring countries; 18438–66: Tristan's chivalric exploits in Germany in the service of the Emperor, which Gottfried explicitly refuses to recount in any detail. These allusions contribute to the picture of a society in which warfare is an ever-present possibility, but the conflicts are described in terms too generalized for any conclusions of substance to be drawn from them.

2 Petrus W. Tax, *Wort, Sinnbild, Zahl im Tristanroman: Studien zum Denken und Werten Gottfrieds von Straßburg*, Philologische Studien und Quellen, 8 (Berlin, 1961).

"Helden" hinzustellen bemüht ist' (p. 44). In the confrontation with the giant Urgan, Tristan displays 'kalt berechnende Unritterlichkeit' (p. 111, note 143), and in the fighting in Arundel he acts 'auf eine listige, und wieder durchaus unritterliche und rücksichtslose Weise' (p. 158), conducting the war with such a degree of 'Heimtücke und Hinterlist' (p. 158) that Tax concludes: 'Der Dichter scheint somit Tristan und sein Heer als Teufelsmacht hinstellen zu wollen!' (p. 160). Less colourful but in much the same vein is the judgement of W. T. H. Jackson: 'There is an element in which he (Tristan) has to prove himself – that of physical combat – and it is in this sphere that the indictment of courtly conventions is particularly strong'.[3] Referring to Tristan's killing of Morgan, Jackson comments: 'His revenge on Morgan is a masterpiece of duplicity but hardly an epic of chivalry' (p. 148); similarly, referring to the Morholt-combat: 'It would be hard to imagine a contest which departed more widely from the courtly tradition' (p. 151). For Tax and for Jackson the reason for Gottfried's divergence from the Arthurian norms is to be found in his more widely based objective of casting a negative light on courtly society, by contrast with which the experience of the lovers represents something at least potentially positive. For Walter Haug, on the other hand, Gottfried's readiness, indeed his very capacity, to invest the depiction of individual combat with features of a negative and questionable kind springs from a fundamental shift in the nature of romance, a shift away from the Arthurian romance of the Chrétien-Hartmann type with its 'Symbolstruktur' and its distinctive concept of chivalric âventiure.[4] Haug argues that, whereas in the traditional Arthurian romance individual combats derive their significance for the hero's progress from their position in the 'Symbolstruktur' and can therefore be depicted in an unproblematic and conventional way, in Tristan each combat has to reveal its significance through the particularities of its conduct. As a consequence 'der Kampfstil wird frei; die Vorgänge können häßlich und gemein werden' (p. 112). And Haug contends that Tristan's military exploits are indeed shown to be 'häßlich und gemein', as he uses all the means at his disposal to cope with a world governed by chance and fate, a world quite different from that presupposed by the Arthurian romance. The idea that Gottfried's distinctive depiction of military events is symptomatic of a shift away from the Arthurian romance is taken up by Peter K. Stein who claims that 'Gottfried ... tut ... alles, um die nötigen und quellenbedingten Waffen-

---

3   W. T. H. Jackson, The Anatomy of Love: the 'Tristan' of Gottfried von Strassburg (New York and London, 1971), p. 147.
4   Walter Haug, 'Aventiure in Gottfrieds von Straßburg Tristan', in Festschrift für Hans Eggers zum 65. Geburtstag, edited by Herbert Backes, BGDSLT, 94, Sonderheft (Tübingen, 1972), pp. 88–125. See especially pp. 88–92 and 121–25.

gänge von Anklängen an die höfische Aventiure freizuhalten'.[5] For Stein, Gottfried's presentation of military events is a vital feature of his 'Absatz-bewegung vom höfischen Roman' (p. 344), a movement which is to be understood as a transcending of the Arthurian romance and its supposi-tions about the relationships between reality and literature which are no longer adequate to deal with the issues that concern Gottfried (pp. 344–50). Finally, building on the observations of the scholars named above, D. H. Green represents Gottfried as one who is in no way taken in by the idealization of knighthood found in Hartmann's *Erec* and who seeks to undermine the Arthurian concepts of chivalry and chivalric *âventiure*: 'Gottfried makes his position clear by composing a romance in which the chivalric quest for adventure plays no part'.[6] Such military events as Gottfried does depict are characterized by 'violence and ruthlessness', 'unredeemed brutality', and 'cunning', leading Green to the conclusion that 'Gottfried, more than any contemporary, depicts knighthood baldly and harshly, stripped of its glittering trappings'(p. 57).

If in what follows I seek to challenge interpretations of the kind just alluded to, it is not because I wish to suggest by way of simple contrast that Gottfried is an enthusiastic exponent of the practices of knighthood and the ideals of chivalry. Such a position would certainly be indefensible. Rather it is because I believe it to be questionable whether Gottfried's depiction of military events is so plainly hostile to knighthood as has been made out, and also whether the conclusions of a literary-historical charac-ter concerning the relationship of *Tristan* to the Arthurian romance which claim support from that depiction are tenable.

Those who have represented Gottfried's attitude towards knighthood as one of outright criticism have compared his depiction of military events exclusively with the Arthurian romance of the Chrétien-Hartmann variety. That such an exclusive comparison provides an adequate basis for forming a judgement of Gottfried's views must be open to doubt. In the first place, it is unlikely that the image of knighthood propagated in the Arthurian works entirely displaced other images of knighthood derived from different kinds of literature and indeed from life itself, and the possibility has to be considered that the conduct of military affairs in Gottfried's work will appear in quite a different light if judged by stand-ards other than those which obtain in the Arthurian romance. Secondly, it is necessary to take into account what Gottfried found in his source, Thomas, and possibly also in the earlier German version by Eilhart von Oberge. At times critics appear to have worked on the assumption that Gottfried had a free hand in describing military events, and that any

5 Peter K. Stein, 'Tristans Schwertleite: Zur Einschätzung ritterlich-höfischer Dich-tung durch Gottfried von Straßburg', *DVLG*, 51 (1977), 300–50 (p. 344).
6 D. H. Green, *Irony in the Medieval Romance* (Cambridge, 1979), pp. 72–73.

deviation from the Arthurian norm can in consequence be held to have the significance of a deliberate contrast. We must remind ourselves here that the Tristan story, for all its occasional links with the Arthurian literature, is inherently a different kind of narrative than the Arthurian romances represent, not least in those aspects which concern the life of the knight as fighting man. Incidents of feudal warfare, wars between princes, the legal and public implications of the challenge to Morholt's demand for tribute, the motive of revenge for a father's death – such things play no part in the early Arthurian romances, and they help to set the Tristan story as a whole, not just Gottfried's version, apart from them. Thirdly, it deserves to be emphasized that Gottfried does not introduce Arthurian criteria into his essentially non-Arthurian material in any manifest way.[7] The setting of the story in a courtly milieu, however superficially brilliant, does not of itself imply that the particular standards of Arthurian chivalry are to define our expectations with regard to conduct in military matters. There is no inevitable link between high courtly accomplishments and the idealism of Arthurian chivalry. Gottfried also does not bring Arthurian standards into his story through any of his characters. In those figures other than Riwalin and Tristan who engage in warfare and combat one looks in vain for any hint of the Arthurian principles of chivalrous conduct, which would, if present, provide a touchstone of judgement. Nor, finally, does Gottfried implant any statements of specifically chivalrous principles by which military conduct might be judged. Neither in the brief account of Riwalin's chivalrous life prior to his attack on Morgan (335–41) nor in the somewhat longer report of Tristan's training in the knightly arts (2103–20) is there any reference to education in a code of chivalrous conduct. Not even Mark's words of advice to Tristan at the time of his knighting (5022–45), which might come to mind, can be considered a contribution to such an education. Although he urges Tristan to give thought to 'ritterlichen pris' (5025), there is nothing in Mark's advice which bears specifically on the practice of knighthood, as there is, for example, in Gurnemanz's advice to Parzival.[8]

These observations will, I hope, suffice to establish that there is a case

7   Green detects irony aimed at deflating the pretensions of chivalry at numerous points in *Tristan*, but the alleged implicit criticism will be lost on those who do not share the presupposition of Gottfried's scepticism towards chivalry. See Green, pp. 52–61 and 72–75. For a cogent criticism of Haug's attempt (see note 4 above) to demonstrate a significant revaluation of the chivalric concept of *âventiure* by Gottfried, see Werner Schröder, '*Die von Tristande hant gelesen*: Quellenhinweise und Quellenkritik im *Tristan* Gottfrieds von Straßburg', *ZDA*, 104 (1975), 307–38 (pp. 324–27).

8   Wolfram von Eschenbach, *Parzival*, edited by Karl Lachmann, sixth edition (Berlin and Leipzig, 1926, reprinted Berlin, 1965), ll. 171, 25–30. Gurnemanz advises Parzival to spare a defeated opponent who offers his surrender, provided he has done Parzival no grievous wrong.

for looking afresh at the military episodes in *Tristan*, placing them in a wider context than that provided by comparison directly with the Arthurian romance. I shall now survey these episodes individually, beginning with the instances of large-scale fighting.

Within a few hundred lines of the start of the text we are taken into the world of military conflict with Riwalin's attack on Duke Morgan. In a studied display of ignorance about the motive for this attack – 'weder ez do not ald übermuot/geschüefe, des enweiz ich niht' (342–43) – Gottfried succeeds in placing the whole venture in an equivocal light, but this serves to characterize Riwalin rather than to qualify the picture of warfare given here. Though Gottfried provides rather more detail than is found in *Tristrams saga ok Ísöndar*, what he describes is in essentials paralleled by the Norwegian version – and was therefore presumably already in Thomas.[9]

Viewing the episode as a whole (335–408), it can be said that Gottfried's account of the conflict between Riwalin and Morgan is an accurate reflection of standard practices of warfare in the Middle Ages.[10] Riwalin pursues a strategy of devastation and siege by which he puts pressure on Morgan and gains increasing domination over his lands. He razes Morgan's strongholds and forces towns into submission, thereby ensuring that few centres of resistance and support for the Breton duke remain. Ransoms from the towns enable Riwalin to increase his forces, presumably through the hiring of mercenaries, and to extend his control further. He ravages the country with fire and pillage. Morgan is forced eventually to go entirely onto the defensive and confine himself to his strongest fortresses, where Riwalin lays siege to him. During the sieges Riwalin

---

9   See F. Piquet, *L'Originalité de Gottfried de Strasbourg dans son poème de Tristan et Isolde* (Lille, 1905), pp. 63–65. The Norwegian prose version by Brother Robert and the Middle English metrical romance of *Sir Tristrem*, which, in different degrees, are important for the reconstruction of the *Tristan* of Thomas, are referred to in the following edition: *Die nordische und die englische Version der Tristan-Sage*, edited by Eugen Kölbing, Part I *Tristrams Saga ok Ísondar* (Heilbronn, 1878), Part II *Sir Tristrem* (Heilbronn, 1882). I shall use the short forms Kölbing I and Kölbing II for references to the *Saga* and to *Sir Tristrem* respectively. For the *Saga* I have also made use of the translation into English by Paul Schach: *The Saga of Tristram and Ísönd* (Lincoln, Nebraska, 1973, reissued in Bison Paperback, Lincoln, Nebraska, 1976). References are to the paperback edition. For the account of the opening scenes of warfare in the *Saga*, see Kölbing I, Cap. I and Schach, p. 3.

10   In what follows I am much indebted to the stimulating account of military strategy in the twelfth and thirteenth centuries by John Gillingham, 'Richard I and the Science of War in the Middle Ages', in *War and Government in the Middle Ages: Essays in Honour of J. O. Prestwich*, edited by J. Gillingham and J. C. Holt (Cambridge, 1984), pp. 78–91. Although they concern a later period, two studies by H. J. Hewitt are of considerable interest for the light which they shed on the conduct of raids or *chevauchées* into foreign territory: H. J. Hewitt, *The Black Prince's Expedition of 1355–1357* (Manchester, 1958) and H. J. Hewitt, *The Organization of War under Edward III, 1338–62* (Manchester, 1966).

stages tournaments and displays of chivalry, no doubt for the dual purpose of providing his own knights with training and diversion and of
intimidating the enemy.[11] Morgan's response to Riwalin's incursion is
partly to counter-attack in the same manner, raiding into Riwalin's territory, partly to seek battle with his army, a strategy suitable for a defender
whose objective is to keep the invading forces together and thus to reduce
the damage they can inflict when moving freely through the countryside.[12] Finally Morgan has to take refuge in his strongholds and sue for
peace to prevent further devastation of his lands. Riwalin returns home in
triumph and laden with booty, the spoils of war with which he richly
rewards his companions in arms.[13]

    The kind of campaign waged by Riwalin in Brittany, with its focus on
devastation, siege, and the taking of booty, represents the routine aspect
of war in the Middle Ages, by comparison with which pitched battles
were exceptional.[14] Chroniclers of contemporary events repeatedly report
such campaigns, showing them to have been conducted by some of the
most highly esteemed military commanders of the time. Charlemagne,
Frederick Barbarossa, Richard the Lionheart, Edward the Black Prince, for
example, all of whom were regarded as models of chivalry, adopted this
strategy as the occasion demanded, which was not infrequently, and no
stigma attached to their choice of this method of warfare.[15] Famous and

11 On such military displays in the context of sieges, see Marjorie Chibnall, 'Feudal
Society in Orderic Vitalis', in *Proceedings of the Battle Conference on Anglo-Norman
Studies, I, 1978*, edited by R. Allen Brown (Ipswich, 1979), pp. 35–48 (p. 44).
12 See Gillingham, p. 85.
13 On the material profit to be had from military campaigns of the kind conducted by
Riwalin, see the numerous references to 'booty' in the Index of Subjects to Hewitt, *The
Black Prince's Expedition*, p. 225.
14 Gillingham estimates that in twenty-five years of campaigning in Europe and on the
crusade Richard I fought at the most three pitched battles (only one of these was in
Europe), being in this respect no exception among medieval commanders (pp. 79–81).
In answer to the question 'What . . . were Richard's twenty-five years of campaigning
all about?', Gillingham states: 'If one looks at Richard's campaigns in Europe, whether
against rebels in Aquitaine or against King Philip of France, this, it is soon clear, is the
pattern to which they conform – a pattern of ravaging and besieging' (pp. 83–84).
Regarding the conduct of war in the high Middle Ages, see also Joachim Bumke,
Höfische Kultur: Literatur und Gesellschaft im hohen Mittelalter, 2 vols (München, 1986), I,
10: 'Die Kriegführung war nur zum kleinsten Teil auf die Bewährung ritterlicher Waf-
fentechnik abgestellt. Brandschatzung und Plünderung waren die üblichen Methoden.'
15 For Charlemagne and Richard the Lionheart (and other renowned commanders),
see Gillingham, pp. 83–85. For Frederick Barbarossa, see Otto von Freising and
Rahewin, *Die Taten Friedrichs oder richtiger Chronica*, translated by Adolf Schmidt,
edited by Franz-Josef Schmale, Ausgewählte Quellen zur deutschen Geschichte des
Mittelalters, XVII, third edition (Darmstadt, 1986), Book II, Chapters 19–20 (pp. 316–
19); Book III, Chapter 3 (pp. 400–03); Book IV, Chapters 38–41 (pp. 594–97); Book IV,
Chapter 48 (pp. 606–07). For Edward the Black Prince, see Hewitt, *The Black Prince's
Expedition*, pp. 43–77 and especially his comments on the devastations which ac-

fabled figures of the past were shown to act no differently. Geoffrey of Monmouth in his *Historia Regum Britanniae* (*c*.1136) tells how King Arthur pursued a strategy of devastation and siege when he launched his campaign against Gaul: 'As soon as he had subdued these countries (i.e. Norway and Denmark) and raised Loth to the kingship of Norway, Arthur sailed off to Gaul. He drew his troops up in companies and began to lay waste the countryside in all directions.' Having put to flight the army which the Tribune Frollo, ruler of Gaul, leads into battle against him, Arthur lays siege to Frollo in the city of Paris. The month-long siege ends when Arthur kills Frollo in single combat. He then proceeds with his campaign, sending Hoel, King of Brittany, at the head of half his army into southern Gaul, where he subdues Guitard, leader of the Poitevins, and the province of Gascony: 'Hoel soon reached Aquitania, seized the towns of that region, and, after harassing Guitard in a number of battles, forced him to surrender. He also ravaged Gascony with fire and sword, and forced its leaders to submit.'[16] In Wace's account of these events in his adaptation of Geoffrey's *Historia*, the *Roman de Brut* (*c*.1155), Arthur is said to act wisely in forbidding his men to ravage and pillage in the regions of northern Gaul that he has just conquered – self-interest, not least, dictates such wisdom, but Paris is put under siege and the lands of Guitard are devastated just as in Geoffrey's *Historia*.[17] In Lamprecht's *Alexander* the great conqueror pursues the same strategy in his long-drawn-out campaign against Darius. He begins by laying waste many lands and cities in Palestine, being brought to a halt only at Tyre, which he invests and eventually conquers and razes to the ground. Similar treatment is later meted out to other cities, including Thebes, which is also razed, and Sardis, which is burned and pillaged.[18]

companied the first raid: 'These practices (i.e. pillage and destruction) were not innovations devised by the prince and his men for use against the people of Languedoc. They were . . . regular features of fourteenth-century warfare and regarded as legitimate and even honourable. The prince and his chief followers had learned the art of campaigning from Edward III. They were "very eager and desirous to acquit themselves well". They were in fact the "flower of chivalry" and many were members of the Order of the Garter. That the "flower of chivalry" should spend a Sunday with a devout brotherhood at Prouille, while their men only a few miles away were burning down the homes of the burgesses of Limoux was not incongruous to the mind of 1355' (p. 72).

16 The two passages from Geoffrey's *Historia* are quoted in the translation by Lewis Thorpe: Geoffrey of Monmouth, *The History of the Kings of Britain* (Harmondsworth, 1966), pp. 223 and 225. For the original text, see *The Historia Regum Britanniae of Geoffrey of Monmouth*, edited by Acton Griscom (London, 1929), pp. 447–48 and 450–51.
17 *Le Roman de Brut de Wace*, edited by Ivor Arnold, Société des Anciens Textes Français, 2 vols (Paris, 1938 and 1940), II, ll. 9895–904, 9971–88, 10117–28.
18 *Lamprechts Alexander, nach den drei Texten mit dem Fragment des Alberich von Besançon und den lateinischen Quellen*, edited by Karl Kinzel, Germanistische Handbibliothek, 6 (Halle, 1884), Vorau manuscript (*c*. 1150), ll. 686–702 and Straßburg manuscript (*c*. 1170), ll. 959–1402, 1910–17, 2258–94.

Set against such a historical and literary background, it is clear that Gottfried's description of the warfare in Brittany is unlikely to have impressed contemporary audiences as anything at all exceptional or as expressing an attitude of hostility towards knighthood and chivalry specifically. It is more likely that they would have seen in Gottfried's account a truthful depiction of warfare as they knew it in reality, an account marked by sobriety rather than glamorization, to be sure, but one which none the less shows Riwalin to have been a skilled general employing recognized methods of war to achieve his objective.

Much the same judgement can be made of the fighting in Arundel which is described towards the end of Gottfried's text, when it is Tristan who shows considerable skill as a commander (18686–948). It is unclear how much of this episode Gottfried found preformed in Thomas. The account in the *Saga* has some points of contact with Gottfried's but it is very much briefer, indeed has the appearance of an abridgement.[19] Eilhart treats this episode at length and agrees with Gottfried in having Tristan divide his forces in order to stage the ambush which proves decisive for his victory.[20] Whether or how far Gottfried is indebted to Eilhart in this episode is impossible to determine,[21] but it is interesting to compare the two accounts and to note that in Gottfried there is no counterpart to the individual combat of Tristrant and Count Ryol in Eilhart (5708–64), and also no account of the carnage wrought by Tristrant and his companions such as Eilhart describes in passages which are redolent of the heroic epic (5973–6072). The comparison with Eilhart shows that Gottfried's account is restrained, avoiding excesses of bloodiness and brutality, and that it stresses Tristan's strategic acumen rather than his physical prowess (though this is acknowledged too).

There are a number of parallels between Gottfried's report of the relief of Arundel from the ravages of feudal rebellion and his earlier account of Riwalin's attack on Morgan, though in the later incident we view events from the perspective of the defending forces. As far as defensive strategy is concerned, the forces of Arundel are too small to offer the invaders pitched battle – 'veltstrit' (18773) – in the way that Morgan did, but Tristan and Kaedin do adopt the same strategy as Morgan pursued when they make raids into enemy territory and attempt by a policy of devastation through pillage and fire to draw the invading forces away from

[19] Kölbing I, Cap. LXIX and Schach, pp. 106–07. On the abbreviated version in the *Saga*, see Piquet, p. 305.
[20] Eilhart von Oberge, *Tristrant*, edited by Danielle Buschinger, Göppinger Arbeiten zur Germanistik, 202 (Göppingen, 1976), 11. 5488–6105. The division and disposition of the forces is recounted in 11. 5864–902.
[21] Piquet claims (pp. 305–09) that Gottfried is heavily indebted to Eilhart in his presentation of this episode, but the lack of evidence regarding Thomas makes it difficult to sustain such a judgement.

Arundel (18772–79). Similar action is taken later by Tristan, after he has disposed his forces for the ambush, when he raids openly into enemy territory to provoke a renewed incursion into Arundel (18817–49). After the invading army has been defeated, the tables are turned on them, and, in a manner reminiscent of Riwalin's attack on Morgan, Tristan and Kaedin launch a punitive raid into enemy lands, subduing all their property, towns, and fortresses, and sending the resulting booty back to Arundel (18912–25). As in the case of the earlier episode, it can be said that all this military action presents typical incidents of medieval warfare and would have implied no particular criticism of Tristan as a knight, or of knighthood itself.

What makes the decisive difference between Morgan's unsuccessful defence of Brittany and the successful defence of Arundel is Tristan's ability to call on reinforcements from Parmenie and his skill in deploying them. Tristan demonstrates here remarkable powers of generalship. He begins by informing himself precisely about the military situation and then occupies a castle belonging to Duke Jovelin which lies on the enemy's approach to Arundel (18752–71). The five hundred knights from Parmenie are brought in under cover of darkness, half of them to be stationed at Karke and half at the castle immediately on the enemy's line of approach. The knights are instructed to hold themselves in concealment until the moment for attack arrives (18793–816). Surprise is of the essence in the strategy which Tristan pursues, as he provokes the enemy to enter Arundel again, thus luring them into the ambush he has laid. The plan is entirely successful and the invading force, brimful of confidence and not expecting to meet resistance, is attacked first by the pursuing Tristan and Kaedin, then by the concealed knights. The enemy are forced to fight on several fronts at once and their formations are soon broken through. Tristan and Kaedin shrewdly focus their energies on capturing the enemy commanders, and under intense pressure the invading forces break up as each man seeks his own salvation (18850–911). The capture of the commanders and the subsequent punitive raid into enemy lands serve to ensure that the victory gained is not reversed, and Duke Jovelin is able to restore order thoroughly by reinvesting his vassals with their fiefs in return for promises of peace.

It would be inappropriate to regard Tristan's actions here as in any way improper or exceptional. That he does not engage the enemy in open battle after the arrival of the knights from Parmenie is no cause for criticism, as has been suggested.[22] His strategy of provocation and ambush is perfectly suited to the situation and secures his and Jovelin's objective without exposure to the vagaries of fortune which attended any pitched battle. This last consideration was one well understood by medieval com-

22 Tax, pp. 158–59.

manders, who found it stated forcefully in the most widely used hand-book on war in the Middle Ages, the Roman Vegetius's *De Re Militari*, and who took it so much to heart that, as has been mentioned earlier, pitched battles were the exception rather than the rule in the conduct of military campaigns.[23] Tristan displays throughout this episode the essential skills of a good general, taking stock of the situation, understanding the enemy's psychology, and deploying his own forces to maximum effect. And Gottfried's presentation of the action complements his hero's efficiency: it is precise and economical; it is vivid in the moments of direct conflict but eschews the heroic gesture and any kind of epic exaggeration. It is an account which does Tristan no little credit and which casts no shadow on knighthood.

I turn now to the final instance of fighting on a large scale, namely that which is associated with Tristan's incursion into Brittany for the purpose of killing Morgan (5267–633). The *Saga* recounts Tristram's flight after the killing of Morgan and the action of Roaldur in sending a relieving force to Tristram's aid in broadly similar fashion to Gottfried,[24] so that it is safe to assume that he derived the events from Thomas, though how much of the detail which distinguishes Gottfried's account from that of the *Saga* is drawn from Thomas is uncertain. As for the events which precede the killing of Morgan, comparison of Gottfried's text with the *Saga* and *Sir Tristrem* suggests that Gottfried remodelled what he found in Thomas quite substantially.[25]

In Gottfried's version it appears that Tristan initially intends an operation of some scale in Brittany. This is evident from the reference to his train ('gezoc' 5324, 5330) and from the presence of ninety or more knights on the expedition (5332–36). Possibly his original plan was to launch a raid similar to that conducted by his father. Learning by chance, however, that Morgan is out hunting, Tristan changes his plan and pursues a course directed exclusively to confronting Morgan and killing him. He first instructs all his knights to prepare for conflict, though their armour is to be concealed beneath their robes, a stratagem no doubt adopted in order to lessen the danger of their being drawn into combat before the time is ripe. He then divides his forces, sending the train, guarded by sixty or more knights, back along the path of their approach, and keeping only thirty knights with himself. The returning party is instructed to proceed steadily

---

23 On Vegetius's advice and its influence on medieval commanders, see Gillingham, especially pp. 82–83.
24 Kölbing I, Cap. XXV and Schach, pp. 35–36.
25 In the *Saga* Tristram is accompanied into Brittany by twenty knights and proceeds directly to confront Morgan in his hall: Kölbing I, Cap. XXIV and Schach, p. 34. In *Sir Tristrem* only fifteen knights accompany Tristrem, who again challenges Morgan immediately in his hall: Kölbing II, 11. 815–20. Eilhart does not recount Tristan's attack on Morgan.

and to stop for no one, presumably meaning that they should avoid any kind of engagement. It would appear that Tristan has in mind that they should act as a reserve from which he can find support if he has to retreat under attack, as indeed happens. Meanwhile, he and his party seek Morgan out. The strategy which Tristan improvises here is a daring one, relying on the element of surprise for its success. It has the advantage of focusing the attack on the true object of hostility, the person of Morgan, and offers the chance of achieving the objective of the expedition swiftly and with little loss of life to Tristan's force. It is, of course, a considerable gamble, and it is not surprising that Gottfried should preface the whole episode with remarks on Tristan's sorrow at his father's death and the susceptibility of young men to the promptings of anger (5069–109).

The risks of the enterprise become apparent when the Bretons respond swiftly and vigorously to the killing of Morgan (5459–89). Tristan and his small company are hotly pursued until they join up with their reserve force and occupy a fortified hill for the night. On the following day, they are constantly attacked on their retreat, with considerable loss of life, and have to take refuge in another stronghold. The numerical superiority of the Bretons now begins to tell, as they lay siege to Tristan and his men. At this point it appears that Tristan's gamble has not paid off, but the watchful Rual now comes unexpectedly to his aid with a force of a hundred knights (5547–66). The Bretons are caught in their camp by Rual's troop and they are subjected to a shattering attack on two fronts, which spells their swift defeat, when Tristan's men sally forth, returning the battle-cry of the relief force. It remains only for Tristan's men to bury their dead and tend to their wounded, before returning to Parmenie with their business accomplished.

It is an exciting passage of arms which Gottfried describes here, in a manner which is again vivid and economical, focusing on the general engagements and the movements of the forces rather than on individual deeds, individual woundings and killings. Criticism of the methods of fighting as such is nowhere evident in this account, and such reservations as we may have about the hazards and costs of the enterprise are attributable to Tristan's impetuosity and daring – personal factors, therefore – rather than to knighthood per se.

In the midst of this episode in Brittany stands the deed which is the raison d'être of the whole venture, the killing of Morgan. This comes about as a result of Tristan's bold strategy in going after his enemy with only a small force and his ruthlessness in catching Morgan unawares and unarmed. Whether the killing is an act of murder or the legitimate execution of blood-vengeance is not to be established from Gottfried's text with final certainty. Gottfried appears to be content to leave the question of legality in some doubt and to represent the killing as an act by which Tristan satisfies his own sense of anger and outrage at the death of his

father and secures de facto control over the lands to which he has succeeded. Rather than pass judgement on the outcome, Gottfried accepts it,
with a certain detachment, as indicative of Tristan's youthful impetuosity
and his ruthless efficiency in pursuing the goals he sets himself.[26]

The blow with which Tristan slays Morgan – a sword stroke which cuts
through skull and brain, penetrating to the tongue, followed by a thrust to
the heart – is almost exactly as in the *Saga*: there Tristan splits Morgan's
head down to the eyes and then thrusts him to the ground.[27] This is a
typical epic blow, examples of which are to be found in untold numbers
in French *chansons de geste* and German heroic poetry. Although such
blows are not found in the Arthurian romances, they do figure in the
French *romans d'antiquité*, in Geoffrey of Monmouth, and in Wace, and it is
more than likely that Gottfried and Brother Robert found such a blow in
Thomas.[28] It would be consistent with the detached posture that Gottfried
adopts towards this incident, if it were indeed the case that he simply
carried this blow over from the source into his account without comment.

While it may legitimately be claimed that the manner of Morgan's
slaying tells us much about the character of Tristan but by itself actually
reveals nothing conclusive about Gottfried's attitude towards chivalry, it
has been observed that the killing of Morgan is Tristan's first action of a
military kind since being knighted, and the inference has been drawn
from this that Gottfried wishes to show how hollow the pretensions of
chivalry are.[29] The sequence of events is certainly telling, but it has to be
borne in mind that the same sequence is found in the *Saga* and *Sir Tristrem*
and may be safely claimed for Thomas; also, more importantly, that
whereas in the *Saga* and *Sir Tristrem* – and presumably in Thomas – the
knighting of Tristan is closely linked to his desire to avenge his father's
death, Gottfried recounts the knighting of his hero without allusion to the

---

26 See the discussion of these issues in Rosemary Norah Combridge, *Das Recht im
'Tristan' Gottfrieds von Straßburg*, Philologische Studien und Quellen, 15, second edition
(Berlin, 1964), pp. 27–28, 44–45.
27 Kölbing I, Cap. XXIV and Schach, p. 35. The verses describing the killing of Morgan
are missing in the manuscript of *Sir Tristrem*: see Kölbing II, 11. 870–880 and the note to
11. 874–75 on p. 138.
28 Instances of heads being split in two, cut through, or sliced off are to be found as
follows (the name of the warrior who strikes the fatal blow is given in each case): *Eneas:
Roman du XIIe siècle*, Classiques Français du Moyen Age, edited by J.-J. Salverda de
Grave, 2 vols (Paris, 1925–1929), 11. 5909–13 (Eneas), 7130–34 (Tarpege), 9811–14
(Eneas); Geoffrey's *Historia*, ed. Griscom, p. 450 (Arthur), p. 472 (Arthur), p. 475 (Gawain twice), p. 493 (Arthur) (in Thorpe's translation pp. 225, 240–42, and 255); *Roman de
Brut*, ed. Arnold, II, 11. 10083–90 (Arthur), 11545–48 (Arthur), 11751–53 (Gawain),
11827–30 (Gawain), 12685–94 (Hyrelgas), 12905–18 (Arthur). The dating of *Eneas* presents difficulties but *c*. 1160 is widely accepted.
29 Tax, pp. 32–38; Haug, p. 109; Green, p. 59.

motive of vengeance.[30] In other words, it would appear that Gottfried has here altered his source with the result that the knighting is dissociated from the theme of revenge. Naturally, it may be argued that the sequence of events still speaks for itself, but it has to be accepted that Gottfried appears to have rejected an opportunity to reinforce an implied criticism of chivalry – this always supposing that his audiences would in any case have viewed Tristan's killing of Morgan as reprehensible.

With the consideration of Tristan's killing of Morgan we have moved away from incidents of large-scale fighting, and it is time now to examine the instances of individual combat in which Tristan engages. The first of these is his encounter with Morholt, the only example in the work of single combat between knights.

Among those who hold Gottfried to be critical of knighthood, much has been made of Tristan's allegedly questionable motivation in this incident and of his allegedly cunning manipulation of the legal and moral issues prior to the combat.[31] These are not matters that I can examine in detail here. It must suffice to say that I am not convinced that Gottfried would have us regard Tristan as guilty of pride, as the party who is in the wrong, or as pursuing personal ambitions above all. Rather I incline to the view of Combridge, who speaks of Gottfried's 'heftige moralische Teilnahme' for Tristan, of a presentation which is 'gänzlich unironisch', and of an incident which shows 'wie sonst selten bei Gottfried, ein Zusammentreffen von Recht und Macht'.[32]

More immediately to our purpose is the question of how the combat itself is depicted. The Morholt-combat is found in Eilhart, the *Saga*, and *Sir Tristrem* as well as in Gottfried. There is such variation in detail among the versions at this point that it is difficult to assess the degree of Gottfried's indebtedness to others, but it is at least certain that the wounding of Tristan by a poisoned weapon and a blow to Morholt's head which leaves a piece of Tristan's sword lodged there, both of which are essential for the further unfolding of the plot, were obligatory features of the encounter. As for the remaining features, it will be best to regard them as original to Gottfried, even though parallels may exist with other versions.

It is beyond doubt that Gottfried depicts here a fierce and vicious encounter with no holds barred on either side (6833–7085). Certainly this is not the kind of combat with which readers of Hartmann, for example, are familiar. But if we widen our basis of comparison somewhat – even without going so far as to encompass the *chanson de geste* and heroic epic, where parallels would not be at all hard to find, we may begin to question

---

30 Kölbing I, Cap. XXIV and Schach, p. 33; Kölbing II, ll. 760–92.
31 Tax, pp. 39–44; Jackson, pp. 149–50; Haug, pp. 109–11; Stein, pp. 340–43; Green, pp. 60, 88–89.
32 Combridge, pp. 48–49.

whether Tristan's part in the Morholt-combat is quite so out of the ordinary and quite so damaging to the image of knighthood as is sometimes suggested. Three examples will serve to make my point. The examples concern chivalric heroes who are presented sympathetically by their authors and whose conduct in combat is in no way subjected to criticism.

My first example is actually an encounter in Arthurian romance, namely Erec's combat with Yders in Chrétien's work.[33] After the initial joust the combatants exchange ferocious blows and soon draw blood. Yders eventually gets through Erec's defences and strikes a blow which glances off his helm and descends to his thigh, penetrating to the flesh. Erec repays this with a blow to Yders' shoulder which penetrates to the bone, so that blood flows down to his waistband. Shortly afterwards Erec stuns Yders with a blow on the helm and follows this with a rapid succession of three blows which cut through to Yders' skull. Erec thrusts the tottering Yders to the ground, removes his helm and would have cut off his head if Yders had not pleaded for mercy. Noteworthy in this account are the wounds to thigh and head, which have clear counterparts in the Morholt-combat, and the general character of the contest, which is every bit as brutal and bloody as Tristan's combat with Morholt.

For all its ferocity, Erec's combat *is* conducted in accordance with the ground rules of the Arthurian romance, but the same cannot be said of my second example, which is the combat of Arthur and the Roman tribune Frollo which gives Arthur possession of the city of Paris. This encounter is found, with no significant variations, in both Geoffrey of Monmouth's *Historia Regum Britanniae* and Wace's *Roman de Brut*.[34] The circumstances of this combat are strikingly similar to those of the Morholt-combat in Gottfried.[35] The encounter of Arthur and Frollo is one between champions and takes place on an island, where it is observed by the supporters of both men, who pray God to aid their cause. The combat opens with a joust which unhorses Frollo but not Arthur. While still mounted, Arthur draws his sword and makes to kill Frollo, but the tribune has retained his lance and with this he pierces Arthur's horse as he rides at him. Arthur is

33 *Les Romans de Chrétien de Troyes, I, Erec et Enide*, Classiques Français du Moyen Age, edited by Mario Roques (Paris, 1977), 11. 875–988. Most of the detail of the blows struck and wounds inflicted is lacking in Hartmann's account of this combat: see Hartmann von Aue, *Erec*, edited by Albert Leitzmann and Ludwig Wolff, sixth edition, prepared by Christoph Cormeau and Kurt Gärtner, Altdeutsche Textbibliothek, 39 (Tübingen, 1985), 11. 833–955.
34 *Historia*, ed. Griscom, pp. 449–50 (in Thorpe's translation pp. 224–25); *Roman de Brut*, ed. Arnold, II, 11. 10017–92.
35 The possibility that Wace's depiction of the Arthur-Frollo combat influenced Thomas's description of Tristan's encounter with Morholt is considered but rejected by Margaret Pelan, *L'Influence du 'Brut' de Wace sur les romanciers français de son temps* (Paris, 1931), pp. 96, 158–59.

THE DEPICTION OF MILITARY CONFLICT

brought to the ground and a sword-fight ensues in which Frollo first wounds Arthur in the forehead so that blood streams down his face, then Arthur strikes Frollo such a mighty blow that he splits his head down to the shoulders, sending blood and brains gushing from the fatal wound. The parallels between this and the Morholt-combat are manifest, but it is interesting particularly to note that Arthur has no more qualms than Tristan does about trying to take advantage of an unhorsed opponent while he is himself still mounted.

My third example is again an episode recounted by both Geoffrey of Monmouth and Wace, though I shall refer to the more detailed version of Wace. At Autun Arthur sends an embassy of three knights, including Gawain, to parley with the Roman Emperor Lucius. After Gawain kills Quintilian in a manner which is, incidentally, reminiscent of Tristan's killing of Morgan, the three knights flee, hotly pursued by the Romans.[36] Two incidents here involving Gawain are of interest. Gawain is chased by Marcellus, who offers to spare his life if he will surrender. Gawain does not heed this but craftily brings his horse suddenly to a halt so that Marcellus outruns him. As he passes, Gawain draws his sword and cleaves Marcellus's head down to the shoulders. As he falls to the ground, Gawain taunts him.[37] A short while later a kinsman of Marcellus seeks to avenge his death, but, as he raises his sword-arm to strike, Gawain is quick to act and cuts through the arm, sending it and the sword flying.[38] Here we may note Gawain's use of cunning, the taunting of his vanquished opponent, and, of course, the parallel with Tristan's hacking off of Morholt's hand and sword.

Such evidence of a comparative nature as I have just presented is necessarily unsystematic. Whereas in examining depictions of large-scale fighting it is possible to discern general strategic and tactical principles which reflect the nature of warfare at the time, in the consideration of individual combats one is faced with a large variety of incidents from which it is difficult to make generalizations. None the less these few examples will suffice to demonstrate that the character of the fighting depicted by Gottfried in the Morholt-combat is not at all exceptional and is unlikely to have appeared so to audiences whose knowledge of fighting was not limited to the nobler encounters of the Arthurian romance.

One final feature of the Morholt-combat requires comment, namely the decapitation of Morholt, which appears to be an innovation on Gottfried's part (7081–85).[39] This act accords well with what we have seen of Tristan's

---

36 *Roman de Brut*, ed. Arnold, II, 11. 11647–760. Geoffrey's account is to be found in *Historia*, ed. Griscom, pp. 474–75 (in Thorpe's translation pp. 241–42).
37 *Roman de Brut*, ed. Arnold, II, 11. 11809–38.
38 *Roman de Brut*, ed. Arnold, II, 11. 11857–74.
39 There is no decapitation of Morholt in Eilhart, the *Saga*, or *Sir Tristrem*.

character in the Morgan episode, in so far as it represents vengeance for the poisoned wound that Morholt inflicted on him. Tristan clearly has this in mind, as it is referred to in his taunting of the defeated Irishman (7065–74). But further, more important perspectives are opened up by his claim, immediately preceding the beheading, that God has passed judgement on Morholt in the defeat of his unjust demands, and that pride – 'hohvart' – has been brought down in this encounter (7075–80). There is evoked here the memory of David's confrontation with Goliath, which ends with the decapitation of the Philistine enemy of God; also of the beheading of Pride (Superbia) by Lowliness (Men Humilis) in the highly influential *Psychomachia* of Prudentius.⁴⁰ It may further be recalled that in Veldeke's *Eneide*, as already in the Old French *Eneas*, though not in Virgil's *Aeneid*, the combat between Eneas and Turnus ends with the decapitation of Turnus. By this act Eneas avenges the death of Pallas and punishes Turnus for his avarice in robbing the dead Pallas of the ring given him by Eneas, the sight of which on Turnus's hand banishes all thoughts of reconciliation from Eneas's mind. In Veldeke's account the beheading of Turnus is an act of justice merited by his wrongdoing.⁴¹ Although Tristan's decapitation of Morholt certainly sets him apart from the heroes of Arthurian romance, whose combats do not end in this way, it associates him with other victors in combat whose cause is godly and just, in a manner which is consistent with Gottfried's portrayal of Tristan throughout the Morholt episode as the champion of justice who enjoys God's support. Viewed in this context, the outcome of the Morholt-combat can be seen to imply no criticism of Tristan or of knighthood.

Tristan's remaining individual encounters – with the dragon and the giant Urgan – will permit of briefer treatment, not least because of the convention which accepts the suspension of the normal rules of chivalrous conduct in dealing with such adversaries.⁴² In neither of these epi-

---

⁴⁰ Echoes of David's confrontation with Goliath (I Samuel 17. 1–51) have been detected throughout the Morholt episode. For details, see Lambertus Okken, *Kommentar zum Tristan-Roman Gottfrieds von Straßburg*, Amsterdamer Publikationen zur Sprache und Literatur, 57, 2 vols (Amsterdam, 1984 and 1985), I, pp. 305–06. For the incident in Prudentius, see *Psychomachia*, 11. 178–309, in *Prudentius*, edited and translated by H.J. Thomson, Loeb Classical Library, 2 vols (London, 1949), I, pp. 290–300. The analogy with David's slaying of Goliath is drawn there, too: 11. 291–304.

⁴¹ *Heinrich von Veldeke*, edited by Ludwig Ettmüller, Dichtungen des deutschen Mittelalters, 8 (Leipzig, 1852), 11. 330, 31–331, 38 (= 11. 12559–606). For the interpretation of this episode, see the careful analysis by Werner Schröder, 'Die Hinrichtung Arofels', in *Wolfram-Studien II*, edited by Werner Schröder (Berlin, 1974), pp. 219–40 (pp. 229–34).

⁴² One may recall here, for example, Iwein's fights with the giant Harpin and with the two giants in the 'Burg zum Schlimmen Abenteuer', in both of which the lion plays a decisive part in securing Iwein's victory: Hartmann von Aue, *Iwein*, edited by G.F. Benecke and K. Lachmann, seventh edition, revised by Ludwig Wolff, 2 vols (Berlin, 1968), I, 11. 4991–5074, 6676–798.

sodes does Gottfried's account differ in essentials from that of the *Saga*, and both dragon and giant are eventually slain. In each case, however, Gottfried's version does contain elements which have no parallel in the *Saga*, nor for that matter in *Sir Tristrem* and Eilhart.[43] These distinctive elements have in common a tendency to make the encounters more difficult for Tristan and more brutal in character than in the other versions.

In the first incident Gottfried makes of the dragon an even more formidable opponent than we find in the other versions. Comparing Gottfried's account with those of the *Saga* and *Sir Tristrem*, Piquet asserts: 'Le poète allemand seul a fait du serpent un monstre de dimensions formidables'.[44] We may furthermore observe that in Gottfried, in contrast to the *Saga*, the initial lance-attack on the dragon does not suffice to disable it. Although Tristan's physical commitment in the charge is beyond doubt – his horse is killed by the impact against the dragon and he barely escapes with his life (8974–83), and although he succeeds in thrusting his lance through the dragon's gullet to reach its heart, the beast cannot be finished off immediately afterwards by a single blow, as in the *Saga*. Rather, the dragon devours Tristan's horse with fire and then flees, causing havoc as it goes, to take refuge under a cliff. There Tristan hopes to kill the dragon, but he meets with such fierce opposition from the beast with its fearsome arsenal of 'weapons' that it is as much as he can do to keep out of its clutches when it emerges to chase him about among the bushes and trees. He finds respite by taking cover, waiting there until the initial wound sustained by the dragon and its subsequent futile exertions reduce it to exhaustion so that he can emerge and end the fight by plunging his sword right up to the hilt into its heart alongside the spear.

In the second incident Gottfried differs notably from the *Saga* and *Sir Tristrem* in having Tristan blind Urgan. He blinds him in one eye at the start of their combat when Urgan leaves himself unarmed after hurling his steel pole at Tristan, then in the other eye shortly before Tristan overcomes him. In spite of gaining these advantages, which are in addition to the hacking off of Urgan's right hand, which occurs in all accounts, and the wound in his thigh, which is peculiar to Gottfried's account, Tristan has to take to his heels to avoid Urgan's blows, running and dodging among the trees after the first blinding, and keeping his distance after the second blinding, until the giant blunders his way to the edge of the bridge from which Tristan pushes him to his death (16037–62, 16152–63).

---

43 For the fight with the dragon, see *Tristan*, 11. 8963–9055; Kölbing I, Cap. XXXVI and Schach, pp. 55–56; Kölbing II, 11. 1409–85; Eilhart, ed. Buschinger, 11. 1619–71. For the combat with the giant Urgan, see *Tristan*, 11. 15963–16174; Kölbing I, Cap. LXII and Schach, pp. 96–99; Kölbing II, 11. 2300–98; Eilhart does not include this episode.
44 Piquet, p. 191, with evidence in support of this on pp. 191–92.

Critics of Tristan's conduct as a knight find confirmation of their view in the features added by Gottfried to these encounters, encounters which are already in their received form and by their nature instances of the more vicious kind of conflict that knights engage in. Gottfried is held to have counteracted the heroic potential native to combats against such opponents by showing Tristan acting, on the one hand with cunning in that he avoids his foe at times and allows the wounds already inflicted to work to his advantage, and on the other with utter ruthlessness in exploiting every opportunity to inflict damage on his adversary.[45] In the main, however, the elements with which Gottfried has enriched his depiction of these combats are such as are to be found in other narratives and in contexts where no criticism of the hero's conduct is implied.

In Hartmann's *Erec*, for example, in his combat with the tormentors of the knight Cadoc, Erec blinds the first giant in one eye with his lance before killing him outright. The second giant proves more resilient and Erec takes advantage of his greater agility to avoid many of his blows and to deliver some of his own to his opponent's leg, which eventually he hacks through, bringing him to his knees; Erec continues to belabour the giant in this position until he topples him to the ground and chops off his head.[46] Geoffrey of Monmouth and Wace both record Arthur's victory over the giant of Mont-Saint-Michel, describing how the giant, blinded by the blood from a wound which Arthur has inflicted on him, gropes around wildly, while Arthur craftily evades his clutches and strikes at him again and again.[47] In Der Pleier's *Garel* the hero seeks protection from the giant's blows among the trees, while in *Wigalois* the hero is driven into a dense thicket, in which safe haven he remains, taking advantage of the fact that he can strike the giant with his sword, whereas the giant cannot wield the branch which he is using as a weapon.[48] In *Wigalois* we have also a vivid demonstration of the power of a dragon to inflict grievous harm, even though wounded by a lance thrust to its heart: the dragon Pfetan, although mortally wounded, catches Gwigalois and crushes him so violently that he is left for dead.[49] In *Diu Crône* Gawein is, like Tristan, more circumspect, and, having penetrated to the dragon's heart with his lance,

---

45 Tax, pp. 48–49, 110–13; Jackson, pp. 152–53.
46 *Erec*, ed. Leitzmann and others, 11. 5501–69.
47 *Historia*, ed. Griscom, p. 472 (in Thorpe's translation, pp. 239–40); *Roman de Brut*, ed. Arnold, II, 11. 11503–48.
48 Pleier, *Garel von dem blüenden Tal*, edited by Michael Walz (Freiburg i. Br., 1892), 11. 5611–19, 5629–33; Wirnt von Gravenberc, *Wigalois der Ritter mit dem Rade*, edited by J.M.N. Kapteyn, Rheinische Beiträge und Hülfsbücher zur germanischen Philologie und Volkskunde, 9 (Bonn, 1926), 11. 2114–31.
49 *Wigalois*, ed. Kapteyn, 11. 5088–122.

he uses his agility to avoid its attacks, waiting for an opportunity to outwit it and kill it.[50]

In all these instances it is clearly held to be proper and in no way unchivalrous for the knight who faces the superior physical properties of the giant or dragon to exploit to the full the resources of intelligence, agility, and courage he possesses in order to triumph over his adversary. The same can be said to hold good of Gottfried's Tristan, who is richly endowed with these resources. In his encounters with the dragon and the giant Urgan Tristan is confronted by exceptionally formidable opponents, and in overcoming them he does no more and no less than was expected of a chivalric hero in such hazardous situations. As in the previous instances considered, there is no reason here to think that his conduct is to be construed as discreditable to knighthood.

My survey of the episodes of military conflict in *Tristan* leads me to the conclusion that Gottfried's attitude to the profession of arms is best described as one of informed neutrality. Although he employs his skills as a narrator to good effect in creating military scenes which are vivid and memorable, he does not go out of his way to glamorize knighthood – but, on the other hand, he does not seek to denigrate it either. His depiction of the scenes of large-scale fighting betrays a keen awareness of the strategic and tactical principles of contemporary warfare, what one would expect from an intelligent, if detached, observer, while in the individual encounters Tristan is shown acting in a manner which bears comparison with the conduct of other literary heroes.

The picture of knighthood that Gottfried presents is certainly different from – indeed, less attractive than – that of the Arthurian romance of the Chrétien-Hartmann variety, but Gottfried's text gives no grounds for believing that that difference reflects a deliberate strategy of undermining the Arthurian ideals. Rather it flows from his commitment to a different kind of story, and from his commitment to a different tradition of writing, one which may be described as clerical (in the sense of educated or learned) and historical rather than chivalric. It seems to me significant that on several occasions it has been appropriate to draw comparisons for Gottfried's depiction of military incidents from Geoffrey of Monmouth's *Historia Regum Britanniae*, Wace's *Roman de Brut*, and, to a lesser extent, the *Roman d'Eneas*, since these works (Geoffrey's at least indirectly through Wace's) are known to have exerted an influence on Thomas.[51]

---

[50] Heinrich von dem Türlin, *Diu Crône*, edited by G.H.F. Scholl, Bibliothek des litterarischen Vereins, 27 (Stuttgart, 1852, reprinted Amsterdam, 1966), 11. 26703–64.
[51] For the relationship of Wace and Geoffrey to Thomas, see Pelan, pp. 72–97, 147–66. For the influence of Wace and *Eneas* on Thomas, see Frederick Whitehead, 'The Early Tristan Poems', in *Arthurian Literature in the Middle Ages*, edited by Roger Sherman Loomis (Oxford, 1959, reprinted 1979), pp. 134–44 (pp. 135, 141).

The evidence does not exist for us to compare the scenes of military conflict in Gottfried's *Tristan* directly with what he found in Thomas, but the fragments of Thomas's work do contain two incidents which give us some inkling at first hand of how he presented such scenes. The first occurs in the context of chivalrous sports held at Mark's court, to which Tristan and Kaherdin have returned in disguise. In the jousting they kill two barons. Tristan's role is not described precisely, but Kaherdin's is: he kills Cariado in revenge for having falsely accused him of cowardice. After the killings Tristan and Kaherdin flee and are able to give their pursuers the slip, returning to Brittany delighted at having exacted vengeance.[52] The second incident concerns Tristan's attack, together with Tristan the Dwarf, on the abductor Estult l'Orgillus and his six brothers. The two Tristans make their approach to Estult's castle but dismount before it on the edge of a wood. There they await their opportunity, and, as two of Estult's brothers pass by on their return from a tournament, the Tristans make a surprise attack upon them and kill them. In the ensuing combat with Estult and the other brothers, all are killed, apart from Tristan, who, however, receives the poisoned wound which is to bring his death.[53] Brief as they are, these incidents – the one a revenge killing in the context of courtly sports, the other an attack launched by knights lying in ambush – give a picture of military action governed by considerations of expediency which accords well with what we have observed in Gottfried's *Tristan* and found supported by examples from Geoffrey, Wace, and the *Roman d'Eneas*. It seems likely that in his depiction of military conflict Gottfried chose to reflect, for the most part faithfully, the style and approach of his source, of which he speaks with such respect in his Prologue (131–66), and that both Thomas and Gottfried stand in this regard, as no doubt in others, in that tradition of clerical, historical writing to which the Latin and French works of the mid-twelfth century that have been cited belong. If this is an accurate assessment of the situation, then it follows that Gottfried's depiction of military conflict in *Tristan* cannot be adduced in support of the argument that he is seeking to transcend the Arthurian romance, rejecting it in favour of something new. Rather than being innovative in this respect, Gottfried stands in a different tradition of narrative, one which antedates the Arthurian romance of the Chrétien-Hartmann variety and which cannot therefore have been designed to subvert the

[52]   Thomas, *Les Fragments du Roman de Tristan. Poème du XIIe siècle*, edited by Bartina H. Wind, Textes Littéraires Français (Geneva and Paris, 1960), Fragment Douce, 11. 795–834.

[53]   Thomas, Fragment Douce, 11. 1017–53. The remaining incidents of combat contained in the Thomas fragments – Arthur's fight with the giant Orguillos and Tristan's fight with Orguillos's giant nephew in Spain – are reported in the briefest of terms (Fragment Sneyd[1], 11. 720–28, 745–52) and yield nothing for the comparison with Gottfried.

conventions of that genre. It is undeniable that by continuing that earlier narrative tradition into the early thirteenth century Gottfried has given shape to an image of knighthood which reinforces our sense of the idealization that is practised in the Arthurian romance, but it would be to misconstrue his purpose, were we to see in this a calculated assault on the Arthurian concepts of chivalry. Gottfried has many targets of criticism in *Tristan*, but chivalry and the Arthurian romance are not among them.[54]

---

[54] Since this essay was completed, John Gillingham has published two further studies which provide valuable insights into the character of medieval warfare and the chivalric mentality: 'War and Chivalry in the *History of William the Marshal*', in *Thirteenth-Century England II: Proceedings of the Newcastle upon Tyne Conference 1987*, edited by P.R. Cross and S.D. Lloyd (Woodbridge, 1988), pp. 1–13, and 'William the Bastard at War', in *Studies in Medieval History presented to R. Allen Brown*, edited by Christopher Harper-Bill, Christopher J. Holdsworth, and Janet L. Nelson (Woodbridge, 1989), pp. 141–158. These studies add substantially to the account given in Gillingham's essay on Richard I, referred to in note 10 above, and can be read with profit by any who would wish to form a judgement of Gottfried's depiction of warfare.

The Renewal of the Classic:
Aspects of Rhetorical and Dialectical Composition
in Gottfried's Tristan

ADRIAN STEVENS

Gottfried's *Tristan* incorporates both exoteric and esoteric senses, and is designed to appeal to two distinct audiences simultaneously. Each of those audiences is addressed in the prologue, one plainly and the other more subtly and indirectly. To lay auditors Gottfried speaks openly of his intention to write the true history of Tristan and Isolt; to clerical sophisticates trained in the art of interpreting sacred and profane Latin texts he speaks literally of history and figuratively of recondite matters of rhetorical style, dialectical invention and allegorical reading. He assumes that the clerics who constitute his readership will be interested not only in the tale but in the technique of its telling; that they will be in the habit of probing beneath the narrative surface or literal sense of texts to discover their deeper, hidden meanings. Gottfried writes as if he regards the Tristan story as a matter of historical fact, but his ambition extends well beyond making available to naive listeners a record of a remote past.[1] His text is constructed so as to reveal itself to subtle analysis as a system of figures which yield access to an implied metacommentary or master narrative which provides an allegorical key to the primary, literal account of the lives of Tristan and Isolt.

To use figures in the way Gottfried does is to write learnedly and allusively, for an élite, while at the same time satisfying the generic expectations of plot and closure routinely associated with narrative by answering the questions: what happened, what happened next and how did it all

---

1   On the relationship between Gottfried's *Tristan* and medieval ideas about the writing of history, see D. H. Green, 'Oral poetry and Written Composition. (An Aspect of the Feud between Gottfried and Wolfram)', in D. H. Green and L. P. Johnson, *Approaches to Wolfram von Eschenbach: Five Essays*, Mikrokosmos, 5 (Berne, Frankfurt, Las Vegas, 1978), 163–264.

end.[2] The fact that Gottfried left the Tristan story incomplete was evidently not to the liking of the German literary public after his death. The thirteenth century saw two completions of his text, by Ulrich von Türheim and Heinrich von Freiberg. Neither was concerned about preserving the distinctive ethos of Gottfried's narrative. Ulrich did not follow Gottfried even to the extent of taking Thomas as his source; Heinrich for his part claimed to have followed Thomas in an Italian adaptation, but if this text actually existed, it was quite remote from the Norman French original in its version of events.[3] Ulrich and Heinrich were required primarily to supply an ending; there was no need for the rest of the story to be interpreted in a manner consonant with Gottfried's design as long as it was brought to a close. This was patently the view of those wealthy enough to commission manuscripts: of the eleven complete copies of Gottfried's poem known to have survived the Middle Ages, no less than ten append continuations. Six add Ulrich's text, three Heinrich's, and one, written in 1461, even provides a complete rendering of the Tristan story by joining to Gottfried's version the end of Eilhart's.[4] Such an arrangement can have been intended only to satisfy the most basic curiosity about story as event.

But it would be a mistake to suppose that Ulrich and Heinrich were themselves naive or incompetent readers of Gottfried's text. They may have been unable to endorse its ideology, but they knew enough to respect its method, as the prefaces to their continuations show. Much the same applies to Rudolf von Ems, who wrote into his love story *Willehalm von Orlens* a critique of *Tristan*, yet attempted as best he could to emulate the formal aspects of Gottfried's artistry.[5] Rudolf and Ulrich are the earliest readers of Gottfried's *Tristan* whose opinions of it are recorded. They were friends, employed together in the service of Konrad von Winterstetten, one of the most powerful of the agents of the emperor Frederick II in Germany.[6] Konrad commissioned Ulrich's *Tristan* and Rudolf's *Willehalm*,

2   For a discussion of plot and narrative closure, see Shlomith Rimmon-Kenan, *Narrative Fiction: Contemporary Poetics* (London, New York, 1983), pp. 6–28.
3   See Thomas Kerth, 'The Denouement of the *Tristan*-Minne: Türheim's Dilemma', *Neophilologus*, 65 (1981), 79–93, and Margarete Sedlmeyer, *Heinrichs von Freiberg Tristanfortsetzung im Vergleich zu anderen Tristandichtungen*, Europäische Hochschulschriften, 159 (Frankfurt, 1976), pp. 261–283.
4   For a description of the MSS, see Gottfried von Strassburg, *Tristan*, edited by Karl Marold and revised by Werner Schröder (Berlin, 1969), pp. viii–lii, 283–302.
5   See Burghart Wachinger, 'Zur Rezeption Gottfrieds von Straßburg im 13. Jahrhundert', in *Deutsche Literatur des späten Mittelalters. Hamburger Colloquium 1973*, edited by Wolfgang Harms et al. (Berlin, 1975), pp. 56–82.
6   See Helmut Brackert, *Rudolf von Ems: Dichtung und Geschichte* (Heidelberg, 1968), pp. 25–33.

and it is likely that both works were finished before his death in 1243.[7] Ulrich and Rudolf share a common judgment of Gottfried's technique which, being like their predecessor clerically trained, they express by citing criteria of literary composition derived from the study of the Trivium. Ulrich says of Gottfried:

8   er was ein künstrîcher man.
           uns zeiget sîn getihte
10   vil künstliche geschihte.
           ez ist eben unde ganz;
           kein getihte an sprüchen ist sô glanz,
           daz ez von künste gê der vür,
           der ez wiget mit wîser kür.[8]

What interests Ulrich about Gottfried is not Gottfried's story, but the way in which he tells it. The narrative artistry which *Tristan* is claimed to exemplify (cf. 'vil künstliche geschihte', 10) is itself dependent on Gottfried's implied mastery of the disciplines of the Trivium: grammar, rhetoric and dialectic. If the language of *Tristan* is smooth and without blemish ('eben unde ganz', 11), it conforms to the criteria of correct usage defined by the rules of grammar; if it is brilliant ('glanz', 12), it is because it deploys the figures of rhetoric; and if the poem is rich in ideas ('sprüche', 12), that is an indication of its author's skill in dialectic, in which the invention or 'finding' of arguments plays a crucial part.[9] The brief reference to rhetoric and dialectic requires elucidation, and here Rudolf von Ems is helpful, since he elaborates on the points made so sparingly by Ulrich. In his *Willehalm* he speaks of Gottfried's hero and heroine:

2187   ... Tristram und Ysot,
           Der liep, der trúwe und ir not
           Er so wol kunde wæhin
2190   Mit wisen worten spæhen.[10]

Wise words are the province of dialectic. Dialectic, as Aristotle puts it in the *Topica*, is the technique of reasoning from generally accepted opi-

---

7   See Brackert, pp. 26–27, 239–44, and Xenja von Ertzdorff, *Rudolf von Ems: Untersuchungen zum höfischen Roman im 13. Jahrhundert* (Munich, 1967), pp. 94–97.
8   Ulrich von Türheim, *Tristan*, edited by Thomas Kerth, Altdeutsche Textbibliothek, 89 (Tübingen, 1979).
9   On the Trivium and the influence of grammar, rhetoric and dialectic on medieval literary composition, see *Medieval Eloquence: Studies in the Theory and Practice of Medieval Rhetoric*, edited by James J. Murphy (Berkeley, Los Angeles, London, 1978).
10 Rudolf von Ems, *Willehalm von Orlens*, edited by Victor Junk, Deutsche Texte des Mittelalters, 2 (Berlin, 1905).

nions. And generally accepted opinions, he explains, 'are those which commend themselves to all or to the majority or to the wise.'[11] Aristotle's *Topica* had established itself by the end of the twelfth century as one of the major texts on dialectic, and it is likely that Rudolf, in common with Gottfried before him, was familiar with its basic ideas and definitions.[12] Wise words, it may be inferred, are the expression in *Tristan* of the generally accepted opinions that form the basis of dialectical reasoning. If those opinions are not only wise but, as Rudolf asserts, brilliantly and beautifully expressed, it is because they are presented with the help of the figures and tropes (often metaphorically designated the 'colours' or 'flowers') of rhetoric, which enhance their attractiveness and appeal.[13] 'Rhetoric', as Thomasin von Zerclære says so succinctly in *Der wälsche Gast*, 'clothes our speech in beautiful colours':

8924   ... Rethoricâ kleit
                unser rede mit varwe schône.[14]

The relationship between narrative artistry in *Tristan* and the disciplines of the Trivium is set out even more explicitly in the lengthy section which Rudolf devotes to Gottfried in the literary excursus of his *Alexander* (probably written in the 1230s, before *Willehalm*):

3153   ... der wîse Gotfrit
                von Strâzburc der nie valschen trit
3155   mit valsche in sîner rede getrat.
                wie ist sô ebensleht gesat
                sîn vunt, sô rîch, sô sinneclîch!
                wie ist sô gar meisterlîch
                sîn Tristan! swer den ie gelas,
3160   der mac wol hœren daz er was
                ein schrôter süezer worte
                und wîser sinne ein porte.[15]

---

11 Aristotle, *Topica*, translated by E. S. Forster, The Loeb Classical Library (Cambridge Mass., London, 1976), p. 273.
12 See Tony Hunt, 'Aristotle, Dialectic and Courtly Literature', *Viator*, 10 (1979), 95–129.
13 On Gottfried's use of the figures and tropes, see Stanislaw Sawicki, *Gottfried von Straßburg und die Poetik des Mittelalters*, Germanische Studien, 124 (Berlin, 1932).
14 Thomasin von Zirclaria, *Der wälsche Gast*, edited by Friedrich Rückert with an introduction and index by Friedrich Neumann, Deutsche Neudrucke, Reihe Texte des Mittelalters (Berlin, 1965).
15 Rudolf von Ems, *Alexander*, edited by Victor Junk, 2 vols, Bibliothek des literarischen Vereins in Stuttgart, 272, 274 (Leipzig, 1928, 1929).

In avoiding all mistakes (cf. 'valschen trit', 3154) Gottfried demonstrates his mastery of grammar; his implied facility in dialectic is attributed to a rich invention ('vunt', 3157) which enables him to produce wise (and therefore by inference generally accepted) arguments and ideas ('wîse sinne', 3162); and his skill in rhetoric is attested by his talent for dressing those ideas and arguments in pleasing language ('süeziu wort', 3161).

Somewhere-behind this characterisation stand the lines from Horace's *Ars Poetica* which provided medieval commentators with an enduring and authoritative definition of the function of poetry:

333   Aut prodesse volunt aut delectare poetae
             aut simul et iucunda et idonea dicere vitae . . .

343   omne tulit punctum qui miscuit utile dulci,
             lectorem delectando pariterque monendo.[16]

(Poets aim either to benefit, or to delight, or to utter words both pleasing and proper to life . . . He has won every vote who has blended profit and pleasure, at once delighting and instructing the reader.)

A mixture of pleasure and profit is precisely what, on Rudolf's reading, Gottfried's *Tristan* provides. Its language is pleasing (Rudolf's 'süeze', 3161, echoes, perhaps intentionally, Horace's *dulce*), and to the extent that it presents the reader ('swer den ie gelas', 3159) with wise ideas, its effect can be said to be beneficial. But to suggest, as Rudolf does, that Gottfried fulfils Horace's ideal of the function of literature is by implication to make an ambitious claim for his *Tristan*: that it has earned for itself, as a text worthy of comparison with the works of the Latin authors of antiquity, the status of a modern classic.

The claim to classic status is one which Gottfried himself seeks both to promote and to justify. He is careful to write into his prologue a number of allusions to the basic postulates of Horace's *Ars Poetica*, and to present himself as being committed to producing a poem which blends profit and pleasure. He undertakes the task of composition, he says, to delight society ('der werlt ze liebe', 46) and to please noble hearts ('und edelen herzen zeiner hage', 47); the story of Tristan and Isolt retains its capacity to delight ('ist noch hiute liep vernomen', 218); it is sweet ('süeze', 219) and as pleasing as bread ('und ist uns daz süeze alse brot', 236); although the lovers are long dead, their sweet name lives on ('ir süezer name der lebet iedoch', 223); their joy and sorrow have continued to give pleasure

---

[16] Horace, *Satires, Epistles and Ars Poetica*, translated by H. Rushton Fairclough, The Loeb Classical Library (Cambridge Mass., London, 1978).

('ze liebe komen', 217).[17] But for all the deliberately contrived echoes of Horace's *dulce* and *delectare*, didactic utility is stressed as firmly as pleasure. Gottfried professes to write not only for the enjoyment of people but for their good ('der werlt ze guote', 6 – a reformulation of Horace's *prodesse*), and he is particularly insistent on the beneficial aspect of his text, the moral gain which 'noble hearts' will derive from reading it:

172	ez ist in sere guot gelesen.
	guot? ja, innecliche guot:
	ez liebet liebe und edelt muot,
175	ez stætet triuwe und tugendet leben,
	ez kan wol lebene tugende geben;
	wan swa man hœret oder list,
	daz von so reinen triuwen ist,
	da liebent dem getriuwen man
180	triuwe und ander tugende van.

Gottfried argues that his poem is good to read in the positive sense that it promotes excellence and nobility of conduct; but in encouraging the pursuit of virtues such as loyalty and constancy it also generates delight (cf. 'liebet', 174; 'liebent', 179), the inference being that true pleasure can be derived only from contemplating attitudes and actions that are judged to be intrinsically good. The arresting phrase 'guot gelesen' (172) is a signal to the clerically educated reader that Gottfried is invoking the interpretative practice of the schools with its characteristic emphasis on the didactic value of the pagan texts of antiquity. Gottfried shares Conrad von Hirsau's view that the 'ultimate benefit' of literary study 'lies in improving the morals of the reader, for if you do not imitate the good which you read, the exercise of reading is in vain': *fructus finalis in correctione morum legentis est: si enim non imitaris bonum quod legis, frustra studium exercetur lectionis.*[18] The positive effect of studying and interpreting the classical authors, Conrad insists, 'will be to encourage the reader, as a consequence of his reading, in the avoidance of vice and in the desire for virtue': *si legentem aversione vitiorum et appetitu ex ipsa lectione virtutum constiterit proficere.*[19] Gottfried at this point chooses to ignore vice, but he leaves no doubt that his interpretation of the story of Tristan and Isolt entails a projection of the lovers as models of virtuous and noble conduct designed to elicit sympathy and approval and to inspire imitation.

The evident parallel between Gottfried's 'guot gelesen' and Conrad's

---

17 Gottfried von Strassburg, *Tristan und Isold*, edited by Friedrich Ranke (Berlin, 1962).
18 Conrad of Hirsau, *Dialogus super auctores*, edited by R. B. C. Huygens (Leiden, 1970), p. 83.
19 *Dialogus super auctores*, p. 83.

bonum quod legis not only underlines the didactic dimensions of *Tristan*; it also clearly indicates Gottfried's commitment to achieving the fusion of invention, ideas and ethics required by the learned literary theory of his age. The argument derived from 'guot gelesen' constitutes in itself a prime example of the technique and practice of dialectical invention. Gottfried 'finds' and cites an authoritative proposition, one which will commend itself to the wise in accordance with Aristotle's definition. But Gottfried, as Rudolf von Ems sees it, is not only adept at 'inventing' wise ideas ('wîse sinne'); he is also a master of the rhetorical art of dressing those ideas in sweet words ('ein schrôter süezer worte'). In practice, Horace's precept that poetry should combine pleasure and profit is dependent on the poet's proficiency in the disciplines of dialectic and rhetoric. In urging the clerical commonplace that the study of classic texts is morally beneficial, and in presenting *Tristan* as a specific example of that general rule, Gottfried does not rely on plain language, but dramatises his case by employing a striking range of rhetorical figures. As so often in *Tristan*, figures of diction, especially those either directly involving or otherwise generated by word repetition, feature in abundance.[20] They include anaphora (the repetition of a word at the beginning of consecutive phrases, cf. 'ez', 174–76); *traductio* (the repetition of a word or root across a variety of grammatical forms, cf. 'guot', 172–73; 'lieben', 'liebe', 174, 179; 'tugenden', 'tugent', 175–76, 180; 'leben', 175–76; 'triuwe', 'getriuwe', 175, 178–80); and *conplexio* (the repetition of a word at the beginning and end of a phrase or sentence, cf. 'guot', 173). The sheer density of repetition itself gives rise to the figure of *similiter desinens* or approximate internal rhyme (e.g. 'guot', 172–73; 'liebet liebe', 174; 'tugendet leben / lebene tugende', 175–76; 'triuwen / getriuwen / triuwe', 178–80). Among other figures used are *isocolon* or parallelism (174–75); *interpretatio* or synonymy (cf. 'tugendet leben / ez kan wol lebene tugende geben', 175–76); and *ratiocinatio* or reasoning by question and answer (173–76). Finally, all of these overlapping figures are themselves subordinated to the dominant structural figure of *expolitio*, the technique of rehearsing a single topic (here the relationship between reading and virtue) while maintaining the illusion that something new is being said.

The art of using the figures has everything to do with creating an appearance of novelty even though the ideas being expressed are familiar; hence the notion prevalent in the manuals of poetic composition assembled by Faral that the function of rhetoric is to dress invention in new and

---

[20] I follow the definitions and terminology of the figures given in the fourth book of the *Rhetorica ad Herennium*, translated by Harry Caplan, The Loeb Classical Library (Cambridge Mass., London, 1954).

attractive clothes.[21] Invention itself is thought of as comprising a body of accepted truths (the 'wise words' of Rudolf von Ems) which in principle are not subject to change, but which in practice, from the viewpoint of the poet, are in constant need of linguistic (figurative and rhetorical) revitalisation and renewal. Mastery of the figures becomes a means of defamiliarising the familiar so as to make it once again interesting and appealing. It is this justification of rhetoric as an enhancement of the axioms 'found' by dialectical invention that lies at the heart of Gottfried's literary excursus.

Much has been written about Gottfried's repeated references in the excursus to the ability of the narrative poets he admires (Hartmann, Bligger von Steinach and Veldeke) to fuse words ('wort') and ideas ('sin', 'sinne').[22] A helpful gloss on this comes from the twelfth-century English humanist John of Salisbury. Discussing the Roman philosopher Seneca, John notes approvingly that he 'assembles authoritative ideas and uses brilliantly ornamented language, so that he cannot displease those who love either virtue or eloquence': *sententias colligit, ornatu uerborum splendet, ut eis displicere non possit qui aut uirtutem amant aut eloquentiam.*[23] In combining eloquence and virtue, rhetorical skill and validity of invention, Seneca establishes himself as a major classic who can be studied both with pleasure and with profit. John is insistent that rhetoric on its own amounts to nothing. 'It is well known and true', he pronounces in the *Metalogicon*, 'that eloquence without wisdom is of no use': *eloquentia sine sapientia non prodesse, celebre est et uerum* (II.ix). Bernard Silvester is equally convinced that 'unless eloquence is joined to wisdom, it is of little profit': *eloquentia enim nisi sapientiae iungatur parum prodest.*[24] Even Matthew of Vendôme, giving instruction on how to compose verse, is unequivocal that 'the conception of the idea comes first, and the devising of verbal expression follows after it': *prior est sententiae conceptio, sequitur verborum*

---

21   See *Les Arts poétiques du XIIe et du XIIIe siècle*, edited by Edmond Faral (Paris, 1924), and the wide-ranging study by James J. Murphy, *Rhetoric in the Middle Ages: A History of Rhetorical Theory from Saint Augustine to the Renaissance* (Berkeley, Los Angeles, London, 1974).
22   The most recent and exhaustive investigations of this subject are by Christoph Huber, 'Wort-Ding-Entsprechungen: zur Sprach- und Stiltheorie Gottfrieds von Straßburg', in *Befund und Deutung. Festschrift Hans Fromm* (Tübingen, 1979), pp. 268–302, and Eberhard Nellmann, 'Wolfram und Kyot als *vindære wilder mære*: Überlegungen zu *Tristan* 4619–88 und *Parzival* 453, 1–17', ZDA, 117 (1988), 31–67.
23   John of Salisbury, *Metalogicon*, edited by C. C. J. Webb (Oxford, 1929), I , xxii. On ideas and themes common to John and Gottfried, see C. Stephen Jaeger, *Medieval Humanism in Gottfried von Strassburg's Tristan und Isolde* (Heidelberg, 1977), pp. 97–104.
24   *Commentum Bernardi Silvestris super sex libros Eneidos Virgilii*, edited by Wilhelm Riedel (Greifswald, 1924), p. 25.

excogitatio.[25] And Bernard Silvester, defining what is necessary to qualify a man for the status of master, is emphatic that 'nobody should lay claim to the title of master before he possesses wisdom and eloquence': *prius enim non debet aliquis nomen magistri praesumere quam possideat sapientiam et eloquentiam.*[26]

In the literary excursus, Gottfried describes Veldeke and those who followed him in establishing the tradition of German poetry as 'vil sinnic und vil rederich' (4725). As Ganz points out, 'sinnic' in this context corresponds to the Latin *sententiosus.*[27] It connotes facility in the inventing of *sententiae* which reflect and promote the cultivation of wisdom and virtue, while 'rederich' stands for eloquence, skill in the use of rhetorical figures. Gottfried's design in the excursus is to promote the idea that the vernacular poetry of the modern age is in the process of enacting a renewal of the classic. But he can only succeed in this if he manages to demonstrate that vernacular texts exhibit the distinctive features of the classic. Specifically, German works with pretensions to classic status are expected to meet the obligation to combine wisdom and eloquence, as Gottfried powerfully implies when he looks back to Veldeke as the first great agent of renewal:

4726	von Veldeken Heinrich
	der sprach uz vollen sinnen;
	wie wol sanger von minnen!
	wie schone er sinen sin besneit!
4730	ich wæne, er sine wisheit
	uz Pegases urspringe nam,
	von dem diu wisheit elliu kam.

In drawing his wisdom ('sine wisheit', 4730) from the spring of Pegasus on Mount Helicon, the source of all authentic literary artistry, Veldeke is not only returning to what was the mythical origin of poetic inspiration for the poets of ancient Greece and Rome, but renewing in the German vernacular their skill in deploying the inventive and figurative techniques of composing texts.[28] Gottfried's references to the wealth of Veldeke's ideas (4727) and to his mastery of the rhetorical language which dresses invention in finely tailored clothes (4729) are clearly intended to

25 Matthew of Vendôme, Ars versificatoria, in Les Arts poétiques du XIIe et du XIIIe siècle, edited by Edmond Faral, III.52, p.180; see Nellmann pp. 32–44.
26 Commentum Bernardi Silvestris, p. 91.
27 Gottfried von Straßburg, Tristan, edited by Peter Ganz after Reinhold Bechstein, Deutsche Klassiker des Mittelalters, Neue Folge, 4, 2 vols (Wiesbaden, 1978), commentary on 1. 4723.
28 See Adrian Stevens, 'Zum Literaturbegriff bei Rudolf von Ems', in Geistliche und weltliche Epik des Mittelalters in Österreich, edited by David McLintock et al., Göppinger Arbeiten zur Germanistik, 446 (Göppingen, 1987), pp.19–28.

project an image of the author of the *Eneide* working within the great tradition of classical letters. But in renewing that tradition, Veldeke is also in an important sense extending its scope and influence by disciplining the German vernacular to its conventions. Within the provincial context of German-speaking Europe, Veldeke can justly be seen as a cosmopolitan innovator, the founding father of German literature who set an example of poetic technique quickly imitated by others:

4733   ine han sin selbe niht gesehen;
       nu hœre ich aber die besten jehen
4735   die, die bi sinen jaren
       und sit her meister waren,
       die selben gebent im einen pris:
       er inpfete daz erste ris
       in tiut[i]scher zungen:
4740   da von sit este ersprungen,
       von den die bluomen kamen,
       da si die spæhe uz namen
       der meisterlichen vünde.

In this densely worked allegorical passage, Gottfried implies that Veldeke's original German graft from the Latin ('daz erste ris / in tiut[i]scher zungen', 4738–39) proved successful, and produced a branch (the *Eneide*) from which further branches (works by other German masters) grew (4740). Repeating the pattern established by the *Eneide*, those branches (works) produced flowers ('bluomen', 4741), rhetorical figures which gave brilliant expression to the wise ideas ('spæhe', 4742) their authors drew from their invention ('vünde', 4743). In the process of literary transmission and imitation, the modern vernacular masters ('meister', 4736) took ('uz namen', 4742) from Veldeke and from each other a profusion of finely expressed ideas, which they adapted to their own use. The result of authors appropriating words and ideas from each other is that by Gottfried's own time the classicising conventions of literary composition have become thoroughly naturalised in the German vernacular:

4744   und ist diu selbe künde
4745   so witen gebreitet,
       so manege wis geleitet,
       daz alle, die nu sprechent,
       daz die den wunsch da brechent
       von bluomen und von risen. . .

The phrase 'witen gebreitet' (4745) continues the metaphor of the branches proliferating from the original graft of the *Eneide*, indicating the rapid expansion of German poetry after Veldeke, while 'geleitet' (4746), a figure alluding to the horticultural practice of training the branches of a tree,[29] stresses the connection between the new vernacular literature and the arts of invention and rhetoric ('diu selbe künde', 4744) basic to its production.

If Veldeke was clerically trained so, too, were the masters ('meister', 4736) who vied with one another to carry on the poetic tradition he inaugurated in Germany. From Gottfried's point of view, the facility in Latin that is the special province of clerks is a prerequisite for any writer whose work aspires to the status of art. German literature is validated on the grounds of its indebtedness to classical models of writing, as is impressively suggested by the allegorical figure of Veldeke's return to the spring of Pegasus, the source of all poetry that derives its claim to legitimacy and cultural distinction from the ancient tradition. Even though the German authors imitate and borrow from one another, and even though, like Veldeke and Gottfried himself, they may use French sources, the skills needed for the composition of literary works are learned initially from the study of Latin texts. It is not from Germany or France but from Rome, from the techniques of reading the classics propagated by the schools, that Veldeke and his successors acquire their status as masters.

The relationship between Gottfried and Veldeke is a case in point. It is Veldeke's intention in key scenes of the *Eneide* to be, in the special sense of the term set out in the classical manuals of rhetoric, demonstrative. Demonstrative argument borrows from ancient philosophy a series of universal definitions of moral conduct; it concentrates, on the basis of those definitions, on the attribution of praise or censure.[30] The fundamental principle of demonstrative argument is that nothing should be praised unless it can be shown to be honourable; equally, anything that can be presented as dishonourable should be censured and rejected. The *Rhetorica ad Herennium* divides honourable issues into what it terms the right and the praiseworthy: *honesta res dividitur in rectum et laudabile*.[31] The praiseworthy is said to have its origin in the right (*ex recto laudabile nascitur*, III.iv.7), while the right itself is defined as what is done in accordance with virtue and duty: *rectum est quod cum virtute et officio fit* (III.ii.3). Specifically, the right is composed of the four cardinal virtues of prudence, justice, courage and temperance: *id dividitur in prudentiam, iustitiam, fortitudinem,*

---

[29] I follow Ganz/Bechstein, 1. 4744 in reading 'geleitet' rather than 'zeleitet' as in Ranke's text.

[30] On demonstrative argument, see Heinrich Lausberg, *Handbuch der literarischen Rhetorik*, 2 vols (Munich, 1960), pp.129–38, and the *Rhetorica ad Herennium* III.vi.10–III.viii.15.

[31] *Rhetorica ad Herennium*, III.ii.3; cf. Cicero, *De officiis*, translated by Walter Miller, The Loeb Classical Library (London, New York, 1913), I.iv.14: *honestum . . . natura esse laudabile*.

modestiam (III.ii.3). Conduct which exemplifies these virtues merits praise; conduct which negates them calls for condemnation.

When in the *Eneide* Dido, abandoned by Eneas, takes her own life in despair, Veldeke 'invents' a heavily censorious commentary on her suicide:

> 77,40   al wâre sie ein wîse wîb,
> 78,1   sie was dô vil sinne lôs.
>   daz si den tôt alsô kôs,
>   daz quam von unsinne.
>   ez was unrehtiu minne,
>   diu sie dar zû dwanc.[32]

In Veldeke's eyes Dido's shame, and her tragedy, is that love causes her to renounce what is right (hence its description as 'unrehtiu minne', 78,4) and to abandon virtue. The prudence that had previously characterised her life (cf. 'al wâre sie ein wîse wîb', 77,40) deserts her in her hour of greatest need. Her suicide is an act of madness ('daz quam von unsinne', 78,3); and being contrary to prudence, it is also an evil act. According to the *Rhetorica ad Herennium*, 'prudence is intelligence capable, by a certain kind of rational judgment, of distinguishing good from evil': *prudentia est calliditas quae ratione quadam potest dilectum habere bonorum et malorum* (III.ii.3). To act imprudently is to act irrationally; to act irrationally is to act evilly. Prudence being reason in action, the two concepts easily overlap. As Thomasin von Zerclære puts it in *Der wälsche Gast*:

> 8842   Râtiô diu kraft kan
>   bescheiden daz übel vomme guot.

The whole basis of Veldeke's demonstrative censure of Dido's suicide is the premise that reason is the essence of morality and honour, and that virtue manifests itself in the prudent exercise of reason, by first discerning and then conforming to the good, which is also the right and the honourable. Evil occurs, and dishonour and disgrace befall the individual when, as in Dido's case, conduct is governed no longer by reason but by passion which, being by definition irrational and subversive of morality, is the source of false judgments and the delusions they generate.[33] Passion blurs the distinction between good and evil which is normally mediated by

---

[32] Heinrich von Veldeke, *Eneasroman*, edited after the text of Ludwig Ettmüller with a translation, commentary and postscript by Dieter Kartschoke (Stuttgart, 1986).
[33] On the relationship between passion and reason, see R. A. Wisbey, 'The *Renovatio Amoris* in Gottfried's *Tristan*', London German Studies I, edited by C. V. Bock (London, 1980), 1–66, which includes extensive references to the secondary literature on the subject.

reason, and evil results from the obscuring of the good. So it is that Dido's sister Anna laments her suicide as the product of passion and unreason:

79,4   'wand ir ûch selbe habet erslagen
79,5   dorch eines mannes minne.
            daz quam von unsinne.
            ir mindet in zunmâzen:
            dorch daz habt ir verlâzen
            ûwern lîb und grôze êre.
            daz mach ich wol klagen sêre.'

As Veldeke's spokeswoman at this point, Anna knows all about the traditional association of reason and temperance within the scheme of the four cardinal virtues that constitute the right. According to Cicero's *De inventione*, 'temperance is a firm and well-considered control exercised by the reason over lust and other improper impulses of the mind': *temperantia est rationis in libidinem atque in alios non rectos impetus animi firma et moderata dominatio.*[34] The *Moralium dogma philosophorum*, a twelfth-century compendium of ancient moral philosophy derived largely from Cicero's ethical treatise *De officiis*, adds the gloss that 'this virtue is life's most splendid adornment, and it stills all violent passions': *hec namque uirtus totius uite ornatus omniumque perturbationum sedatio.*[35] Dido's intemperance (cf. 'ir mindet in zunmâzen', 79,7) renders her defenceless against the destructive passion for Eneas that is explicitly identified as the consequence of unreason ('daz quam von unsinne', 79,6), and as she throws away her life, she abandons with it her honour and her reputation ('grôze êre', 79,9). Anna in her demonstrative rejection of Dido's suicide assumes with Cicero and the author of the *Moralium dogma philosophorum* that honour and virtue are practically synonymous: *uirtus igitur et honestum nomina diuersa sunt, res autem subiecta prorsus eadem.*[36] Dido's defection from virtue entails the loss of her honour; and she loses both her honour and her virtue because prudence and judgment have, in her, been overwhelmed. Veldeke insists on the point:

79,40   dô het ir rât unde ir sin
80,1   ubel ende genomen,
            dô si dar zû was komen.

It is, says the *Moralium dogma philosophorum*, the role of prudence as the

34 Cicero, *De inventione*, translated by H. M. Hubbell, The Loeb Classical Library (London, Cambridge Mass., 1949), II.liv.164; cf. *Rhetorica ad Herennium*, III.ii.3: *modestia est in animo continens moderatio cupiditatem.*
35 *Das Moralium Dogma Philosophorum des Guillaume de Conches*, edited by John Holmberg (Uppsala, 1929), 8,21f.
36 ibid., 7,14f; cf. Cicero, *De inventione*, II.lii.159.

rational guarantor of moral discrimination to advise, and of justice, courage and temperance to act on her advice, as prudent counsel should always precede and inform any practical undertaking: *consilium autem preuenire debet actum* (8,3). Precisely because Dido in her frenzy lacks reason ('sin', 79,40) and prudent counsel ('rât', 79,40), she suffers disgrace and ruin.

Gottfried, like Veldeke, is schooled in these ethical commonplaces; in *Tristan* as in the *Eneide* they provide a metacommentary on much of the action, an allegorical key to its understanding. When Marke recalls Tristan and Isolt from the cave of lovers to his court he, no less than Veldeke's Dido, is a victim of intemperance and passion. The passion at work in Marke, destroying the control of reason, is explicitly identified by Gottfried as lust (cf. 17591ff). Great emphasis is placed on the fact that the pleasure Marke takes in Isolt's return to court is entirely sexual, and that it is bought at the expense of his honour and reputation:

17723   Marke der was aber do vro.
    ze vröuden hæter aber do
    an sinem wibe Isolde,
    swaz so sin herze wolde,
    niht zeren, wan ze libe.

As in the *Eneide*, honour and virtue are regarded as being interdependent. Lust, the personification of intemperance, overrides prudence, reason and virtue in Marke and dishonours him (cf. 'niht zeren', 17727) in the process. Marke's conduct is subjected to a lengthy and detailed demonstrative censure; he becomes a paradigm of the destructiveness of vice:

17728   ern hæte an sinem wibe
    noch minne noch meine
17730   noch al der eren keine,
    die got ie gewerden liez,
    wan dazs in sinem namen hiez
    ein vrouwe und ein künigin
    da, da er künic solte sin.
17735   diz nam er allez vür guot
    und truog ir allez holden muot,
    als er ir vil liep wære.

In pretending to himself that his relationship with Isolt is good ('diz nam er allez vür guot', 17735) when patently it is not, Marke is behaving imprudently, failing to distinguish between good and evil in the way that reason, virtue and honour demand. And his moral failure, Gottfried implies, is a failure on his part to love Isolt. Love as created by God is honourable (cf. 17728–31); but it can be honourable only as long as it is virtuous. Lust of the type which claims Marke as a victim is a passion that

obliterates reason and restraint, and is therefore by inference a vice; as a
source of shame and degradation it is the antithesis of love, since love is
honourable and confers virtue. In recalling Isolt to court, Marke is behaving wrongly and immorally. Gottfried is emphatic that his action incurs
nothing but shame and dishonour:

17753	wem mac man nu die schulde geben
	umbe daz erlose leben,
17755	daz er sus mit ir hæte?
	wan zware er missetæte,
	der ez Isote seite
	ze keiner trügeheite:
	weder sin trouc in noch Tristan;
17760	er sach ez doch mit ougen an
	und wistes ungesehen genuoc,
	dazs ime dekeine liebe truoc
	und was sim doch liep über daz.

To live, as Marke is said to live, a life without honour (cf. 'daz erlose
leben', 17754) is to live a life without love in the special sense that Gottfried gives to love. Love, dependent on virtue, is destroyed by vice.
Marke's lust isolates him from all genuine communication with Isolt; he is
content merely to pretend to himself that she loves him (cf. 17735–37). Yet
love is nothing if not mutual; it involves in an absolute way the sharing
and returning of emotion, as the prologue makes explicit (cf. 58–63). Isolt
does not reciprocate Marke's desire, and no longer attempts to deceive
him into thinking that she does (cf. 17756–63). Marke knows this, yet he
ignores it (17760–63). If he were to acknowledge that Isolt does not love
him, the only prudent and honourable course open to him would be to
put an end to their relationship. But doing what, within the logic of
Gottfried's argument would be the right thing would, of course, run
counter to lust, and it is lust which both binds Marke to Isolt and at the
same time blinds him to the shamefulness and futility of his situation:

17764	'war umbe, herre, und umbe waz
	truoger ir inneclichen muot?'
	dar umbez hiute maneger tuot:
	geluste unde gelange
	der lidet vil ange,
	daz ime ze lidene geschiht. . .
17797	swaz man von blintheit geseit,
	son blendet dekein blintheit
	als anclich unde als ange
17800	so geluste unde gelange.

Although Gottfried contrives by dialectical subtlety to transform him into a paradigm of vice and thereby convict him in a moral sense of wrongdoing, Marke is, according to the criteria of judgment more routinely and mundanely applied in twelfth-century society, the innocent and injured party, and Tristan and Isolt are the transgressors. In defining the customs and obligations of marriage, both secular and canon law in Gottfried's time prohibited adultery, and imposed particular restraint on the wife.[37] In suggesting that Marke's desire to resume marital relations with Isolt is wrong and dishonourable, Gottfried is by implication using the authority of one moral order to subvert the authority of another. The logic of his case is that love may in certain circumstances be more important than adultery. Love of the kind exemplified by Tristan and Isolt involves fineness of conduct and honourable (if unorthodox) self-fulfilment, whereas marriage as Marke practises it, although it may be supported by legal, social and ecclesiastical sanctions, is degrading. When he argues that his poem is 'guot gelesen' (172), Gottfried presents the love of Tristan and Isolt as exemplary by aligning it with the scheme of virtue inherited from classical antiquity. This is perhaps the most significant dialectical move in the entire work. The claim is that the relationship of the lovers, being good and noble in itself, has the capacity to inspire virtuous conduct in the reader or listener (cf. 'edelt muot', 174; 'tugendet leben', 175). But for Tristan and Isolt to be praised in the prologue as representatives of the honour of love presupposes that love itself can be perceived as a virtue, and be distinguished by reason as innately good. Gottfried insists that it can, and emphasises that not only is love virtuous and honourable in itself, it is the condition that makes the attainment of virtue and honour possible, the ultimate spur to moral conduct:

187   liebe ist ein also sælic dinc,
           ein also sæleclich gerinc,
           daz nieman ane ir lere
190   noch tugende hat noch ere.

To the extent that it presupposes a close familiarity with the moral philosophy of the ancients, Gottfried's text assumes a clerically trained reader conversant with classical Latin literature. As the insertion of the acrostic G DIETERICH (composed of the initial letters of the first ten stanzas of the prologue) shows, the expectation is that this implied reader will not be content simply to scan the manuscript consecutively and establish its literal sense, but will peruse it backwards and forwards to discover hidden links. The acrostic itself, presumably a reference to the names of

---

37 On marriage in feudal society, see now Georges Duby, *The Knight, The Lady and The Priest: The making of Modern Marriage in Medieval France* (Harmondsworth, 1985).

Gottfried and his patron, constitutes one such link, but there are also verbal connections, thrown into prominence by Gottfried's chosen rhetorical form of writing. The figure of *traductio* foregrounds a number of terms, among them *guot* and *übel*, *ere* and *lop*, in a way that requires explanation. Word repetition that draws attention to itself by its unusual density is calculated to interrupt continuous left-to-right reading and to encourage the search for an interpretation within which the foregrounded terms may plausibly be related. One example would be the unusually heavy emphasis on 'guot' in the stanza:

5   Der guote man swaz der in guot
             und niwan der werlt ze guote tuot,
             swer daz iht anders wan in guot
             vernemen wil, der missetuot.

Gottfried's implied reader might associate 'der guote man' with the commonplace classical description of the ideal orator as 'a good man skilled in the art of speaking' (*vir bonus dicendi peritus*).[38] The 'good man' by inference skilled in rhetoric would then be Gottfried himself; and what Gottfried does with a good intention ('in guot', 5) for the good of society ('der werlt ze guote tuot', 6) is to write his *Tristan*. But readers and listeners, the society for whose benefit *Tristan* is intended, will perceive the good that constitutes the poem only as long as they allow themselves to be guided by reason and virtue. Gottfried's ideal reader must be characterised by prudence, the first of the cardinal virtues, and distinguish between good and evil:

17   Tiur unde wert ist mir der man,
             der guot und übel betrahten kan. . .

In his prudence he will be properly responsive to the good that *Tristan* offers him, and he will arrive at a just assessment of Gottfried as author and of his positive moral intention ('in guot / vernemen', 7–8). In writing the ethical character of his ideal reader into the text, Gottfried is not simply expressing a personal preference; he is implicitly invoking (and 'inventing') the authoritative classical humanist criteria of moral excellence, and trying to establish a normative community of attitude and interest between himself and those interpreters subtle enough to look beyond the letter of the poem. Intimating that he no less than his ideal

---

38 On the commonplace idea of the ideal orator as *vir bonus dicendi peritus*, see Lausberg, *Handbuch der literarischen Rhetorik*, op. cit., fn. 30, vol. I, pp. 550–51; cf. Isidore, *De rhetorica*, in: *Rhetores Latini Minores*, edited by Karl Halm (Leipzig, 1873), pp. 505–22, III.1, p. 507: *Orator est igitur vir bonus, dicendi peritus. Vir bonus consistit natura, moribus, artibus. Dicendi peritus consistit artificiosa eloquentia.*

reader is a man of wisdom and virtue, Gottfried indicates that his *Tristan* will be morally discriminating, but that this will be fully understood only by somebody willing and able to evaluate human conduct in the way that tradition demands. As well as being a man of prudence, Gottfried's implied reader is required to be a man given to judging justly. The phrase,

19   der mich und iegelichen man
                    nach sinem werde erkennen kan,

is a calculated allusion to the cardinal virtue of justice, which Cicero defines as 'a habit of mind which gives every man his desert': *iustitia est habitus animi . . . suam cuique tribuens dignitatem* (*De inventione*, II.liii.160).

Gottfried encourages the assumption that *Tristan* will exemplify in practice the rational scheme of virtue it proposes in theory. But the virtue of the poem cannot guarantee its success; the role of the implied reader is vital. For Gottfried art is completed, can only achieve its design as art, in the acclaim of the public:

21   Ere unde lop diu schepfent list,
                    da list ze lobe geschaffen ist:
                    swa er mit lobe geblüemet ist,
                    da blüejet aller slahte list.

To merit praise, art must promote virtue; but it must also be promoted by the virtuous. The poet and his public must share a common evaluation of good and evil, and to do this they must, all of them, be good themselves. As the *Moralium dogma philosophorum* observes in a gloss on temperance, 'a man can perceive nothing that is good unless he is good himself': *nichil enim homini bonum sine se bono* (53,11). But a man can see what is good only so long as he continues to be guided by prudence; hence Gottfried's acknowledgement that only those capable of rational judgment, of being able to distinguish between good and evil, will judge *Tristan* on its true merits:

29   Ir ist so vil, die des nu pflegent,
                    daz si daz guote zübele wegent,
                    daz übel wider ze guote wegent:
                    die pflegent niht, si widerpflegent.

His poem depends for its success and even its survival, he intimates, on the action of prudence, the mediator of goodness and for that reason the first and foremost of the ancient virtues.

Sophisticated clerical literature of the type Gottfried produces is not intended to be interpreted only on a surface level. The study of grammar and rhetoric that was an integral part of the Trivium inculcated the theory that all canonical texts, whether secular or religious, have the generic capacity to signify something more (and more illuminating) than they explicitly state.[39] Texts were regarded by the schoolmen as rhetorical constructs. Composed of figures, they have hidden figurative meanings, what Bernard Silvester called *misterium occultum*,[40] and Thomasin von Zerclære (who was speaking of courtly romances) 'tiefe sinne'.[41] Discussing the use of the figures, Isidore of Seville noted that 'the things which are to be understood are concealed in figured garments, so that they may exercise the mind of the reader and not lose their dignity by being exposed naked to public view': *ea quae intelligenda sunt, propterea figuratis amictibus obteguntur, ut sensus legentis exerceant et ne nuda atque in promptu vilescant.*[42] Fulgentius, himself one of Bernard Silvester's sources, enlarges further on the practice of figurative reading:

> Non incommune carmina poetarum nuci comparabilia uidentur; in nuce enim duo sunt, testa et nucleus, sic in carminibus poeticis duo, sensus litteralis et misticus; latet nucleus sub testa: latet sub sensu litterali mistica intelligentia; ut habeas nucleum, frangenda est testa: ut figurae pateant, quatienda est littera; testa insipida est, nucleus saporem gustandi reddit: similiter non littera, sed figura palato intelligentiae sapit.[43]

> (The songs of the poets are not uncommonly thought to be like a nut; for just as in a nut there are two things, the shell and the kernel, so there are two aspects to poems, a literal and a mystical sense; the kernel is hidden beneath the shell: beneath the literal sense is hidden

---

[39] See Hennig Brinkmann, *Mittelalterliche Hermeneutik* (Darmstadt, 1980), pp.154–259; Christoph Huber, 'Höfischer Roman als Integumentum? Das Votum Thomasins von Zerklære', *ZDA*, 115 (1986), 79–100, and Jon Whitman, *Allegory: the Dynamics of an Ancient and Medieval Technique* (Oxford, 1987).

[40] Bernard uses the phrase *misterium occultum* in his commentary on Martianus Capella, in which he expounds the theory of hidden figurative meanings, and argues that such meanings are a feature of both sacred and profane texts. I quote from Brinkmann, *Mittelalterliche Hermeneutik*, p.169: *Figura . . . est oratio quam involucrum dicere solent. Hec autem bipartita est: partimur namque eam in allegoriam et integumentum. Est autem allegoria oratio sub historica narratione verum et ab exteriori diversum involvens intellectum, ut de lucta Iacob . . . Integumentum vero est oratio sub fabulosa narratione verum claudens intellectum, ut de Orpheo. Nam et ibi historia et hic fabula misterium habent occultum.*

[41] *Der wälsche Gast*, 1108. I accept the argument advanced by Huber (cf. fn. 39) that courtly romances could be read, at any rate by clerics, as integuments.

[42] Isidore, *Etymologiae*, edited by W. M. Lindsay (Oxford, 1911), I. xxxvii.1–2. Linda M. Patterson, *Troubadours And Eloquence* (Oxford, 1975), argues that the Provençal poets who cultivated the *trobar clus* intended their songs to provoke a search for hidden figurative meanings.

[43] Fulgentius, *Super Thebaiden*, edited by R. Helm (Stuttgart, 1970), 180.12f. Brinkmann, *Mittelalterliche Hermeneutik*, pp. 294f.

the mystical meaning; to obtain the kernel, the shell must be cracked; for the figures to be exposed, the letter must be broken; the shell has no taste, but the kernel gives an enjoyable flavour; similarly it is not the letter but the figure which appeals to the discerning palate.)

Stories presented through the medium of the figures relate one thing and mean another. The figures turn narrative into extended allegory, but the allegory can be missed or ignored by those who lack the literary training to recognise and understand it. Gottfried's allusions to the cardinal virtues of prudence and justice are a case in point. Suggesting meanings that are supplementary to the literal sense of the text, they are clearly intended to offer hints as to the kind of figurative or allegorical reading capable of linking the moral generalisations contained in the prologue, and of establishing their relevance as a potential interpretative key to the narrative which follows. But that kind of reading was available only to a privileged minority; although apparently disseminated among a wide public, Gottfried's poem was conceived primarily as a poem for clerics. Only a cleric could be expected to have the degree of familiarity with ancient moral philosophy that the prologue assumes; and only a cleric could have been expected to appreciate the way in which Gottfried, by uniting the disciplines of invention and figurative writing, dialectic and rhetoric, was attempting in his *Tristan* to renew the classic.

Not that Gottfried neglects his lay auditors. He promises that he will tell them the Tristan story as it actually happened: 'wie dirre aventiure was' (166). But he promises also to tell it correctly, as other authors (with the one honourable exception of Thomas) have not told it:

149   sin sprachen in der rihte niht,
             als Thomas von Britanje giht.

This does not simply mean, as has been generally supposed, that the unnamed authors of the rival versions of the Tristan story did not go to the trouble of reading Thomas and so got their facts wrong.[44] Inaccuracy and untruthfulness are certainly being implied, but Gottfried's complaint cannot be fully reconstructed unless it is realised that the assertion 'sin sprachen in der rihte niht' (149) makes an allusion to the standard definition of (Latin) grammar as the art of speaking correctly. In the succinct formulation of Thomasin von Zerclære: 'Grammaticâ lêrt sprechen rehte' (*Der wälsche Gast*, 8921). The definition can be traced back to classical sources. According to Quintilian, the study of grammar involves two

---

44   See, for instance, Werner Schröder, '*Die von Tristande hant gelesen*: Quellenhinweise und Quellenkritik im "Tristan" Gottfrieds von Straßburg', *ZDA*, 104 (1975), 307–338.

distinct but related disciplines: learning the rules of correct speech (*recte loquendi scientia*), and reading and interpreting the works of canonical authors, which he terms *lectio*.[45] Hrabanus Maurus concurs, saying that 'grammar is the knowledge of how to interpret the poets and historians, and of how to write and speak correctly': *grammatica est scientia interpretandi poetas atque historicos et recte scribendi loquendique*.[46] In claiming that his rivals and predecessors failed to speak correctly (149), Gottfried is insinuating that they either broke or were ignorant of the rules of grammar. Their language, divorced from Latin and from Latin literary culture, is unrefined and provincial; and their works, being ungrammatical, can know nothing of rhetoric or of dialectical invention, since grammar forms the indispensable basis of the Trivium. It is, in the words of John of Salisbury, 'the source of all the liberal disciplines', *origo omnium liberalium disciplinarum*.[47] To lack grammar is to lack competence in all the essential skills of literary composition, as Gottfried is eager to remind his implied clerical reader:

131   Ich weiz wol, ir ist vil gewesen,
        die von Tristande hant gelesen;
        und ist ir doch niht vil gewesen,
        die von im rehte haben gelesen. . .

146   aber als ich gesprochen han,
        daz si niht rehte haben gelesen,
        daz ist, als ich iu sage gewesen.

Part of Gottfried's charge is that the competing versions have not told the Tristan story correctly because the people who compiled them did not (and perhaps could not) read the relevant historical sources, unlike Thomas,

151   der aventiure meister was
        und an britunschen buochen las
        aller der lantherren leben
        und ez uns ze künde hat gegeben.

---

45 See Lausberg, *Handbuch der literarischen Rhetorik*, op. cit., fn. 30, vol. I, pp. 35f. The theory and teaching of grammar in the Middle Ages is exhaustively treated in James J. Murphy, *Rhetoric in the Middle Ages. A History of Rhetorical Theory from Saint Augustine to the Renaissance* (Berkeley, Los Angeles, London, 1974), pp. 22–193; see also Paul Zumthor, *Langue, Texte, Énigme* (Paris, 1975), pp. 93–124.
46 Hrabanus Maurus, *De institutione clericorum*, edited by Alois Knoepfler, Veröffentlichungen aus dem Kirchenhistorischen Seminar München, 5 (Munich, 1900), III.18.
47 John of Salisbury, *Metalogicon*, op. cit., fn. 23, I.xiii.15–17.

Thomas is distinguished from the rest by his knowledge of the material, but also by the fact that he is, as a fully trained cleric, a master of the art of narrative ('aventiure meister', 151). He had at his disposal the literary skills acquired from the study of the Trivium, and used them to interpret and present the story in the 'correct' manner. Gottfried's 'lesen' in this context acquires, in addition to its settled meaning 'to tell', the connotation of reading in the sense of interpreting (i.e. reading as *lectio*). It is only in relation to the question of literary competence derived from the study of Latin that Gottfried's attitude towards Thomas can be fully understood. Gottfried not only claims to have followed Thomas's example in undertaking a thorough investigation of the source material; he presents himself as being just as concerned as the French master to produce a work of art, a poem that conforms to the 'correct' standards of composition as defined by the Trivium:

155	Als der von Tristande seit,
	die rihte und die warheit
	begunde ich sere suochen
	in beider hande buochen
	walschen und latinen
160	und begunde mich des pinen,
	daz ich in siner rihte
	rihte dise tihte.

The reintroduction and subsequent emphatic repetition of 'rihte' (156, 161–2), extending and reinforcing the earlier allusion to grammar as the art of speaking correctly ('in der rihte', 149), underlines Gottfried's commitment to achieving a work which, like Thomas's ('in siner rihte', 161), will be exemplary in its implementation of the formal, Latin-based rules that govern the writing of classic texts. Important though the verification of the facts of the Tristan story may be to Gottfried, his ambition extends much further than the simple recording of events, as the renewed play on the senses of 'lesen' subtly hints:

163	sus treip ich manege suoche,
	unz ich an eime buoche
165	alle sine jehe gelas,
	wie dirre aventiure was.
	waz aber min lesen do wære
	von disem senemære:
	daz lege ich miner willekür
170	allen edelen herzen vür,
	daz si da mite unmüezic wesen.

Whether the 'one book' Gottfried mentions (164) is a complete manuscript copy of Thomas or Thomas's own source, the essential point is that having read the facts as presented by what might be called the Thomas branch of the Tristan story ('alle sine jehe gelas', 165). Gottfried proposes to offer his own interpretation ('min lesen', 167) of them. His aim is not to reproduce Thomas's text, but to rewrite it, displaying his own mastery of the arts of rhetoric and dialectical invention and presenting his version of 'die rihte und die warheit' (156). And in the process he will, he intimates to his implied learned reader, attempt a renewal of the classic in keeping with the tradition of clerical vernacular narrative inaugurated by Veldeke.

Goethefried von Straßburg?
Appropriation and Anxiety in
Wagner's Tristan Libretto

ARTHUR GROOS

Most scholars familiar with the history of Tristan and Isolde would probably agree that Gottfried von Straßburg's romance and Richard Wagner's
opera constitute the two major artistic realizations of this apparently
universal myth. They might not agree on anything beyond this generalization, medievalists observing that only the first act of *Tristan* bears any
extensive relationship to Gottfried's romance, musicologists countering
with Wagner's low opinion of that romance[1] and the rather different
nature of his opera. Such polarized opinions are a common feature of
debates on the relative merits of literary works and their adaptations:
advocates of the source invariably lament how little has been retained in
the adaptation; proponents of the adaptation rejoice in transcending the
source's limitations. Such adversarial stances seldom afford much critical
insight, since they are usually based on details of plot without sufficient
regard for larger and often overriding differences in historical context,
genre, and medium. Yet these differences account for the most remarkable feature of the relationship between Gottfried's and Wagner's *Tristan*:
the very paucity of the detailed correspondences that normally comprise
the stock-in-trade of comparisons. The following pages will suggest some
of the strategies that determine their absence in Wagner's *Tristan*.

I

Libretti traditionally have a much more uncertain status than conventional literary texts, in part because their genesis and reception involve

This article has been published, in revised and expanded form, in *Reading Opera*, edited
by Arthur Groos and Roger Parker (Princeton University Press).

[1] See the discussion in *Mein Leben*, edited by Martin Gregor-Dellin (Munich, 1963),
p. 594.

them in a different complex of considerations. We normally isolate two distinct sets of relationships in discussing nineteenth-century libretti: 1. that between the literary source and the libretto, and 2. that between the libretto and its music. The inherence of both sets of relationships in opera generates the familiar conflict between librettists, concerned with the integrity of their text vis-à-vis its source, and composers, concerned about the text's articulation with musical expectations.[2] Although the source-libretto relationship plays an increasingly important role in the genesis of nineteenth-century operas, the finished libretto is normally subsumed in its reception by the libretto-music relationship, a status suggested by the fact that libretti invariably appear in print in conjunction with the first performance of an opera.

Wagner's mature libretti, however, command a different status. Whereas the title pages of first editions through *Lohengrin* (1850) identify the libretto as a part of a musical work by designating it as an 'Oper', the title pages of subsequent libretti avoid any such limitation. Indeed, their publishing history provides them with an independent status well before the first performance of the operas,[3] the most famous example being the *Ring*, whose libretto appeared in 1853, twenty-three years before the first performance of the entire cycle at Bayreuth. But even at the time of the performance, Wagner's libretti often appear in two discrete editions, one 'für den Buchhandel', one 'für die Aufführung', suggesting a dual existence of his libretti – one independent of and one dependent on its musical realization.

The situation is no different with *Tristan*. The libretto first appears in Leipzig in January 1859 without any indication of its future musical status ('*Tristan und Isolde* von Richard Wagner'),[4] well before the edition for the Munich premiere in 1865 and the edition of the *Gesammelte Schriften und Dichtungen Richard Wagners* in 1871. Other evidence, such as Wagner's letter of 15 April 1859 to Mathilde Wesendonck, also broaches the work's dual status.[5] Although the general comparison 'zwischen einem Gedicht, das ganz für die Musik bestimmt ist, und einem rein dichterischen

[2] A classic example of this tension is *La Bohème*, which resulted in two carefully articulated 'literary' acts (I and IV) presenting Murger's novel and play, and two 'musical' acts (II and III) with traditional musical structures (concertato finale, etc.) not based on Murger's works. See Arthur Groos and Roger Parker, *Puccini: La bohème* (Cambridge, 1986), p. 60.
[3] The following is based on Horst F. G. Klein, *Erst- und Frühdrucke der Textbücher von Richard Wagner*, Musikbibliographische Arbeiten, 4 (Tutzing, 1979).
[4] The title-page is reproduced in Klein, p. 30. The subtitle, 'Eine Handlung', which commentators consider a literal translation of the Greek *drama* and link with the 'innere Handlung' of the action, was added later.
[5] *Richard Wagner an Mathilde Wesendonck: Tagebuchblätter und Briefe*, edited by Wolfgang Golther, 33rd edition (Berlin, 1908), pp.124–26.

Theaterstück' outlines the limits of a libretto vis-à-vis a play, and thus the ultimate unity of the libretto and its music, the larger context of the letter which precipitates this comparison, Wagner's reading of *Tasso*, also documents the alternate reception of both Goethe's work and *Tristan* as *Lesedramen* independent of their intended performance media.[6] As we shall see, Wagner's comparison of his libretto with a play by Goethe is not accidental.

Wagner's *Tristan* differs from libretti by other composers not only in its independence from the music, but also in its independence from its source. Since mid-to-late nineteenth-century libretti increasingly derive from famous or well-known works of literature, they usually reflect a relationship with those works, either celebrating the source by keeping it more or less intact, or celebrating its revision or transposition to another medium.[7] In either case, the association with 'literature' serves to legitimize the more tenuous status of the libretto, validating it by means of its source. *Tristan*, however, celebrates itself. To begin with, the paucity of references to Gottfried von Straßburg among the hundreds of *Tristan*-references in Wagner's essays, letters and diaries implies an opinion which the famous letter of 29–30 May 1859 to Mathilde Wesendonck states in no uncertain terms. Leafing through San Marte's *Parzival* translation causes him 'sogleich von der Unfähigkeit des Dichters schroff abgestoßen zu werden. (Schon mit dem Gottfried v. Straßburg ging mir's in bezug auf Tristan so)'.[8] Similarly, Cosima's diaries record discussions of the medieval poem on only three occasions (12–14 March 1870; 18 October 1877; 21 June 1879); the only reading, stimulated by her reminiscence of a quote, ends with another version of Gottfried-bashing: 'Abends in T[ristan] und I[solde] gelesen, wobei mir immer deutlicher erhellt, wie großartig und ihm eigen R[ichards] Konzeption ist'.[9]

It is important to emphasize, as Germanists have recently done, that this attitude is shared by informed contemporary opinion, formed by such eminent scholars and literary historians as Lachmann, Eichendorff,

---

6   Goethe's plays, especially *Tasso* and *Iphigenie*, were generally considered to be untheatrical, i.e. reading texts, an opinion that was fostered by seminal discussions in Hegel's *Aesthetik* and Gervinus' *Geschichte der deutschen Literatur*. See Karl Robert Mandelkow, *Goethe im Urteil seiner Kritiker*, II: *1832–1870* (Munich, 1977), 157 and III: *1870–1918* (Munich, 1979), 5–6 and the entries s.v. 'Tasso'.
7   For a model study of the latter kind of transposition, see the book by Caryl Emerson, *Boris Godunov: Transpositions of a Russian Theme* (Bloomington: Indiana University Press, 1986).
8   In the edition by Golther, p. 146, n. 6.
9   Cosima Wagner, *Die Tagebücher*, edited by Martin Gregor-Dellin and Dietrich Mack (Munich, 1976–77), I, 209. Given the uncertainty whether Wagner used the *Tristan* translation of Hermann Kurtz, which was in his Dresden library, or that of Karl Simrock (Leipzig, 1855), it is interesting to note that Cosima's quote of lines 5067–69 recorded for 12 March 1870 is from the latter (I, 208).

and Gervinus.[10] Basing *Tristan* on a work not generally considered to be 'high literature' in the contemporary canon provides the libretto with the same unusual degree of independence vis-à-vis his source that it has with respect to the music. This does not mean that the libretto has no relationship with Gottfried's poem, only that the nature of that relationship has shifted. References in the letter of 29–30 May 1859 to Mathilde Wesendonck, asserting that medieval narratives are 'unreif' or 'nicht fertig', and as such products of their age, imply their true 'fruition' or 'completion' only in Wagner's contemporary and representative transformation.

But not only the medieval narratives. The fact that Gottfried's poem remained literally incomplete, and also that August Wilhelm Schlegel, then Friedrich Rückert, August von Platen, Karl Immermann, and finally Robert Schumann had attempted to write or compose works on Tristan during Wagner's lifetime, but left them 'unfinished',[11] posed a cumulative challenge to posterity that would have been obvious to any self-promoting artist in the 1850s. It was certainly obvious to Wagner, whose simultaneously arrogant and obsequious letter to Ludwig II of 13 June 1865 triumphantly celebrates the completion and perfection ('Vollendung') of their unique masterpiece 'Am zweiten Tristantag', the day of the second performance, but also – by implication – on the second day of the new era:

> Dieser wunderliche Tristan ist – vollendet. Sie wissen, wer noch am Tristan dichtete, hinterliess ihn unvollendet – von Gottfried von Strassburg an. Fast schien das alte Misgeschick sich auf mein Werk ausdehnen zu wollen: denn – vollendet war es erst, wenn es ganz und leibhaftig, als Drama, vor uns lebte und unmittelbar zu Herz und Sinnen sprach. – Diess wär' erreicht. Das uralte Liebesgedicht, da lebt es und spricht laut zum Volk, das mir durch rührende Zeugnisse seine Ergriffenheit kundgiebt. Was Wir – mein edler Geliebter – **mit** dieser Vollendung leisteten, werden Sie einstens noch ermessen! Ich sage es kühn: **Unsrem** Tristan, wie er heute

---

10 See, for example, Marianne Wynn, 'Medieval Literature in Reception: Richard Wagner and Wolfram's *Parzival*', *London German Studies*, 2 (1983), 94–114.

11 On Schlegel's rendition, which did not progress beyond the story of Riwalin and Blanchefleur, see his *Sämmtliche Werke*, edited by Eduard Böcking (Leipzig, 1846), I, 100–26. Friedrich Rückert's attempt to continue Schlegel's fragment, published in the journal *Die Jahreszeiten* (summer, 1839), itself remained a fragment. Platen's attempts, known today only from the poem 'Tristan', include both poetic and dramatic fragments – see the *Sämtliche Werke*, edited by M. Koch and E. Peret (Leipzig, 1909), VIII, 269–75 and X, 375–82. On Immermann's fragment, see the *Werke*, edited by Robert Boxberger, 13 (Berlin, n.d.). Schumann's scenario to the opera, written in 1845–46 by Robert Reinick and well known in Dresden intellectual circles frequented by Wagner, was published in *Die Musik*, 17 (1925), 753–60. For a survey of modern 'Tristans' in general, see Michael S. Batts, *Gottfried von Straßburg* (New York, 1971), pp. 109–50.

wieder ertönen und erbeben wird, ist nichts Gleiches dieser Art an die Seite zu setzen.[12]

We might accordingly consider Wagner's *Tristan* not as a simple 'adaptation' or 'transposition' of Gottfried's romance, but rather as a work that *appropriates* the medieval fragment into a definitive modern realization. In the following pages, I hope to illustrate Wagner's strategy of appropriation by examining literary reminiscences in the climaxes of Acts I and II, which subsume Gottfried's *Tristan* fragment while simultaneously establishing Wagner's work as the culmination of a modern literary tradition whose most important antecedent member is Goethe's *Faust*.

II

An appropriation shares many characteristics with traditional forms of adaptation, such as some degree of transposition and modernization. Berlioz – to take an example of a contemporary composer-librettist – considered *Les Troyens* as 'Vergil Shakespearized', i.e., the classical Latin epic transposed to drama as well as updated to the Romantic standard of dramatic genius. A similar process can be posited for Act I of *Tristan*, where the medieval narrative has not merely been transposed to dramatic form, but specifically to nineteenth-century analytic drama (such as that of Hebbel), whereby events in the 11,000 lines of Gottfried's romance before the love potion become Tristan's and Isolde's reminiscences, and the linear structure of the narrative, although retained in the objective fact of the ship's progression toward its destination, becomes merely the setting for the circular journey of the hero's and heroine's subjective consciousness.

What differentiates Wagner's *Tristan* libretto as an appropriation from a transposition is an underlying teleological conception of the source-libretto relationship. In a normal transposition, a 'high' literary source and adaptation are different primarily in a generic sense, and modernization does not seriously alter our evaluation of their relative and distinct status. In an appropriation such as *Tristan*, however, Gottfried's romance and Wagner's libretto reflect the development from medieval narrative to modern drama posited by *Oper und Drama*; i.e., they recapitulate the historical process in which the Middle Ages merge into the modern world, in this instance the source being subsumed by the libretto. In

---

12 *König Ludwig II. und Richard Wagner: Briefwechsel*, edited by Winifred Wagner, I (Karlsruhe i. Br., 1936), 106.

accordance with the highly rhetorical style of Gottfried's romance,[13] this process is noticeable particularly through identifiable reminiscences with chiasmus.

The passage following the drinking of the love potion in Act I.5 exhibits one of the most brilliant uses of language in opera. Whereas Gottfried uses oxymoron to narrate the external compulsion of the potion, and then exemplifies that compulsion with an extended allegorical psychomachia[14] that dramatizes the lovers' struggle against it, Wagner renders the internal process whereby the lovers become aware of their long-repressed attraction to each other, first using dramatic and physical chiasmus to dramatize their affinity in a spontaneous exchange of exclamations and embraces which the potion triggers:

ISOLDE:	Tristan!
TRISTAN:	Isolde!
ISOLDE:	(an seine Brust sinkend): Treuloser Holder!
TRISTAN:	(mit Gluth sie umfassend): Seligste Frau!

(Sie verbleiben in stummer Umarmung.)[15]

After an interruption by the chorus and by Brangaene, Tristan and Isolde 'fahren verwirrt aus der Umarmung auf', only to repeat this chiastic process again in a long double cursus that leads to their increasingly conscious awareness of each other and a mutual affirmation of their spiritual union as well.

The initial part of this double cursus (pp. 27–28) proceeds separately through three pairs of simultaneous utterances, as the strict syntactical parallelism suggests; at the same time the decreasing lexical parallelism, from identical lines to anaphora and then to mere alliteration, implies a decreasing isolation. The ensuing passage represents the increasingly conscious affinity between Tristan and Isolde by means of two rhetorical devices, rhyme in alternating lines and a second dramatic chiasmus:

---

13 The most recent – and provocative – study of Gottfried and rhetoric, Winfried Christ, Rhetorik und Roman: Untersuchungen zu Gottfrieds von Straßburg 'Tristan und Isold', Deutsche Studien, 31 (Meisenheim am Glan, 1977), also surveys previous contributions to this subject.

14 See especially Peter Ganz, 'Minnetrank und Minne. Zu Tristan, Z. 11707f.', in Formen mittelalterlicher Literatur: Siegfried Beyschlag zu seinem 65. Geburtstag, edited by Otmar Werner and Bernd Naumann, Göppinger Arbeiten zur Germanistik, 25 (Göppingen, 1970), pp. 63–75; and Wiebke Freytag, Das Oxymoron bei Wolfram, Gottfried und andern Dichtern des Mittelalters, Medium Aevum, 24 (Munich, 1972), pp. 186–91.

15 Cited from the critical edition of the Tristan libretto, Richard Wagner: Sämtliche Schriften und Dichtungen, 7 (Leipzig, 1911), pp. 26–27. In cases where there is a major elaboration of a line, I use variant lines according to the orchestral score in Richard Wagners Werke, edited by Michael Balling (Leipzig, 1917), here V, 110.

TRISTAN:	Isolde!
ISOLDE:	Tristan!
TRISTAN:	Süßeste Maid!
ISOLDE:	Trautester Mann! (p. 28; Balling, pp. 115–16)

These lines seem to represent a deliberate reminiscence of Gottfried's prologue (in Kurtz's translation): 'Ein Mann ein Weib, ein Weib, ein Mann, / Tristan Isold, Isold Tristan'.[16] Their presence here is not fortuitous: Wagner portrays the initial emotional effects of the potion at the beginning of our passage with a long recapitulation of the prelude to the opera; he now signals the beginning of the hero's and heroine's consciousness of that compulsion with the most characteristic lines from his source's prologue.

Yet this highly self-conscious musico-dramatic citation of beginnings also relativizes the medieval text by making it only a prologue to the ensuing development of Tristan's and Isolde's love. The concluding section of the cursus again renders their parallel reactions, but far more intensely – Tristan and Isolde are now, so to speak, completely attuned to each other, as the continued rhyme, absence of the first person pronoun, and univocal expression suggest. The conclusion of the duet articulates the couple's climactic realization and affirmation of their love:

BEIDE:	Jach in der Brust
	jauchzende Lust!
	Isolde! Tristan!
	Tristan! Isolde!
	Welten-entronnen
	du mir gewonnen!
	Du mir einzig bewußt,
	höchste Liebes-Lust!

The most obvious expression of this realization is the use of rhymed couplets to underscore the congruence or harmony of the lovers' desire, the past participles *entronnen* / *gewonnen* in particular suggesting the completion of an irreversible process: namely, that the lovers have escaped from the feudal world and found each other, moving from the public sphere of medieval society to the exclusive and more intense realm of their private relationship. The unrhymed lines with the lovers' names emphasize that they now comprise a separate unity 'consonant' only with each other, while the chiastic doubling of their exchange of names in the duet suggests that this new state represents an intensification and culmi-

16 Cited from Hermann Kurtz, *Tristan und Isolde. Gedicht von Gottfried von Straßburg*, third edition (Stuttgart, 1877), p. 3. On the quotation, see Peter Wapnewski, *Der traurige Gott: Richard Wagner in seinen Helden* (Munich, 1982), p. 75.

nation of the love intimated earlier by the reminiscence of Gottfried's romance.

But how do we evaluate this relativization of the medieval romance within the larger context of the libretto, i.e., what is the nature of the love of which Gottfried's text is only the precursor? That a conscious subsuming of medieval patterns into Romantic ones is taking place is suggested in general terms not only by the transformation of the linear narrative of the romance into the circular pattern of the libretto throughout Act I, but also by a similar structural appropriation in Act II, the dawn-song framework updated to include – as recent scholarship has shown – reminiscences of modern conceptions of love and death from Lessing and Schiller through Novalis, Schlegel, and Schopenhauer.[17]

The climax at the end of the metaphysical explorations of the *Liebesnacht* in Act II.2 initially proceeds by binary opposition: Tristan and Isolde long to negate the frustrations of the day world, suggested by the series with 'ohne', and replace them with a future state that affirms their longing, suggested by the adjectives in alternating lines:

> Ohne Wähnen
> sanftes Sehnen,
> ohne Bangen
> süß Verlangen;
> ohne Wehen
> hehr Vergehen,
> ohne Schmachten
> hold Umnachten;
> ohne Scheiden
> ohne Meiden,
> traut allein,
> ewig heim,
> in ungemess'nen Räumen
> übersel'ges Träumen.   (p. 50)

Yet the actual transition from a medieval world that both would like to do 'without' to a realm beyond time ('ewig heim') and space ('in ungemess'nen Räumen'), a realm adumbrated by Novalis' second *Hymne an die*

---

17   See Thomas Mann, 'Leiden und Größe Richard Wagners', in *Wagner und unsere Zeit*, edited by Erika Mann (Frankfurt a. M., 1963), pp. 96–97; Dieter Borchmeyer, 'Welt im sterbenden Licht – *Tristan* und der Mythos der Nacht', in his *Das Theater Richard Wagners: Idee – Dichtung – Wirkung* (Stuttgart, 1982), pp. 261–87; for an expanded discussion of the Lessing (and Schiller) reminiscences in the torch and light imagery of Acts II and III, see my 'Wagner's *Tristan*: In Defence of the Libretto', in *Music and Letters*, 69 (1988), 465–81.

Nacht ('zeitlos und raumlos ist der Nacht Herrschaft'),[18] requires a further narrowing and intensification of their already isolated subjectivity.

In striving for this (post-)Romantic time-space beyond physical boundaries, the lovers inevitably broach the necessity of transcending the limitations of individuation in death. Although the potion enabled them to find each other in Act I as 'Tristan *und* Isolde', that same conjunction – philologists would call it a copulative – which reminds them of their conjoined fates also reminds them of their separation from each other by self-consciousness.[19] In affirming death as a way of destroying the separation of individuation ('Doch das Wörtlein: und, / wär' es zerstört' [p. 47]), the lovers again move through an exemplary rhetorical pattern, inevitably progressing from conjunction to chiasmus as the vehicle for realizing a union beyond consciousness.

It has long been recognized that their expression of that chiastic union at the end of Act II.2 represents the clearest reminiscence of Wagner's source in the entire libretto, the scene in the garden near the end of Gottfried's fragment, in which Tristan and Isolde, having been discovered by Marke, take leave of each other for the last time, using the conceit of a *Personenwechsel* (18355ff) in order to overcome spiritually the physical necessity of separation. In Isolde's words:

> Nun gehet her und küsset mich:
> Tristan und Isolde, Ihr und ich,
> Wir Zwei sind immer Beide
> *Ein* Wesen in Lieb und Leide.
> Der Kuß soll ein Insiegel sein,
> Daß ich Euer sein soll und Ihr mein
> In Stete und Treue bis an den Tod,
> Nur Ein Tristan und Eine Isot.[20]

As in Act I, Wagner's placement of this reminiscence from Gottfried establishes a self-conscious and highly appropriate structural irony: his lovers unwittingly recapitulate the parting exchange of their medieval counterparts a few moments before their own King Marke will discover them in the garden, precipitating the separation that will find its resolution only in death.

Wagner's adaptation further reveals characteristic differences from the medieval source. The most obvious is that the shift from narrative to

---

18 From the beginning of the second hymn, edited by Gerhard Schulz, second edition (Munich, 1981), p. 42.
19 See the excellent discussion of this nexus in Wapnewski, *Der traurige Gott*, pp. 71–79.
20 Kurtz, p. 209

music-drama enables the revelation of the lovers' inseparability to be presented, not in successive monologues, but simultaneously in a duet – hence the shift from the romance's description of their *Personenwechsel* by oxymoronic play with unity and duality to the libretto's expression of it through chiasmus. And whereas the romance's rhetorical figures suggest a static pattern of anticipation and fulfillment between the potion and garden scenes,[21] the libretto's increasingly elaborate chiasmus suggests a continuing process of intensification:

> ISOLDE: Du Isolde,
> Tristan ich,
> nicht mehr Isolde!
> TRISTAN: Tristan du,
> ich Isolde,
> nicht mehr Tristan! (p. 50; Balling, pp. 271–73)

On the surface, Tristan and Isolde yearn to become 'nicht mehr Tristan' and 'nicht mehr Isolde' respectively, i.e., they seem to long for death, that state which according to Schopenhauer affords 'die große Gelegenheit, nicht mehr Ich zu sein'.[22] But Schopenhauer's conception of death as the mere negation of consciousness does not adequately characterize Wagner's lovers, since they desire to merge personalities with each other. Isolde expresses this wish in the form of a chiasmus, as does Tristan; both exchanges of the speaker's personality, through a reversal of the sequence in Isolde's chiasmus and Tristan's, also combine chiastically to establish a metachiastic relationship between the two in which – by denying *self*-consciousness – they become *one*-conscious, 'ein-bewußt'.

As they strive toward this disembodied relationship, in which each will exchange consciousness with the other and be subsumed into a larger unity, first and second person pronouns – the characteristic expression of the Romantic consciousness' division of the world into *Ich* and *Nicht Ich* – disappear from their discourse, and Tristan and Isolde invoke a metaphysical journey beyond ('ohne') the division of individuation into the brave new world ('neu') of night beyond the limitations of space ('endlos') and time ('ewig'):

> BEIDE: ohne Nennen,
> ohne Trennen,
> neu Erkennen,

---

21 See Freytag, *Das Oxymoron*, pp. 190–91.
22 'Ueber den Tod und sein Verhältnis zur Unzerstörbarkeit unsers Wesens an sich', in *Schopenhauers sämtliche Werke*, edited by Max Frischeisen-Köhler, III.4 (Berlin, n.d.), 526.

neu Entbrennen;
endlos ewig
ein-bewußt:
heiß erglühter Brust
höchste Liebes-Lust!   (p.51)

In both climaxes to Acts I and II, then, Wagner has incorporated reminiscences of his medieval source into a larger modern context, shifting attention from the static relationship between the lovers to the progressive development of their common subjectivity. Wagner makes this particularly clear at the end of the major climaxes in Acts I.5, II.2, and III.3, whose final position emphasizes the precise development of this consciousness through a remarkably similar series of concluding lines:

ACT I.5	ACT II.2	ACT III.3
Du mir einzig bewußt,	ein-bewußt:	unbewußt,
	heiß erglühter Brust,	
höchste Liebes-Lust!	höchste Liebes-Lust!	höchste Lust!

In each case, the penultimate rhyme word derives from the root *bewußt* and articulates the basic concern with the consciousness of the hero and heroine. The exclamation at the end of Act I, 'du mir einzig bewußt', characterizes the effect of the love potion, which makes Tristan and Isolde 'conscious' of their attraction for each other at the same time that it makes them aware of nothing else. The ecstatic 'ein-bewußt', which climaxes – in every sense of the word, as the 'heiß erglühter Brust' suggests – their exploration of love and death in Act II, evokes the transcendent union of 'one-consciousness' that they can realize only by casting off the shackles of individuation that separate them. Finally, the *Liebestod* at the end of Act III calls upon the heroine quite literally to expire 'unbewußt' into the surrounding universe, thus becoming 'un-conscious'. These simple variations, *bewußt*, *ein-bewußt*, and *unbewußt*, epitomize in telegraph style the trajectory of consciousness and desire that begins with Tristan's and Isolde's awareness of their love and concludes with its realization in death.

III

In characterizing *Tristan und Isolde* as a paradigmatic tragedy of post-Romantic consciousness, however, these final couplets do more than appropriate Gottfried's romance by relativizing it as a precursor of Wagner's libretto: they also indirectly take issue with the one work of German literature capable of contesting the unique position claimed for his opera –

Goethe's *Faust*,[23] establishing a variant of what Harold Bloom has called the 'anxiety of influence'.[24] The major reminiscence is provided – not surprisingly – in the final line of our first two climaxes by the unusual word *Liebeslust*, which as the final word of two duets receives an emphasis substantially greater than in normal discourse. The word *Liebeslust* first appears, according to Grimm's *Wörterbuch*, in three famous passages of *Faust I* and *II*, which is furthermore the only locus cited for this lemma. The initial occurrence is the famous description of the Faustian character:

> Du bist dir nur des einen Triebs *bewußt*;
> O lerne nie den andern kennen!
> Zwei Seelen wohnen, ach! in meiner *Brust*,
> Die eine will sich von der andern trennen,
> Die eine hält, in derber *Liebeslust*,
> Sich an die Welt mit klammernden Organen;
> Die andre hebt gewaltsam sich vom Dust
> Zu den Gefilden hoher Ahnen.   (1110–17)

The second passage centers on Faust's command to Mephisto after meeting Gretchen to procure him 'ein Halstuch von ihrer *Brust*, / Ein Strumpfband meiner *Liebeslust*!' (2661f); the third – at the very close of *Faust II* – involves the final resolution both of the problem of Faustian striving and the Gretchen tragedy in the petition of the Doctor Marianus that the Mater Gloriosa accept 'was des Mannes *Brust* / Ernst und zart beweget / Und mit heiliger *Liebeslust* / Dir entgegenträget' (12001–04). In *Faust*, then, this unusual compound word also traces the course of the action and epitomizes it.

Wagner's striking motivic counterpoint with a unique compound word suggests what other documentary evidence confirms: that he also considered *Tristan und Isolde* as a corrective to and improvement on a substantial element of Goethe's *Faust*. Cosima's diary makes it clear that Wagner followed contemporary opinion, which from the 1830s on elevated *Faust* to the central work of the age,[25] in designating it as *'das Buch'* (13 April 1882).[26] But Wagner's high estimation of *Faust* did not deter him

---

23 See Dieter Borchmeyer, 'Idee eines *Faust*-Theaters', in *Das Theater Wagners*, pp. 48–56.

24 *The Anxiety of Influence: A Theory of Poetry* (New York, 1973).

25 On the following, see Karl Robert Mandelkow, *Goethe in Deutschland: Rezeptionsgeschichte eines Klassikers*, I (Munich, 1980), 240ff.

26 Other references praise the work as 'das schönste Buch in deutscher Sprache' (30 September 1882), 'eine Art Evangelium' (12 November 1878). In fact, *Faust* should be the modern equivalent of the Luther Bible, 'die neue Bibel ... ein jeder sollte jeden Vers daraus auswendig wissen' (22 March 1873). Although Wagner's reading of the work would be considered highly selective by modern scholarly standards, there is no doubt that he held a high opinion of the passages cited above. Of the 'Osterspazier-

from asserting – at a crucial moment in the genesis of *Tristan und Isolde* – that Goethe's ultimate concern with the totality of Faust's striving obviated the even more significant potential of the original love tragedy. The letter to Mathilde Wesendonck of 3 April 1858 attempts to clarify a heated argument the previous evening about the 'versäumte Gelegenheit' of *Faust*, namely redemption through love, Wagner's constant and unremitting theme. Instead of remaining 'bei der ersten, so schönen Gelegenheit, der Liebe Gretchens', Goethe extricated Faust from this love,

> damit er nun die eigentliche große Welt, die antike Kunstwelt, die praktisch-industrielle Welt, mit möglichst Behagen vor seiner recht objektiven Betrachtung *abspielen* lassen könne. So heißt dieser Faust für mich eigentlich nur die versäumte Gelegenheit; und diese Gelegenheit war keine geringere als die einzige des Heiles und der Erlösung. Das fühlt auch der graue Sünder schließlich, und sucht das Versäumte durch ein Schlußtableau nachzuholen, – so außerhalbliegend, nach dem Tode, wo's ihn nicht mehr geniert.

Inherent in this criticism is a fundamental antithesis between the objective 'große Welt' and the subjective 'Seelentiefe der Liebe': by objectifying Faust's striving, Goethe neglected – according to Wagner – the true realm of salvation, the subjective consciousness, since in Faust's episodic progress through the world, 'das Subject nie dazu kommt, das Object, die Welt in sich aufzunehmen'.

According to *Mein Leben*,[27] Wagner sent this letter to Mathilde with the pencil sketch for the opera's prelude in celebration of sending the orchestration of Act I of *Tristan und Isolde* to the engraver, i.e., adding to the letter's criticism of Goethe's *Faust* his own realization of the 'versäumte Gelegenheit', namely 'die einzige des Heiles und der Erlösung'. Directed to his biographical Isolde-surrogate (in whose eye 'ich mich hinein versenke! Dann giebt es eben kein Object und kein Subject mehr; da ist Alles Eines und Einig, tiefe, unermeßliche Harmonie!'), Wagner's letter echoes in turn the realization of Isolde's own empathetic transfiguration. That transfiguration, modelled – as Dieter Borchmeyer has shown – on the end of *Faust II*,[28] culminates not in a transcendent salvation, but in the 'Weltwerden des Subjects', immersion in 'die Tiefe des Heils'. Ignoring the real world surrounding her, Isolde '*heftet das Auge endlich auf Tristan*',

---

gang', Cosima reports 'R. zu Tränen ergriffen, wie er sagt, vom jedesmaligen Umgang mit einem solchen edlen Geist! Bewunderung und Verwunderung über beinahe jedes Wort' (2 April 1875), and specifically of Faust's definition of his two drives, ' "das", sagt er, "ist der Faust, der uns fesselt" ' (9 April 1882). The Gretchen tragedy, in particular, represents 'die ganze Macht der Sinnlichkeit' (12 September 1880).

27 Edited by Gregor-Dellin (n.1), pp. 652–53.
28 See Borchmeyer, pp. 281–84.

drawn first by his 'holdes Auge' and then by his 'süßer Athem' to sink unconscious into the all-encompassing tide of the world-breath:

> in des Welt-Athems
> wehendem All –
> ertrinken –
> versinken –
> unbewußt –
> höchste Lust!

Wagner's extension of his appropriative technique to include Goethe's *Faust* represents in one respect no unique occurrence in mid-nineteenth-century intellectual life. The *'Faust-*fever' of the 1830s and 1840s, which constituted the formative experience of a generation of students and helped establish it as *the* work of German literature, inspired not only the young Wagner to begin his first *Faust*-compositions, but countless others as well, so that Gervinus felt obliged to observe in his 'Literaturgeschichte':

> Jeder fand sich bei seiner Erscheinung, wie es Niebuhr von sich aussagt, in seinen innersten Regungen ergriffen und fühlte sich geneigt, es fortzusetzen; man versuchte die eigene Kraft daran, und Jeder glaubte, dem geheimnißvollen Dichter erst nachgeholfen zu haben, wenn er ihm seine eigenen Empfindungen unter- und anschob. Aber alle die unendlichen Nachbildungen, die Faust erfahren hat, waren nicht Lösungen des ungelösten Räthsels, es waren nicht Fortsetzungen, sondern, wie Göthe selber sagte, Wiederholungen. (V,105)

As the preceding argument has suggested, Wagner's *Tristan und Isolde* differs from such adaptations or 'repetitions' in the attempt to subsume Goethe into the larger context of his work and his life. Numerous subsequent events, such as celebrating the anniversary of Goethe's death and the stylizing of Cosima's diaries as a counterpart to Carlyle's biography or Eckermann's conversations, suggest a conscious attempt also to institutionalize his position as Goethe's successor. The ensuing libretti also testify to a continued and even intensified program of appropriation. This is particularly true of *Parsifal*,[29] which incorporates its medieval source even more independently than the manner outlined above, and by means of the most appropriative form of nineteenth-century thought, extra-Biblical typology, even subsumes religion into the institution of art. But that is the subject for another study.

---

[29] The process has been observed in *Die Meistersinger* by Peter Wapnewski, 'Wagners Sachs in Goethes Werkstatt', in *Richard Wagner: Die Szene und ihr Meister*, second edition (Munich, 1983), pp. 67–74; on *Parsifal* in general as a 'summation' see Borchmeyer, pp. 287–301.

Marke's Royal Decline

THOMAS KERTH

Critics seem to be of one mind regarding the character of King Marke in the opening episodes of Gottfried's *Tristan*. He is called variously 'ein im höfischen Sinn untadeliger König',[1] 'ein ideal[er] Artus-ähnlich[er] Herrscher',[2] and Gisela Hollandt summarizes: 'Er ist ein Hüter der Ordnung und der Tugend, er ist tapfer als Führer des Heeres im Kriege, er hält auf Ansehen und königliche Würde, und die jungen Fürsten der Nachbarländer dünken sich glücklich, an seinem Hofe leben und lernen zu dürfen'.[3] According to this same view, however, Gottfried later abandons the idealized portrayal of Marke the public figure, what one may call *rex inquam rex*, and concentrates on Marke's degeneration into *rex inquam homo* (terminology from Engelbert von Admont).[4] Now, according to Hollandt, 'Gottfried entwirft eine Studie des argwöhnischen Gatten, er argumentiert jetzt psychologisch' (p. 65), this in order to enhance Marke's role as foil to Tristan. Thus, the ideal king degenerates into an ineffectual cuckold who can give Isolde to Gandin for a song and perch in a tree to eavesdrop during the orchard scene. Marke becomes the passive figure to Tristan (p. 57), whose actions govern the plot; his decline is necessary to 'der nun dominanten Minnethematik' (p. 63). The cause of this degeneration is 'die liebende Zuneigung zur Person Tristans und die Fürsorge für dessen Wohlergehen' (p. 57). Although Hollandt's study is now some twenty years old, its importance is hardly diminished because her discus-

---

1 Helmut de Boor and Richard Newald, *Geschichte der deutschen Literatur*, II, *Die höfische Literatur: Vorbereitung, Blüte, Ausklang 1170–1250* (Munich, 1953), p. 141.

2 Rüdiger Krohn, 'Erotik und Tabu in Gottfrieds *Tristan*: König Marke', in *Stauferzeit: Geschichte, Literatur, Kunst*, edited by Rüdiger Krohn *et al.*, Karlsruher Kulturwissenschaftliche Arbeiten, 1 (Stuttgart, 1978), pp. 362–376 (p. 368).

3 Gisela Hollandt, *Die Hauptgestalten in Gottfrieds 'Tristan': Wesenszüge, Handlungsfunktion, Motiv der List*, Philologische Studien und Quellen, 30 (Berlin, 1966), p. 55.

4 See Erna J. Buschmann, '*Rex inquam rex*: Versuch über den Sinngehalt und geschichtlichen Stellenwert eines Topos in *De regimine principum* des Engelbert von Admont', in *Methoden in Wissenschaft und Kunst des Mittelalters*, edited by Albert Zimmermann, Miscellanea mediaevalia, 7 (Berlin, 1970), pp. 303–333.

sion of the psychological factors of the Marke/Tristan relationship remains *the* seminal study of the 'psychologische Realität' (p.11) of Gottfried's characters.

But such psychologizing is predicated upon two tacit assumptions: first, that these characters possess psychological integrity and can be compared to human beings embedded in historical reality; and second, that the reality portrayed in the work is identical with historical reality. I propose to demonstrate, however, that the psychologizing critics have chosen in their analyses of King Marke to sacrifice historical reality in their search for psychological integrity and have thus been led to make assumptions about his literary kingship that bear only little resemblance to the historical assumptions of the medieval audience.

To examine Marke's kingship in terms of the text and its contemporaneity and not in the context of modern sensibilities, one could judge it against the idealized vision of those philosophers who sought to educate to kingship through the *Fürstenspiegel*. One must, of course, be very careful in the choice of any treatise on kingship as a model for the ultimate Good King, because the hidden assumptions of the compiler often skew his vision; e.g., Giraldus Cambrensis' hatred of Henry II and indeed of the whole *stirps Normannica* explains much of the vituperation of his *De principis instructione*.[5] The most prudent solution may be to refer to one of the earliest and most often quoted medieval treatises on kingship, that of the Pseudo-Cyprian, since its very popularity bespeaks the general acceptability of its premises.

The *De duodecim abusivis saeculi*[6] was written between 630–700, probably in Ireland. In the sixth *abusio*, which concerns the lord without strength ('dominus sine virtute'), the Pseudo-Cyprian defines that strength as both exterior and interior, that is military and moral: the king must rule through fear, order and love ('terrorem . . . et ordinationem et amorem'). Marke as we know him from the earlier episodes of *Tristan* clearly conforms to the general standards of the Pseudo-Cyprian. He is 'erbære' (421) and 'werde' (453); his English lords serve him 'vorhtliche' (447), and he defends his realm against foreign invaders with his external, military, strength (1119–34).

Marke's position in England is itself proof of this. Already the hereditary ruler of Cornwall, he became overlord of England at the request of the governed. Once the Saxon warriors had driven out their common foe, the Britons, the victors had begun murdering each other ('slahen unde

---

5 Wilhelm Berges, *Die Fürstenspiegel des hohen und späten Mittelalters*, Schriften des Reichsinstituts für ältere deutsche Geschichtskunde, Monumenta Germaniae historica, 2 (Leipzig, 1938; reprint Stuttgart, 1952), p.10, n. 2, p.150 and passim.
6 Edited by Siegmund Hellmann, Texte und Untersuchungen zur Geschichte der altchristlichen Literatur, 34¹ (Leipzig, 1909), pp. 43–45.

morden starke', 443) in a lawless struggle to fill the power vacuum. They turned to Marke to achieve political stability (*ordinationem*): '[si] bevulhen ouch do Marke / sich und daz lant in sine pflege', 444f. The success of this arrangement – and Marke's ability to fulfill his obligation of ensuring the peace in England – is attributed to the loyalty of the governed (*amorem*): 'sit her diendez [Engelant] im alle wege / so sere und so vorhtliche, / daz nie kein künicriche / eim künege me gediende baz', 446–49). Marke's justice is feared even by his own sister Blanscheflur, who sees Marke as the incorporation of the law and its executor (*terrorem*). And it is precisely Marke's kingly virtue that draws the flawed Riwalin to his court.

It is not, however, for any violations of royal responsibility that Marke is criticized by scholarship, but rather for something more intangible – if no less undesirable in a king – namely weakness as a result of personal obsession with a subject, with Tristan. Marke offers Tristan rich rewards in exchange for his entertaining companionship:

> an dir ist allez, des ich ger;
> du kanst allez, daz ich wil:
> jagen, sprache, seitspil . . .
> harpfen, videlen, singen,
> daz kanstu wol, daz tuo du mir;
> so kan ich spil, daz tuon ich dir,
> des ouch din herze lihte gert:
> schœniu cleider unde pfert,
> der gibe ich dir, swie vil du wilt. (3722–35)

What Marke expresses here is the knowledge that Tristan has a cultural superiority in 'höfschlichen dingen' (3729), which the king himself lacks. An apologist could even suggest that Marke is here actually serving his court by enhancing the cultural environment. That the courtiers approve of Marke's actions and of Tristan as the receiver of royal favors[7] is clearly stated in the text: 'swaz er [Tristan] getet, swaz er gesprach, / daz duhte und was ouch alse guot, / daz ime diu werlt holden muot / und inneclichez herze truoc' (3746–49). The courtiers are also overjoyed for Tristan upon Rual's arrival with the news that Tristan is their prince (4326ff).

Once Tristan's identity is revealed, it is only right – and perfectly legal – for Marke, with becoming royal 'milte', to lavish upon his nephew those material possessions suitable to his rank (although Rainer Gruenter

---

7 Rainer Gruenter, 'Der Favorit', *Euphorion*, 58 (1964), 113–128, maintains to the contrary, 'Marke . . . schadet Tristan durch seine bevorzugende Behandlung am Hofe mehr, als Tristan sich durch die unbestreitbaren Verdienste, die er sich um den Hof erwirbt, beliebt machen kann . . . Die Vorzüge Tristans hätten hingereicht, um eine Gesellschaft zu alarmieren, in der wir ja immer eine Art Versicherung und Schutzgemeinschaft gegen den Ungewöhnlichen zu sehen haben' (p.116).

speaks here of Marke's 'eigentümlicher Überschwang' and 'fast unter-
würfige Zärtlichkeit'[8]. Marke offers him 'stiure' (4460): 'min lant, min liut
und swaz ich han, / trut neve, daz si dir uf getan' (4461–62). Notice,
however, that Marke is not at this point speaking of the transference of
royal power, but rather of financial support for the knighting of his im-
poverished heir. Notice also that there is no trace of a jealous reaction by
the courtiers, but rather praise for both Marke and Tristan: 'si buten im
unde baren / ere unde lop mit schalle: / "künec Marke", sprachens alle, /
"du sprichest, als der höfsche sol: / diu wort gezement der crone wol" '
(4492–96).

When Tristan then departs for Parmenie to regain his patrimony, it is
with the promise that, should he return safely, Marke will make him
co-regent ('daz ich dir min guot und min lant / iemer geliche teile',
5154–55). Although Marke's action is often cited as evidence for his exag-
gerated affection for Tristan, it must not necessarily be understood as
such. The official sharing of royal prestige as well as royal power with the
heir was, in fact, a common practice both in England and in the Empire
throughout the Middle Ages. Thus, Marke's offer does not have to be
construed as a corruption of his kingship because of excessive love for
Tristan.

Further, Marke promises Tristan the succession upon his own death
(5156–61). This promise is not idle talk; Marke makes a contract with
Tristan by taking his hands in the gesture of fealty: 'se mine triuwe in dine
hant' (5153). The promise, however, has a condition: Tristan must return
to Marke, once his affairs in Parmenie are concluded. That Marke desig-
nates his sister's son as his heir is also consistent with historical practice in
England and in Brittany, possibly Thomas's own homeland, where in fact
there was in the century preceding his *Tristan* epic a remarkable dearth of
legitimate male heirs.[9]

But it is important to remember that these lavish favors, Gruenter's
immodica donatio (p.122), are not conferred upon just any court favorite,
but upon the consanguineous heir presumptive to the throne. To maintain
even at this point that the barons become jealous of Marke's favorite is to
ignore the fundamental change that has occurred in Tristan's status at

8 'Der Favorit', p.117.
9 Conan II (†1066) was succeeded by his sister's son Alan Fergent IV (1084–1112),
whose grandson Hoel III (1148–1156) was succeeded by his sister's son Conan IV
(1158–1169) after a short interregnum, and Conan IV himself was eventually succeeded
by his daughter's son Artur I Plantagenet (1196–1203). A similar pattern can be observed in historical England, when Henry I (†1135) is succeeded by his sister's husband
Stephan II of Blois (1135–1154), after whom the succession again passed through the
female line by means of Henry's daughter Mathilde to his grandson Henry II (1154–
1189). See H. Grote, *Stammtafeln* (Leipzig, 1877; reprinted Leipzig, 1983), pp. 318–19,
394.

court. Previously he was the merchant's son who became the king's constant companion and the receiver of rich presents, a twelfth century Piers Gaveston. That would certainly have been ample grounds for jealousy among the competitive barons. Now, however, Tristan has, by right of birth, a legitimate claim to share in the wealth of Cornwall, something of which none other can boast. Such jealousy would be foolhardy – Tristan is the only legitimate heir; to incur the wrath of one's future king is not very prudent – and it would be simply illogical: no courtier could hope to take the place ordained for a prince of the royal blood . . . and keep his head!

However, as we know, there is a distinct shift in Gottfried's portrayal of King Marke, and that shift occurs suddenly, without any narrative preparation, namely, after Tristan's return from Parmenie. We suddenly discover that Marke, hitherto described as a strong king, owes tribute to Gurmun of Ireland. Gottfried somewhat minimizes the political impact of this legal subordination on Marke's kingship by stating that it was instituted when Marke was a boy and thus unable properly to defend his realm against Gurmun's onslaught. This is an acceptable excuse, for even the Pseudo-Cyprian exclaims, 'Vae enim terrae, cuius rex est puer . . .' (p. 52), 'woe to that country, whose king is a boy'. The Old Norse translation of Thomas goes even further, claiming that this tribute was first extracted during the reign of a previous king, thus exculpating Marke totally.[10] It is also important to observe that Marke's legitimate claim to kingship, by virtue of heredity and the consent of the governed, is contrasted to Gurmun's. Gurmun is nothing less than a violent, foreign usurper in Ireland, who solidified his power base by marrying Isolde Mother, sister of the powerful Irish Duke Morolt, and making Morolt his champion (*vorvehtære*).

Critics generally maintain that Tristan's duel with Morolt gives him a moral claim to the throne, because of Marke's weakness.[11] There is, however, nothing inherently unkingly in the fact that Marke seeks a champion for England and Cornwall to defeat Gurmun's own and, thereby, to end the paying of tribute to Ireland. Paradoxically, no one claims that Gurmun is weak because his champion fights for him; and historically, an official King's Champion can be documented in England from the coronation of Richard II (1377).[12] The focus of the narration here is, no doubt, the barons' cowardice in the face of Morolt's inhumane demand as well as

---

[10] *Die nordische und die englische Version der Tristan-Sage*, I , *Tristrams Saga ok Ísondar*, edited by Eugen Kölbing (Heilbronn, 1877), p. 30 (chapter 26).

[11] Rosemary N. Combridge, *Das Recht im 'Tristan' Gottfrieds von Straßburg*, Philologische Studien und Quellen, 15 (Berlin, 1964), p.124; Gruenter, p.121; and Krohn, p. 376, among others. Combridge, p.123, n.14, further notes that the dictum *rex non pugnat* specifically deals with legal quarrels between a king and his subjects and therefore might not be applicable here.

[12] The post is still held by the lord of the manor of Scrivelsby; however, the gauntlet

Marke's inability to deal effectively with the situation; and, consequently, Tristan's nobility is heightened when he – who has himself no sons to surrender – selflessly offers to save the barons' sons for them. It need not necessarily follow, however, that Tristan here shows himself a better *king* than Marke merely because he offers himself as the king's champion and makes a fiery speech in defense of English liberty. However, just such a program seems to be Gottfried's intention.

First of all, Marke tries (in vain) to dissuade Tristan from risking his life to save his people: 'hie begunde in Marke leiten abe / mit allen sinen sinnen' (6242–43). Not a very kingly attitude. Furthermore, Marke is compared to a 'timid woman' in his fear for Tristan's survival: 'Der guote künic Marke / dem gie der kampf so starke / mit herzeleide an sinen lip, / daz nie kein herzelosez wip / die not umb einen man gewan' (6521–25). Marke then assumes the role of a squire (*getriuwer dienestman*) when he, with tearful heart – no less – assists Tristan in his preparations for the duel: 'zwen edele sporn starke, / die spien im sin vriunt Marke / und sin getriuwer dienestman / mit weinendem herzen an' (6547–50).

That these are meant to be understood as negative characterizations of the king is proven *ex negativo* by their absence in Robert's translation of Thomas, because Robert – unlike Gottfried – programmatically eliminates or at least ameliorates negative references to Marke.[13] In Robert's version, Marke does not try to dissuade Tristan from the duel, he is not compared to a woman, and he does not put on Tristan's spurs. Rather, Robert's Marke promises Tristan the succession *because* he is willing to champion the English cause, and he girds him with one of the kingdom's most precious possessions, the sword of Marke's father, Tristan's grandfather, with which to fight. Two vassals (*lendir menn*) bind on the spurs.[14] Thus, although we cannot say for certain that Thomas wanted to portray Marke negatively at this point, since his version of this episode survives only in Robert's translation, Gottfried certainly does. Marke's playing the role of squire is not just a metaphorical humbling, but it constitutes what Gernot Müller, in another context, calls a symbolic 'Schauspiel', visual evidence that reflects the truth of the matter: Marke publicly assumes the role of squire; thus, he is the true squire, and Tristan the true king.[15]

The conflict with Morolt does mark the turning point in the portrayal

---

was thrice thrown down and the challenge issued last at the coronation of George IV in 1821.

[13] Michel Huby, *Prolegomena zu einer Untersuchung von Gottfrieds 'Tristan'*, Göppinger Arbeiten zur Germanistik, 397, 2 vols (Göppingen, 1984), I, 111–114.

[14] Kölbing, p. 34, l.9ff (chapter 28).

[15] G. Müller, 'Zur sinnbildlichen Repräsentation der Siegfriedgestalt im Nibelungenlied', *SN*, 47 (1975), 88–119 (p.107). See also Jan-Dirk Müller, 'Sivrit: *künec – man – eigenholt*: Zur sozialen Problematik des Nibelungenliedes', Amsterdamer Beiträge zur älteren Germanistik, 7 (1974), 85–124 (p.105, n. 51).

of Marke, but Tristan's popularity lingers until his return from the first voyage to Ireland. Gottfried tells us that envy, 'der verwazene nit' (8319), is the source of the barons' turning against him. Many critics[16] seem to feel that their accusation of witchcraft is a trumped-up charge, although their circumstantial evidence would seem convincing enough in a medieval world where the black arts are viewed as a real threat to the common weal; the Pseudo-Cyprian, for example, in the ninth *abusio*, 'rex iniquus', warns expressly against the king who listens to the superstitions of magicians, soothsayers and demonic spirits ('magorum et hariolorum et pythonissarum superstitionibus non intendere'). How could Tristan defeat the invincible Morolt, fool his mortal enemy Isolde Mother into healing him and return safely from an Ireland where all Englishmen are slain on sight? These questions are perfectly justified, since the barons do not know the extent to which deception has been part of Tristan's character from the beginning. It is a mistake to criticize them for not knowing the text as we do and for not having our sophistication in the realm of supernatural phenomena.

The purpose of these baronial accusations is to get Marke to produce a direct heir: they advise him 'beidiu vruo und spate / mit vlizeclichem rate, / daz er ein wip næme, / von der er zerben kæme / einer tohter oder eines suns' (8353–57). There is nothing sinister in this. Marke's reply is that God has already provided an heir (8358–60) and that he will never take a queen as long as Tristan lives. The fault thus lies with Marke and not with Tristan or the barons. The Old Norse version emphasizes the seriousness – and justice – of the barons' demand, by having them refuse to serve the king should he persist in his refusal to follow their counsel. His recalcitrance intensifies, naturally, the barons' hatred of Tristan and leads both to Tristan's urging of Marke to accede to their wishes (8379ff) and to his threat to leave Cornwall altogether (8424ff). The barons' proposal that Marke seek the hand of Isolde, though motivated by their desire to see Tristan defeated ('niwan durch Tristandes tot', 8453), is not without a certain socially redeeming quality. They see Isolde as the key to the greater glory of England and Cornwall; namely, since Isolde is Gurmun's only heir, Ireland comes with her. Should Marke marry Isolde, he would be able to add Ireland to a greater Britain, thus increasing his nation's prestige and power: the Irish tributes would then fill English coffers. For the barons, a wooing expedition headed by Tristan cannot fail: if he succeeds in winning Isolde, they have the prospect of another heir as well as of Ireland itself; should he be unsuccessful, he would be out of the way and Marke would be forced to marry or leave no legitimate succession, thus plunging Cornwall and England again into civil war and destruc-

---

16 Most recently C. Stephen Jaeger, 'The Barons' Intrigue in Gottfried's *Tristan*: Notes toward a Sociology of Fear in Court Society', *JEGP*, 83 (1984), 46–66 (p. 61).

tion. The barons may be blinded by their hatred of Tristan, but they are
not to be dismissed merely as representatives of the 'evil and dangerous'
world of the court, characterized by its 'shallowness, sensuality, materi-
ality, ruthless clambering for preferment, inhuman machinations'.[17]

Despite Marke's conviction that envy is the lot of all good men ('haz-
zen unde niden / daz muoz der biderbe liden . . .', 8395–96), the barons
express on their way to woo Isolde quite another and more serious reser-
vation about Tristan's character, and thus about his capacity to rule:

> 'wisheit unde vuoge
> derst harte vil an disem man.
> ist daz uns got gelückes gan,
> wir mugen vil wol mit ime genesen,
> wolter dekeiner maze wesen
> an siner blinden vrecheit;
> der ist ze vil an in geleit:
> er ist ze vrech und ze gemuot,
> ern ruochet hiute, waz er tuot;
> ern gæbe niht ein halbez brot
> umb uns noch umb sin selbes tot.' (8660–70)

They grant Tristan wisdom and ability, but they view his lack of cir-
cumspection as a threat. If a king does not care for his own life, how can
he be made to care for theirs? Further, one must remember that the life of
the king is the guarantor of security for the realm. Tristan is at present the
only legitimate heir to the throne. Should he die in this or in any other
adventure, what would then become of England? In fact, the situation
would be worse if the court were to continue under the present circumstances and lose Tristan when Marke was too old to produce another heir.
These barons are not just the evil courtiers of a court novel;[18] although
their motives may be corrupted by hatred, their concerns for their country
are understandable enough.

The barons are objecting to Tristan as a man – and as heir to the throne
– because he values his own whim above the good of the whole, *rex
inquam homo* above *rex inquam rex*, as does the now fallen King Marke.
However, to introduce such historical / philosophical concepts into the
discussion of kingship in *Tristan* illuminates the problem. The great stum-
bling block to interpretation is History itself. Gottfried's Cornwall is more
fiction than reality, what a semiotician would no doubt label a ho-
monymic heterotopia[19] or 'allotopia' (Umberto Eco) which has some par-

17 Jaeger, p. 63.
18 Jaeger, p. 54.
19 Hugh J. Silverman, 'From Utopia/Dystopia to Heterotopia: An interpretive Essay',
Philosophy and Social Criticism, 7,2 (1980), 169–182.

allels to kingdoms as his audience would know them – knighthood, ordeals, fealty, music and art, power and riches, the hunt – but this literary Cornwall is also governed by processes which lie totally outside historical reality.

A flagrant example is Marke's inactivity after Blanscheflur's abduction.[20] Abduction was one of the four medieval crimes involving Carolingian blood law (along with murder, theft and arson), and the king was bound to separate couples who had not been joined together peacefully and in accordance with the prescribed rites so as to prevent possible family feuds resulting from the crime.[21] Well into the twelfth century, the union between an abductor and his victim was considered illegal. The *Decretum* of Burchard of Worms (1008–12) offers in book xix, the *Corrector* or *Medicus*, a list of punishments for sins, organized in hierarchical order according to their severity. Abduction received the severest penalty, the same meted out for bestiality, adultery and murder.[22]

Imagine, then: the king's own sister is abducted, and he does absolutely nothing to pursue her abductor, makes absolutely no inquiries as to her whereabouts for fourteen years. This is contrasted negatively, of course, with faithful Rual's long search for the kidnapped Tristan. Blanscheflur's abduction is not only a matter of breaching the social order, which would in itself be bad enough, but it is also a political matter of the highest order. As a royal bride, her person offers Cornwall the possibility of valuable foreign alliances and power. No medieval king – outside fantasy literature – would allow this valuable national asset to be stolen. Gottfried is also not unaware of this aspect when he lets Rual compliment Riwalin on his greater *ere*, *werdekeit* and *pris* (1613–14) as a result of this union. Furthermore, Blanscheflur offers the only possibility for providing a legitimate

---

20 The legal term here is *raptus in parentes*. According to Rudolf Köstler, *Die väterliche Eheeinwilligung: Eine kirchenrechtliche Untersuchung auf rechtsvergleichender Grundlage*, Kirchenrechtliche Abhandlungen, 51 (Stuttgart, 1908), neither Roman law (p.162) nor Salic law (p. 37) distinguished between the abduction of a willing victim (elopement) and kidnapping. The basis of this identification was the absence of the necessary consent of the bride's guardian. Two Councils of Rome (721 and 743) and the Council of Ravenna (877) confirmed this position in canon law, even when the victim was a widow (p. 70, n.3; p. 71). Peter Lombard (*c*.1100–64) was the first theologian to maintain that only the consent of the partners was necessary for legal marriage, because marriage, as a sacrament, was by definition open to all believers (p.104). Rolandus Bandinellus, later Pope Alexander III (1159–81), supported this change, with the condition that the bride be over 12 years of age, the age of consent (pp.113–19). That *raptus in parentes* was still an important issue in the pre-courtly literature of the High Middle Ages is demonstrated by the presence of the abduction *topos* in *Salman und Morolf*, in *Orendel*, and in *König Rother*.
21 Georges Duby, *Le Chevalier, la femme, et le prêtre: Le mariage dans la France féodale* (Paris, 1981), p. 43.
22 Duby, p. 75.

heir to the throne, since Marke has not yet married. For a country that has only recently risen above fractious anarchy, this loss could promise tremendous upheaval for the future.

The issue of King Marke's bachelorhood normally attracts critical attention only as it is connected with Tristan's career in Cornwall. There is ample evidence to suggest, however, that for the medieval audience, the absence of a queen, and, therefore, the impossibility of a legitimate heir would have been the focus of concern, not to say disbelief at Marke's dereliction of royal duty,[23] long before the appearance of Tristan, whose legitimate claim through his mother would offer the barons in the *real* world the consolation of continuity, even if he were not their ideal choice. Marriage was not only desirable for the protection of the soul of the man, 'It is better to marry than to burn' (I Corinthians 7.9), it was essential for the king. A eulogy of King Louis VII of France, composed c.1171, gives adequate documentation of the contemporary obsession with producing legitimate male heirs. Having chosen incest (when mere adultery would not suffice) as the grounds for his divorce from Eleanor of Aquitaine, the mother of his two daughters, and having been left a widower by his second wife, who bore him two more daughters, King Louis took a third wife, five weeks after the death of his second. The eulogist tells us that the king decided to marry again this third time because he was ' "counseled and urged by the archbishops, bishops, and other barons of the kingdom", for his marriage was not just his own affair but that of his whole house, in this case of the immense network of vassalic bonds stretching over the whole of northern France'.[24] God's reward for all this sacrifice for France was the birth of his son Philip. Ivo of Chartres had given a similar message to Louis' father, Louis VI, in a letter (no. 239) regarding his indecision about taking a bride: were he to produce no successor, the

---

23 That the providing of an heir was integral to the medieval concept of kingship can be demonstrated by the presence of a specific petition for royal fertility in some coronation rituals for hereditary monarchies, e.g. the English *Ordo* of St Dunstan (960–973): 'et plenus erit benedictione Domini in filiis', quoted in Percy Ernest Schramm, 'Ordines-Studien II: II. Die Krönung bei den Westfranken und Angelsachsen von 878 bis um 1000', *Zeitschrift der Savigny-Stiftung für Rechtsgeschichte*, 54 (1934), 117–242 (p. 218). Similarly, a prayer for the king's progeny is included among the *laudes hymnidicae* for Charles the Bald and the *laudes imperiales* written at the time of Louis the Pious ('Exaudi Christe [R/] Eius precellentissimis filiis regibus vita'), quoted in Ernst H. Kantorowicz, *Laudes regiae: A Study in Liturgical Acclamations and Mediaeval Ruler Worship*, University of California Publications in History, 33 (Berkeley and Los Angeles, 1958), pp. 74 and 105 respectively.

24 'Le roi d'abord se décida, "conseillé et incité par les archevêques, évêques et autres barons du royaume"; le mariage du patron en effet n'est pas sa seule affaire, c'est l'affaire de toute sa maison, ici de cette immense maison qui par les liens de vassalité s'étendait sur tout le Nord de la France', Duby, p. 203. English translation by Barbara Bray (London, 1984), p.192 (adapted here).

kingdom would be divided against itself.[25] That the nobility was also not above exploiting a childless king is seen from the example of Emperor (Saint) Henry II. The overly pious prince Henry, reared by churchmen at the cathedral of Hildesheim, had avoided marriage until the age of twenty-three, when as heir to the duchy of Bavaria he was compelled to enter into it. Henry's childless marriage to St Kunigunde made him an ideal candidate for the electors, who hoped for another break in the line of succession[26] and chose him to succeed his childless cousin Otto III, thus bringing to an end the Saxon imperial dynasty. One may disapprove of Marke's barons, but they are obviously like Louis VII's 'good' barons, who seek to ensure the preservation of the kingdom and not like the 'bad' electors, who prefer a childless emperor so they can exert their own political influence.

In actuality, Marke's bachelorhood and his subsequent decision not to marry would have been incomprehensible to his audience had he been an historical king. In fact, I can find only one example in French and English history of a mature bachelor king, and that is William II Rufus, whose contemporary reputation – not without certain reason – suffered as a result. All the other monarchs who survived puberty married, and in some cases married several times, for the sole purpose of providing the nation with a legitimate heir.

Marke seems unconcerned, and this lack of concern for the future welfare of his kingdom would make Marke a bad king in the eyes of the contemporary public long before Tristan enters the tale. But Gottfried tells us that Marke was a good king, feared and loved by his barons, and we believe him. This belief is necessary for the role Marke must play in the Riwalin episode, but must be discarded as soon as the 'Minnethematik' becomes Gottfried's central preoccupation. Gottfried is much less kind to his Marke than Hartmann is to his Artus, who has similar marital difficulties. Although Artus is occasionally portrayed in medieval literature with a touch of narrative whimsy – one may think of his penchant for dozing off, for example – his fitness for kingship is not questioned. But Marke cannot remain a good king – or a good man, for that matter – because he is to be cuckolded; kingship is not the focus of the tale, but rather forbidden love.

The structure of such love literature demands that the audience not be sympathetic to the betrayed husband; such sympathies are only invoked in modern literary texts peopled by more intricately conceived characters with more problematic relationships. Gisela Hollandt was correct in her assertion that Marke's character is sacrificed to the plot, although he does retain certain sympathetic qualities; however, such a sacrifice is only

25 Duby, p.179.
26 Duby, p. 64.

possible when his kingly nature is detached from historical reality. The adequately documented medieval obsession with legitimacy would have been inconsistent with the sympathy for the lovers that Gottfried wishes to evoke. Marke, then, is from the very beginning cloaked in attributes that make his kingship a clearly literary one. Once this kingship is divorced from historical reality, all the historical measures by which one can evaluate his character and his kingship are rendered invalid. That we accept Marke as a king, and Cornwall and England as places, is a tribute to Gottfried's convincing artistry. Measuring Marke against any reality, literary or historical, which lies outside Gottfried's fiction and seeking psychological explanations for his royal decline may be interesting for scholarly speculation and interpretation, but only for that. Such speculation only heightens the disparity between the literary and historical realities of the text and demands a consistency in characterization which is simply not part of medieval narrative technique.

The Role of King Marke
in Gottfried's Tristan – and elsewhere

MICHAEL BATTS

Since it is my contention that the role of Marke in Gottfried's version of what is frequently referred to as the eternal triangle is crucial to the survival of this work into the modern period in varied forms, I must begin by analysing briefly the various combinations available to any author planning to use this situation as a basis for a plot.

Given the situation of a woman between two men – the wife, the husband, and the lover – an author may portray the husband or the lover as ignoble and appeal to the audience's sympathy for the other. A happy end is then achieved if the ignoble husband or ignoble lover is eliminated and the lovers united, or the husband and wife re-united. There is a tragic outcome if the ignoble husband finds out and encompasses the death of one or both the lovers, or if these inadvertently bring about their own demise. Equally tragic, but rarely depicted, is the outcome if the wife abandons her noble husband for the sake of an *ig*noble lover, and realises her mistake too late.

The situation is less clearly definable when neither man is portrayed as an unsympathetic character, and the wife is possibly even in love with both of them. Only in this scenario is a *ménage à trois* conceivable (it can occur with a noble lover and an ignoble husband, but normally only in farce). The difficulty here is to retain the sympathy of the audience for the heroine, especially if she is in love with both men, or vacillates between the two of them. It is my view that the lovers' decision in *Tristan und Isolde* to accept the three-cornered relationship necessitated a depiction of Marke as a relatively sympathetic character, and that it is this factor that ensured that the story would survive and be recreated in a variety of forms. The concentration of critical interest on the lovers, however, has tended to obscure the vital role played by the man who stands between them. In order to show this, I must of necessity recount at least portions of the plot, but I will do this as briefly as possible, consistent with my aim of elucidating Marke's character.

The King is introduced very early in the story as a ruler par excellence, the respected lord of Cornwall and England: 'kein künec so werder was als er' (453). It is Marke's reputation that induces Riwalin, himself a ruler successful in establishing his authority, to seek out his court in the expectation of being able there to extend his experience and to improve his qualities. This is, of course, a not unfamiliar theme for a medieval story: a young adventurer sets out for the court which represents to him the acme of chivalry.

Gottfried then does his best to justify Riwalin's expectations by his enthusiastic, encomiastic, description of the *hohgezit* at Tintagel, and the frequent references to Marke, *der mære, der tugende riche, der guote, der höfsche hochgemuote,* and so forth. Marke is, moreover, valorous, as evidenced by the alacrity with which he rides into the field against his enemy. The only mildly discordant note at this stage is the attitude of Riwalin and Blanscheflur to Marke. Riwalin apparently does not want the relationship between himself and Blanscheflur to become known – Gottfried gives us no hint as to why – while Blanscheflur fears that her brother's concept of honour is so rigid, that he would have her either executed – 'der heizet mich verderben / oder lesterliche ersterben' (1473–74) – or at least disinherited – 'und er mich niht ersterbet, / daz er mich aber enterbet' (1479–80). Her own position appears to be equally categorical, though, for she considers disinheritance to be a worse fate than death, and bewails the dishonour that would befall her brother's kingdom, should she bear an illegitimate child. She is clearly aware of Marke's very keen sense of honour.

It is approximately fifteen years later when Marke re-enters the story, and little seems to have changed. He is still *der lobebære, der wol gemuote, der tugende riche;* however, there are subtle indications that his standing is no longer what it was. To begin with, whatever one might think of the scene in which Tristan dismembers the hart, it suggests that Cornwall has fallen behind the times. Marke himself is shown only in an *un*warlike mood; he seems bent solely on the pursuit of pleasure, and the avidity with which he welcomes Tristan suggests a lack of self-control or feelings of inadequacy. He is laughed at when he wishes to appoint Tristan his court huntsman (3370–71); he *does* make Tristan his harper. In fact Tristan becomes *everything* to him:

> an dir ist allez, des ich ger;
> du kanst allez, daz ich wil:
> jagen, sprache, seitspil.
> nu suln ouch wir gesellen sin . . .   (3722–25)

This pact of friendship is superseded during the accolade ceremony when Marke adopts Tristan, taking the responsibility of knighting him, equipping him for his struggle to regain his lands, and promising to remain single, so that Tristan may inherit his kingdom. Four times in the passage where Rual is received at court prior to the accolade ceremony Marke is called *der guote* and the court sings his praises (4489ff).

When Tristan, following in his father's footsteps, secures his land and then leaves it for Cornwall, there is an essential difference between the two situations. To Riwalin, Marke had been a respected example of chivalry, from whom he hoped to learn. For Tristan, Marke is a father figure from whom he has received virtually everything he possesses, and *for* whom he plays the virtuoso, hunter, harper, singer, and so forth. He is *de jure* nephew and *de facto* son and heir. The situation is *similar* to the extent that Tristan also fights for Marke. Earlier, however, Riwalin had merely accompanied Marke into battle and been wounded; now Tristan must take on the task alone, as neither Marke nor his barons can face Morold. This presents Marke with his first dilemma: he would like to be rid of the tribute, but not at the cost of risking Tristan's life – which is surely a positive trait, since he is presumably honestly convinced that Tristan cannot succeed. Here, and subsequently, it is Tristan who overrules him. It is indicative of the status of equality that Tristan has now attained with Marke that the King is referred to both before and after this event as *sin vriunt* (6548, 8232) – in the first instance Marke is also called 'sin getriuwer dienestman'. From this point on Marke rapidly becomes increasingly indebted to Tristan. Having defeated Morold, Tristan goes on to win Isolde for Marke, and to recover her then from Gandin, since again neither Marke nor any of his men dares to challenge Gandin.

Prior then to the series of episodes which charts the deteriorating relationship between the protagonists, it is established that Tristan owes everything to Marke, but that Marke, in his turn, owes a great deal to Tristan, in particular his freedom from tribute and his queen. Marke himself seems to have aged to the extent of being less valiant than in the time of Tristan's father – he will face neither Morold nor Gandin, though in the latter case perhaps for legalistic reasons. However, he is still strong enough to resist the pressure from his nobles, to risk their displeasure in order to protect Tristan's position. It is Tristan himself who rules Marke, and their roles have become in a very real sense reversed. There is, however, no overt criticism of Marke, ineffectual as he may seem to have become. The adjectives applied to him have not changed, and they only begin to change with the arrival on the scene of Marjodo.

When Marjodo tells Marke that people are talking of Tristan and Isolde, the King is immediately assailed by doubts and characterised here as 'der getriuweste unde der beste, / der einvalte Marke' (13652–53). He does not *want* to believe that the story can have any foundation. The audience can sympathise with Marke at this stage, but the sympathy must necessarily begin to decline somewhat, as he first tries his own hand at trapping Isolde, then enlists the aid of Marjodo, and finally of both Marjodo and Melot. The adjectives applied to Marke in this sequence are *einvalt, geloubec, verdaht, verirret*; he is also called *der zwiveleære* and finally *der trurige Marke* (the last when he has been convinced that he has *falsely* suspected her, that is, he regrets that he has suspected her). It is made abundantly clear, however, at this point that it is his honour as much as his feeling for Isolde which is at stake.

Marke is therefore portrayed as easily led into suspicion by others (bearing in mind always that there are grounds for this suspicion), but he is still not without the ability to take action on his own behalf. It is Marke, after all, who consults his nobles, calls the council, and agrees to the trial; and it is also Marke who, when he sees that the evidence of the trial is contrary to his own experience, again takes matters into his own hands and sends Tristan and Isolde from court. Opinions vary about Marke's motives in banishing the lovers, but, taken at face value – and I see no reason why it should be taken otherwise – his statement is quite plain: he sees that Isolde loves Tristan better than himself and he is not prepared to suffer 'diz laster und diz leit' (16577); they should leave him, since he loves them too well to want to do them any harm. One can argue here that he has mellowed with age if he can make such a magnanimous gesture now, one that, according to Blanscheflur, he would not have made earlier, but again it is his honour which is at stake – 'ine lide dirre unere / nach dirre zit nimere' (16581–82).

Again it seems reasonable to pause here and consider dispassionately the audience's response to Marke's actions. They *know* he is being deceived, and *how*, and *why*. They also know that his attempts to catch out the lovers are not initiated by him but by others less worthy than he. His only formal attempt to solve the dilemma once and for all fails to convince him, for he is able to see *after* the trial that the truth did not emerge there. At this point it must be borne in mind that the King's hands are effectively, because judicially, tied. As the ruler, Marke cannot possibly take any action that would seem to impugn the validity of the oath sworn by Isolde, but as an individual who is directly and emotionally involved he sees the truth. He cannot, therefore, inflict any punishment on either Isolde or Tristan, although he could inhibit their relationship (as he later does). Instead, he summons up all the nobility of which he is still capable and sets them free. This is again a public act, and in a sense it is his last act as King, for he is concerned here not only for his own feelings but also for the honour of his position.

The turning point comes of course with the grotto episode, and here we have a strange situation inasmuch as the lovers, who wanted nothing better than to be alone together away from Marke, now would like to come back to court, while Marke, who is presumably regretting having banished them – he is referred to again here as *der trurige* – would presumably be glad to have them back. The irony of the situation is thus that all three are happy to have an excuse to go back to the previous three-cornered situation, and therefore respond immediately when the opportunity presents itself. True, Marke goes through the formality of a protestation of having erred and being convinced of their innocence, but his nobles are well aware that he wants them back, innocent or not:

> sin rat enstuont sich al zehant,
> wie sin wille was gewant
> und daz sin rede so was getan,
> daz er si wider wolte han. (17669–72)

All sides share therefore in this complicity, and to this extent Marke is no more blameworthy than Tristan and Isolde, for they too are willing to resume the old ways. However, Marke's attitude now changes.

As an *unknowing* obstacle to their love Marke was acceptable. Even when others instigated his simple traps, he was not a danger, since he could easily be deceived and satisfied. The position is quite different now that Marke *knows* what the situation is, but wishes to be able to pretend that it does not exist, and therefore requires restraint of them. He insists on bodily possession of Isolde, knowing that her affections lie elsewhere, and yet wishes to deny the lovers any show of affection. It is here and only here in my view that Marke becomes an unsympathetic figure, although one might also argue, in rather more modern terms, that he begins to become a tragic figure.

Let me recapitulate once more: Marke is portrayed sympathetically to the extent that he is noble and honest, though not necessarily, as he becomes older, a dashing figure, a man greatly concerned, as King, for his honour or the honour of his position. The mutual obligations of Marke to Tristan and Tristan to Marke are stressed, so that the combination of these factors makes the mock marriage and lovers' deceit acceptable. They become no less acceptable during the various plots and counterplots, since the King is not shown as the instigator of these. At most his intelligence is belittled by the ease with which he is deceived and undeceived. When he acts on his own, he behaves in a manner which can only be considered reasonable (before and during the trial) and later magnanimous (in setting them free). He becomes *culpable* only after the grotto episode.

What we have after the grotto episode is a conflict between two kinds of love. Tristan and Isolde were suddenly overwhelmed by love after drinking the love-potion, though clearly predestined for the experience. Marke, too, is overtaken by love, after having entered into marriage for strictly pragmatic reasons. There seems no reason to doubt that his attraction to Isolde and his respect for her are genuine – whatever his reasons may have been for choosing her in the first place – and his suffering at losing her equally genuine:

> swaz zornes er hæte,
> so was im ie sin liebez wip
> liep unde lieber dan sin lip.   (16524–26)

To this extent, then, his situation is a tragic one, for he is confronted with a kind of passion which is far beyond his comprehension. His situation can engage the sympathy of the audience as long as he doubts and wishes to have his doubts removed, because he has reasonable cause both as an individual (love) and as King (honour), but after the grotto scene his doubts are no longer genuine, but contrived. He has to insist on separating the lovers in order to maintain a situation whereby his belief in their innocence may *seem* to be justified, even though he knows they are *not* innocent. He is led to this pass by the strength of his carnal passion, and this is not only *his* undoing but the undoing of the lovers, for they, in turn, are affected to the extent that their love is distorted also into carnality, which then manifests itself openly and thus deprives the King of his ability to deceive himself, even knowingly. Whether or not the nobles believe the King's story of having found the lovers together in the orchard is at this stage irrelevant; honour is no longer at stake; Marke knows the truth.

This is not, of course, the end of the story, but it is in my view the climax. This brings us back to my point of departure, namely, the concept of the triangle situation as one with which these characters *must live*. It also brings us back to the question of the potion and its function in the story. Whether or not the potion is viewed as both the cause of the love and cause of the lovers' death is from my perspective not important. What *is* important is on the one hand the response to the potion's effect and on the other the response of Marke to that effect. Gottfried's version is after all not the only one and certainly not the most widely known one in the later Middle Ages. In one tradition the (full) effect of the potion wears off after a few years, and such a version naturally lends itself to a depiction of the lovers as feeling compelled to a love they do not really want. All is blamed, even by the lovers, on the potion. But even where the effect does *not* wear off, the tendency in the centuries immediately after Gottfried is to view the potion as an 'unseliger Trank' and the death of the lovers as an 'unseliger Tod', directly attributable to the potion. The love is viewed in other words in these traditions in a strictly negative light, so that the role of the husband is necessarily reduced. Whether or not or to what extent his affections are engaged is not important.

In a third tradition the effect of the potion does *not* wear off and the lovers do *not* feel regrets about their love, but Marke takes direct action and kills Tristan. In this version it is clear that the main characters cannot all be sympathetically portrayed. Either the lovers must be shown as unsympathetic characters and Marke as an upholder of what is right and proper – a rarely considered alternative – or Marke – which is more usual – portrayed as thoroughly unsympathetic, for his act in killing Tristan is hardly acceptable under any circumstances. This particular tradition has been strong in England, and it presumably accounts for the more limited interest in the work in the modern period, at least until the end of the nineteenth century; most modern versions follow the other tradition.

The crux of the story, the detail on which all else hinges, is not so much the potion, or indeed the effect of the potion, but the reticence of the lovers *about* the potion. They never disclose its effect, and Marke never learns of it from other sources. And yet, curiously enough, as even in the Eilhart version, casual bystanders at the death of the lovers are able to tell King Marke all about the 'kraft vnd würckung des vnsåligen getranckes' (5138–39); and he then utters the cry that echoes down the centuries: 'das du mir nicht gesagt hastt von dem vnsåligen tranck' (5150).[1] Although there has been a great deal of discussion about the role of society in determining the lovers' actions, for example in relation to their decision gladly to return to court from the love grotto, there has been virtually no discussion of the lovers' (and Brangane's) immediate and apparently irrevocable decision to conceal from Marke the fact of their having drunk the potion.

The 'fatal flaw' is, of course, essential to the plot, and it is one of the reasons why the story could be transposed (with or without potion) to modern situations. If the lovers told their story, then Marke's relationship to them would be quite different and in modern terms extremely difficult (until recent times) to accept. He would not in fact be an obstacle to their love at all but purely peripheral to it. But, because they do *not* tell him, they are somehow under an obligation to him. Because Marke does not know, he cannot relinquish his claim; and because they do not tell Marke, they must accept living out their life *with* him. But this scenario is only possible as long as Marke can be portrayed as a sympathetic character. Gottfried laid the basis for this by his portrayal of Marke up to the grotto episode as a primarily sympathetic, though not necessarily strong, character, and it is to be assumed that Gottfried too would have ended his work with Marke's regret at not having known the true facts.

Whether or not we assume this kind of ending to Gottfried's incomplete work, I would like to argue that a major factor in the success of

---

[1] From the 1484 'Volksbuch', *Tristrant und Isalde*, edited by Alois Brandstetter, Altdeutsche Textbibliothek, Ergänzungsreihe, 3 (Tübingen, 1966).

Gottfried's portrayal of Marke (and ultimately of the success of the work in the future) lies in the distinction made between the public and the private man. When we first see Marke, he is a representative of an ideal state, a man obsessed apparently with the honour of his position and the reputation of his family. He begins to become more human through his relationship with Tristan, and the process of humanisation or individualisation, if I may call it that, continues as he is increasingly torn between his personal love for Tristan and for Isolde. While I have argued on the one hand that he makes a magnanimous gesture in setting the lovers free, he does this in public, citing his desire to submit no longer to dishonour: 'ine lide dirre unere / nach dirre zit nimere' (16581–82). When, however, the narrator says that Marke possessed Isolde after the return from the grotto, 'niht zeren, wan ze libe' (17727) and says that the King possessed neither Isolde's love 'noch al der eren keine' (17730), then he is making a distinction between public and private honour, between public reputation and, if you will, self-respect.

It is Gottfried's great achievement to have portrayed Marke as a character who both functions as a representative of society or of the social class in which he has his being and is also an intensely human individual. He unwillingly enters into a marriage, when he would rather have had Tristan as his sole heir, but, having entered into marriage for public reasons, he becomes personally involved, first with Isolde and then in a conflicting relationship with both of them. The record of Marke's royal decline, as it has been called, no matter whether or not his record as king is good or bad, is the record of one whose personal feelings gradually come to take precedence over his office. The dual nature of his role made it possible for later writers to adapt the figure of Marke to changing circumstances. Depending on these circumstances he would be more or less of a sympathetic character and more or less of a public, or, alternatively, private figure.

The chapbook and similar versions deriving from Eilhart, although they record Marke's pious expressions of regret, nevertheless tend to stress the pernicious nature of this kind of love and the death as a punishment and a warning to others. There was no need here for a sympathetic Marke, for the love is depicted as illicit and immoral, and Marke primarily as a representative of the accepted stance of society, who, while he may express regret for what had happened – of course through no fault of his own – nevertheless reflects a general rather than personal opinion. In late medieval and Reformation times, then, the emphasis is on Marke as a representative, and this tradition remains dominant into the nineteenth century, when, especially in France, there are numerous versions in which law and order triumph, albeit tragically perhaps, over love. However, the 'tragedy' of Tristan and Isolde – and most of the German dramatic works at the end of the nineteenth century are sub-titled either 'Tragödie' or

'Trauerspiel'[2] – marks the introduction of a modern concept derived from classical models and Romantic ideas. The lovers are driven to death or suicide as a result of their conflict with society, not brought to death by chance as in Gottfried. In such a situation society is represented by Marke, and Marke is consequently much less of an individual and not necessarily sympathetic. In almost all cases, too, the medieval situation is retained, primarily, it seems, in order to present situations that would not be morally acceptable, if situated in the present.

It is not until the twentieth century that a major change takes place in this attitude, and the causes lie evidently in the influence of Nietzsche, Freud, and others. In the first place there is a movement back to a simple structure and a minimum of characters. The action is again concentrated around the three protagonists and not dispersed among a multitude of minor figures and confusing sub-plots (especially prevalent in the nineteenth century), while the medieval background is discarded in favour of a modern *mise en scène*. Already Georg Kaiser, though outwardly retaining the medieval court situation, moved far from the medieval context in his Freudian analysis,[3] and later writers move fully into the modern era and portray Marke as a business tycoon or a doctor, even as a university professor. In such works Marke is no longer a mere blocking figure in the older sense, a representative of a society which is opposed to the lovers, but one who, as in Gottfried's work, is directly and emotionally involved. The characters' beliefs and attitudes reflect, of course, the social situation in which they live, but they play out their roles on the personal level.

After the Second World War things changed once more, as the social order developed to the point where the marriage bond was no longer seen to be any obstacle at all to an extra-marital love affair. With no taboos, except perhaps for incest or nymphet love, no conflict was possible, and Hans Erich Nossack's novel *Spätestens im November* (Berlin, 1955) or Albert Cohen's novel, *Belle du Seigneur* (Paris, 1968), suggest that not the impediment to love but the love itself is what creates the problem for the lovers; the husband is irrelevant. In the one case the love brings about an existential crisis; in the other the overwhelmingly exclusive nature of the love relationship creates a burden that can only be relieved by suicide. In these works Marke no longer has a role, but, by creating a situation in which the eternal triangle had to be lived out and by creating in Marke a believably sympathetic character who stands, as it were, as a measure of the other

2   e.g., Ludwig Schneegans, *Tristan. Trauerspiel* (Leipzig, 1865); Albert Gehrke, *Isolde. Tragödie* (Berlin, 1869); Adolf Bessell, *Tristan und Isolde. Trauerspiel* (Kiel, 1895); Friedrich Roeber, *Tristan und Isolde. Eine Tragödie . . .* (Leipzig, 1898).
3   *König Hahnrei. Tragödie* (Berlin, 1913).

love, whether on the social or purely personal level, Gottfried had sup-
plied a model which enabled later generations to take the old plot, to
adapt the figure of Marke to contemporary circumstances, and thus to fill
the old story with new meaning time and again. I suspect that, despite
Nossack and others, we have not seen the last of King Marke.

Gottfried's Heroine

MARIANNE WYNN

The heroines of medieval German fiction present a broad spectrum of individuality. Far from exhibiting monotonous sameness, they are cast by their authors in highly individualised moulds. Their personalities are distinctively outlined; their profiles projected with considerable precision. This transmission of a fictional character's uniqueness is achieved by the different poets in a vast variety of ways. It may be effected through careful and detailed psychological analysis, as in the case of Gottfried's Blanscheflur.[1] An author may decide to record principally behaviour and gestures, and to typify speech, as Wolfram does in his portrayal of Orgeluse, and obtain the same result. Direct description of a character may be combined with that character's self-revelation in an extended speech, and a singular fictional identity will establish itself. This is what happens with the figure of the girl in Hartmann's *Der arme Heinrich*. A narrator may also allow a character to individualise itself predominantly through action, as Kriemhild does in the *Nibelungenlied*. The authors of medieval Germany composing in the vernacular experimented with many forms of character-portrayal. The finest among them achieved brilliant results in that they managed to create plausible and memorable figures of fiction. These are memorable in the sense that they imprint themselves on memory because they carry a particular pattern of features, each one carefully selected by the poet. It is these skilful and varied combinations of specific attributes, culled from a wide range of possible human qualities, which make these characters unique, non-interchangeable. They thus allow the listener/reader to experience them as individuals. On occasions a figure may be made to fill a social role, but certain traits will have been added to remove it from the danger of remaining

---

[1] For an analysis of Gottfried's portrait of Blanscheflur, see Marianne Wynn, 'Nicht-Tristanische Liebe in Gottfrieds *Tristan*: Liebesleidenschaft in Gottfrieds Elterngeschichte', in *Liebe – Ehe – Ehebruch in der Literatur des Mittelalters*, edited by Xenja von Ertzdorff and Marianne Wynn, Beiträge zur deutschen Philologie, 58 (Giessen, 1984), pp. 56–70.

confined to the cage of a type. In this way Hartmann's Enite may be said to be seen by the author as the perfect wife. Yet at the same time he takes care to individualise her through plotting the growth of her inner strength, and through outlining her proclivity towards sensuousness with considerable precision. His Laudine, presented as the liege-lady *par excellence*, is still given a personality all of her own through the capacity for feeling deeply which Hartmann attributes to her. The poet of the *Nibelungenlied* too details the aspects of his heroine's character with care, and furthermore applies a highly specific perspective of human individuality in the description of it. Kriemhilt, one might say, owes her uniqueness to the fusion of two persons into one. She is portrayed first and on the one hand as the shy and charming girl of the court romance and second, and on the other hand, as the vengeful woman of heroic literature. The transition from one to the other is convincingly motivated – catastrophe releases the wildness of her passionate nature. Even the implied heroines of the love lyric declare themselves in the work of different poets with such exactitude that they almost appear individualised. Certainly at the core of every corpus of songs there is a dominant female figure. The sharp differentiation between these patterns of femininity lends them aspects of individuality. Walther's love-poetry is dominated by his ideal of the sweet and loving girl. Neidhart's willing and over-eager wench is light years removed from Reinmar's *princesse lointaine*. In the handful of dawn-songs which Wolfram left, a passionate woman reveals herself willing to run enormous risks of discovery for the sake of her love. The creation of such highly individualised women characters, and such clearly outlined figures within lyrical fiction represents an outstanding achievement on the part of the German poets, an achievement made possible through the patient perfection of a variety of techniques. Basically, of course, this achievement must be traced back to the extraordinary gifts of this small group of poets, to their sharp sense of the details of a personality, of its facets, and to their grasp of psychological patterns. A statement like the one made by Gertrud Jaron Lewis: 'eine detailliert psychologische Charakterstudie von Seiten des mittelalterlichen Dichters ist freilich nicht zu erwarten'[2] seems strange, for the best of the German medieval poets have managed precisely such studies, albeit not in the manner of extensive and circumstantial analysis of postmedieval writers who will probe a personality at length. The success of these authors in creating distinctive female figures of fiction may be measured by the lack of success in this same area by near-contemporary poets elsewhere. In a survey of the

---

2 Gertrud Jaron Lewis, '*daz vil edel wîp*: Die Haltung zeitgenössischer Kritiker zur Frauengestalt der mittelhochdeutschen Epik', in *Die Frau als Heldin und Autorin: Neue kritische Ansätze zur deutschen Literatur*, edited by Wolfgang Paulsen (Berne/Munich, 1979), pp. 66–81; here p. 66.

heroines of thirty late thirteenth-century Middle English romances, Adelaide Evans Harris has this to say of their central women characters: 'Essential as she was to the story, she was often of so little importance as an individual that she was not even given a name. A title, such as "the daughter of the King of Hungary" or "the wife of Sir Isambras", sufficed, and was indeed more descriptive than a name of her own, in that it indicated her dependence upon these two relationships.' She concludes that these heroines are generally 'peerless in grace and beauty, [yet] are . . . so lacking in personality that in retrospect they blend almost imperceptibly into one'. She is forced to decide that 'Chaucer's Criseyde . . . is the only one to possess distinct individuality. Although she is no more lovely and far less virtuous than any of the others, she alone in all that shadowy group is vividly alive.'[3] So by comparison, the gallery of female portraits in medieval German literature is indeed impressive. Isot, Gottfried's heroine, is part of it.

The critical analysis and assessment of Isot's delineation in Gottfried's work has been overshadowed by the preoccupation of scholars with the poet's thematic concerns and his stylistic virtuosity. Indeed, Gottfried's technique of character-portrayal as a whole has attracted far less interest and attention than his themes, concepts, and style. A glance at the bibliographical aids to *Tristan*-research will testify to this.

Hans-Hugo Steinhoff's bibliography of 1971 and its sequel of 1986[4] show three major rubrics relevant to the present context: Philosophy of Life (*Weltanschauung*), Language and Form (*Sprache und Form*), and Sources (*Stoffgeschichte*). There is a fourth of considerable length: Individual Problems (*Einzelprobleme*), but the entries here do not list any of the characters. It is only under the sub-section Ordeal (*Gottesurteil*) that Isot receives mention in some of the titles. The sequel which covers Tristan research of the period 1970-1983 does have a small section entitled Individual Figures (*Einzelne Figuren*). Yet the shortness of the list, only twenty-one entries as against over fifteen hundred of the total bibliography, speaks for itself. Isot is mentioned four times only.[5]

---

3 Adelaide Evans Harris, A.M., 'The Heroine of the Middle English Romances', *Western Reserve University Bulletin*, New Series, 31 (August 1928), Literary Section Supplement, no. 8, Western Reserve Studies, 2, no. 3, Cleveland, Ohio, pp. 1–43 (here pp. 5 and 40 respectively).

4 *Bibliographie zu Gottfried von Straßburg* (Berlin, 1971); II: *Berichtszeitraum 1970–1983* (Berlin, 1986), volumes 5 and 9 respectively of Bibliographien zur deutschen Literatur des Mittelalters, edited by Ulrich Pretzel and Wolfgang Bachofer.

5 Three of these papers will be discussed below. The fourth by Joan C. Dayan, 'The Figure of Isolde in Gottfried's *Tristan*: Towards a Paradigm of "Minne" ', *Tristania*, 6,2 (1980/81), 23–36, was not accessible to me. Judging by its title, however, it would seem that its main concern lies in circumscribing the leading idea of Gottfried's work, rather than in defining his projection of the heroine's personality.

Similarly, the research report of 1974 by Reiner Dietz, *Der 'Tristan' Gottfrieds von Strassburg: Probleme der Forschung (1902–1970)*[6] amply demonstrates that the main thrust of *Tristan*-scholarship has been directed towards the isolation of the leading ideas of the work. There are surveys here of contributions on the subject of Gottfried's attitude towards classical antiquity and on the relation between his view of love and the interpretations of that sentiment as formulated in contemporary love-song. The significance of the principle of honour and the importance of social prestige in the work may be seen to have been widely investigated. In addition, Reiner Dietz's summaries show the massive amount of research devoted to the theme of passion in the work, to the love philtre, to death, to the lovers' paradise, and to the problematic relation of Gottfried's world of thought to Christianity. One entry, and one entry only, refers to a character in the work, to King Mark. There is no mention of Isot. The account of *Tristan*-scholarship by Beatrice Margaretha Langmeier of 1978, 'Forschungsbericht zu Gottfrieds von Strassburg *Tristan* mit besonderer Berücksichtigung der Stoff- und Motivgeschichte für die Zeit von 1959– 1975'[7] does not change the picture transmitted by the other two bibliographical reference-works, nor does the Wege der Forschung volume edited by Alois Wolf of 1973,[8] or the Metzler review by Gottfried Weber and Werner Hoffmann of 1981.[9] The brief report by Michael S. Batts entitled 'Research since 1945 on Gottfried's *Tristan*'[10] confirms the impression gained from all bibliographical aids on Gottfried's *Tristan*: the weight of *Tristan* scholarship lies squarely on the ideological substance of the work. This is eminently understandable. There can be no doubt that the theme of passion in it is paramount. To document, discuss, and understand its nature is Gottfried's chief concern. Its presentation poses innumerable problems of interpretation which have attracted a large number of attempts to solve them, and which will continue to do so. Yet character portrayal in the narrative is by no means of mere peripheral significance. After all, passion here is not considered in the abstract, but applied to reality. It manifests itself in the thought, action, and behaviour of two individuals, both of whom are carefully delineated.

The only major study so far which concerns itself exclusively with Gottfried's art of character-portrayal is that by Gisela Hollandt, *Die Hauptgestalten in Gottfrieds 'Tristan': Wesenszüge, Handlungsfunktion, Motiv der*

6   Göppinger Arbeiten zur Germanistik, 136, edited by Ulrich Müller, Franz Hundsnurscher and Cornelius Sommer (Göppingen, 1974).
7   Dissertation, University of Freiburg (Switzerland), published Zürich, 1978.
8   *Gottfried von Strassburg*, Wege der Forschung, CCCXX (Darmstadt, 1973).
9   *Gottfried von Strassburg*, Sammlung Metzler, 15, fifth edition (Stuttgart, 1981).
10 *Tristania*, 9, 1–2 (1983–84), 40–48.

List of 1966.[11] Most unfortunately the author approaches her task with a preconceived notion, namely this, that the concepts of character and personality in literature are modern and may not be applied to medieval writing. (Why this should be so is not explained.) Moreover, in a passage which seems curiously contradictory within itself, she claims that while Gottfried manages to individualise his leading figures, he nevertheless does not create individuals:

> ... personale Wesensart darf mit modernen Begriffen wie 'Charakter', 'Persönlichkeit' oder gar irgendeiner Art von psychologischem Typus keineswegs gleichgesetzt werden. Doch wird die Untersuchung zeigen, daß die Romanfiguren, trotz mancher übereinstimmender Züge, Eigenschaften haben, die an die einzelne Gestalt gebunden sind und diese von allen anderen unterscheiden. Dies gilt nicht nur für Tristan und Isolde, sondern auch für die Nebenfiguren. Marke ist von anderer Wesensart als etwa Riwalin oder Rual; Brangaene hat Züge, die Blanscheflur oder der irischen Königin fehlen. Gottfrieds Gestalten sind zwar noch keine Individuen im vollen Sinne des Wortes, wohl aber ist jede einzelne unverwechselbar sie selbst mit ihren Begabungen und Fehlern, ihren Stärken und Schwächen.[12]

This prejudice that medieval authors are incapable of adequate character portrayal seems widespread among Germanists. That the poets of the middle centuries can handle psychological analysis and development of personality in fiction has frequently been denied.[13] Critics of English literature, on the other hand, appear to labour under no such difficulty. They approach the text expecting to find proper characterisation of the figures in it, and are disappointed if they do not, as we have seen. With Germanists, the expectation has often been a negative one.[14] Certainly the

---

11 Philologische Studien und Quellen, 30, edited by Wolfgang Binder, Hugo Moser, Karl Stackmann (Berlin, 1966).

12 p. 9.

13 See e.g. Friedrich Ranke, *Tristan und Isold*, Bücher des Mittelalters, 3 (Munich, 1925), pp. 192–193: 'Es ist ... im allgemeinen nicht die Art mittelalterlicher Dichter, die Menschen ihrer Romane als einheitliche und eigenartige oder gar sich von innen heraus entwickelnde Charaktere zu erleben und zu zeichnen'; also Max Wehrli, 'Der Tristan Gottfrieds von Strassburg', *Trivium*, 4 (1946), 81–117 (p. 116): '... [man] darf ... in einem mittelalterlichen Roman keine Einheit der Charakterzeichnung erwarten'.

14 The positive view has also been expressed. See e.g. Karl Schmid, 'Über das Verhältnis von Person und Gemeinschaft im früheren Mittelalter', in *Frühmittelalterliche Studien*, 1 (1967), 225–249 (p. 239): 'Die Alternative, "typische" oder "individuelle" Personendarstellung im Mittelalter hat eher Verwirrung gestiftet als Klärung gebracht. Es wäre nämlich unsinnig, den mittelalterlichen Menschen die individuelle Prägung, d.h. Individualität und jegliches Personen- und Persönlichkeitsbewußtsein einfach ab-

techniques of character portrayal which may be observed in medieval literature are less explicit than those found in works of the later period. There is less use of the inner soliloquy, and less space is given to authorial commentary than in postmedieval literature. Epithets and adjectives are not as heaped as they often are in the novel; after all, the highly differentiated vocabulary of the modern linguistic medium was as yet not available. Nevertheless, even though the means of character portrayal may be different with medieval authors from those of later writers, the objective and result are the same – a fictional figure distinguished from others by attributes of its own, an individual that commands credibility. Such a one is Gottfried's heroine.

Gisela Hollandt's chapter on this figure is largely devoted to the theme of cunning, to the ability to deceive, and to the forms of deception associated with Isot. She shows convincingly that Isot has a particular gift for language and is highly adept at handling the double-entendre. According to her, she uses deception to safeguard her love and because of this end her means are exonerated by the author.[15]

Wilfried Wagner, in an article of 1973, 'Die Gestalt der jungen Isolde in Gottfrieds *Tristan*'[16] bases himself on the observation by Friedrich Ranke that Gottfried in his portrayal of Isot before the love-potion employs the technique of characterisation through contrast. The personality of Isot outlines itself through juxtaposition with her mother. Against the background of her mother's diplomacy and expertise, her caution and experience of life, Isot appears as inexperienced and immature. It is not until she finds herself in the grip of an overpowering passion that her personality changes. She becomes calculating and deceitful.[17] Wilfried Wagner takes Ranke's proposition further, pointing out that until her departure for Cornwall, Isot is regularly described by the poet as *junc, schœne, süeze, wunneclich* and *lieht*, but is also shown by him as emotional and helpless.[18] Wilfried Wagner relates this her early characterisation to the characterisation of passion in the work and concludes: 'Das Lob der *minne* als einer befreienden, fast reinigenden Macht, die das Leben "sinnvoll"

zusprechen. Die großen historischen Gestalten des Mittelalters sind dafür Beweis genug.' Indeed the question of whether the critic may, or may not, speak of characterisation in medieval literature has over the years given rise to much theoretical discussion. For a most useful survey of the course and the aspects of this controversy see Otfrid Ehrismann, *Nibelungenlied: Epoche – Werk – Wirkung*, Arbeitsbücher zur Literaturgeschichte (Munich, 1987), pp. 212–224.

15 Hollandt, pp. 119ff, 128ff, 146, 151ff.
16 *Euphorion*, 67 (1973), 52–59.
17 Ranke, op. cit., pp. 201ff.
18 Wagner, p. 55.

macht . . . erfordert die vorherige Zeichnung der jungen Isolde in all ihrer Abhängigkeit und Unausgeglichenheit . . .'[19]

C.B. Caples in a paper published in 1975 with the title 'Brangaene and Isold in Gottfried von Strassburg's *Tristan*'[20] follows in the footsteps of Friedrich Ranke and Wilfried Wagner. He too traces a development in the character of Isot. In his description of the heroine, Gottfried, so he argues, uses the 'aspectual technique',[21] i.e., as the plot progresses, aspects of Brangaene's character infiltrate Isot's personality to become a permanent part of it. He stresses the fact that Gottfried allotted a more substantial role to Brangaene than the authors of the other Tristan narratives, and concludes that 'her character is essential to Gottfried's version of the heroine Isold's development'.[22] He points out that Gottfried persistently draws attention to Brangaene's loyalty and unselfishness, qualities which Isot does not possess in the early part of the story, but which she displays later on, having absorbed these virtues from Brangaene.[23]

Most recently Nancy Zak has devoted a chapter to Gottfried's heroine in her Berkeley dissertation of 1981, 'The Portrayal of the Heroine in Chrétien de Troyes's *Erec et Enide*, Gottfried von Strassburg's *Tristan*, and *Flamenca*'.[24] She stresses the particular aspect of Isot as the creature of passion, claiming that 'her association with "Minne", her creatrix [represents a] relationship [which] determines her role and her position throughout the poem'.[25] In support of this assertion she cites images and figures of speech used by Gottfried when describing the link between the goddess Love and the heroine. In the second section of the chapter she analyses the description of Isot's beauty.

None of these special studies concerned with Isot have given a full account of Gottfried's heroine. None have outlined the precise details of her individuality, and the sum of it, as Gottfried wished it to be seen. There are still many questions to be answered here. What is this distinct personality which Gottfried gives his heroine? What are the attributes that make it up? What are the specific techniques of portrayal that he uses to characterise her? In what manner does he remodel the blueprint for his heroine as found in Thomas? What is it that he adds? What does he elaborate? What does he suppress? Where does he place his accents as

---

19 ibid., p. 58.
20 *Colloquia Germanica*, 9 (1975), 167–176.
21 ibid., p. 174.
22 ibid., p. 168.
23 ibid., pp. 172–173.
24 Since published under the same title in Göppinger Arbeiten zur Germanistik, 347 (Göppingen, 1983).
25 ibid., p. 59.

against Thomas? Is the result of his changes a totally different figure, or at least one reminiscent of its model, and if so, in what way? Does he idealise Isot, or portray her realistically, or does he fuse idealisation with realistic treatment? Does he evaluate her aesthetically and morally? Does he criticise her? What is the author's attitude towards his heroine? What likely impact did this figure have on contemporary audiences?

Clearly, the answers to all these questions would fill a sizeable monograph. Their quantity and weight would go far beyond the bounds of a mere paper. So I must content myself with merely sketching some of them.

The starting-point for any assessment of Gottfried's Isot must be Thomas's heroine. We are all familiar here with the crippling difficulty that faces the critic trying to compare Gottfried's work with his source. Thomas's romance is extant only in fragments which together account for no more than approximately one sixth of the total work. We possess its latter part, beginning with Tristran's inner conflict when contemplating marriage with Ysolt of the White Hands, and ending with the lovers' death.[26] The remainder of the work is accessible only through the translation of 1226 into Norwegian prose by Friar Robert.[27]

In the last part of the romance the characterisation of the heroine shows components which Gottfried retained. She is a woman of exceptional beauty (3076–77). Her beautiful hands merit particular mention (845). She has the gift of music, is an accomplished singer, and able to accompany herself on an instrument. Her sophistication is evident in the elegant turn of phrase which she employs in speech (843–932) and in her adept argumentation (1349ff). She is dominated by her love for Tristran (701–712) and in turn dominates his thinking (53–388). Love is the keynote of her existence. She is capable of deep emotion and grieves for her lover (701–712). She is clever and deceitful (2695–2705; 1571–1610) and lives in constant fear that her adulterous love might be discovered (1824–1829). In her

---

26 All line references are to the edition of the fragments in volume I of Joseph Bédier's work, Le Roman de Tristan par Thomas: Poème du XIIᵉ siècle, 2 vols (Paris, 1902–1905). There have since been two further editions by Bartina H. Wind, published in 1950 and 1960 respectively, of which the later one, Les Fragments du Roman de Tristan: Poème du XIIᵉ siècle, Textes Littéraires Français (Geneva/Paris), reduced in size, but revised, has here been used to supplement Bédier's edition.
27 Chapter references are to Tristrams Saga ok Ísondar, part I of Die nordische und die englische Version der Tristan-Sage, edited by Eugen Kölbing (Heilbronn, 1878–82), pp. 113–204. Kölbing's edition has been compared here with Paul Schach's translation of the saga, The Saga of Tristram and Ísönd (Nebraska, 1973), which is based not only on the three editions of the saga by Eugen Kölbing, Gísli Brynjúlfsson (Copenhagen, 1878) and Bjarni Vilhjálmsson (Reykjavik, 1954), as well as on all extant manuscripts, but takes note also of the Reeves Fragment and leaf two of AM 567 4to, XII.

loyalty to Tristran she tries to impose hardship on herself as she knows that he suffers (2009–2048). Her most striking feature in this last part of Thomas's romance is her ability to conduct lengthy self-analysis, meditation, and argument. As this is so pronounced a part of her portrayal in the concluding section of the narrative it seems reasonable to assume that it was a feature of her characterisation throughout the work. Nevertheless, it cannot be said that Thomas tried to individualise her by this means, for this astonishing capacity for circumstantial probing into the mind, and for extensive reasoning, is seen to be shared here by his other characters as well, by Tristran and Brengvein. So a dominant feature which could have established an individuality in Thomas's heroine is not used by him for this purpose. Gottfried, it would seem, judging now by the reflection of Thomas's style of portrayal in the Norwegian prose version, has restricted this aspect of the characters generally. However, in the description of hero and heroine much is still made of it, while in that of Brangaene it is greatly reduced. Through this imbalance Gottfried achieves an effect of individualising the heroine, as also the hero, setting her and him off against Brangaene, an effect which Thomas either could not manage, or did not intend to introduce. At any rate Gottfried in this way gives hero and heroine an intellectual dimension which Brangaene does not possess. Such differentiation between the characters cannot be found in Thomas. Indeed Brengvein in Thomas's work is by no means a subsidiary character, at least not in the extant part of the narrative, where she is very much a figure of the foreground. In her violent scene with the heroine in which she berates her, deploring the indignities to which she has been subjected, she steals much of the limelight, because of her articulate vehemence and the just nature of her complaints (1265–1616). The encounter is a meeting of equals, and it is difficult to imagine that Thomas gave Brengvein this stature vis-à-vis the heroine suddenly. It is much more likely that he adumbrated the narrative balance between the two figures long before. The final eruption of tension between the two women would then be fully motivated, and Thomas was a master at motivation. Gottfried on the other hand, accords Isot far greater importance than Brangaene, does not allow the latter to rival her in any scene, and keeps Isot throughout in a position of uniqueness.

Thomas, in the end, draws his heroine into a complex network of stresses. Not only has Tristran also become adulterous through *his* marriage, but Brengvein too takes a lover, Caerdin, friend of Tristran and brother to his wife. Dissembling and deceiving now involves six characters linked by marriage, friendship, vassalage, blood relationship, and relationship by marriage. Considering the structure of Gottfried's narrative and its leading ideas it would appear unlikely that he would have placed his heroine into a situation where so many aspects were competing for attention. An audience's interest in her might have become substantially reduced.[28]

So much for the last and extant part of Thomas's work. What can we glean of his heroine through the medium of Brother Robert's translation? While it is considered that Robert followed Thomas's text faithfully in all details of the story, it is also accepted that he abridged here and there. Very probably this occurred predominantly in those parts where the characters indulged in the type of discursive self-examination and disputation of which the extant section of Thomas's work gives an example. In this way we may have lost a considerable amount of self-revelation on the part of his heroine, and of her portrayal through the reaction of other characters to her.

It is quite a vivid figure that emerges from Robert's translation, in particular when taken in conjunction with the last and extant part of Thomas's work. On first mention of her the heroine is described as 'beautiful and well-bred' ('fríða ok kurteisa') and much stress is laid on her desire to learn and be instructed. She is clever, widely renowned for her intelligence, and can hold her own in discussion with learned men. She learns to write, to compose letters, and to play stringed instruments. Clearly, she is gifted, is intellectually inclined, and has poise (30). In her refusal to consider the steward as suitor she speaks out with boldness and makes a determined bid for independent action (37, 41). She argues shrewdly with her mother that it would be more politic for *her* to kill Tristram than for her mother, as he is not in her safe keeping but in the queen's (44). When persuading Bringvet to stand in for her, her cleverness is once again underlined: 'En frú Ísond var hin hyggnasta kona' (46). Ruthlessly and cunningly she plots Bringvet's death and shows the same lack of mercy when dealing with the thralls who were to have carried out the deed (47 and 48). In answer to the increasing rumours at court concerning her relationship with Tristram Ísönd practises pretence and displays her skills at deception (52–57). Her accomplished handling of danger and trickery culminate in the ordeal (58 and 59). No particular facets of Ísönd's character are then revealed during the description of her life with Tristram in the wilderness. When the lovers are finally surprised by the king and Tristram has to flee, she shows her capacity for suffering,

---

28 The study by Pierre Jonin, *Les Personnages féminins dans les romans français de Tristan au XIIᵉ siècle: Études des influences contemporaines* (Aix-en-Provence, 1958), is only partially relevant to the present enquiry. Although the work contains many interesting observations on Thomas's heroine, the author's chief concern is not the art of characterisation of the various poets. His main interest lies in establishing Béroul's and Thomas's originality vis-à-vis Eilhart, and furthermore to isolate 'l'influence des réalités historiques, des courants littéraires et du climat religieux dans tous les épisodes et événements où interviennent les personnages féminins' (p. 14).

sheds tears and grieves, and expects nothing but misery for the rest of her days (67 and 68).

Many of the characteristics of Ísönd were taken up by Gottfried for his heroine. I do not have to rehearse which ones. However, they were used in a manner different from Thomas. The chronological listing of attributes in the description of the heroine, whether by direct statement, or by implication, has a structure in Gottfried. And this is vital. He plots a development of this figure, a feature which is missing entirely from Thomas's narrative. Friedrich Ranke already noticed this as early as 1925.[29] Gottfried's Isot before her departure for Cornwall has no poise, no self-assurance like Ísönd, while still in Ireland, but is on the contrary uncertain, timid, and helpless. She gains that poise after the drinking of the love-potion. When in constant confrontation with danger she is forever compelled to protect herself, her lover, and her love. Isot changes, not suddenly, she develops. The Isot of the latter part of Gottfried's romance is no longer the same as the one of her first appearance in the narrative. In the course of time she has experienced conflict, has questioned herself on moral precepts, and has developed a high, and constantly increasing degree of inner awareness. She has loved, feared, suffered, gambled, and sacrificed. And while almost all these emotions and actions characterised the heroine also in Thomas's work, Gottfried has vastly extended their description, thereby outlining her personality strikingly and precisely. Furthermore, as the action progresses, Isot loses much of her early orientation towards self. The Isot whom Tristan first meets is different from the one he leaves. The girl whose chief objective it had been to centre her energies upon her own self, and to dazzle the court with the newly improved and acquired accomplishments of that self (7962ff)[30] is now a woman who in an agonising cry of despair is able to push aside that self. With admirable magnanimity, she considers Tristan's suffering to be greater than her own (18490ff, in particular 18554–18566). Development lends a fictional character credibility. By introducing it Gottfried has added to his heroine's individuality.[31]

There are many other ways as well whereby he has extended it. His heroine is more fully documented by authorial commentary than either Ysolt or Ísönd, and in this way her personality is revealed in greater

---

29 Ranke, op. cit., p. 200: '[Gottfried] . . . versucht . . . etwas wie eine Charakterenwicklung zu zeichnen, von der bei Thomas noch nicht die Rede war'.
30 Reference throughout is to Gottfried von Strassburg, *Tristan und Isold*, edited by Friedrich Ranke (Berlin, 1930).
31 Even C. Soeteman ('Das schillernde Frauenbild mittelalterlicher Dichtung', *Amsterdamer Beiträge zur Germanistik*, 5 (1973), 77–93) who together with other scholars insists that medieval poets are in general incapable of creating more than a stereotype, concedes that Gottfried's Isot is a 'profilierte Persönlichkeit' (p. 85). He even calls her 'völlig emanzipiert' (p. 86).

detail. He has added her dimension for self-torture as it shows itself for example in her self-analysis after the drinking of the potion. He has elaborated her flair for the arts, her artistic bent, and her talents. Tristan finds in her not merely an apt pupil, but one with sufficient gifts to enable him to raise her to his own level of perceptiveness. A deeply sensuous nature is attributed to her. It declares itself in particular in the two temptation scenes, in the lovers' first meeting after the potion, and in their final meeting in the garden. In both cases the heroine is shown in the guise of the temptress, a feature absent from Thomas's text. Yet despite her sensuousness Gottfried portrays her also as capable of profound spiritual experience, as he shows in the description of her behaviour in the lovers' paradise. This aspect too is missing from Thomas's work. There is moreover a complex duality that governs the character of Gottfried's heroine, which he transmits with great sophistication. She acknowledges in her bearing the split nature of her existence. She responds to the two notions of *êre* which dominate Gottfried's interpretation of the received narrative. The public personage in her answers to the ordinary world, the world about her, of diplomacy, malice, and intrigue – to the court. She answers with hypocrisy and pretence, with deception and betrayal, with ruthlessness and brutality. The private individual in her, however, reacts to the world of love and to its particular moral code, to *its êre*, with total integrity, loyalty, devotion, and utter genuineness. So on the one hand Gottfried portrays an evil woman who will shrink from nothing, a queen who will abuse her position of power, and who will murder. On the other hand he idealises her as perfect in loving, and as one whose sheer femininity on one occasion prevents her from committing murder, justified though it might be. He idealises her furthermore in references to her beauty, where in one case in particular he goes far beyond the traditional eulogising phrases that had become the norm among medieval poets when describing female appearance. In a passage which must surely be one of the most beautiful and melodious in medieval German poetry, he utters a hymnic praise of her beauty, claiming that it outshines that of the fabled Helen of Troy:

> 'ine geloube niemer me,
> daz sunne von Mycene ge;
> ganzlichiu schœne ertagete nie
> ze Criechenlant, si taget hie.'   (8273–76)

Yet elevate her though he might, and idealise her with reference to that for him most important of all values, with reference to perfect loving, the poet's attitude towards his heroine is still ambivalent. Flawless as Isot might be in her service of love, she is after all a woman, and perfection according to Gottfried's thinking cannot be found in the female. He makes this abundantly clear, so it seems to me, in his commentary on female behaviour.[32]

All women, so he claims, are Eve's daughters and share her nature. What is forbidden, they desire. Prohibition is for them a goad to action. Eve's immoral act – and it is specifically stated that her plucking of the fruit was immoral (17960: 'dar ans ouch alle ir ere gaz') – has tainted all her daughters. Her folly, her sinfulness, and her inability to practise restraint have descended to all women: 'sus sint ez allez Even kint,/ die nach der Even gevet sint' (17961–62). They have descended also to Isot. Gottfried's commentary on the nature of women forms the introduction to the very scene in which his heroine will prove him to be correct in his evaluation of female frailty. Prompted by her proclivity to sensuousness, inherited from Eve, and showing like Eve that disastrous flaw, the inability to endure restraint and to accept restriction, she organises the lovers' meeting in the garden which will be their undoing. At high noon, when the sun is in its zenith, at the hour of *accidia* (18126–18138) she summons her lover, and they are discovered. She engineers and re-enacts another fall, and loses another paradise.

In his assessment of the nature of women Gottfried follows the dominant thinking of his own time on this subject. Boldly independent in much of his thought, he accepted here the ruling and conventional view. The acceptance of it – which cannot have been an unthinking one – must have meant a considerable conflict for him when idealising his heroine. How entrenched this view was is shown by Hartmann. Early on, during his harsh, yet uncalled for treatment of his wife, his hero Erec expatiates on this notion that women will attempt that which is forbidden:

> 'daz ich von wîben hân vernomen,
> daz ist wâr, des bin ich komen
> vol an ein ende hie:
> swaz man in unz her noch ie
> alsô tiure verbôt,
> dar nâch wart in alsô nôt
> daz sis muosten bekorn.
> ez ist doch vil gar verlorn

---

32 Understanding the so-called *huote*-excursus (17858–18114) has remained a vexed question. Any interpretation of any part of it is likely to prove controversial. However, at least the verses on which the above argument is based (17925–17962) appear to me to be straightforward. For a full survey and discussion of research on the excursus see Rüdiger Schnell, 'Der Frauenexkurs in Gottfrieds *Tristan* (V. 17858–18114): Ein kritischer Kommentar', ZDP, 103 (1984), 1–26. Most recently the excursus has been analysed by Janet Wharton, 'The Role and Function of King Marke in the Tristan Narratives of Eilhart von Oberg and Gottfried von Strassburg' (Dissertation, University of London, 1987).

swaz man iuch mîden heizet,
wan daz ez iuch reizet
daz irz enmuget vermîden:
des sult ir laster lîden.
swaz ein wîp nimmer getæte,
der irz nie verboten hæte,
niht langer si daz verbirt
wan unz ez ir verboten wirt:
sô enmac sis langer niht verlân.'   (3242–3258)[33]

However, Hartmann, unlike Gottfried, does not appear to share this view, for he uses it as a symptom to illustrate his hero's immaturity.

Finally a word about the likely impact of such a heroine as Gottfried's on a contemporary audience. An adulterous heroine of high station must have been a delicate subject to handle. To idealise her into the bargain cannot but have seemed extraordinarily bold. Even the select and sophisticated audience to whom Gottfried addressed himself must have had their reservations. Adultery was condemned by the Church as a sinful act, and in secular law it was considered a punishable crime.[34] The widespread practice of concubinage in the middle centuries makes it clear that this interpretation of adultery as a punishable crime was applied to women only. The example of the emperor Frederick II may illustrate this. He was married four times and had ten legitimate children. However, in addition to these he also had nine illegitimate ones with eight other women.[35] While society turned a blind eye to masculine adultery, it viewed feminine marital infidelity as a serious offence. On occasion it occurred that a woman had to pay for it with her life.[36]

Adultery as a subject for literature was clearly felt to be questionable in medieval Germany. It seemed safest to laugh at it, as the many fabliau-type narratives of the thirteenth century prove. It may be significant also that the only work by Chrestien de Troyes which no German poet attempted to adapt was his *Lancelot*.[37] Taking adultery as one of his major themes and treating it as a serious problem, describing and discussing the suffering it causes, and moreover insisting on the inevitability, indeed necessity, of it within the context of contemporary dynastic marriage was

---

[33] Hartmann is quoted according to Albert Leitzmann (Ludwig Wolff / Christoph Cormeau), Altdeutsche Textbibliothek, sixth edition (Tübingen, 1985).
[34] Joachim Bumke, 'Liebe und Ehebruch in der höfischen Gesellschaft', in *Liebe als Literatur: Aufsätze zur erotischen Dichtung in Deutschland*, edited by Rüdiger Krohn (Munich, 1983), pp. 26–45 (here p. 26), and *Höfische Kultur: Literatur und Gesellschaft im hohen Mittelalter*, 2 vols (Munich: DTV, 1986), II, 551.
[35] Bumke, 'Liebe und Ehebruch', p. 31.
[36] ibid., p. 32, also *Höfische Kultur*, II, 551.
[37] Bumke, *Höfische Kultur*, II, 553ff.

a move as innovative on the part of Gottfried as it was courageous. The brittle nature of the experiment may have been one of the reasons why he decided that a restricted group of listeners would serve his work best. It might have been the safest course for him. Even so, even though the audience whom he addressed was a small, sophisticated, and closed circle, it is difficult to imagine how its members coped with a heroine whose behaviour they saw not merely as scandalous, but as a transgression of extreme gravity, and whom the author at the same time glorified.

I have only skimmed over the surface of some of the many problems which Gottfried's presentation of his heroine poses. I have asked many questions and left most of them unanswered. I hope to answer some of these at a later stage.

'Daz lebende paradis'?
A Consideration of the Love of Tristan and Isot in the Light of the 'huote' Discourse

JANET WHARTON

In Gottfried's *Tristan* the meeting of Tristan and Isot which leads to Marke discovering them *in flagrante delicto* is presented as a re-enactment of the Fall.[1] Tristan and Isot are referred to as Adam and Eve; the setting is a garden; the hour is midday, a time which was frequently associated with the Fall in the exegetical tradition. Such details might seem fortuitous; however, the evidence of the *Tristrams saga* suggests that Gottfried radically remodelled the incident in order to establish clearer parallels with the Genesis account of the Fall. It is almost certain that if there had been any reference to the Fall in Thomas's version, Brother Robert, as a religious, would have included it in his adaptation of the work, but there is no mention of it. Brother Robert simply recounts:[2]

> Tristram could by no means restrain his will and desire and therefore he made use of every opportunity he could find. It happened one day that he and Ísönd were sitting together in an orchard, and Tristram held the queen in his arms.

Gottfried's narrative shows two significant differences, which make the sequence of events more closely resemble those of the Fall: Tristan and Isot's meeting in the orchard is not one of many meetings, but a single, isolated occurrence; the meeting is not primarily the result of Tristan's desire but of Isot's and is instigated by her (18129–61).[3]

---

1 Gottfried von Strassburg, *Tristan und Isold*, edited by Friedrich Ranke, fourteenth edition (Dublin and Zürich, 1969), 18126–64. All references to Gottfried's work are from this edition.
2 *The Saga of Tristram and Ísönd*, translated with an introduction by Paul Schach (Lincoln, Nebraska, 1973), p. 104.
3 Peter W. Hurst gives a very full analysis of the parallels between Gottfried's portrayal of the scene and the biblical account of the Fall (including contemporary exegesis) in 'The Theme of the Earthly Paradise and Associated Traditions in Middle

Gottfried's portrayal of the scene also evokes the earlier discovery of the lovers by Marke at the cave. One particularly striking link between the two scenes is the vivid image of the two suns, which occurs in both but with very different significance. For at the cave Gottfried identifies Isot with the sun of love as her radiance blends with the sunlight, whilst in the orchard she is no longer in harmony with the sun but suffers under the rival onslaught of the natural sun and the sun of love.[4] Tristan and Isot's sojourn at the cave is depicted as an interlude of perfect love and paradisial happiness ('wunschleben', 16846, 16872). The two scenes thus linked appear to present a paradise of love and a fall from that paradise.

Although Gottfried provides a frame of reference from which his audience can assess the significance of the Fall metaphor with his discussion of the Fall in the *huote* discourse (17858–18114), there have been widely varying interpretations of the scene in the orchard. For Gottfried Weber[5] and more recently Dietmar Mieth[6] the Fall metaphor indicates the inherently sinful nature of Tristan and Isot's love. Positions at the opposite extreme are represented by Ingrid Hahn[7] and P.A. Thurlow,[8] who interpret the passage to show that Isot is being portrayed as a fundamentally good woman, that her conduct of her love is ideal, but unfortunately brings her into conflict with ill-conceived controls on her and so results in unhappiness. We must consider then whether the metaphor is used to show the lovers' sinfulness, to absolve them of blame for their plight – or to convey something else entirely.

In fact Gottfried's analysis of the Fall focuses on two quite specific aspects of the incident; namely, the reason for and consequences of Eve's disobedience. Her act is said to have established a mode of behaviour which will recur whenever a woman is subjected to prohibitions:

> ir erste werc, dazs ie begie,
> dar an so buwetes ir art
> und tet, daz ir verboten wart . . .
> sus sint ez allez Even kint,

High German Literature, with Particular Reference to the *Wiener Genesis*, Hartmann's *Erec* and Gottfried's *Tristan*' (unpublished Ph.D. dissertation, University of Cambridge, 1975). Here in particular see pp. 177–83.

4   17580–86; 18129–34.

5   Gottfried Weber, *Gottfrieds von Strassburg 'Tristan' und die Krise des hochmittelalterlichen Weltbildes um 1200*, 2 vols (Stuttgart, 1953), I, 280.

6   Dietmar Mieth, *Dichtung, Glaube und Moral: Studien zur Begründung einer narrativen Ethik mit einer Interpretation zum Tristanroman Gottfrieds von Strassburg* (Mainz, 1976), pp. 205–206.

7   Ingrid Hahn, ' "Daz lebende paradis" (*Tristan* 17858–18114)', *ZDA*, 92 (1963–64), 184–195.

8   P.A. Thurlow, 'Some Reflections on "huote" and "êre" in the "scheiden und meiden" Episode of Gottfried's *Tristan*', *GLL*, 35 (1982), 329–42.

die nach der Even gevet sint.
hi, der verbieten künde,
waz er der Even vünde
noch hiutes tages, die durch verbot
sich selben liezen unde got!   (17950–52; 17961–66)

The question of the perverse nature which women have inherited from Eve underlies the discourse. In the first part Gottfried exposes the problematic nature of *huote* in the light of this female trait, using imagery associated with the Fall ('distel', 'dorn') to show the inevitable, disastrous consequences of applying prohibitions, and discussing how a man should treat his wife if she is to retain her honour (17858–924). Then, after considering the Fall itself, Gottfried examines how women, given their nature, can conduct themselves with propriety (17967–18087).

It is in this final part of the discourse that Gottfried discusses the possibility of a paradise deriving from love, in which the events of the Fall would be rendered insignificant. The fact that much of the argument is couched in abstract language, with certain terms recurring at various points with modified significance has led to a multiplicity of interpretations. Here Gottfried's argument is traced as he presents it in the hope of showing the precise nature of the ideal which he is expounding.

The first possible mode of conduct which Gottfried considers is that women should show complete restraint and abstain from any illicit sexual activity:

und sit in daz von arte kumet
und ez diu natiure an in vrumet,
diu sich es danne enthaben kan,
da lit vil lobes und eren an.
wan swelh wip tugendet wider ir art,
diu gerne wider ir art bewart
ir lop, ir ere unde ir lip,
diu ist niwan mit namen ein wip
und ist ein man mit muote.   (17967–75)

The formulation is rather vague here: 'daz' (17967) and 'es' (17969) refer to behaving like Eve and doing what is forbidden. However, lines 17972–73 – 'diu gerne wider ir art bewart/ir lop, ir ere unde ir lip' – make it clear that Gottfried is referring specifically to what is forbidden in the context of sexual mores. Gottfried's attitude here reflects the general view of his age, which saw sensuality as being more deeply rooted in the nature of woman than of man. Superficially he is full of praise for the woman who overcomes this trait and behaves like a man, and he introduces a string of laudatory adynata:

> da honiget diu tanne,
> da balsemet der scherlinc,
> der nezzelen ursprinc
> der roset ob der erden.   (17982–85)

Although such a denial of womanly nature may have represented an ideal associated with female saints, martyrs and abbesses,[9] Gottfried is in fact less enthusiastic about it and reserves higher praise for the woman who does not sacrifice her womanly nature in order to retain her honour. Indeed, he is quite categorical that a woman should not do this:

> ezn ist niht ein biderbe wip,
> diu ir ere durch ir lip,
> ir lip durch ir ere lat,
> so guote state so si des hat,
> daz si si beidiu behabe.   (17997–18001)

Rather, a woman should exercise *maze* (moderation), in order to do justice to the opposed claims of *lip* (sensuality) and *ere* (reputation). She must show self-restraint and work extremely hard to achieve the requisite balance, experiencing both *liep* and *leit* (17986–18012). However, it is an achievement well worth striving for:

> maze diu here
> diu heret lip und ere.   (18013–14)

Gottfried's highest praise is given to the woman who conducts her life according to the dictates of *maze* and furthermore esteems herself:[10]

> Ezn ist al der dinge kein,
> der ie diu sunne beschein,

---

9   Rüdiger Schnell, 'Der Frauenexkurs in Gottfrieds *Tristan* (V. 17858–18114): Ein kritischer Kommentar', *ZDP*, 103 (1984), 1–26 (pp. 16–21); Thurlow, pp. 334–35.

10   Several critics who have analysed this discourse in detail, Lore Peiffer, *Zur Funktion der Exkurse im 'Tristan' Gottfrieds von Strassburg* (Göppingen, 1971), pp. 207–209, Schnell (pp. 21–23) and Thurlow (pp. 335–36), consider that Gottfried only puts forward two alternative modes of behaviour for a woman: those of total abstinence or moderation in extra-marital sexual activity. However, there are three distinct parts to Gottfried's argument. Each is introduced by a mark of praise, the last two with a capital letter emphasizing a new element in the argument: 17969–70, 17986–87, 18015–16. There is here a clear climax, the final possibility representing the ultimate good, which cannot be transcended. The climax is further emphasized by the greater length at which each successive element is discussed. Hahn (pp. 190–92) and Ferdinand Urbanek, 'Die drei Minne-Exkurse im *Tristan* Gottfrieds von Strassburg', *ZDP*, 98 (1979), 344–71 (p. 367), recognize three elements in the argument, but their interpretation of the final, ideal possibility and its realization is problematic.

so rehte sælic so daz wip,
diu ir leben unde ir lip
an die maze verlat,
sich selben rehte liebe hat.   (18015–20)

This proper regard for herself is manifested in her attitude to her sexuality. Gottfried still uses the term *lip*, but now *lip* is not directly opposed
to *ere*. Whilst in the preceding section the woman was praised because she
did battle 'wider ir libe/mit ir eren' (17988–89), now Gottfried suggests
that the woman who denies her body ('wider ir libe tuot', 18025) is unworthy of regard (18025–32). The true nature of woman comprises an
element of sensuality which should not be denied. However, this is not a
licence for unrestrained sexual indulgence, for such behaviour is condemned as 'bœse getelœse' (18040). Only a woman who finds the correct
path between abstinence and lechery displays a true regard for her wo-
manhood. Gottfried's ideal woman who does this behaves in such a way
that her sexuality enhances her entire being and draws the praise of the
whole world:

ein wip, diu ir wipheit
wider ir selber liebe treit
der werlde zuo gevalle,
die sol diu werlt alle
wirden unde schœnen,
blüemen unde crœnen
mit tegelichen eren,
ir ere mit ir meren.   (18051–58)

Such a woman is able to create a paradise for the man whom she loves
(18059–67).
   The paradise which the woman creates is stripped of all the negative
manifestations of the Fall; there are no thorns:[11]

diu rosine suone
diu hat ez allez uz geslagen:
dorn unde distel unde hagen.   (18076–78)

With the euphemism of 'rosen brechen' Gottfried suggests that the man
can find sexual fulfilment without any unpleasant consequences:

---

11 In biblical exegesis thistles and thorns are interpreted as signs of the wrath of God;
the sinful nature of man; vices, especially lust. R.A. Wisbey, 'The "Renovatio Amoris"
in Gottfried's *Tristan*', in *London German Studies, I*, edited by C.V. Bock (London, 1980),
pp. 1–66 (pp. 21–25), analyses the use of imagery connected with the Fall in the work to
show that Gottfried contrasts the corrupted love of his time with the pure love of an
earlier terrestrial paradise.

> dern darf dekeine sorge haben,
> daz in der hagen iht ange,
> sor nach den bluomen lange;
> daz in der dorn iht steche,
> so er die rosen breche.   (18068–72)

Moreover, this paradise is unassailable: there is no danger of a fall since there is no forbidden fruit:

> dan ist niht obezes inne
> wan triuwe unde minne,
> ere unde werltlicher pris.   (18085–87)

As Friedrich Wodtke has shown, this paradise, which exists in the heart ('der hat daz lebende paradis/in sinem herzen begraben', 18066–67), bears strong parallels to the descriptions of a spiritual paradise which occur in medieval sermons.[12]

The discourse concludes as Gottfried compares this paradise of the heart with the situation of Tristan and Isot and finds that it at least equals it, for the woman cherishes the man supremely well. Once more it is emphasized that in this paradise the woman keeps the man free of the evils connected with the Fall (*distel, dorne*) and the vexations of love:

> ern dörfte niht sin leben geben
> umb keines Tristandes leben;
> wan zware ein rehte tuonde wip
> an swen diu lat ere unde lip
> und sich der beider dar bewiget,
> hi, wie si des von herzen pfliget!
> wie hat sin in so süezer pflege!
> wie rumets alle sine wege
> vor distel und vor dorne,
> vor allem senedem zorne!
> wie vriet sin vor herzenot,
> so wol so nie dekein Isot
> dekeinen ir Tristanden baz.   (18097–18109)

The use of the names Tristan and Isot in the comparison to refer to a particular kind of lover (18107–09) makes it clear that Gottfried is here

---

[12] Friedrich Wodtke, 'Die Allegorie des "inneren Paradieses" bei Bernhard von Clairvaux, Honorius Augustodunensis, Gottfried von Strassburg und in der deutschen Mystik', in *Festschrift Josef Quint anläßlich seines 65. Geburtstages überreicht*, ed. by Hugo Moser, Rudolf Schützeichel and Karl Stackmann (Bonn, 1964), pp. 277–290.

positing a relationship which is fundamentally different from theirs.[13] However, even though the ideal woman of the discourse might create greater happiness for the man, there is no denigration of Isot, for in the next lines the name Isot is used to typify the woman who can offer all that a man can desire in love (18110–114). The reason why the paradise of the discourse is superior lies not in the individual nature of the lovers but rather in the nature of their relationship.

Gottfried twice describes the circumstances in which a woman creates paradise for a man:

> an swen ouch diu genendet,
> an den si gar gewendet
> ir lip unde ir sinne,
> ir meine unde ir minne;   (18059–62)

> an swen diu lat ere unde lip
> und sich der beider dar bewiget . . .   (18100–01)

It occurs when her commitment to the man is absolute. Their relationship takes account of her whole being: there is no dichotomy between the claims of *lip* and *ere*, for both are entrusted to the same man. This then is the key difference between the two women who live according to *maze*: she who also shows a true regard for herself is involved with only one man in any way. The ideal which Gottfried is here advocating is that of a lasting relationship between lovers, one which is entered voluntarily and is sanctioned by society – and this surely is in effect marriage based on affection.[14]

Gottfried's analysis of the various modes of life available to women helps elucidate Isot's conduct of her life and love throughout the work and particularly in the orchard scene. Most importantly, the fact that she is married to Marke, whom she does not love, precludes her being able to

---

13 This point is corroborated by the fact that there is no possibility of a fall from the paradise of the heart (18085–87), whereas Tristan and Isot *do* fall.

14 As early as 1954 Gerhard Meissburger argued that Gottfried regards marriage based on affection as the ideal, indeed the only possible way of finding happiness in love (*Tristan und Isold mit den weissen Händen: Die Auffassung der Minne, der Liebe und der Ehe bei Gottfried von Strassburg und Ulrich von Türheim* (Basel, 1954), pp. 24–29). However, Meissburger's evidence, which is drawn almost exclusively from the portrayal of Tristan's relationship with Isot of the White Hands seems slight and inconclusive on its own, and his view has been little regarded. Contrasting views are advanced by Hahn, who suggests that the paradise of the heart can be achieved by a married woman devoting herself wholeheartedly to her lover (pp. 191–92), and by Tomas Tomasek, who sees the realization as being possible only in a future society and as being dependent upon the development of the individual (*Die Utopie im 'Tristan' Gotfrids von Strassburg* (Tübingen, 1985), pp. 187–211).

achieve the ideal happiness of the *lebendez paradis*. However, Gottfried's portrayal of the woman who shows complete restraint suggests that it would have been totally unnatural for her to deny her love for Tristan, even if she had been able to do so. Thus Isot's position is of necessity that of the second woman, who constantly strives to reconcile the claims of love and honour. The intensity of her passion for Tristan and the gross deception in which it has involved her may superficially make the idea of her life being governed by *maze* seem ridiculous. Yet in so far as Isot's sensuality has not been responsible for any major indiscretion up to the discovery in the orchard, then it must be regarded as fair. Isot's deviation from this mode of behaviour is signalled just before she initiates the fateful meeting in the orchard as Gottfried reintroduces the image of a battle and shows her faced with a conflict between her desire and the inappropriateness of the time. Now, however, she does not, as the good woman of the discourse, join battle 'wider ir libe/mit ir eren' (17988–89), but tries to circumvent the conflict.

Although Tristan and Isot cannot attain the absolute ideal of the *lebendez paradis*, their life at the cave approaches it in all but one respect. For at the cave, during the period when Isot is able to devote herself entirely to the man whom she loves and the ties of her marriage are broken, she and Tristan enjoy a *wunschleben* of perfect love. Nothing can transcend the quality of their love, nor anything which they do impair it (17235–41). This happiness is inferior to the paradise of the discourse merely in that the lovers only enjoy it as exiles from society. They lack the *werltlicher pris* which is one of the fruits of the *lebendez paradis* (16875–77; 18085–87). Because their relationship is not sanctioned by society, when Tristan and Isot return to court, their paradise is vulnerable. A fall, impossible in the *lebendez paradis*, is now possible for them; indeed, as Gottfried made clear in the first part of the discourse with the Fall imagery, it is the inevitable lot of any woman subjected to *huote* as Isot is.

In his portrayal of Tristan and Isot's life at the cave and of the *lebendez paradis* Gottfried draws on models from Christian theological writing.[15]

---

15   Friedrich Ranke, 'Die Allegorie der Minnegrotte in Gottfrieds *Tristan*', Schriften der Königsberger gelehrten Gesellschaft, Geisteswissenschaftliche Klasse, 2. Jahrg., H.2 (Berlin, 1925), 21–39, shows the similarity of the allegorization of the cave to medieval church allegories and suggests that Gottfried is creating a religion of love. Julius Schwietering demonstrates the influence of St Bernard's mysticism in 'Der Tristan Gottfrieds von Strassburg und die Bernhardische Mystik', in J.S., *Mystik und höfische Dichtung im Hochmittelalter* (Tübingen, 1960), pp. 1–35. More recently Ulrich Ernst, 'Gottfried von Strassburg in komparatistischer Sicht: Form und Funktion der Allegorese im Tristanepos', *Euphorion*, 70 (1976), 1–72, has isolated the manifold influences on the allegory, which include classical sources and images from St Augustine's 'City of God', and has shown how Gottfried draws them all together to depict his new ethic of love.

However, although the ideals which he sets up are analogous to his Christian models, they are purely secular. The *lebendez paradis* with its virtues of *triuwe, minne, ere* and *werltlicher pris* exists solely in connection with love between a man and a woman, even though the love may be imbued with a spiritual dimension. It is in the context of this concept of paradise that Gottfried presents Tristan and Isot's meeting as a fall, and it is in this context, not a purely theological one, that the nature of the flaw which causes their fall must be assessed.

As he sets the scene for the discovery, Gottfried comments:

> ez was an einem mitten tage
> und schein diu sunne sere,
> leider uf ir ere.   (18126–28)

Although discovery clearly would involve social disgrace for the lovers, it is questionable whether *ere* here can be interpreted in the limited sense of social standing. It has long been established that *ere* does not denote a single uniform concept throughout the work and that the sense must be assessed from the context.[16] In this scene with its strong connection with the lovers' paradise, the honour of the cave must also be considered:

> da lachet in der süeze schin,
> diu sælige gleste,
> ere, aller liehte beste . . .   (17066–68)

Since the sunlight which symbolizes this honour passes through three windows representing the *güete, diemüete* and *zuht* of ideal love, we must conclude that the honour is dependent on these qualities being present. It is an honour associated solely with love, its quality and its conduct. Thus, although Tristan and Isot as exiles from court have lost their social standing (16875–77), they nevertheless have the honour of love. After their return from the cave, Tristan and Isot once more receive honour from the courtiers: their social standing is restored. However, as this has so often been in question, it seems unlikely that it is merely the potential loss of social honour which Gottfried views with such sorrow (18126–28). Moreover, the use of the Fall metaphor implies a transgression which is committed for the first time. This is certainly not applicable to an action which involves only the loss of social honour. It seems probable then that the honour of love is at stake here, and this is supported by the symbolism connected with *sunne*, not least by the image of the two suns and its changing significance.

Its position introducing the incident combined with the slow measured

---

16 Friedrich Ohly, 'Besprechung von: Maria Bindschedler, "Gottfried von Strassburg und die höfische Ethik" ', *ADA*, 68 (1955–56), 119–30.

tone of the narrative here lends great stress to the statement that the incident occurs at midday (18126). This time was regarded as particularly dangerous both in folklore[17] and in Christian thought. In the latter, it was associated not only with the biblical Fall, but also with the sin of *accidie* and concupiscence.[18] According to St Bernard the demons of noonday are particularly dangerous since they 'simulate the day and even the midday in order to deceive'.[19] Moreover, they constitute the temptation which besets those who are perfect and have overcome other temptations. The implication is that with the meeting in the orchard Tristan and Isot debase their perfect love and are guilty of concupiscence.

Throughout Gottfried's work physical love is portrayed as intrinsically good and an essential aspect of a love relationship. However, it is also made clear that it should be practised with propriety and discretion. This is evident in the allegory, where the honour of love is associated with *zuht* (17065), and also in the narrator's stance: for whenever physical love is praised or sympathetically portrayed, it is indicated that there is a suitable opportunity, that decorum is observed.[20] The question is discussed in greatest detail when Tristan and Isot display the requisite qualities just before the banishment:

> diz ist diu rehte trutschaft,
> diz sint die besten sinne
> an liebe und an der minne:
> swa man der tat niht haben müge,
> da nach als ez der minne tüge,
> daz man ir gerne habe rat
> und neme den willen vür die tat.   (16420–26)

---

[17] *Handwörterbuch des deutschen Aberglaubens*, edited by Hanns Bächtold-Stäubli, 10 vols (Berlin and Leipzig, 1927–1942), VI (1934–35), 400–403.
[18] Reinhard Clifford Kuhn, *The Demon of Noontide: Ennui in Western Literature* (Princeton, 1976), pp. 39–59, traces the concept of *accidie* and its linking with the devil of noontide in writers from Evagius of Pontus to St Thomas Aquinas. In Hartmann's *Erec*, too, the midday sun illuminates culpable sexual indulgence (Hartmann von Aue, *Erec*: *Mittelhochdeutscher Text und Übertragung*, translation by Thomas Cramer (Frankfurt am Main, 1972) 3013–15). On the demon of noonday in Gottfried, see also Hurst, pp. 178–183.
[19] *Life and Works of Saint Bernard, Abbot of Clairvaux*, edited by John Mabillon, translated and edited with additional notes by Samuel J. Eales (London, 1896), Sermon 33, 9 (p. 220); Sermon 33, 13 (p. 221).
[20] For example, when they are on board ship Gottfried commends the lovers because they do not restrain themselves (12369–79), but only after he has emphasized the propriety of their behaviour: 'swes gelieben gelanget,/des tribens under in genuoc,/so sich diu zit also getruoc:/so si zir state kamen . . .' (12366–69) The narrator's stance in the flour-on-the-floor scene, where the love-making lacks propriety, however, is ironic and detached (e.g. 15186–90). The same importance is attached to the lovers' discretion in the parental history too (1367–69).

It is implied that there are occasions when it would be possible to come together, though not in a way commensurate with true love and that in these cases, abstinence is preferable. In other words, the quality and value of the love act are affected by the circumstances in which it takes place. The honour of love is diminished by lack of decorum, that is, if considerations of external honour are not observed.

Before the orchard scene, Isot is clearly fully aware that the time is not appropriate for a meeting:

> sus wolte si dem strite,
> dem muote unde der zite
> mit einem liste entwichen sin.   (18135–37)

Her attempt to circumvent the conflict between her desire and the hour shows her deviating from the model of the good woman described by Gottfried in the discourse. She may seek external circumstances which mitigate the impropriety, but the meeting is obviously not 'als ez der minne tüge'. That Isot's precautions are totally inadequate is underlined by Brangaene's sorrowful reaction and by Marke's rapid discovery of the lovers. We must conclude then that the physical union of the lovers in this scene becomes concupiscence because of the lack of regard for propriety. This view is substantiated by a number of evocative details in Gottfried's portrayal of the scene. For example, the description of the sumptuous regal bed calls to mind the flour-on-the-floor scene where, with critical irony, Gottfried characterizes Tristan's leap into Isot's bed as blind sensuality.

It is made abundantly clear in the narrative that Isot's excessive desire is generated by Marke's *huote* (17833–57; 18116–23). The *huote* discourse emphasizes that Isot's reaction to *huote* is that of all women. In this way Gottfried lessens the guilt attaching to Isot, and makes Marke in a large measure responsible for the lovers' lapse from the ideal love which they manifest at the cave.

It is implied in the discourse that it would be possible for a couple such as Marke and Isot to live in harmony and honour, but only if the husband trusted his wife to conduct her life with discretion:

> ja sol ein ieclich biderbe man
> und der ie mannes muot gewan,
> getruwen sinem wibe
> und ouch sin selbes libe,
> dazs aller slahte unmaze
> durch sine liebe laze.   (17911–16)

In other words, scandal can be avoided and honour maintained if the woman is allowed sufficient freedom to satisfy her desire. She can then behave as the good woman of the discourse, avoiding potentially compromising situations.

Nevertheless, this offers at best a life of reasonable contentment, of happiness interspersed with frustration and sorrow or, as Gottfried puts it in the *minne* discourse, 'rosen bi dem dorne' (12271). The bliss of enduring happiness and social respectability can only be achieved where a partnership based on affection receives the approbation of society. This presupposes a society in which women have considerably more control over the choice of their husbands than Isot had. Gottfried, however, by no means suggests that radical change would be necessary: he implies merely that the onus lies on men to seek out their women more carefully:

> der suohte, alse er solde,
> ez lebeten noch Isolde,
> an den man ez gar vünde,
> daz man gesuochen künde.   (18111–14)

This may appear to assume a love with a far more rational basis than that of Tristan and Isot. Yet the example of Riwalin and Blanscheflur demonstrates the possibility of such a match. With his vision of the *lebendez paradis*, of the perfect happiness deriving from love in society, Gottfried offers an ideal which transcends the concept of love outlined in the prologue and experienced by Tristan and Isot; and it is an ideal which, he claims, is readily accessible to his audience.

'Tristan- und Siegfriedliebe':
A Comparative Study of Gottfried's Tristan
and the Nibelungenlied

GEORGE GILLESPIE

I

Who could imagine Tristan beating Isolde or loosing a bear among the cooks at the end of a hunt in the course of which he has killed every head of game that breaks cover? By the same token it would be difficult to imagine Sîfrit singing love songs or conversing elegantly in a foreign language while playing chess. Sîfrit and Tristan represent two types of archetypal hero: the guileless and not over-intelligent physical type such as Achilles and the resourceful and devious type such as Ulysses. Each is the victim of his own basic defects: Sîfrit lacks insight into the reactions of others to his actions, whereas Tristan is shown in the end to be a hollow actor, whose integrity evaporates once he is parted from Isolde. Yet these two apparently antipathetic heroes are involved in stories, the plots of which show striking similarities. The authors of the early thirteenth-century versions of their stories in Germany have, in their different ways, attempted to attune them to the prevailing chivalric culture and to depict their love relationships within the conventions of courtly love; the intentions of the authors are revealed in their treatment of their material.

The drawback to much comparative study is excessive abstraction, by means of which the plots of complicated imaginative works can be reduced to the bare bones so that spurious similarities are produced that give an illusion of relationships, which can be seen to be false as soon as the texts are read in full. In the case of Gottfried's *Tristan* and the *Nibelungenlied*, however, beside fortuitous resemblances, there are many striking similarities, which derive from the traditional structures of their respective material.[1] Before we go into the details of such similarities the follow-

---

1 See H. de Boor, 'Die Grundauffassung von Gottfrieds Tristan', *DVLG*, 18 (1940), 262–306, and Hugo Kuhn, *Tristan, Nibelungenlied, Artusstruktur*, Bayerische Akademie

ing correlation of the *dramatis personae* of the two stories may make the discussion clearer:[2]

The king and suitor	Gunther (Gunnarr)	Marke
The hero, the king's helper	Sîfrit (Sigurðr)	Tristan
Father of the hero	Sigemunt (Sigmundr)	Riwalin
Mother of the hero	Sigelint (Hjördís)	Blanscheflur
Foster-father of the hero	(Reginn)	Rual
Slayer of the hero's father	(Lyngvi)	Morgan
Enemy or enemies of the king	Liudegêr, Liudegast	Morolt
Courtier(s) hostile to hero	Hagen (Högni)	Marjodo, Melot
The bride won for the king	Brünhilt (Brynhildr)	Isolde von Irlant
The bride of the hero	Kriemhilt (Guðrún)	Isolde as blanschemains

Each hero arrives from outside the society in which he appears as a saviour – he is also known to have killed a dragon, and in *Tristan* does so in the course of the tale; as is usual with such a 'Heilbringer', his origins are mysterious, even dubious, and he causes disruption in the society he enters.[3] Each performs great deeds and defeats the king's enemies, but engenders envy at the court of the king he serves; ultimately he is unable to outwit his adversaries at court, though the interest of Tristan's story consists of his continually fending them off. Tristan is born from the union of his mother Blanscheflur with the badly wounded Riwalin and is brought up by foster-parents, Rual and Floræte, while Sîfrit in the *Nibelungenlied* has been given a spurious courtly upbringing with his parents at the court of Worms – in the *Þiðrekssaga* his mother Sisibe dies at his birth and he is suckled by a hind, while in Old Norse Eddic tradition he is begotten by his dying father on the battlefield and is then brought up at the Danish court where he proves so unruly that he is subsequently brought up by the smith Reginn.

Both heroes are connected with the symbolism of the boar, a fact which may well be fortuitous, though it does indicate that the origins of the two tales reach back into primitive roots. The boar is not only an image of

der Wissenschaften, Philosophisch-Historische Klasse, Sitzungsberichte 1973, Heft 5 (Munich, 1973).

2   The roles here are represented by persons in Part I of the *Nibelungenlied*. One could also include some from Part II, where Etzel is the suitor, Rüedegêr the helper, and Kriemhilt the bride; furthermore, Sîfrit undertakes a bridal quest for Kriemhilt on his own account.

Persons from the Old Norse Nibelungen material are shown in brackets.

3   See Kuhn, pp. 12–13. The challenge of an unknown warrior at court is frequently the starting-point of a story in Celtic and Old Norse literature: see W. Mohr, 'Tristan und Isolde', *GRM*, 55 (1976), 62.

warlike courage[4] but also of sexuality,[5] even being related to the devil in the Bible.[6] In Germanic art the boar is the emblem of the warrior; it is also the holy beast of the ancient Celts, being early connected with the Tristan story in the Welsh Triads, where it is the battle emblem of Drystan.[7] In the Old French Tristan story Iseut dreams of the head of a great wild boar covering her lap with blood when she is on her last vain voyage of rescue to Tristan.[8] The dream of the boar is already in the version of Thomas, Gottfried's main source,[9] but Gottfried is the first to make it Tristan's heraldic beast,[10] where in Marjodo's dream (13511ff) it represents the adulterer who soils Marke's marriage bed. In the *Nibelungenlied* itself the image of the wild boar is used variously: it occurs in Kriemhilt's warning dream where it represents the murderers of Sîfrit (str. 921),[11] but his murder is later compared to the killing of a beast of the chase: *ein tier, daz si sluogen, daz weinten edliu kint* (str. 1002,3); the *Þiðrekssaga* is more explicit: Sigurðr is murdered shortly after he has killed a large boar, and Högni alleges that it is the boar that killed him. It appears that Sîfrit-Sigurðr, as a great warrior, is here represented by the boar, the killing of which is a pre-enactment of his own death – in the hunt in the *Nibelungenlied* he actually kills a great boar among other game.

A bridal quest on the basis of hearsay ('Hörensagen') and involving disguise and deception is the typical structural feature of the type of narrative to which the Tristan and Siegfried stories both belong. Tristan assumes the roles of merchant and minstrel under an assumed name, while Sîfrit pretends to be Gunther's vassal and, invisible in the *tarnhût*, overcomes the Amazonian Brünhilt in athletic contests and later in the bridal chamber. Such bridal quest schemes are common to the 'Spielmannsepik' and the 'Heldenepik';[12] in the former the outcome is usually happy, as in the Arthurian epic, whereas in the latter it is mainly tragic. The bridal quest with the triangular relationship between suitor, bride, and helper is international, but it was particularly favoured in the subliterary story-telling of mediaeval Germany; the tragic outcome is, however, uniquely shared by *Tristan* and the *Nibelungenlied*.

4 See M. Zips, 'Tristan und die Ebersymbolik', *BGDSLT*, 94 (1972), 149–50.
5 P.W. Tax, *Wort, Sinnbild, Zahl im Tristanroman* (Berlin, 1961), pp. 83–84.
6 Tax, p. 85.
7 Zips, pp. 144–45.
8 Zips, pp. 138–39.
9 Zips, pp. 135–36.
10 Zips, p. 145.
11 *Das Nibelungenlied*, edited by H. de Boor (Wiesbaden, 20 1972).
12 See G.T. Gillespie, 'Spuren der Heldendichtung und Ansätze zur Heldenepik in literarischen Texten des 11. und 12. Jahrhunderts', in *Studien zur frühmittelhochdeutschen Literatur*, edited by L.P. Johnson, H. -H. Steinhoff and R.A. Wisbey (Berlin, 1974), pp. 248ff.

Sîfrit, and ultimately Tristan, die because of a love intrigue based on deception – Sîfrit's 'Steigbügeldienst' and use of the *tarnhût* comes close to Tristan's trickery. In each case there is an unanswered question: did Tristan and Isolde fall in love before drinking the love-potion or was their love solely the result of its magic power; and did Sîfrit have an earlier meeting with Brünhilt before the bridal quest to Iceland, as in the old Norse versions – he knows the route to Îsenstein and its customs (str. 331, 378)? Whatever we may think, both brides are won by deception, but the crucial difference is that Tristan ends up in love with the bride, whereas Sîfrit only wins her for Gunther in return for the hand of his sister, Kriemhilt. In the Old Norse version of the Nibelungen story it is the mother of Guðrún (MHG Kriemhilt) who gives Sigurðr a potion that causes him to forget his vows to Brynhildr, whom he later wins for Gunnarr (MHG Gunther) – the *Nibelungenlied* poet leaves the former relationship between Sîfrit and Brünhilt vague, though he and his audience may well have known more than he cares to reveal in his epic; in *Tristan* the potion prepared by the bride's mother brings about the passionate attachment between the bride and the helper through an accident. In *Tristan* it is the king who is deceived, in the *Nibelungenlied* the bride with the connivance of the king. Thus a potion is involved in a deception in both stories originally – Gottfried leaves us to wonder about its real or symbolic meaning, while the *Nibelungenlied* author omits it entirely (if he ever knew it). What is more, a substitution in the bridal bed reinforces the deception in each epic. In *Tristan* deception continues in defence of the lovers against the morality of the court; in the *Nibelungenlied* it merely constitutes the knot which is gradually unravelled in murder and vengeance.

In both *Tristan* and the *Nibelungenlied* the relationship between the hero/helper and the bride causes the murder of the hero in the latter and the continued tension between the lovers and courtly society culminating in the death of both in the former. This short-circuit, as Hugo Kuhn terms it, of the normal bridal quest scheme is found only in these two tales, where the helper is shown to be more suitable for the bride than the suitor/king; hence the tragic outcome.[13] In each case the king is a vacillating ruler and an inferior lover: in the *Nibelungenlied* this necessitates a substitution in the bridal bed where Sîfrit overpowers Brünhilt in order that Gunther may enjoy his conjugal rights (Av. 19–20); in *Tristan* Brangæne is substituted for Isolde to preserve the semblance of her virginity, although Marke cannot tell the difference between the two, since love for him seems to be identical with lust (12588ff. In fact the heroes win the respective brides twice for their kings: Sîfrit in the athletic contests and also in the bedchamber; Tristan on the initial bridal quest to

---

13 Kuhn, pp. 12ff.

Ireland and the second time when he wins her back by his minstrelsy from Gandin; his admonition of Marke is somewhat arrogant, considering his own relationship to Isolde at the time, *'und hüetet miner vrouwen baz'* (13450). Sîfrit, likewise, is at no pains to conceal his scorn for Gunther at the opening of the Saxon campaign, which he conducts for the king: *'belîbet bî den frouwen und traget hôhen muot'* (str. 174)

The plots of the two epics hinge on adultery: in the *Nibelungenlied* marriages are normal and contractual; only Gunther's is apparently broken; in *Tristan* Marke's marriage is really broken but remains a hindrance to the lovers. The substitution in the bridal chamber in each case leads to tragedy: Marke is deceived in *Tristan*, but the preservation of the lovers' honour proves impossible to maintain, so that their parting and death ensues; in the *Nibelungenlied* this deception leads to Sîfrit's murder, though he is innocent of adultery, being guilty of foolhardiness in taking Brünhilt's ring and girdle and presenting them to his wife, Kriemhilt, an act which causes him to be accused of boasting that he has deflowered Brünhilt. Thus adultery is left uncertain in the *Nibelungenlied* – in the *Þiðrekssaga* Sigurðr actually deflowers Brynhildr in the bridal chamber – and Sîfrit is apparently murdered for boasting to that effect. In *Tristan* the love-potion is the pivot of the story and the precarious adulterous relationship of the hero and the bride the basis for the episodic continuation of the story; Sîfrit's murder is central to the *Nibelungenlied*, for its consequences dominate Part II of the epic.

Another motif is connected with the theme of the relationship between the helper and the bride: in the Old Norse Eddic version of Siegfried's story the sword placed between Sigurðr and Brynhildr at their second meeting is a genuine earnest of Sigurðr's loyalty to Gunnarr; it would seem that this well-known motif, which occurs elsewhere in connexion with the bridal quest scheme,[14] has been replaced with the somewhat burlesque athletic contests and bridal chamber struggles by the *Nibelungenlied* poet. In *Tristan* the sword placed between the 'sleeping' lovers in the Cave of Lovers is a gesture that deceives Marke, whose vision is coloured by suspicion and lust for Isolde so that he suppresses his doubts in a state of wishful uncertainty about her fidelity.

In both epics an ambiguous oath is connected with the adultery, assumed or real: in the *Nibelungenlied* Sîfrit is prepared to swear an oath to the effect that he is innocent of adultery with Brünhilt, but Gunther, knowing full well that he is innocent, pronounces him guiltless even before he actually swears the oath (str. 860); in *Tristan* Isolde's deceptively worded oath at Caerleon saves her life and preserves the deception of her relationship with Tristan for a while. Like the oath Sîfrit does not swear it

---

14 See Gillespie, p. 251, regarding its use in *Orendel*.

deceives those not in the know, namely the bystanders in the tale, not the reader or listener.

The death of each hero is brought about by the machinations of a jealous woman, though in the *Nibelungenlied*, as opposed to the Old Norse versions of the story, Brünhilt's role in the plot to murder Sîfrit is played down and Hagen is made the chief plotter; in *Tristan* it is Isolde as blanschemains who delivers the false message that causes the wounded Tristan to die of grief. The women in the triangle, on the whole, show more determination, even ruthlessness than the men: Isolde even attempts the murder of Brangæne to preserve her reputation at court and has to be restrained from using his own sword against her 'enemy' Tristan. In the Old Norse version Brynhildr is the ruthless architect of Sigurðr's murder; in the *Nibelungenlied*, because of the poet's alteration of Kriemhilt's rôle to one of revenge on her brother for Sîfrit's death rather than on Etzel for the death of her brother, this ruthlessness has been transferred to her: she not only urges the Huns on to slaughter the Burgundians; she has the hall set on fire over their heads, and finally has Gunther beheaded, and decapitates Hagen herself with Sîfrit's sword, for which she is cut down by Hildebrant. In each case the main female characters are unwavering and lethally consistent: in *Tristan* the hero is uncertain of his own identity and that of his beloved when he is out of contact with her at Arundel; Kriemhilt, after Sîfrit's murder, uses people, especially the uxorious Etzel, to further her plan of vengeance; the fact that she meets her match in the relentless Hagen causes the general slaughter of the main protagonists in the *Nibelungenlied*.

Unity in death is reserved for the lovers in the part of the Tristan story not completed by Gottfried,[15] and Eilhart gives the traditional ending, where a rose and a vine are said to entwine above their common grave. In the Eddaic versions of the Nibelungen story Sigurðr and Brynhildr are laid together on the same funeral pyre; unity in death has been introduced symbolically in the *Nibelungenlied*, when Kriemhilt seizes Sîfrit's sword from Hagen and beheads him with it, an act that not only binds the originally separate two parts of the epic, but vividly brings back the memory of Sîfrit, her *vriedel* (str. 2372,3).

II

It is usual to infer that the *Nibelungenlied* poet used oral sources: the opening line of the poem suggests this unequivocally: *Uns ist in alten mæren* . . . (str. 1, 1), while references to hearing the story occur throughout

15   See Mohr, p. 295.

the epic. Gottfried in his *Tristan* sometimes says he has read certain matters (1314, 1806, 4576f, etc.), but at other times he refers to hearing them (4539, 6140, 9511, etc.). In spite of the fact that Gottfried's known source is a literary one, namely the version of Thomas, the Tristan story, like the story of Siegfried's death and the downfall of the Burgundians, had oral and variant versions, which may well have been recited by the same performers who purveyed the 'Spielmannsepen', in contrast to the mainly literary transmission of the Arthurian epic in Germany. The *Nibelungenlied* thus stems from oral poetry much akin to the branch of the Tristan story as related by Béroul and Eilhart in the late twelfth century. In this connexion it is interesting that the compiler of the *Þiðrekssaga* uses the personal names *Tristram* and *Isollde* for various characters in his work, which is packed with bridal quest themes reminiscent of the 'Spielmannsepik'; by the same token Eilhart refers to Dietrich and Hildebrant in his *Tristrant* (5973ff).[16] In each case one may assume varying repertoires to do with each hero, so that the heroes' characters would not be by any means consistently represented in each episode.

The author of the *Nibelungenlied* discards the adventurous exploits of Sîfrit's youth, leaving Hagen to outline the essentials for the mechanics of the plot (str. 87–100); he concentrates on the inevitable course of events and the interaction of the characters; he even satirises the Iceland bridal quest adventures and Sîfrit's feats in the bridal chamber to entertain his public; Sîfrit's barbaric style of hunting, too, somewhat downgrades the hero in the eyes of a courtly and sophisticated audience. Gottfried rejects the impossible 'spielmännisch' motif concerning Isolde's blonde hair being brought from Ireland to Cornwall by a swallow as nest-building material; but the elimination of such a detail does not interfere with the basic bridal quest structure and the series of adventurous deceptions of Marke inherent to the original story.

The *Nibelungenlied* and Gottfried's *Tristan* are each the ultimate courtly refinement of earlier somewhat cruder tales. In both epics an attempt is made to transcend the material, hence both abound in ambiguities, since the plots consist of basically episodic entertainment. The *Nibelungenlied* poet makes his attitude to his material clear by irony, burlesque, and non-committal observations; his main concern is the remorseless logic of events set in motion by the actions of the characters themselves. Sîfrit's murder and Kriemhilt's revenge reveal the anarchic power-seeking of a superficially courtly and Christian society, although the qualities of loyalty and honour are not ignored when it comes to the general conflict – honour and loyalty towards Sîfrit go by the board when Hagen's loyalty to Gunther and his own honour appear to be at stake; the illusory concept

16 Edited by F. Lichtenstein (Strassburg, 1877).

of *êre* destroys *minne* and *triuwe* at the end; but the poet does achieve his object, which is to show the desolate final judgement on a power-motivated society.

Both the *Nibelungenlied* and Gottfried's *Tristan* are the result of the developments in a type of story-telling outside that of the Arthurian romance; yet they were composed in the same cultural milieu and exhibit much of the same concern with courtly manners and chivalric values apparent in the Arthurian epics. The *Nibelungenlied* poet and Gottfried (much influenced by Thomas) have freed themselves to a large extent from the type-casting and stereotyped role-acting that they would have found in the older sources. Their poems in their very different ways are designed for sophisticated audiences, probably at the bishops' courts of Passau and Strassburg. Courtly society saw itself idealised in tales of antiquity and the chivalric world of Arthurian epic, both modelled on French prototypes.

The accommodation of the heroic epic with its native roots and different compositional traditions presented considerable difficulties when the attempt was also made to grapple with problems of contemporary society; in the *Nibelungenlied* there is a certain imbalance and resultant ambiguity arising from the conflict of genres; courtly love is overlayed on a stark tale of intrigue, murder, and violence. In *Tristan* the problem is similar, though the accommodation, already begun by Thomas, is taken further by Gottfried, who is more successful in achieving some sort of coherence in his characterisations than the *Nibelungenlied* poet, who has been more radical in altering the plots from his sources, thus constructing a well balanced and aesthetically satisfying work. In each case a courtly setting is given to a basically uncourtly and immoral tale; the level of irony with which the poets view this incongruity is not always easy to determine.

As Hugo Kuhn has pointed out,[17] the Arthurian romance has a mythical or fairytale structure, namely that of the 'Descensusmärchen', in which the woman is a partner of the hero in his reintegration into society; the 'Minneehe' introduced into this scheme by Chrétien de Troyes and the realisation by the hero of his proper place in courtly society is not found in either *Tristan* or the *Nibelungenlied* – Kriemhilt does little to transform Sîfrit fundamentally and is the innocent accomplice in his murder. Unlike Arthurian heroes, Sîfrit and Tristan learn nothing and do not develop through experience: Tristan remains a ruthless and charming trickster fettered, after drinking the love-potion, by a consuming passion beyond his control; Sîfrit remains oblivious to the hostility his prowess and over-

17   Kuhn, p. 16.

bearing, not to say loutish, behaviour arouses, a lack of perception that costs him his life.

Unlike the 'Spielmannsepik' and the Arthurian romance, both epics end in tragedy; the *Klage* attempts to resolve the Nibelungen tragedy in a Christian sense with a lament for the dead and their proper burial, while the part of the Tristan story uncompleted by Gottfried attempts to resolve the tragedy of their final parting through the union of the lovers in the grave. In both epics a tragic ending is foreordained, which is in direct contrast to the fate of Arthurian heroes who surmount all their curious difficulties. 'Alle Vorausdeutungen sind einheitlich auf die entscheidende Wirkung des Minnetrankes gerichtet: sie alle reden von Lösung aus der Welt, von Leid und Tod', states de Boor of Gottfried's *Tristan*.[18] Similarly, the overwhelming majority of 'epische Vorausdeutungen' in the *Nibelungenlied* point to Sîfrit's murder and Kriemhilt's subsequent revenge, which stem from the initial deception of Brünhilt contrived by Sîfrit with the use of the *tarnhût*. In each epic the tragic theme of *liebe unde leit* is mooted in the prologue (*NL* str. 1–19; *Tr* 1–244), but the train of tragic events is brought about through magic objects, which symbolise the inevitability of fate beyond human control.

Both poets knew the *Eneide* of Veldeke, in which the problems connected with passionate love are discussed. In Kriemhilt's discussion of her mother's interpretation of her dream of the falcon the *Nibelungenlied* poet has reworked a scene from Veldeke's *Eneide*,[19] in which Lavine discusses the nature of love with her mother, and her words,

> 'Muter, gebe daz sie muze
> Mich lange vormiden,
> Wie mochte ich die not alle geliden?' (9866–68)

are reflected in those of Kriemhilt to Uote:

> 'âne recken minne   sô wil ich immer sîn.
> sus scœn' ich wil belîben   unz an mînen tôt,
> daz ich von mannes minne   sol gewinnen nimmer nôt.'
> (str. 15,2–4)

and the argument of Lavine's mother:

> 'Nicht ne vurchte das ungemach,
> Mercke wie ichz bescheide.
> Michil liep kompt von leide . . .' (9870–72)

---

[18] de Boor, p. 288.
[19] Edited by G. Schieb and T. Frings, 3 vols (Berlin, 1964–70).

is reversed in Kriemhilt's reply to her mother's assurance that she will gain happiness through *mannes minne*:

> 'ez ist an manegen wîben   vil dicke worden scîn,
> wie liebe mit leide   ze jungest lônen kan.
> ich sol si mîden beide,   sone kan mir nimmer missegân.'
> (str. 17,2–4)

In the last two strophes of this first 'âventiure' the inevitable course and theme of the whole epic is stated, namely that, in spite of forswearing love for a time, Kriemhilt did become the wife of a brave warrior, whose murder she would avenge on her nearest kinsmen, causing the slaughter of many men (str. 18f). In this opening the seal is set on the whole course of the epic, and the importance of the love relationship between Sîfrit and Kriemhilt is emphasised, for it is Kriemhilt's excessive devotion to Sîfrit and her obsession with revenge for his murder that brings *leit* that began with *liebe* – the loss of Sîfrit's love together with the loss of his treasure and her own loss of status as his wife constitutes her *leit* (the tragic theme of love lost has, in the *Nibelungenlied*, been transferred from Brünhilt to Kriemhilt, if we regard the Old Norse versions of the Sigurðr-Brynhildr tragedy as representing the original story). Here the basic theme of sorrow following on the joy of love is superimposed on the inevitability of events in the traditional plots known to the audience, which are now welded into one whole by Kriemhilt's new role as avenger of Sîfrit's death. The theme runs as a leitmotif throughout the epic, particularly through the use of 'epische Vorausdeutungen' and is clearly restated at the end:

> mit leide was verendet   des küniges hôhgezît,
> als ie diu liebe leide   z'aller jungeste gît.   (str. 2378,3–4)

Gottfried also makes this theme central, and, in his prologue, he suggests that the superficial courtly world cannot accept the sorrow involved and thus forgoes the true experience of love (55ff). In *Tristan* love itself involves suffering: *leit* is integral to *liebe*, and it begins with the drinking of the love-potion – in the *Nibelungenlied* it begins with Sîfrit's murder. Even before Tristan's birth his mother Blanscheflur, apostrophising *minne*, has declared:

> 'din ende daz ist niht so guot,
> als du der werlde geheizest,
> so du si von erste reizest
> mit kurzem liebe uf langez leit . . . '   (1406–09)

Tristan and Isolde, having drunk the love-potion,

... waren beide einbære
an liebe unde an leide
und halen sich doch beide ... (11730–32)

but they are ensnared and their fate is sealed: *Tristan* becomes from then on the history of their *liebe* and their *leit* in conflict with their *êre*, their reputations at court, which, of course, cannot be maintained indefinitely. Put another way, their story consists of a string of episodes in which they skilfully hoodwink the cuckolded king, an aspect that Gottfried manages to blur.

III

In both epics the concept of *minne* stems from the lyric.[20] This concept of *hôhe minne* in the love lyric, which existed in ephemeral artistic performance, concentrates on the love relationship between a man and a woman within courtly society, but, because of the nature of the genre, in a short-winded way with aesthetic considerations largely, if not exclusively, in mind. Its conventions are rather uncomfortably accommodated to the narratives of both epics, which operate in a critical manner towards courtly society.

The rather male-orientated early Danubian lyric, such as that of the Kürenberger in a strophic form akin to that of the *Nibelungenlied*, is more closely related to that epic than is the lyric of 'hoher Minnesang'. The image of the falcon for the man is found in both (*MF*, 8, 33; *NL*, str. 13), and the adjectives *starc*, *schœn*, and *wilde*, with which Kriemhilt describes the falcon of her dream, would seem to characterise Sîfrit perfectly. In the supernatural world he robs the Nibelungen of their treasure and tricks Brünhilt into marriage with Gunther; in courtly circles he is the handsome epitome of good manners, uprightness and loyalty; yet, in contrast to his idealised courtship of her, he beats Kriemhilt for her part in the quarrel with Brünhilt.

The 'Minnehandlung' the poet has introduced for Sîfrit and Kriemhilt follows the conventional pattern of *hôhe minne*: Sîfrit's service with Gunther in the Saxon War and on the bridal quest to Iceland is, in fact, service (*dienst*) for the favour of Kriemhilt; when Kriemhilt first greets Sîfrit, love appears to be an ennobling experience: dô wart im von dem gruoze vil gehœhet der muot (str. 292,4). This is in direct contrast to Gunther's purely sensual love for Brünhilt. The poet presents Kriemhilt and Sîfrit as ideal courtly lovers:

20 de Boor, pp. 280–81.

> Er neig ir flîzeclîche;   bî der hende si in vie.
> wie rehte minneclîche   er bî der frouwen gie!
> mit lieben ougen blicken   ein ander sâhen an
> der herre und ouch diu frouwe.   daz wart vil tougenlîch getân.
>
> (str. 293)

which is offset by the rather earthy thoughts of some onlookers:

> Do gedâhte manec recke: 'hey wær' mir sam gescehen,
> daz ich ir gieng' enebene,   sam ich in hân gesehen,
> oder bî ze ligene!   daz liez' ich âne haz.'   (str. 296,1–3)

One wonders whether the poet is 'sending up' the highflown notions of *hôhe minne* here.

Gunther's lust is touched on with strong irony in the *Nibelungenlied* through the use of courtly love cliché when he picks out Brünhilt among her ladies watching the arrival of visitors at Îsenstein:

> 'Sô sihe ir eine   in jenem venster stân
> in snêwîzer wæte,   diu ist sô wolgetân;
> die welent mîniu ougen   durch ir sccenen lîp.
> ob ich gewalt des hête,   si müese werden mîn wîp.'   (str. 392)

However, his humiliation on the wedding night is complete when he is left hanging till daybreak by a nail on the wall, a scene which the poet described in terms that recall the dawn shining through a window on fulfilled lovers, a reference which an audience familiar with the contemporary *tageliet* would not have missed:

> dort muost' er allez hangen   die naht unz an den tac,
> unz der liehte morgen   durch diu venster schein.   (str. 639,2–3)

The real contrast to the newly fashionable code of courtly love comes when Kriemhilt's feelings for Sîfrit are shown to be so excessive that they can no longer constitute a courtly pastime: her passionate devotion drives her to overstate Sîfrit's superiority (str. 815) and provokes Brünhilt to utter her suspicions about Sîfrit's feudal relationship to Gunther, which leads on to their public quarrel and Sîfrit's murder; after the murder this excessive passion turns to an obsession with vengeance. The sophistication of courtly love is exposed as empty dalliance under the harsh wind of reality – after all Kriemhilt herself was used as a bargaining counter to retain Sîfrit's service at the Burgundian court, and she uses Etzel's uxorious infatuation for her in pursuit of her vengeance.

The love-potion and its magic power over Tristan is mentioned in the early lyrics of Veldeke and Bernger von Horheim (*MF*, 58,35ff; 112,1ff), which derive from a French source, namely Chrétien de Troyes; but it is employed there as a conceit emphasising the lover's genuine devotion as opposed to that of Tristan brought about by the potion. In *Tristan* the part played by the potion is uncertain, and courtly love outside the sphere of marriage is taken to its ultimate, even absurd conclusion, for the *hôhe minne* of 'Minnesang' can really only be sustained in the space of a song, though it is artificially sustained by Gottfried throughout the epic through masterly fiction; in the final analysis, it involves adultery and a clash with conventional society.

In *Tristan* concepts of courtly love are pursued as consistently as the story will allow, for the love-potion and the indulgence in sexual love have little to do with *hôhe minne* evident in such lyricists as Reinmar; and the theme of *Tristan* is, in fact, conflict with society, not compliance with courtly conventions. After drinking the love-potion the moral values of society are rejected by the lovers; with their banishment and their sojourn in the Cave of Lovers, they can live in perfect harmony with their inner life, separated from court. Through music they are lifted beyond the actual world, symbolised by the court, *ir aller werlt* (50), the world of accepted morality, even beyond the world of Arthurian romance (16763ff). As Werner Schröder has pointed out[21] such defiance of society and the poet's defence of it could more plausibly stem from the letters of Heloïse than from the mystical utterances of St Bernhard, this being an earthly tragedy demonstrating the devotion of the lovers to one another, even beyond sexual pleasure, in which the unconditional love of the woman and the disintegration of the man are revealed.

Gottfried overlays the basic problem with notions concerning the *edele herzen*, who alone can comprehend the concept of absolute love outside marriage in opposition to society: *hövescheit* subsumes the sensitivity they possess. His work is intended for educated courtiers, who might understand this attitude to a tale of representative lovers, but would hardly have followed their example, since it proved impossible for them to retain their reputation at court and at the same time pursue their love indefinitely. Gottfried's *Tristan*, in the first part a sophisticated 'Spielmannsgeschichte' still retaining many standard motifs of the genre, becomes, after the drinking of the love-potion, a work enshrining in symbolic language the relationship between ideal lovers and society and relating their experience of absolute love to music, the most abstract as well as the most sensuous of arts.

By blackening those in opposition to the lovers, Gottfried persuades us

---

21 Werner Schröder, *Text und Interpretation: Das Gottesurteil im 'Tristan' Gottfrieds von Straßburg*, Sitzungsberichte der wissenschaftlichen Gesellschaft an der Johann Wolfgang Goethe-Universität Frankfurt am Main, XVI, no. 2 (Wiesbaden, 1979), pp. 52ff.

to take their part, and he castigates Marke for his excessive surveillance of his wife (*huote*) (17848ff); Marke's love for Isolde is *valsch* according to the values of absolute love because it is sullied by suspicion and is motivated by physical desire alone. Gottfried, indeed, polemicises against superficial love in literature and purely physical lust without spiritual harmony,[22] the meeting of true minds; so Marke is condemned for his less than spiritual love for his wife. The lovers maintain their position in conventional society through deception; in the Cave of Lovers they live by a different set of rules in an aesthetic realm devised by the poet.

Despite their adulterous situation, the lovers, paradoxically, are still deeply concerned with their reputations in the eyes of courtly society; the narrator comments enigmatically:

> Swie sanfte uns mit der liebe si,
> so müezen wir doch ie da bi
> gedenken der eren.   (12507–09)

The balance between *minne* and *êre* cannot, however, be maintained indefinitely in this situation, and the end is unavoidably tragic.

In the *Nibelungenlied*, on the other hand, excessive *minne* and the deception of Brünhilt set off the train of events that ends in tragedy; the upholding of honour is based on an illusion (Sîfrit's supposed adultery) and is proceeded with unnecessarily: the foolhardy acceptance of the invitation to Hungary is criticised with common sense by Rûmolt; in the subsequent conflict the adherence to concepts of loyalty (*triuwe*) ensures the deaths of all the participants in the final conflict.

IV

Both poems go 'against the grain' in that they stand in contrast to the solutions of Arthurian romance. They differ considerably in their themes: *Tristan* is concerned with absolute love as opposed to marriage, while the *Nibelungenlied* deals with destructive power-politics. Both tragedies stem from excessive love, and in both works a tragic light is thrown upon the chivalric world with its concepts of courtly love, honour, and loyalty. To offset this tragic inevitability temporarily each author has indicated an ideal state of affairs by the introduction of an idyllic interlude before tragedy overwhelms the main characters, a tragedy which the audience would be awaiting; in each case images of ideal love are called up.

At Bechelâren, in the interlude inserted by the *Nibelungenlied* poet, the luxury and courtly manners of an ideal feudal society provide a background for young love; the betrothal of the youthful pair, Gîselher and

22 See de Boor, p. 290.

Rüedegêr's daughter, when Volkêr earns the gift of arm-rings with his love-songs, suggests what could be possible if the illusion of *êre* were not the overriding factor in the course of events, whereby the Nibelungen march on to their doom. In *Tristan*, Gottfried, following Thomas, has replaced the hardship of banishment to the forest wilderness by a sojourn in an idyllic setting, a *locus amoenus*, far removed from the chicanery and intrigue of court life and the tension of the lovers' efforts to continue their adulterous association undetected. However, their own courtly conditioning, which causes their concern for their reputations and the discovery of their place of seclusion by Marke necessitate their return to the life of hazard and conflict and ultimately to their parting and death.

Gottfried states his intention in his almost programmatic prologue, but does not really carry it out satisfactorily. In *Tristan* the author is dealing with a tale consisting of unending deception and skilful avoidance of exposure. The public of the original story and, perhaps, some of Gottfried's listeners would have been primarily interested in such typical escapades ('Schwänke') – it is, of course, noteworthy that it was Eilhart's *Tristrant* that was most widely read and became the basis for the later printed version of the story. Gottfried attempts to lift this picaresque tale – prompted by Thomas – to a different level, to a reflection on the nature of human love and the relationship of one human being to another within the restrictions and conventions of society; hence the enormous ambiguities in his poem and the inability of the critics to analyse it to a satisfactory conclusion. Like Tristan himself Gottfried is defeated, and this may be the reason for the unfinished state of his epic: the material cannot be bent to his stated intention; too much depends on pure chance, because the entertaining tale consists of linked adventurous episodes which the audience knew and expected.

In his idyll the *Nibelungenlied* poet presents the possibility of uncomplicated married happiness, denied to Kriemhilt herself and finally destroyed for the young couple by the illusory pursuit of honour, whereas Gottfried presents a mystical vision of absolute love divorced from the reality behind the situation of his story, namely an adulterous association continued in the face of the opposition of courtly society, whose ideals on honour and loyalty it is flouting. In the *Nibelungenlied* it is a defective society that is out of joint; in *Tristan* it is the lovers who behave in a socially disruptive manner; Gottfried tries to persuade us otherwise, but he achieves only partial success through various excursuses, possibly because he fails to alter the basic plot of his story radically, as the *Nibelungenlied* poet does – the episode of the Cave of Lovers is but an interlude. Gottfried Weber's assertion:[23] 'Dergestalt stellt sich Gottfrieds *Tristan* als

---

[23] Gottfried Weber, *Gottfried von Straßburg* (Stuttgart, 1962), p. 71.

Spiegel und Mitträger der Krise des hochmittelalterlichen Weltbildes dar, die in ihrem Zentrum eine Krise des Liebesphänomens, eine Krise um Eros und Agape ist', exaggerates and generalises the problem to do with a highly individual work. Hugo Kuhn, when summing up the main ingredients of the two epics comes nearer the mark,[24] when he states, 'Dort Hofintrigen und ein Ehebruchsprozeß in der Mitte – hier Machtkämpfe und ein Mord in der Mitte'; but this, too, is, perhaps, an oversimplification, since all four elements are to be found in each epic, if one includes Tristan's brutal assassination of Morgan. Our two poets have dealt with given plots in their different ways and have altered them to suit their different purposes, which tend towards criticism of certain concepts that we extrapolate from 'Minnesang' and Arthurian romance, but which may or may not have been generally accepted among courtly audiences.

[24] Kuhn, p. 7.

'Ez ist ein zunge, dunket mich':
Fiction, Deception and Self-Deception
in Gottfried's Tristan

JOAN M. FERRANTE

'Ez ist ein zunge, dunket mich.' It is appropriate that Brangaene identifies the poisonous tongue (9422) which would have killed Tristan, and that this is her first utterance in the poem. The tongue is a significant symbol for both of them. On the narrative level a tongue is implicated in their near-deaths, and on the symbolic level it represents their ability to use words to manipulate people and truth. Eloquence, in the mouth of a character or of a poet, can be good or bad, it can protect or deceive. The ambivalence of the symbol is inherited from Christian tradition, on the one hand the gift of tongues at Pentecost to spread the Word of God and Christ himself as the Word, on the other the tongue as a dangerous weapon (Psalms 52.2: 'Your tongue plots destruction; it is like a sharpened razor, you who practice deceit') which cannot be controlled (James 3.8: 'No man can tame the tongue. It is a restless evil, full of deadly poison.') The same ambivalence is reflected in Gottfried's attitudes towards words and speech, even towards the mode of fiction.[1]

Gottfried is not alone among serious medieval narrative poets in raising questions about his chosen mode. Chrétien de Troyes before him and

---

1 For various views on this topic, see Philip Grundlehner, 'Gottfried von Strassburg and the Crisis of Language', in *Spectrum Medii Aevi. Essays in Early German Literature in Honor of George Fenwick Jones*, edited by William C. McDonald (Göppingen: Kümmerle, 1983), 139–55; Samuel Jaffe, 'Gottfried von Strassburg and the Rhetoric of History' in *Medieval Eloquence*, edited by J. J. Murphy (Berkeley: University of California, 1978), 288–318; and Sherron E. Knopp, '*Daz honec in dem munde*. The Narrator and his Audience in Gottfried's *Tristan, Colloquia Germanica*, 16 (1983), 131–147, which I unfortunately did not see before I had written this paper and which makes similar points about the steward and Gandin. For an unusual and rich perspective on medieval views of truth, lies, fact and fiction, see Giles Constable, 'Forgery and Plagiarism in the Middle Ages', *Archiv für Diplomatik*, 29 (1983), 1–41.

Dante after, subvert their own authority and the validity of their message by having their leading characters abuse their powers of speech, and by setting up surrogate narrators who use fiction to serve their own not always elevated purposes. These poets were alert to the power of the Word (and of the word), and therefore, perhaps, wary of their own gifts. Anxious to persuade the audience of their message, they used the powerful tool of their eloquence, but aware of how easily that very eloquence might lead the audience astray, they simultaneously undercut it.

Though Gottfried goes out of his way to impress on us the importance of his story, particularly in the religious analogies of the prologue, and in the allegories of the investiture, the combat with Morolt, and the Minnegrotte, which suggest the deeper level of truth in his fiction, he also forces us to question his authority and the truth of his story by various means, of which I shall discuss three general areas. 1. He has all his leading characters, even the most honorable and the most sympathetic, abuse speech, by making rash promises and not keeping their word, by manipulating people and events through verbal traps, false inferences, and lies. 2. He sets up a series of surrogate narrators, story-tellers who use fiction to serve their own needs and to disguise the truth, and a hero who continuously provides a different version of his own story, all the while claiming that he (Gottfried) is telling the true version of the story. And 3., he uses the loaded symbol of the tongue in a series of episodes running through the poem, to stand for languages, poetry, music, eloquence, deception, and destruction. I shall now list various examples of these categories, since the sheer quantity is significant, and note the questions they raise.

Promises, oaths, are a constant motif, treated surprisingly casually by figures in authority, kings, queens, princes. Morolt accuses the Cornish of breaking their *triuwe* and *eit* (6355) to send tribute every year, an agreement Marke had been forced to make when he was unable to defend his land. Tristan answers the legal point, arguing that the agreement held only so long as the land could not be defended, and excuses Marke in this instance. But Marke continues to make promises he either will not be able to keep or hopes not to be held to: he has made Tristan his heir, not foreseeing the need to marry; when he is pressured to marry, he swears to have no one but Isot, thinking this can never happen (8520–22). Later when he is convinced of the lovers' innocence, he promises not to doubt them again, but of course he will. And least excusable of all, he makes an unqualified promise to Gandin, simply for the entertainment of the court, without any thought to the implications; when he tries to get out of it, Gandin offensively reminds him of the importance of a king's word and implies that he is unfit to rule (13222ff). Though Gandin is a *trügenære* (13202), who will be similarly deceived by Tristan, the emphasis in the episode is on Marke's fault, as king, in making such a promise. Gilan, also a ruler, makes the same kind of unqualified promise to Tristan (15946;

15954–56), though it is in the higher cause of saving his land. Nonetheless, when Tristan claims his dog, Gilan tries, somewhat ignobly, to buy his way out, pretending to offer more (half the land and his sister), whereas in fact nothing is so valuable to him as Petitcreiu (see 15908–11).

The Irish king, Isot's father, makes a very careful promise, a model in the context of this poem, to give his daughter to anyone who rids the land of the dragon, provided he is noble (8905–13). But even this oath gives rise to a series of claims and counter-claims, and covert promises, an episode filled with allusions to truth, reassurances of good faith, and lies, which do not show his court in the best light. Not only does his steward claim the princess, knowing he has not killed the dragon, with much talk of 'warheit: / küneges wort und küneges eit' (9817–18), but the queen, a woman of honor and responsibility, exacts promises both from Tristan, whom she has a right to distrust, and also from her own husband, whom she manipulates into promising more than he is comfortable with. He offers 'ich volge, swes ich volgen sol; / swaz ir wellet, deist getan.' But she insists 'habet irz danne an mich verlan?' until he says 'ja, swaz ir wellet, daz sol sin' (10634–38). One might argue that she will not use his promise against him, indeed she will help him to keep his original oath, and certainly she does not otherwise use words to manipulate people. But she does attempt to manipulate them in another way, by the potion, and by keeping its existence a secret, by hiding the truth about it, she accomplishes the single most destructive act of all.

Her daughter Isot provides the most glaring example of the misuse of an oath by a figure of authority, in this case a queen. But even before she swears the public oath with God as her collaborator, a 'gelüppeter eit' (15748) that is not only false in spirit, if true to the letter, but is also cast as a rather coarse joke suggesting a lack of respect for the official procedure and therefore for her position, she has already abused that position and the trust of a friend, by hiring two men to murder Brangaene. She makes them 'swern eide und eide, / triuwe über triuwe geben' (12716–17) that they will do her bidding – that is kill Brangaene, promising to knight them in repayment; but when they return, pretending to have done what she ordered, she turns on them and accuses them of murder. They are only saved from her wrath because they failed to keep their oath, an oath she should never have made them take. The horror of the attempted murder is compounded by the abuse of faith. Why does Gottfried make so much of these royal oaths? After all, if we cannot trust the words of kings and queens, why should we trust the words of a poet?

But it is not only by oaths and promises that characters in the story catch each other. There are less flagrant verbal snares: both Blanscheflur and Isot use veiled words (Blanscheflur's offended friend, 754–56, Isot's *lameir*, 11986ff) to draw Riwalin and Tristan into declarations of love; Marjodo and Brangaene manipulate Marke and Isot in a game of words, one to trap, the other to escape. They are like directors guiding their actors, Brangaene even changing Isot's script: 'einen niuwen brief sir aber do las, / waz aber ir rede solte sin' (14154–55), but the women's words prevail on the nights when physical caresses precede the conversation, that is when Marke is vulnerable to Isot's 'truth', which is false, and rejects Marjodo's true truth as lies.

It is of course disturbing that characters we do not respect, Marjodo, Melot, tell the truth, but far more disturbing that the ones we do respect lie. Although Gottfried tells us that Marke is better off when he does not know the truth, although Marke allows himself to be deceived by Minne, by his lust for Isot, we still cannot excuse Tristan and Isot for lying to him. Nor for lying to others. When Tristan tells various fictions to cover his arrivals in Ireland, we can accept them as harmless self-protection, but when he announces that he must lie ('den muoz ich liegen disen tac, / swaz ich in geliegen mac', 8705–06), he risks lowering himself to the steward's level. Why does Gottfried blur the already dim line between truth and fiction? Why does he make it difficult for us to make a distinction between fiction, which we can accept, and lying which we must deplore? Is he forcing us to look more closely at our own use of words, to make a distinction between the harmless fictions we tell and the destructive lies?

Is that why so many of the characters in the poem are story-tellers? All of them have some ulterior motive for telling their stories, most have something to gain by them. Some, like Marke and Melot, make up stories to deceive and trap their audience; others, Brangaene with the allegory of the 'zwei gewant' and Rual with his tale of Tristan's life, tell the truth as if it were a story, Brangaene to save her life, Rual to restore Tristan's identity. Rual is the only character who uses fiction for selfless motives. He had, in fact, created a fictional identity for Tristan in order to protect him and his land, and as soon as it is safe to do so, he reveals the truth, though even he cannot resist playing on the audience like any performer, building up the suspense of his tale to the climax of producing the ring. (In this case Tristan, the arch-performer, is simply part of the audience for the true story of his own life.)

Tristan, Isot, and Gandin, are performers of others' tales, but their talents give them potentially harmful powers, Gandin to take the queen, Tristan and Isot to control (distract) men's thoughts; Isot is compared to the sirens (an analogy that suggests very destructive powers) and Tristan's talents seduce Marke, the Irish, and, at the end of the poem, the unwitting Isot as blanschesmains, all of whom suffer as a result. In the case of the second Isot, Tristan is indulging himself with his art, singing about his first love, giving no thought to the fact that the girl of the same name who is listening will assume the songs are meant for her, taking no responsibility for the effects of his art. It is in fact only in the Minnegrotte, where they have no audience, that Tristan and Isot can perform without harm to others. But what does all this say about the poet's role? Does he, in fact, create fictions to satisfy himself and attract his audience, to win him favor and protection, fictions which may be comforting to the most receptive members of that audience, the *edelen herzen*, but which may well lead others astray? Does he have any sense of responsibility for the effects of his art on his audience? It is surely no coincidence that Gottfried describes both narrative poets and the goddess Minne as 'verwære' (4691; 11908); both use color to attract and to deceive.

What is the relation between content and embellishment, between truth and fiction in his story, or even between surface fiction and allegorical truth? The very word Gottfried uses most often to describe his story, *mære*, is highly ambiguous. It means, at different moments in the poem, 'story', 'report', 'rumor', 'news', any of which may be true or false. His source is sometimes *buoch*, sometimes *istorje* (particularly when he is speaking of national events, Morolt and the Roman sanction of the tribute, 5880, the war in Arundel, 18692, and Urgan's attacks on Gilan's land, 'diu ware istorje . . . von Tristandes manheit', 15915–16), but mostly it is *mære*, *daz ware mære*, or just *mære*. Gottfried frequently criticizes earlier versions (except for Thomas's) or rejects them out of hand, but he constantly refers to 'daz mære' as his source. Does he mean us to take his source as 'true' or simply as the correct version of the story, the one with the most true meaning in it, or the one with the message he prefers? Does he imply that its 'truth' derives from historical events (which I think unlikely) or from his interpretation?

Gottfried carefully sets up an identification between himself and his story-telling hero: in the prologue, when he criticizes those who envy art and cleverness instead of honoring and praising them, as his world presumably does, and as Tristan's certainly does to him – one might even say that it is envy and criticism which ultimately turn Tristan's talents against his friends. Later, at the time of the investiture, instead of describing the ceremony, Gottfried describes his hero's clothes allegorically and goes on to a long discussion of contemporary poets, reserving his highest praise for lyric poets – for him, as for his hero, music and poetry are more important than chivalry.[2] Gottfried uses allegory at key moments in the poem, in the prologue, the investiture, the battle with Morolt, and the Minnegrotte, to suggest a deeper level of truth to his fiction. Indeed, he

---

2 For studies of Tristan as an artist, see Hannes Kästner, *Harfe und Schwert. Der höfische Spielmann bei Gottfried von Straßburg* (Tübingen: Niemeyer, 1981), Wolfgang Mohr, 'Tristan und Isold als Künstlerroman', *Euphorion*, 53 (1959), 153–74, W. T. H. Jackson, 'Tristan the Artist in Gottfried's Poem', *PMLA*, 77 (1962), 364–72, and my 'Artist Figures in the Tristan Stories', *Tristania*, 4 (1979), 25–35.

uses the allegorical interpretation of the encounter between Morolt and Tristan (the four against four) to claim a greater truth for his version than for any others ('swie ich doch daz nie gelas / an Tristandes mære, / ich machez doch warbære,' 6874–76). In his reliance on allegory at crucial moments, Gottfried may be suggesting yet another connection with his hero, whose fictions frequently hide a truth, though he may not be aware of it.

Tristan's major fictions come at his arrival in Cornwall and on his two trips to Ireland, where he is attempting to create an identity for himself that will either protect him or help him get what he has come for, and in each case the fiction contains allegorical truths. He tells the first people he meets in Cornwall, the pilgrims, that he was born in this country, that he was supposed to hunt but lost his way, that his horse plunged down a gulley and disappeared, leaving him to wander without direction. We know, as he does not, that he was in fact conceived in this country, that he is on a quest (hunt) to find his destiny, that passion (the horse) will plunge him into danger and disgrace, and that he will go off into exile. To the next group he meets, the hunters, he tells another story, which begins like a tale, 'jensit Britanje lit ein lant' (3097), as though he were beginning to enjoy his new role. Because they are of this land, he cannot claim to be, so he tells them the reverse of the tale he told the pilgrims, saying he is the son of a merchant and curiosity led him to wander abroad. Curiosity did lead him to the kidnappers' ship and he will later play the role of a merchant, a minstrel-turned-merchant. In a sense, a minstrel is a merchant, selling himself and his wares to a receptive audience, a messenger between cultures. In another sense, Rual, the only father Tristan knows at this point, can be considered a merchant: in his political role he trades and bargains to make the best deal for his land and his young lord. (He accepts this identity, metaphorically, later when he tells Tristan 'ich han lange . . . mine marschandise . . . durch dinen willen her getriben', 4353–57). Tristan will also be a merchant in the political sense in his relations with the Irish, by arranging the marriage between Isot and Marke, selling them a political alliance they do not want, and bargaining for the return of all the Cornish hostages as Isot's dowry. But he is a merchant in a more insidious way: he traffics in people and their affections. Isot will say bitterly that she was bought and sold ('ine weiz, wie ich verkoufet bin, / und enweiz ouch, waz min werden sol', 11590–91); and Gottfried says that Tristan and Isot traded on Marke's love for Tristan to hide their affair ('mit der verkouften si vil, / mit der ertrugens ir minnenspil', 13003–04).

When he goes to Ireland to be cured of the first wound, Tristan spins an elaborate set of fictions, pretending to go to Salerno, pretending to be dead (he will return 'ein niuborner man', 8313), saying he is a minstrel who became a merchant's partner out of greed (many at court would see his relationship to Marke in that light). He tells the queen he is 'Tantris', and certainly the minstrel is the reverse side of the knight; finally, he gets himself away from the Irish court, whose hold over him is becoming too strong, by claiming a wife at home, probably a reference to his loyalty to Marke which is endangered by his new relationships. And when he returns on the bride-quest, he presents himself to the coastguard as a merchant seeking goods (Isot in fact), and as a helpless minstrel-turned-merchant to the queen, suiting his story to his audience.

By embedding a truth at an allegorical level in these fictions, is Gottfried being the hidden glossator of Tristan's story, asking his audience to dig for the real meaning beneath the surface fictions? Are we to do the same with his poem? And if we are, why does he cast such doubts on Tristan's motives? We are at first inclined to contrast him, despite his fictions, with the steward, who lies for the most obvious self-serving purpose, to marry a woman he does not deserve, claiming to have killed a dragon he cannot overcome even after it is dead. But is there such a difference between them (off the battlefield)? Tristan has certainly killed the dragon, but he has done so in order to win Isot for the enemy of her country, to get himself off the hook with Marke's courtiers, as if she were simply a political commodity and not the highly gifted individual he helped form. It is no accident that Tristan is nearly killed by the serpent's tongue he put in his bosom, with its implications of the destructiveness of deceptive fictions. Though it is the tongue in Tristan's possession which gives the lie to the steward's claims, it also raises serious moral questions about his use of fiction and therefore, inevitably, about the author's use of fiction. Is Gottfried also fashioning such a beautifully seductive tale to serve his own purposes in his own court, pretending to offer an exalting example of love to his audience, but less concerned with the harmful effect such a story might have on them than he is with putting down his rivals and securing his own place? It is surely significant that the last deception the poet-hero practices with words in the poem is self-deception, when he allows himself to confuse the second Isot with the first because of her name. As Tristan falls into that trap, Gottfried stops/ends the poem.

The symbolism of the dragon's tongue in Tristan's bosom is related to the other 'tongues' in the poem. The 'tongue' references seem to cluster at certain points in the story, in the description of the hero's youth, in the literary excursus, on the bride-quest, in the attempted murder of Brangaene, in the Minnegrotte, and at the separation. *Zunge* means both the physical organ, which is connected with the expression of words and of music, and also language.

In the excursus, *zunge* refers to all three, in the gifted use of contemporary poets. Tristan has the same gifts and will use them to win favor in all the foreign courts he visits. Though it is in the limited sense of language that Gottfried uses *zunge* in Tristan's early life, his gift for foreign tongues seems to be connected with his gift for story-telling and for playing a variety of musical instruments. His ability to express himself in different modes, to give different versions of the same material (he plays and sings in Breton, Welsh, Latin, and French, 3627–28) is related to his tendency to present himself in different guises and roles. It is therefore also connected with his ability to deceive, perhaps with magic powers as well; on the bride-quest he can speak the Irish language but the Cornish barons cannot (8533, 10874), therefore he can manipulate people and events, while they can only wait. That he is always a foreigner, always an outsider, is emphasized by the fact that people instinctively address or describe him in French, as they do Isot, as though the talents of both of them and later their love made them different, exotic, as though their love made them more at home in French romance (the *geste*, 8942), than in German. Other characters who have some connection with romantic love, Gandin, Gilan, even the steward, also use French. Tristan is moved to French by the sight of Tintajel (3159–60), where his parents met, and the temple of love, the Minnegrotte, is the 'fossiure a la gent amant' (16700).

The first two clusters of *zunge*, in Tristan's youth and in the excursus, are positive, suggesting only the ability to communicate, to please. There is no hint of the darker side, the side that predominates in the next two clusters, around the dragon-killing and the attempted murder of Brangaene. Here the tongue's power to harm and destroy the user as well as the object of its attack, dominates. Although the tongue is the proof of Tristan's claim to have killed the dragon, and therefore represents his power to win Isot (by languages and music more than by arms), it also represents the dangers of verbal powers. Why does Tristan take the tongue, rather than the head? Of course it is more portable, easier to handle as words are easier to manipulate than wisdom, but the steward goes for the head without even thinking of the tongue, and later when he defeats Urgan, Tristan will take the hand, the symbol of action, which points to the new direction his life is taking. If the head represents wisdom and the tongue eloquence, it is clear that the head without the tongue (wisdom without expression) is impotent, but the tongue without the head (eloquence without wisdom) is dangerous. The steward makes a fool of himself, Tristan is nearly killed, and the court in which they meet is thrown into a confusion of lies, insults, hidden identities and conflicting promises. The negative aspect of the tongue points ahead to the life of deception and danger Tristan will lead because of his affair with Isot.

The attempted murder of Brangaene picks up the same themes. Isot commands Brangaene's head to be cut off and her tongue to be brought back as proof of her death (12732–35). But Brangaene uses both while she still has them to buy time with the killers and to convince Isot of her loyalty. So the tongue which Isot had feared as a threat, because of its ability to reveal the truth and betray her, becomes a major instrument in disguising the truth and protecting her. When Brangaene finally runs out of words in the orchard, Marke discovers the lovers in bed. That is the end of the physical (and the deceitful) phase of the love.[3]

But with the gift of Petitcreiu, the love had already begun a new stage in which the lovers could subsist on the knowledge of mutual desire and of shared suffering. In this stage the lovers' tongues can return in the Minnegrotte to their early, pure meaning, of poetry and music. They play and sing with hands and tongues, they are entertained by the 'süeziu zunge' of the birds (the metaphor Gottfried had used for poets in the excursus), 'diu da schantoit und discantoit / ir schanzune und ir refloit' (17370–72), the purest music of all, nature's wordless art.

But the lovers cannot remain alone in the Minnegrotte, with the purity of their tongues. They must return to the world and ultimately accept separation. At the moment of separation, they make their first (and last) long declarations of love (18266–85; 18288–358), sealed by a kiss and Isot's gift of the ring. Isot's grief is now beyond words, 'ir zunge in ir munde / diu gesweic ir dicke zuo der not' (18482–83), as Blanscheflur's was when Riwalin died ('ir clage starp in ir munde; / ir zunge, ir munt, ir herze, ir sin, / daz was allez do da hin', 1738–40). The grief of the women is too deep for words, but Tristan goes off with his tongue ('Tristandes zunge und min sin / diu varnt dort mit ein ander hin', 18527–28), and uses it to assuage his grief by singing about Isot. Unfortunately his songs deceive the other Isot ('Tristan hæt ir so vil gelogen / mit disen . . . handelungen der ougen unde der zungen', 19398–400), and she devotes all her skills to winning him. Having deceived her with his tongue, he then elaborately deceives himself, to justify accepting her love. Though he withstands her advances three times, he gives in on the fourth, persuading himself that the queen has failed him. What seems to trouble him most is that she has not sent a message to him, as though she did not care what had become of him. What he needs then, is her words to keep his love alive. Without them, he looks elsewhere for comfort.

It is on that bitter note of betrayal and self-deception that Gottfried stops the poem. If, as some of us believe, he chose to end the poem here, why did he leave a story that began with such exalted claims on such a negative note? Had he, like his poet-hero, with his great gifts and high aspirations, finally just deceived himself and his audience? Is his poem, the most effective expression of the most powerful love-story in the

---

3 There are structural hints in the two long digressions, 11.12183ff and 17770ff, which mark off the physical affair between the drinking of the potion and the separation in the orchard, that there would be no more sexual contact after, as there had been none before, hence that the returns which take up much of the remaining story would not be appropriate.

Middle Ages, finally, for all its beauty and artistry, a tale of self-indulgence and self-deception? And why did he choose to tell it? Was it to guide the *edele herzen* to a higher form of love, or to demonstrate his gifts and his powers over his audience, no matter where it led them? Did he finally undo himself and his work by the gifts of his own tongue?

Finding, Guarding, and Betraying the Truth: *Isolde's Art and Skill, and the Sweet Discretion of her Lying in Gottfried's* Tristan

LESLIE SEIFFERT

> When my love swears that she is made of truth,
> I do believe her, though I know she lies,
> That she might think me some untutor'd youth,
> Unlearned in the world's false subtleties.
>
> Thus vainly thinking that she thinks me young,
> Although she knows my days are past the best,
> Simply I credit her false-speaking tongue:
> On both sides thus is simple truth suppress'd.
>
> But wherefore says she not she is unjust?
> And wherefore say not I that I am old?
> O Love's best habit is in seeming trust,
> And age in love loves not t'have yeares told.
>
> > Therefore I lie with her, and she with me,
> > And in our faults by lies we flattered be.
>
> W. Shakespeare, Sonnet 138

Shakespeare's lyric lover is allowed the privilege both of effecting some sort of accommodation with circumstances in which both he and his partner are being less than straightforwardly truthful, and also – more pleasingly and more effectively still – of enshrining this accommodation in an equivocal dialectic; this in turn is worked through in the framework within which a sonnet can capture an instant and make it immortal. He thus pulls off an intellectual coup whose sophistical benefits Tristan's uncle and Isolde's husband King Marke – a figure of romance who must respond to fresh circumstances with each new episode – could never quite be allowed the luxury of enjoying.

'Simply I credit . . .': if only, for *der einvalte Marke*, it could be just as simple as that! If only, like our Shakespearean figure, he could just seek to hold on to some such simple version of the marriage of love and truth. It would no doubt be at best no more than relatively simple, and a moral problem would still remain, but the resultant *Lebenslüge* would avert the pitiful situation into which he finds himself manoeuvred. For the lovers in their turn there would be the prospect of averting the tragic outcome of frustrated *triuwe* that cannot but lead to their deaths from one or other form of *leit*.

Or again: 'O Love's best habit . . .': if only Marke, in the not inconsiderable *bescheidenheit* remaining to him, had been able to reach even so unworthy an accommodation with at any rate a 'seeming' trust!

Thus, although so many of the equivocations in the sonnet prompt us to recall the romance, the contrast of genres also confronts us with telling differences. Of course these might, in a back-handed way, serve to highlight the extent to which some such *zwivel* might yet have been commended to Marke; but since Gottfried's story, unlike the sonnet, tells us so much about the whole situation, it would after all be idle for us to indulge, with Shakespeare's protagonist, in any such game of 'wherefore'. For one thing, we know very well why Isolde does not admit 'she is unjust': by so damaging an admission she would, as a confessed adulteress plainly guilty of high treason, be offering herself to the executioner. Nor is Marke's age, as such, an issue: one may glimpse something of a generational anomaly in his marriage, upon which there further supervenes a relationship between his nephew and this wife whom that nephew was sent to court and win for him; but it does not emerge from this that his age is being set off in any disabling or disqualifying way against Isolde's youth.

Christopher Ricks, whose observations on this Sonnet 138[1] first prompted the train of reflection that has led to my making it the epigraph of this paper, pointed out certain properties of the pun of *lie* with *lie* which has been such a feature of the English language since *c.*1300 and which, by thus marrying love-making with truth and untruth, is such a testing pun, and one of great potential power:[2] it does not, like *whole/holy*, call for recognition of an original 'congruity which prevailed in [the] etymologi-

---

1   Christopher Ricks, 'Lies', *Critical Inquiry*, 2 (1975), 121–42; a different type of problem, focusing less on cognition and art than on the question of how far men may be exculpated for lethal acts they perform under authority or within a system of discipline (the 'Nuremberg defence'), is addressed by Stephen Vizinczey in the title essay (pp. 281–96) of his collection *Truth and Lies in Literature* (London: Hamish Hamilton, 1986).

Chapters in Sissela Bok, *Lying: Moral Choice in Public and Private Life* (Hassocks, Sussex: Harvester, 1978) of particular relevance are viii 'Lies in a Crisis' (pp. 107–22), ix 'Lying to Liars' (pp. 123–33, with Sonnet 138 as one of its epigraphs) and x 'Lying to Enemies' (pp. 134–45); this wider range of problems would prevent me from containing the discussion within the bounds of this paper (but can be taken up on other occasions of the kind alluded to in my final remarks).

2   Bok, p. 133 and *passim*; there is a vast literature on the evident inescapability of puns and their integrality to natural languages (cf. now Walter Redfern, *Puns* (Oxford: Blackwell, 1986).

cal root' of the two terms;[3] nor is it of that 'right-angled or antithetical kind' that enables *cleave* 'cut apart' to play against *cleave* 'cling together';[4] nor yet again does it offer 'intimations of a metaphorical relationship, in which each of the two words may be seen under the aspect of the other', as when *heart/hart* and *dear/deer* may interplay so as to allow love to be viewed as a chase (or to allow the chase to be viewed as some analogue of lovemaking).[5] (Though it is not uninteresting to be told that a technical term 'to lie' has reference to a posture of self-defence in fencing, so that Shakespeare's pun may have some further sporting resonance.)[6]

And as Ricks further points out, taking up a point from Edmund Leach, the pun does not appeal to the sort of linking or associative opposition that can operate among the names of beings that are subjects or objects of taboo (as when the females – or feminine/effeminate beings – referred to by *queen/quean* have a common feature of 'abnormal status', taken respectively in a positive, highly virtuous sense, and in a negatively charged sense or even, for some users, a dubious or sinful sense having reference to uncertain sex or depraved character).[7]

Yet precisely this sense of handling matters of great power may after all pervade the way this perhaps historically accidental pun of English *lie* with *lie* proved over many centuries so challenging and so fascinating; and Shakespeare offers a complex instance of a poet choosing, almost to

---

3   Ricks, p. 132; the whole word-field of 'patient'/'patience' and 'suffering' is built around equivocations of this kind (cf. A. V. C. Schmidt, 'The Inner Dreams in *Piers Plowman*', *MAe*, 55 (1985), 24–40, commenting that '[*Piers Plowman*] will go on to show that if there *is* an answer to the problem of why God "suffers" evil, it must lie in the possibility that God can also, in a more literal sense, "suffer" ' (pp. 34, 39, n. 33); similar word-fields, germane to the topic of this paper, are grouped around the terms 'trial' and 'temptation', and about various senses of the word 'case'; a German example with considerable bearing on our topic turns on the etymological link of *lügen* with *(ver)leugnen*, cf. remarks below (and also n. 45 below) on *daz guldine lougen*.

4   Ricks, p. 132; and cf. 'arms' that embrace in love and 'arms' that seek offensively or defensively to kill in war – alike in Chaucer (T. McAlindon, 'Cosmology, contrariety and the Knight's Tale', *MAe*, 55 (1985), 41–57 (p. 53)) as in recent posters making a point about 'all the arms we need'.

5   Ricks, p. 132; readers of *Sir Gawain and the Green Knight* need no reminding of how the chase and love-making can be played off against one another: cf. W. R. J. Barron, '*Trawthe' and treason: the sin of Gawain reconsidered. A thematic study of 'Sir Gawain and the Green Knight'* (Manchester: U.P., 1980), ch. I 'Hunting and wooing' (pp. 1–35); Marcelle Thiébaux, *The Stag of Love: The Chase in Medieval Literature* (Ithaca, N.Y.: Cornell U.P., 1974); Gerald Morgan, 'The Action of the Hunting and Bedroom Scenes in *Sir Gawain and the Green Knight*', *MAe*, 56 (1987), 200–16.

6   Ricks (pp. 130f) cites Douglas Hamer's review of P. Martin, *Shakespeare's Sonnets: Self, Love and Art*, *RES*, n.s. 25 (1974), 78 (though he does not endorse all of Hamer's conclusions).

7   Edmund Leach, 'Anthropological Aspects of Language: Animal Categories and Verbal Abuse', in E. H. Lenneberg, *New Directions in the Study of Language* (Cambridge, Mass.: M.I.T. Press, 1964, p/b 1966), pp. 23–63 (p. 25), cited in Ricks, p. 133.

the point of obsession, to lay its ambiguities and ambivalences under contribution.

Our contemporary culture (unless the psychiatrist's couch counts as 'the modern secular counterpart to the confessional's kneeling'),[8] may have different obsessions about the postures appropriate to truth; nevertheless Ricks can conjure up an ample tradition in which recumbency has marked 'the great moments or endurances of truth: the child-bed, the love bed, the bed of sleep and dreams, the sickbed, the death-bed, the grave'.[9]

But while such a pun – alluding to recumbency as the seemly posture of truth and to mendacity as its seeming antithesis – evidently enjoys an immense fullness of power in its playful way with truth, this must after all owe something to a poetic justice that highlights a pre-existent dialectic whose philosophical value would hold independently of the availability of such a pun – in German therefore without this pun as much as in English with it. In such a dialectic, a lie, as a finely tuned antithesis to whatever truth is its putative thesis, might so admirably serve the ends of truth – revealing truths in the form of paradox, unmasking other lies, discrediting false pretensions, sorting out astonishing but true events from mere frauds[10] – as to sustain a claim to be 'made of truth'.

It may be no more than a wonderful coincidence that Modern English readers, as witnesses to Isolde's poisoning of truth with her oath,[11] can think of her, in such Shakespearean terms, as 'lying with' two men: her lord and king (who, in not the best of faith, has responded to her offer to submit to any form of judgement that his council might propose by subjecting her, his queen, to the rigours of this shameful form of law) and her lover the king's nephew (who, in somewhat treacherously good faith, has come to be fleetingly but tellingly at her side as she prepares for her ordeal); and since the drifts and tides of phonological and analogical change in our two cognate languages have not enduringly yielded the

---

8   Ricks, p. 131.
9   Ibid.
10 Christopher Ricks's paper had been read to a meeting of anthropologists, philosophers, politicians, historians and poets on 'Lying and Deceit' (St Catherine's Society, Cumberland Lodge for the Royal Anthropological Institute) studying issues such as self-deception, testing the truth value of miracles, separating valid miracles from frauds, and ensnaring a villain by an elaborate lie constructed by the detective (Mary Douglas, 'Is one man's truth ever another man's lie?', *THES*, 8.3.1974, p. 2); on 'lying to unmask liars', cf. Bok, pp. 123–25.
11 'ir gelüppeter eit' (15748). Quotations are from the edn by Rüdiger Krohn (*Gottfried von Strassburg, 'Tristan', nach dem Text von Friedrich Ranke neu herausgegeben, ins Neuhochdeutsche übersetzt, mit einem Stellenkommentar und einem Nachwort* (Stuttgart: Reclam, 1980)); reference will also be made to the commentary in the edn by Peter F. Ganz (*Gottfried von Straßburg, 'Tristan', nach der Ausgabe von Reinhold Bechstein* (Wiesbaden: Brockhaus, 1978)); translations are cited from A. T. Hatto's Penguin Classics rendering (1960).

same pun in both of them, it might seem difficult to share this coincidence with German readers except through our common pride in Shakespeare.

MHG *ligen* and *liegen* could of course have merged in sound, while being kept apart in writing: for a time they did so, even in High German, and when you read your Luther, you have to be watchful not to mistake the force of *ich liege*.[12] But Standard German has maintained the distinction, adopting for the verb of mendacity an originally regional rounding of [i:] to [y:]. If you view a language as the means by which a community receives and creates (or recreates) its system of values, and look therefore in diachronic study not just to the mechanics of sound change or to the chance fortunes of borrowing, but also to proportionality and analogy in the system of signs and the values of which those signs are the medium, then the link of the verb to the noun (MHG *lüge*/ NHG *Lüge*) is a clue to a motivation for this preference for the rounded variant, which reconstitutes the analogy holding between verb and noun (the more so as the levelling of MHG *louc/lugen* under NHG *log/logen* meant that there was no longer any vowel in the verb system to match the umlauted *ü* of the noun).

But if Standard German, in the interests of maintaining proportion and analogy within a derivational word-field, has passed up a poetic opportunity for a rich and revealing word-play between *liegen* and *lügen*, it has not thereby lost the philosophical capacity for operating with the dialectics of truth and untruth. Moreover, on another front, German has maintained a morally crucial consonance historically obtaining among another highly significant set of words, a foursome (two nouns, two verbs) central to a heavily loaded and highly valued word-field: for the rhyming match of MHG *liegen* and *triegen* has been kept up in the NHG verbs *lügen* and *betrügen*.

(Admittedly, as between the cognate nouns of this word-field, the simplexes in the archaic phrase *Lug und Trug* have maintained the rhyme more perfectly than have the currently standard forms – not even of the same gender! – of the *nomina actionis die Lüge* and *der Betrug*. However, vowel modification as between cognate words – only slightly obscuring the basic vocalic identities that are in play – is a morphological commonplace that plays its elegantly harmonic part among the system-building features of word-formation, while the derived *nomina agentis Lügner* and *Betrüger* have with the perfect harmony of their vowels at any rate maintained assonance.)

---

12 'Vnd das nicht yemand hie dencke / ich liege', *Sendbrief vom Dolmetzschenn* (Nuremberg, 1530; Wittenberg, 1530), edited by Karl Bischoff (Tübingen: Niemeyer, 1965), pp. 12/13: clearly, whether or not he could help standing, he was not to be caught lying.

I
FINDING, GUARDING AND BETRAYING THE TRUTH

Finding truth in a king's own 'great matter' [13]

We need to consider one further conceptual issue before we turn to the details of that episode in which Isolde, with God's conniving aid, purges (and perjures) herself by submitting to the humiliation of the ordeal by red-hot iron. What is being brought to light in this episode, despite the disingenuously calculating way in which some of the participants try to work on God as the guarantor of truth, is not some pure form of God's truth alleged to exist *sub specie aeternitatis*. Nor can we accept an argument that God, in helping Isolde, has been deceived, or has deceived himself: any blasphemy in Gottfried's presentation of God's and Christ's decision for Isolde (and against her traducers) cannot run to implying that the persons of the Trinity, even as personages in the story, do not know at least as much as Gottfried's hearers do – which as far as this 'great cause' or 'weighty matter' is concerned is effectively the whole truth.

But King Marke, on whose degree of conviction all possibility for action in the story turns, enjoys no such privilege. Nor do even those members of his court who could be said to know what is really going on, for they still have their work cut out to establish that their case is indeed the case: the story turns on an elaborate interplay between suspicion hardening into certainty in the minds of certain representative members of the court, and a scruple of doubt entertained along with many other scruples and fancies and hopes (or despairs) by the King.

Now this very social romance has not only set its two most highly profiled individual figures in a society that they need, and which even needs them, but to which they come as aliens or interlopers and in which they remain strangers (both of them at different times subjected to banishment and exile),[14] but it has also set the King in a most complex relation to

---

[13] Variants on expressions like 'great cause' or 'weighty cause' occur in the exchanges in 1533 between Henry VIII and his newly appointed Archbishop of Canterbury, Thomas Cranmer, when the annulment of the King's marriage with Catherine of Aragon was at last to be expedited (Jasper Ridley, *Henry VIII* (London: Constable, 1984), p. 218; John Bowle, *Henry VIII* (London: Allen & Unwin, 1964), p. 168; and J. J. Scarisbrick, *Henry VIII* (London: Eyre & Spottiswoode, 1968), p. 310); Scarisbrick uses the expression 'great matter', which is the form of words in which this phrase, with Cranmer's obsequiously discreet epithet, has become proverbial (cf. Ridley, heading to ch. 11, and Bowle, heading to ch. X).

[14] Wolfgang Mohr, 'Tristan und Isold als Künstlerroman', *Euphorion*, 53 (1959), 153–74, on the tension arising because the lovers are born for their society and need it, yet suffer from a 'Disproportion' obtaining 'zwischen den beiden Einsamen und dem Leben in der grossen Welt' (p. 163); cf. the theme of 'Disproportion mit dem Leben' that had been the subject of an exchange between Mohr ('Parallelen zwischen deutscher

his court: as Herbert Kolb observes, he may be, but he does not have to be, the centre of the court,[15] and the court is never more likely to find its own centre than when making itself guardian of its own and of its King's honour.[16] Yet before public opinion can be given executive effect, action has to be mounted with the King after all at its centre.

And so, in the complex interactions of so social a romance, what is most pointedly at issue is the way knowledge gets to be established in the minds of earthly knowers who, being in the story, have no vantage point (such as an author or hearer might be deemed to share with God) from which to judge the matter. But if they enjoy privileges like royal office and dignity, then it may be incumbent upon them to act in a very determined way once what is the case has supposedly been determined, and they will not escape very harsh judgement (by other persons in the story, by hearers, by the author) if they fail to act in a manner consonant to the case.

Marke's problem begins with the constitutional nicety, noted by Herbert Kolb, that he cannot, as a private individual might, set aside his own suspicions or act on his own fond hopes: in his responsibility to his court, he must allow suspicions publicly entertained to crystallize as charges to be purged before a court.[17] One can go further: even as a private individual, Marke ought not to act rashly or damagingly on the basis of mere suspicion; all the more so as King, whose word might mean someone's death, must he be content with nothing less than truth, safely and soundly established. Establishing knowledge in such a framework means working on the mind of a knowing subject, and we have here a case study of an especially delicate kind, for that subject is the King; what is at issue is the King's own 'great matter'; and the person whose supposed betrayal of trust is so humiliatingly under examination is his lady the Queen.

Moreover, once a form of judicial process has been invoked, with the King as *Gerichtsherr*, and once knowledge of a certain kind is established for certain in his and the public mind – and especially if what is thus established is that the Queen, as an adulteress, is *eo ipso* a traitress as well,

Dichtung des Mittelalters und der Neuzeit', *Euphorion*, 50 (1956), 129–61 (p. 143)) and Emil Staiger ('Lessing: *Minna von Barnhelm*', now in E. S., *Kunst der Interpretation* (Munich: dtv, 1971), pp. 63–81).

15 Herbert Kolb, 'Der Hof und die Höfischen. Bemerkungen zu Gottfried von Strassburg', *ZDA*, 106 (1977), 236–52 (p. 238); cf. now (on a 'Doppelgesichtigkeit' of society, to which the lovers respond not by fleeing society once and for all, but by seeking to return to it, as leading members in it and supporters of it) Walter Haug, 'Gottfrieds von Straßburg "Tristan": sexueller Sündenfall oder erotische Utopie?', in *Kontroversen, alte und neue*, Akten des VII. Internationalen Germanisten-Kongresses, Göttingen, 1985 (Tübingen, 1986), vol. 1, pp. 41–52 (pp. 46–47).

16 Kolb, p. 240.

17 Kolb, p. 241.

guilty of a high crime or misdemeanour – then the King will be bound, unless his prerogative of mercy can be properly invoked, to act to judicially murderous punitive effect. (The sentences Ísönd defiantly invokes in the *Saga*, ch. LVI,[18] are burning at the stake, or quartering.) So we are dealing not just with knowledge to be established, but with knowledge that, as it confirms a public scandal, will in consequence crown Isolde's ordeal by putting her into jeopardy of a cruel and degrading death.

Isolde's resourcefulness in her ordeal

Isolde's loneliness and indignity, with such a fearful prospect before her in the event of failure, cannot but highlight the extent to which this trial partakes of the character of a degradation ritual: like thieves and robbers, for whom no simple oath will suffice to purge their guilt, she is expected to submit to one of the recognised forms of ordeal.[19] She is in fact not utterly alone, despite the nicely-judged sarcasm of her reply to the Bishop of Thamise – those taunting remarks that of course she needn't go looking for friends or kindred at a court where, being after all an exile, she can't help being talked about and slandered (15491–96); but once recourse is had to such an ordeal (rather than to a vindicating oath sworn as in Béroul over sacred relics), even those who take her side in the debates in council are being denied all opportunity to act as compurgators.[20]

---

[18] In the *Saga*, it is Ísönd herself who first volunteers mention of this form of ordeal, though even so, the King need not have chosen it, as he does, in preference to other procedures (ch. LVI); references to the *Saga* are to Eugen Kölbing, 'Tristrams saga ok Ísondar', mit einer literarhistorischen Einleitung, deutscher Übersetzung und Anmerkungen (Heilbronn: Henninger, 1878).

[19] Cf. Robert Bartlett, *Trial by Fire and Water. The Medieval Judicial Ordeal* (Oxford: Clarendon Press, 1986), esp. pp. 30–33 on the distinction between persons who were 'oath-worthy' and those – including strangers! – who would be compelled to undergo the ordeal; also pp. 13–15 for political cases affecting high-born persons, with the actual ordeal sometimes undergone vicariously for them. For a close analysis of the forms of the ordeal and the problematic character of their application (or even of their applicability) in a work of the imagination see the meticulous study by Rosemary N. Combridge, *Das Recht im 'Tristan' Gottfrieds von Strassburg* (Berlin: Erich Schmidt, 1964), esp. in this connection pp. 83–113; on the issue of the categories of person for whom the particular procedure was normally deemed fitting, cf. Kolb, p. 249, for relevant passages from the *Sachsenspiegel*; and see also Krohn, vol. 3 (Kommentar), pp. 146f (*ad* 15634ff) for further studies on the ordeal in law and literature.

[20] Kolb, p. 246; one of a myriad of particulars in which Gottfried's version departs from that in Béroul, *Tristan*, ed. by Ernest Muret, Classiques français du moyen âge (Paris, Honoré Champion, 1947), 4217–31, where 'tuit cil qui l'ont oï jurer' – most particularly *la mesnie Artus* drawn up around the cloth on which the relics are displayed – can put up with no more, averring that in what she has sworn she has more

Isolde can accordingly hardly help attempting to win support by other means. We thus see her fostering public sympathy to make up for such friendlessness and, of more operative importance still, carefully setting up within that sympathetic public an amply witnessed knowledge that will provide a version of the truth she can use in her ordeal. Focusing on her rough clothing, exposing so much of her arms and feet (15656–67, cf. also *Saga*, ch. LIX), may be somewhat theatrical, but it duly makes its point (and in fact is less demonstrative than the lavish staginess of Béroul's *mise-en-scène* of the corresponding episode); as for her attempt to curry favour with God by comprehensive acts of charity (15643–50; *Saga*, ch. LIX), this may be admired as a refusal to yield to despair (which would be the negative face of that spirited sarcasm with which she had taunted the council). It is also no mere defiance, but a most carefully constructive mind that is at work in her show of consideration (15603–19) for that poor, infirm pilgrim which provides (as in the *Saga*, ch. LVIII) so calculatedly appealing a framework for her comment that of course this accident (this *Fall* that is being presented as an *Unfall*) will compromise any terms in which her oath could conceivably be couched.

Though when it comes to complications that compromise, let us note how compromised and compromising – even for the King – are the personal and social relationships of the two central figures one of whom is seeking to establish what his truthful view should be, unclouded by any *wan* or *zwivel*, of the other's truth- and faithfulness. In what Isolde takes to be her want of friends and kindred, the one figure above all to whom she could ordinarily and legitimately look for loving friendship and support should be her husband, lord and king. Hence the forethought of her family in Ireland, as they sent her away from home to marry into historically hostile Cornwall, in deploying the arts they understood so well and providing the love-potion; and the misapplication of that device goes only so far to explain, and serves in no way at all to excuse, the astonishing way in which Marke has opted for, of all things, the rigorous course of this bizarre and dubious law with its cruel and (at least for such as his wife) unusual devices.

In this, Marke may not have specifically betrayed his kingly office: he is no doubt exercising his prerogative, and we must always remind ourselves just how much of his conduct is governed by punctilios of a constitutional kind. He has however lost sight of something that in the image

than met the accusations of *li fel* (4222 and *passim*) who, on pain of attracting sure vengeance from Arthur and his court, must henceforth say not another word in her detraction. Gottfried's contrasting representation of Isolde's isolation makes this, of all contexts, the one in which her cunning is most manifestly defensive, cf. Gisela Hollandt, *Die Hauptgestalten in Gottfrieds <Tristan>: Wesenszüge, Handlungsfunktion, Motiv der List* (Berlin: Erich Schmidt, 1966), pp. 119ff (esp. pp. 131–35).

of feudalism is hardly less entitled to his most scrupulous observance, namely a duty arising from personal relationships. And there is in Gottfried's account no King Arthur (as there is in Béroul) to call Marke to account for being too easily influenced by disloyal counsellors and for allowing this outrage to go on for far too long.[21] This is the context in which God's *courtoisie* comes to Isolde's rescue; and far from being shocked at some supposed blasphemy, we may marvel at this as something wholly in accord with the true and proper being of the kind of God one would expect a chivalrous society to worship, if one supposes that such a society's best opinion of earthly majesties might equally embrace the attributes *tugenthaft* and *hövesch*.[22]

Moreover, God's response vindicates something else besides Isolde's carefully phrased appeal to his complete sense of justice and total knowledge of the truth; but to see what else he is endorsing, we must notice that, in the occasion to which God is thus responding, events have not come about in exactly the way that the unfettered scheming of Isolde's accusers had been seeking to contrive them. We shall shortly examine in more detail this scene in which Isolde comes to be able to propose – for her husband's royal assent! – her own wording for the terms of her oath: let us for the moment simply sketch in the pointed contrast Gottfried draws between the purportedly pious malignity of Isolde's accusers and the more chivalrous conduct of another party that has evidently come into being in her defence.

Now the Queen's accusers would no doubt have wished to be represented as simply invoking God's putative way of allowing his transcendent knowledge of all truth to express itself through a justice that – so it was argued – immanently informs the trials and experiments that men and women set up in their world.[23] But others appear to wonder at what we might still describe as their gall (and cf. Gottfried's phrase 'diu bitter nitgalle' applied to Marjodo, 15686f); and so the particular course of Isolde's ordeal has instead been crucially affected by the way the malign conduct of these accusers – better called traducers – has been thwarted by a more chivalrous element in society which, to its credit (cf. 15690–92, cited below), has refused to go along with the downright malice that – as

21 Cf. Béroul, 4141–69, where Marke shows himself suitably impressed by King Arthur's admonition.
22 Cf. Krohn, vol. 3 (Kommentar), *ad* 15552 ('*gotes höfscheit*'), Ganz, vol. 2, p. 328, *ad* 15556 for examples from many literatures (Ganz cites e.g. Dante on God as *Sire della cortesia*) of the non-blasphemous character of such a notion; Hollandt, p. 134, holds that Gottfried's criticism is directed against those whose way of appealing to the institution of the ordeal shows that their conception of God is no better than a caricature.
23 Bartlett, pp. 162–6: the true issue for those questioning the ordeal was not whether such a principle 'made sense' of it, but what the warrant was for God's having actually ordained it.

is only too plain – quite manifestly informs the manoeuvrings of Melot and Marjodo.

Isolde's version of the truth thus fills a gap provided by courtesy of – and through the courtesy of – such friends as she does after all turn out to have on the council; and the God who loves courtesy and truth is responding to the only seemly elements in this entire sordid business: truth (of a sort!) framed by courtesy in the unlikely surroundings of a ritual otherwise all too malevolently set up to hurt and degrade.

But let there be no mistake about it: Isolde's carefully fabricated version of the truth is indeed and in truth a lie, embodying both of the twin aspects under which a lie may present itself, *suppressio veri* as well as *suggestio falsi*. The word-field membership that links MHG *liegen* with its rhyming-partner MHG *triegen* is also not forgotten: in the very moment when Gottfried is with such dramatic pointedness inviting us to contemplate that amazing grace – that miracle of courtesy, that astonishing condescension, or maybe simply that extraordinary favouritism – with which God endorses Isolde's words by keeping her unharmed in the ordeal, he carefully plants, in his own narrator's voice (both with generalizing reference (15742), and with specific reference to Isolde (15747)) the word *trügeheit*.

Nor is it going to be easy, for all the hostility to herself that Isolde rightly discerns at this foreign court to which she has been given away in marriage, to absorb her contrivance into that category of *list* that is *tugenthaft* because it belongs to the craft of the warrior: there is a difference between honest cunning and fraudulent cheating. Gottfried further characterizes Isolde's oath as a *gelüppeter eit*: her family has shown as marked a propensity to traffic in poisoned weapons as she herself is now displaying to the poisoning of oaths, in a recourse to foul and unfair devices designed to obscure – rather than to encounter – the fullest consequences of some test, and to obviate – rather than to confound – the strict application of its terms.[24]

Awareness of such attempts on Isolde's part at avoidance and obviation cannot but add to any unmasking of the untruth at the heart of her conduct the further opprobrium of recourse to foul, unjust or improper means. The deception is indeed complete, and involves two of the principal senses of the English verb *to cheat* that the synonymy of German distributes between 'betrügen (um etwas)' and 'täuschen':[25] the court and all present are cheated of their expectation that the truth will at last be established; Isolde is also stated as cheating in the sense of irregularly and improperly displaying something as being other than it is. *Betrug* and

---

[24] Krohn, vol. 3 (Kommentar), p. 151, *ad* 15748.
[25] R. B. Farrell, *Dictionary of German Synonyms* (Cambridge: U.P., 2nd edn, 1971), pp. 89f, *s.vv.* 'deceive, cheat, delude'.

Täuschung are both involved: a deliberate and contrived falsehood is being improperly invoked to pervert the course of a form of law. The charge-sheet could not be more comprehensively damning if Gottfried had set the matter out in casuistic detail rather than in a perfectly timed phrase of just two words.

God's perfect courtesy and an imperfectly chivalrous court

Yet the more we highlight the mendacious and deceitful quality of Isolde's performance, the more signal a miracle it will be seen to be that God works in this most astonishing of causes. Hence the basic dilemma that has been with us since what we conventionally take to be the beginnings of the modern study of mediaeval literature, a dilemma whose terms recur in varyingly expressed but essentially identical formulations through the successive research orientations which have guided the history of our discipline.[26]

Are we dealing here with a naive or maybe even reckless blasphemy that takes delight in Isolde's 'frivoles Spielen mit allem was heilig und ehrwürdig ist'?[27] Or, supposing that it is a blasphemy, has it perhaps after all been more carefully calculated from some consideration of progressiveness or enlightenment such as would be willing to think the hitherto unthinkable: is this a critical spirit setting out to shock people into reconsidering the terms in which to view God (allowing him to be, say, *hövesch* or even *galant*), or alternatively to shock them into reconsidering the moral and social order of their world?[28] (Or are we merely dealing in sophistries like wondering whether Isolde had after all ever truly been Marke's wife?)[29]

---

26   The range of opinions is very amply illustrated by Beatrice Margaretha Langmeier, *Forschungsbericht zu Gottfrieds von Strassburg 'Tristan' mit besonderer Berücksichtigung der Stoff- und Motivgeschichte für die Zeit von 1759–1925* (Zurich: Juris, 1978) (through the succession of historicist, positivist and hermeneutic research paradigms); the record can be updated by reference to Krohn, vol. 3 (Kommentar), pp. 148–50, *ad* 15733ff.

27   So Bartsch (cited Langmeier, p. 63); Hollandt, p. 132, rightly dismisses one view that goes so far as to think of God as being bribed by some hypocritical display of charity on Isolde's part.

28   So Lorenz/Scherer (cited Langmeier, p. 63); and cf. again Hollandt, p. 134, on the debased conception of God evidenced in the conduct of Isolde's opponents. G. T. Gillespie, 'Why does Tristan lie?', *Trivium*, 12 (1977), pp. 75–91 (esp. pp. 83–84) makes us aware of a complicity in which 'courteous' Christ and the reader conspiratorially join the two lovers in approving what they know (all four of them!) to be a deception, in the interests of protecting a love superior to existing social morality; I shall be arguing that Isolde, at this climax in a very socially conscious romance, is manifesting a very needful variety of that highly social quality or virtue *bescheidenheit*.

29   So Mone (cited Langmeier, p. 31) – a legalism transporting us very forcibly into the

Or alternatively to all that, are we in the presence of some not so much critical as ironizing spirit whose path towards whatever 'tiefere Bedeutung' he is going to lead us to will pass via 'Scherz' or 'Satire'? We may have all manner of reasons for supposing that Gottfried – or at any rate the narrator's voice he projects in the work he has composed – is casting doubt or even heaping opprobrium on the institution of the ordeal. Or at the very least he may be cultivating an irony that rejoices in seeing an ill-informed or misguided faith – or worse still: a basely abused, foolishly misdirected or sinfully misapplied one – supply the very means by which it is put to confusion in the story itself, and held up to the scorn of its perhaps enlightened (or at any rate by this very means better-to-be-informed) audience.

It is quite attractive to adopt a construction that suggests that this very institution, being to a boldly critical narrator and his open- or fair-minded audience such a dubious arrangement, is ideally suited to a presentation in which, precisely by being so maliciously abused, it can be worked so as to frustrate the misconceived designs of those who so readily embrace the idea of having recourse to it. Even so, we would then expect Gottfried, in the interests of the most perfect demonstration of such a point, to take its essential components perfectly seriously.

As an artist, Gottfried may underplay or omit or regroup some details, for aesthetic effect: to keep Isolde centrally in focus, he may avoid shifting attention unduly to the mere realia of the institution or to the officious personages doing their various duties in due order. One cannot expect to use such an account as a faithful representation or accurate documentation of how a regularly constituted ordeal was actually administered, and by the same token it is unprofitable to argue that some apparent omissions or irregular orderings of prescribed phases of the exercise are evidence, on their own, of the poet's critical stance. What is more important is to concentrate on what Gottfried has been scrupulous to observe, beyond the essentials of having Isolde successfully swear an oath under circumstances of great moral and physical jeopardy, with secular and especially spiritual authority combining to legitimate and even to sanctify the instruments and the procedures to which she has submitted.

Notice, for instance, amidst so much else that is passed over, with what constitutional propriety the King withholds the use of his prerogative until his divided council has defeated itself and is manifestly unable to discharge its duty of advising the King what his will and pleasure should

---

atmosphere of King Henry's 'great matter' (cf. n. 13 above, and C. N. L. Brooke, *The Medieval Idea of Marriage* (Oxford U.P., 1989, pp. 162–9) on the 'extremely confused, confusing, and sordid story' (p. 162) of 'The Marriages of Henry VIII').

4

be. It is, by comparison, relatively less important for the poet, after showing us Isolde grasp the iron, to build in a three days' wait, and then to tell
us rather clinically that the wounds were healing and not festering;[30] we
do not need that in order to be satisfied as to whether or not justice, or at
any rate poetic justice, was being done. As things stand, the miracle is the
more dramatically presented, and our attention is directed rather to what
matters – to something of greater moment (but also far more astonishing
and puzzling) than conundrums about whether Gottfried had meant the
exercise to appear invalidated by having the clergy bless the iron at the
wrong point in the ceremony.

For the remarkable thing to note is that, in working the miracle, God
does so not by tempering justice with mercy, but because he has been
offered a courteously presented version of the truth able to supplant a
more damagingly revealing truth that has, however, discredited itself by
its hate-filled (and thus sinful) lack of true chivalry. God in his chivalry, in
short, covers[31] this mendaciously truth-constructing Isolde, and takes her
into his protection and care, to the discomfiture of her enemies, who have
sought to bring the truth to light, but in their malice have contrived not to
reveal the truth, but only to betray it. Already once before, in the orchard
scene, the lovers had called upon God's power to give protective covering
(cf. *beschirmen*, 14638, 14706), when first Tristan and then (through Tristan's comportment) Isolde had become aware of the trap laid for them:
with the King so carefully *verborgen*, the lovers may then all the more
desperately have needed God's covering and concealing hand. So now in
the ordeal, exposed to such public shame (and with Tristan, as so often,
protected by disguise and thus avoiding discovery), the friendless Queen
again receives God's protective and covering favour in an hour of need
when all other protection has been withdrawn from her.

Isolde's constitutional opportunism and her enemies' flawed case

But how had Isolde come to have the opportunity for formulating her
oath thus played into her own hands? Such formulation is supposed
normally to have rested with the judges or with the accuser,[32] and yet

---

30   Combridge, p. 99; Krohn, vol. 3 (Kommentar), p. 148, *ad* 15733.
31   Cf. Haug, p. 49: '[Isolde] legt also alles auf einen Betrug Gottes an und bittet ihn
zugleich, dabei mitzuspielen. Und er tut es, er deckt den Ehebruch vor der Öffentlich-
keit.' For God's 'covering' hand, cf. Psalm xxxii.1, cited by St Paul at Romans iv.7, and
echoed by the more poetically expanded vocabulary of protection and shadowing in
e.g. Psalm xci.4.
32   Combridge, pp. 98ff.

from one version to the next we see Isolde contriving to by-pass any such provision (Gottfried), or to intervene before things go too definitively against her cause (*Saga*), or simply to propose an alternative that suits her better (Béroul). In Gottfried she does this very adroitly: there is, for example, none of the blatant contrast, seen in Béroul, between the terms proposed explicitly to Yseut by King Arthur (4191–96) and the transparently more qualified terms she promptly goes on to use in swearing (4197–216) which, however, those present enthusiastically endorse as being more than her accusers had required of her!

Gottfried's account differs also from that in the *Saga* (ch. LIX), where Ísönd intervenes when she notices that a majority in the council is set to carry the day against her interests, and the public pity she has mobilized on her behalf proves important as moving the King to agree that the oath she has offered needs no amplifying. What is distinctive in Gottfried is the use he makes not of a threat to Isolde from some emerging majority in the council, but of an opportunity presented to her by a failure of the council to agree the terms of the Queen's oath.

In this, Gottfried highlights more than just adroitness on Isolde's part: it is also a matter of finely calculated good judgement (the obverse side, even the shadowy side, of that much praised virtue *bescheidenheit*); and by no means the least indication of the calculated good judgement that she shows in her approach to the affair can be seen in that very moment when she is about to propose the terms for her oath herself. At this of all points she sees fit to remind Marke – who was doubly in a position to propose such terms to her, both as the aggrieved lord and husband whose grounds for doubt must be disposed of, but also as the King upon whose will and pleasure all the proceedings must turn – of the powers that in the last resort are reserved to the crown:

> 'künec herre' sprach diu künigin,
> 'min eit muoz doch gestellet sin,
> swaz ir dekeiner gesaget,
> als iu gevellet unde behaget.' (15697–700)

– a royal pleasure to which she does not scruple to give an orientation convenient to her own cause.

But we must neither overstate nor understate the extent to which what falls out is of Isolde's own contrivance. True, we credit her with the prudence that makes its scheming dispositions so as to be prepared for such opportunities as arise. Even more crucially, we credit her with the good judgement (*bescheidenheit* again) that can turn those opportunities to account when they occur: in Béroul Yseut had given elaborate instructions to Tristran (3294–312) as to how he should be disguised and how he should act in that disguise, but Isolde's message in Gottfried is simply that Tristan should be there, watching out for her (15555–59),[33] and it is up to her to make a well-judged response to the appearance he actually presents on the occasion.

But in noticing how tellingly prepared Isolde is, both in herself and in the dispositions she has made, for whatever chances or opportunities may betide, let us also notice how circumstances outside herself play into her hands. These turn out, when considered in their own terms, to be no mere matter of chance, for much of what creates this present opportunity for Isolde arises from a specific set of failings in her accusers that are entirely in keeping with their behaviour throughout.

It is also in keeping with the way they are represented in all the versions, but Gottfried differs from the *Saga*[34] in highlighting certain particulars of motivation in just this context (so that if there had been explicit interest in any such motivation at this point in Thomas, the saga man has passed it over, but our author has played it up).

> Nu waren da genuoge
> so grozer unvuoge,
> daz si der küniginne ir eit
> vil gerne hæten uf geleit
> ze schaden und ze valle.   (15681–85)

The passage beginning with these words introduces a keynote term *unvuoge*, alluding to the social failing of unmannerliness and the social-cum-moral failing of 'Bosheit' or 'baseness', which almost says it all.[35] Notice

---

33 Her only qualification – 'swa er die vuoge næme' (15556) – might be read either as a saving clause (he should not do it at all if it could not be done discreetly) or as in fact urging him to come, but to do so with all discretion; either way the keynote of *vuoge* is struck, cf. n. 35 below.

34 The *Saga*, ch. LIX, simply records that some ('sumir') were inclined to press in closely upon her (imposing presumably the strictest form of words) and some (again 'sumir') were trying to help her, while the majority ('flestir') were going along with the King in imposing the harshest form of oath: the epithet 'sem frekastan' applied to this projected oath – otherwise used of the roughness of a woodworker's tool or the voracity of a wolf – fits the motivation of the King who is stern and severe, even covetous and pugnacious; but it is on the king, not the counsellors, that the saga-narrator lavishes such epithets. With Gottfried, the focus shifts, at least here, to the malice of the accusing party at court, which, as Hollandt, p. 142, n. 58 notes, is paradoxically going to work to Isolde's advantage.

35 Cf. Hollandt, pp. 144ff, on the unethical bases of Marjodo's and Melot's conduct; Gottfried underscores the importance of *vuoge* and *unvuoge* through the polyptota or *figurae etymologicae* (cf. Krohn, vol. 3 (Kommentar), p. 151, *ad* 15737–39) that lend such sarcastic verve to his comments on the outcome of the ordeal:

> er [Crist] vüeget unde suochet an,
> da man'z an in gesuochen kan,
> alse gevuoge und alse wol,
> als er von allem rehte sol. . .

next how Gottfried stresses the excessive and relentless manoeuvrings of Marjodo: the phrases 'sus unde so / und manege wis' (15688–89) conjure up all the intricate shifts and shiftinesses with which he and his party (and there were quite enough of them too!) worked so deviously and persistently at maximizing the harm and ruin to be brought upon the Queen. He also notes in the midst of all this base behaviour the undue presence of an excess of desire (*vil gerne*, 15684), and caps it all by the presence of *nit* in *nitgalle* (15686), with the hint of actual sinfulness compounding the social and moral failings.

All of these clues – all in Gottfried, none of them in the *Saga* – point to those irrational, unethical, passionate elements that distort perception and cloud judgement. And all this in the King's own 'great matter' where the knowledge, will and judgement of these people's sovereign lord are to be given shape! It is indeed to the credit of the court – though no thanks to the Melots and Marjodos among them – that this unmannerly, base and sinful conduct has provoked a chivalrous reaction:

> da wider was aber da manic man
> der sich an ir erte
> und ez ir ze guote kerte.   (15690–92)

The result is a hung council, unable to form a clear view of what its advice to the King is to be; and this, in Gottfried (again differing from the *Saga*, where a majority was emerging, siding with the harsh and pugnacious spirit of the King), is how Isolde gets her opportunity to intervene.

In her very way of turning to the King, there may be a hint of a traditional right for Marke, as aggrieved husband, to assert the accuser's privilege of framing the terms of the oath; we have preferred to stress rather the constitutional point on which, in fact, her words to the King actually turn. Spelt out more fully than she does, this point is that – however nicely and finely Marke has merged his personal interest in that of his council, doing nothing other than by and with the advice of his princes and leading retainers both temporal and (since it is a *concilje*) spiritual[36] – in the last resort what counts is the King's pleasure, and in such an impasse as has now been reached in council, the King must exercise what is not just his personal privilege but his royal prerogative.

> daz wart wol offenbare schin
> an der gevüegen künigin.   (15737–40, 15745–46)

For *höfscheit* and *vuoge* (7562) in Tristan's words when explaining himself (shortly before he introduces himself in Ireland as Tantris!), cf. Mohr, 'Künstlerroman', pp. 156–57.
36 On the composition and competence of a *concilje*, cf. Krohn, vol. 3 (Kommentar), pp. 144f, *ad* 15303, with references to R. His (*Strafrecht des deutschen Mittelalters*, 1935) and Combridge.

Isolde is of course opportunistic enough to help along in her own best interests that process in which the King's will and pleasure is formed and her oath formulated to accord with such will and pleasure: but Gottfried does highlight her moral advantage over her accusers by the sweet irony of having her echo (15723) the very phrase *sus oder so* that he had earlier employed to point up Marjodo's zestful pursuit of her destruction and ruin. For Isolde's use of this phrase shows, by contrast, a courteously constructive spirit: she will improve on the terms of her oath (cf. 'ich bezzer iu den eit', 15722) in any way her lord and husband pleases.[37]

Isolde's best hope, once these proceedings had been embarked upon, had always lain in an appeal to God's *höfscheit* (15552); and it is to a matching courtesy on her part, evidenced not least by her concern for *vuoge* at all stages, that such *höfscheit* on God's part can respond, tempering justice with the wider quality of chivalry that indeed also embraces mercy. As for the opposition, they have been put to confusion as they deserved to be, by virtue of their unchivalrous, discourteous, spiteful, malicious and sinful conduct. It is one of the many paradoxes of this whole episode that those who are indeed in possession of the truth harm the cause of truth by their irrational and unethical conduct, while Isolde – alone and defenceless and so perhaps needing to guard her honour (if not quite yet, at this stage, her actual life) with any device that she can contrive – even in going beyond honest cunning to actual cheating, deception and fraud, does so with such a careful construction so courteously framed as to invoke God's covering hand over her, her lying self thus endorsed as being, in our dialectical sense, 'made of truth'.

II

ON THE CROWNED VIRTUE OF *BESCHEIDENHEIT*

The charming discretion of Isolde's bewitching guile

One courtly virtue – or at any rate *virtù* – has increasingly emerged from our consideration of the way in which Isolde fabricates her lie and practices her deception with this oath that is so manifestly laced with the poison of untruth. For not only has she appealed, with well-placed foresight, to every chivalrous sentiment that can be found in the mind of God

---

37 She will no doubt be able to turn any such request for emendation to her own account, having already shown a capacity to adjust the terms in which she is prepared to swear to God in this matter, in the orchard scene, where her talk had been of having room in her heart for only one man (the man who had deflowered her, 14760–66). She now improves the match of her words to the circumstances: the world now knows of two men, for her arms, at one time or another, have indeed found room for more men than her heart has done.

or of men and women: she has also, in calculating to a nicety what is needed to catch out the flawed and debased truthfulness of those who are intriguing against her, shown such finely tuned good judgement that God, who is not mocked, here or anywhere else – the same God, moreover, whom the episode of the combat with Morolt had been at such pains to establish as being on the side of those who are in the right, and whose chivalrous aspect is now being revealed (*goffenbæret*, 15733) and verified (*bewæret*, 15734) – does not have his verified and verifying courtesy stretched so far as to endorse a literal lie.

The discreet charm of this virtue of good judgement, which was much advocated by moralists – for Freidank, indeed, it was not so much the crowning as the crowned virtue: 'bescheidenheit,/ diu aller tugende krone treit'[38] – no doubt showed its sovereign merits in helping things go smoothly even at the best of times; but such merits would be as nothing to those it might display when what is at stake is survival at an intriguing and hostile court. This is the nearest we may come to seeing honest virtue in Isolde's stratagem: not by aligning it with the cunning that is so good a part of the warrior's valour (we have already shown a reluctance to shelter it under such a rubric), but rather by seeing in it, for all that our qualms about Isolde's deceptive handling of the truth may make this seem the rather shadowy side of such *virtù*, the discretion that is so valuable a part even of the peacetime courtier's valour.

It is a nuisance, working greatly to the discomfiture of those of us who like to do our word-field studies by counting and classifying actual occurrences of words, that Gottfried harps so little on the term *bescheidenheit*;[39] this does not mean that the notion does not unspokenly inform his personages' conduct, or that the virtue itself (one cannot properly call it a 'thing') is not in play (or at work) in their actions. What we are handling is a semantic structure in which the words people use and the ways they act circle around a term that was either so banal that it could be taken for granted, or so highly charged that it was commonly – not to say discreetly – avoided. In so far, however, as the discussions at this symposium have addressed to me the question of finding a characterization of the precise kind of intelligence and intellectuality to which Gottfried aligns the love-

38 Freidank, *Bescheidenheit*, edited by H. E. Bezzenberger, 1, 1f.

39 It is not absent from Gottfried's text: cf. the quadruple *muot, (vollez) guot, bescheidenheit* and *hövescher sin* repeatedly invoked when Tristan is made knight; the cognate *bescheidenliche* (14633: Hatto translates 'distinctly') has a bearing on the discernment that enables Tristan to distinguish the shadowy figures of Marke and Melot in their hiding-place, so that the abstract excellence sententiously invoked on solemn occasions is echoed by a specific (cognate!) term referring to some practical predicament in which danger is discerned (and discerningly met).

life of his protagonists[40] (and insofar as I drew from the Shakespearean epigraph of my paper a model for an intellectual coup that Marke was not quite privileged enough to pull off), then for the most aptly characterizing expression available from Gottfried's contemporary German I cannot avoid coming back again to the term *bescheidenheit*.

Some further remarks, therefore, to accommodate the dialectics of this scene, and to subsume the paradoxes upon which it plays, within a wider interest Gottfried shows not only in the intellectuality and intelligence that is at the heart of such prudent courtliness, but also, *per contra*, in the emotions and passions that may variously support and enhance, or disorder and subvert, such courtly discretion and judgement. For when viewed in such a wider framework, Isolde's *trügeheit* emerges as merely the instrument by which her good judgement enables her not only to outface and outwit her enemies, but also to dominate the fear and worry with which she had good reason to respond to the grim and fraught predicament to which first the gossip of courtiers and now the deliberations of learned and reverend men in the *concilje* have brought her. More particularly, it is an instrument both suitably and needfully adapted to the specific jeopardy in which her most basely intriguing opponents are bidding fair to place her.

A special quality of *bescheidenheit* enables Isolde – who even in her darkest moments is never less than the *gesinne* or *wol gesinne* (15469–70) who had been able to find words with which to face the council – to triumph over the *vorhte, sorge, leit, swære* and *angest* that are the variously emotive but also objectively present constituents of her *not* (cf. 15319–20, 15534–49). Good sense and good judgement thus enable her to triumph over both her fears within herself and the dire circumstances that beset her from without.

Case studies in bescheidenheit and its want:
(i) the truth in the lovers' eyes

It is not given to everyone in the story to have judgement thus dominate damaging emotion. I do not wish to claim any one moment as marking Marke's 'royal decline' in any especially signal way;[41] but a very suggestive moment comes some time after the *gerihte zem glüejenden isen* has thus allowed the King, for a space, to set aside the doubts clouding his fond hopefulness – and after the gift of Petitcreiu has led to the Queen's prevailing upon her husband to agree to Tristan's return – when once again

---

40 I am grateful to Stephen Jaeger for highlighting this issue at the symposium.
41 Thomas Kerth, 'Marke's Royal Decline', pp. 105–16 in this volume.

der minnen [unmüezege] arcwan bears its ample fruit (16455ff), and eye and heart start seeking each other out as surely and as tellingly as the finger seeks out the seat of pain (16473ff).

For now, Marke cannot help noticing in the lovers' glances the balm of Love: he thus becomes an eye-witness, dependent no longer on gossip, or on traps and ambushes designed to produce corroborative evidence, or on proofs that might be equivocal or purgations that might be perjured, but is himself able to see, beyond every scruple of doubt, the truth that is in the lovers' hearts and to which the heart's friend, the eye (16490),[42] gives privileged access:

> durch daz er nam ir allez war.
> sin ouge daz stuont allez dar:
> er sach vil dicke tougen
> die warheit in ir ougen
> und anders aber an nihte
> niwan an ir gesihte. (16501–06)

There is, incidentally, something less than *bescheidenlich* in the lovers' comportment at this stage: Gottfried again does not apply this exact term, but the narrative voice registers with its *leider* (16489) the baleful character of this development as, in the blindness of their love (16453), Tristan and Isolde are taken beyond the limits within which it had been possible for them to conceal their love and guard it from discovery by King or court. Not satisfied with the prudence that waits for suitable opportunities and, in the meantime, places trust in the *gemeiner wille* (16443) that lovers share, they yield, in the behaviour of their outer senses – the organs of sight and (metaphorically) of touch or feeling – to those pangs of love that will betray themselves by glance or gesture.

Now one of the principal offices of *discretio*, discretion, modesty or *bescheidenheit*, sustained through all the semantic shifts to which those matched terms have otherwise been subject, has been precisely to counteract or – since prevention is the soundest policy of all – to inhibit the indiscretions to which our sensual being may be inclined. In her ordeal, Isolde had, against all the odds, most carefully guarded her tongue,[43] and Tristan, too – also rather against the odds, but with Isolde's much praised courteous response to his supposed indiscretion playing its

---

42 Ruth H. Cline, 'Heart and Eye', *RPh*, 25 (1972), 263–297; and on a single poetic complex taking in light- and mirror-imagery as well cf. Antonín Hrubý, 'Historische Semantik in Morungens "Narzissuslied" und die Interpretation des Textes', *DVLG*, 42 (1968), 1–22 (pp. 12ff).

43 Walther's palindromic 'Hüetent iuwer zungen' (87,9f) did not quite embrace so subtle a view of what it meant to bolt this gate and allow no base words to escape; cf. Alexandra Barratt, 'The Five Wits and their Structural Significance in Part II of

helpful part – had been most effectively able to keep his whole person from discovery; so carefully and so effectively that in the event it was their opponents who had been caught wrong-footed and off guard, and had ended up betraying the cause of truth they had so zealously thought to be serving. But now it is the reunited lovers that have dropped their guard sufficiently to betray in another sense the truth that is in their hearts.

And what is Marke's no better judged response to this sight of the truth that thus unguardedly finds expression in the lovers' eyes? It is an access of such raging, senseless hatred, envy and anger that his own judgement becomes blinded: lost to all sense and proportion (16516), suffering indeed a very death of his senses (16517), he cannot properly effect a balance between the fury into which his jealousy drives him and the love he still feels (dearer than life itself) for his wife, and, thus tormented, he casts aside not just every scruple of doubt and suspicion, but also every care even for the very distinction of truth from falsehood:

> doch brahte in disiu swære
> und diz vil tobeliche leit
> in also groze tobeheit,
> daz er sich es gar bewac
> und niwan an sime zorne lac:
> ern hæte niht gegeben ein har,
> wære ez gelogen oder war. (16528–34)

Whatever the morality of Isolde's handling of the truth, the very way she had played with the terms of her oath had called for the most acute observation of contrasts, between true and false, open and hidden, sincere and feigned.

And yet, even 'in disem blinden leide' (16535), and at the centre of the incensed and sarcastic speech Marke addresses to the lovers, it can be acknowledged that, in moderating the retribution he imposes (16583–85) and settling for the lesser sentence of banishment, he has not so much departed from his rights out of mere fondness for the guilty pair (despite 'da sit ir mir ze liep zuo', 16590) as shown a measure of kingly *bescheidenheit*. In addressing them as 'neve Tristan, min vrouwe Isot' (16587), he touches on the public, even politic sense (alongside any personal emotional sense) in which they are – and must be – 'liep' to him: for as his nephew and his wife they are the centrepieces of successive policies he

"Ancrene Wisse" ', *MAe*, 56 (1987), 12–24 (esp. pp. 19–20), for confessional writings and their treatment of the sins of the tongue, and for discretion guarding the mouth as the gate of the body. (Such writings would not of course have been looking to *discretio* for the purposes I have in mind here.)

has adopted (or been made to adopt) for satisfying his royal duty of providing for the succession.[44]

Moreover, as Marke's marriage has remained childless, Tristan's importance for this aspect of policy is undiminished (though his problematic character as an evidently not universally welcome potential successor is undiminished, too). Furthermore, the joint presence of both wife and nephew at Marke's court is an ironic reminder of his not wholly right royal kingliness (admixed even with an element of bad faith) in his first allowing such a sister's son to emerge as heir presumptive and then – letting his barons persuade him to adopt a different policy – so far going back on what would be his next avuncular duty of finding a suitable consort for his heir as actually to allow that sister's son to undertake the dangerous courting of a consort, but on the King's own behalf. The story has of course gone on to show Love – making good her claim over Tristan as, by inherent right, his *domina protectrix* ('erbevogetin', 11765) – seize the occasion of the drinking of the love-potion to get right, after a fashion, what Marke's various shifts of policy had, after their fashion, got wrong; but there still remains something more than merely personal fondness in the interest the King has in the continued life – even at the cost of their continued living together! – of his sister's son and his wife.

Case studies in bescheidenheit and its want:
(ii) the return from the fossiure

If the banishment scene allows us, in a back-handedly ironizing way, to credit even an insanely incensed Marke with a measure of royal discretion, the scenes later ending the episode of the Minnegrotte and bringing the lovers back to court show his understanding of the best-judged response to his position in a still more heavily qualified and compromised light. Watching the sleeping *gent amant* as he spies on them in their *fossiure*, and fascinated especially by Isolde, who had never seemed to her estranged lord 'so lustic und so lustsam' (17607) as she does now, he allows himself to be bewitched by Love's 'golden Denial' ('daz guldine lougen', 17542) that so soothingly disaffirms what it would be too painful for him to acknowledge; he allows, too, both eyes and sense to be seduced by this gilding of innocence ('diu guldine unschulde', 17552) that so enticingly (cf. 'mit ir gespenstikeite', 17554) offers him the more comfortable of

44 In this and the following paragraph, I am grateful to Thomas Kerth for illuminating comments made in his paper (pp. 105–16, above) and in discussions throughout the London Symposium.

the choices facing him in the dilemma of 'yea' and 'nay' (17530f) in which he has become 'wegelos'.[45]

With the King at all stages refusing knowledge of what is the case (cf. 17752), we find even his counsellors ('as wise men do', 17673) recognising the quality of the advice that their lord's beguiled heart desires to hear: allowing wish and desire to inform the will of their King, who will not allow knowledge to inform it, they indulge his evident desire for the lovers' return. He displays great relish for this luxury of reconciliation, and plainly enjoys the presence of such a consort as Isolde at his side, so gratifying alike to the private yearnings of his heart, the sensual desires of his body and (in a more carefully circumscribed way) the public clamourings of his honour.

And it is the mention of just this carefully circumscribed way in which honour is satisfied that ushers in Gottfried's blunt and damaging criticism of Marke's blindness and self-deception. For, despite the zeal with which court and retinue do honour to the lovers, and despite or even because of all the care that is taken to spell out the terms of a suitably discreet *modus vivendi* – the lovers are urgently (*genote*, 17713) commanded and entreated, for God's sake and the King's, to show seemly restraint in their conduct – the whole arrangement is just so much less royally magnanimous than the unstinted honour and unreserved indulgence with which Isolde had been returned to the King's love, and been 'praised, lauded and esteemed among the people',[46] after the ordeal. For now, the joy that Marke has with Isolde at his side may be all his heart could want – but it is 'niht zeren, wan ze libe' (17727):

> ern hæte an sinem wibe
> noch minne noch meine
> noch al der eren keine,
> die got ie gewerden liez,
> wan dazs in sinem namen hiez
> ein vrouwe unde ein künigin
> da, da er künic solte sin.   (17728–34)

This gives rise not only to Gottfried's description of such demeanour on the King's part as 'diu alwære,/diu herzelose blintheit' (17738f) – it is the proverbial blindness of love, together with the more particular miraculous beauty of Isolde in the flower of her age, that blinds both the outer and the inner senses (17740–42, 17804–08) – but also to an express exoneration of both Tristan and Isolde from any charge of deception practised on

---

45 Rainer Gruenter, 'Das "guldine lougen". Zu Gotfrids *Tristan*, vv. 17536–56', *Euphorion*, 55 (1961), 1–14.
46 15753–55, in the translation of A. T. Hatto.

the King. For Marke can see with his own eyes, and for that matter also knows the circumstances perfectly well even without the evidence of his eyes; yet he still has such capacity for self-deception as to cherish in this vain way the wife who has no love for him. But then this threesome – this companionship which the King's own judgement, made in a mixture of rage and good judgement, had earlier deemed to be gross vulgarity if acquiesced in knowingly by a king (16614–16) – has been resumed in circumstances where the King's own better judgement had been set aside under the seductions of an indulgent and self-indulging love.

Let us go back to that moment in which the King feels prompted to end the lovers' banishment, for in what leads to that impulse we shall be able to recognise an analogy that will draw in turn on what we have learnt from our discussion of Isolde's skilful and well-judged contrivance in the ordeal. Central to this point is, however, in both scenes where an ill-founded reconciliation follows the practice of some more or less transparent deception, our further recognition of the way in which emotions that are variously constructive, or seductive, have (respectively) enhanced, or subverted, the judgement that (again respectively) the lovers and the King apply in their conduct.

Marke's readiness to be taken in by so transparent a device as the sword between the lovers is fed by the emotions in a heart that is only too ready to be soothed by Love's gilded deceptions ('daz guldine lougen' (17542) again): Love, made up in her own fairest colours, offers a démenti which gives the lie to the truth, and invests Isolde in the golden aura of innocence ('diu guldine unschulde', 17552) by which, however guilty, she is again exculpated.[47] But Marke's frame of mind has made him vulnerable to such deception: the dreary torpidity of his conduct casts a shadow over – and in its own way gives the lie to – the seeming activity of the hunt and its joys. For has he not embarked on the chase, not because he seeks its delights for their own sake, but to seek distraction from his continued hankering after Isolde? Has not his conduct – as Gottfried's later narration and comments indicate – been inspired after all only by a craving for the pleasures and the empty dignity that her presence at his side will bring him? His heavy heart is filled with vain desires, and to such a heart Love's beguiling power will present the vainest hopes and fancies in the most glowing and golden of colours.

The lovers, on the other hand – through the King's earlier judgement of banishment, in such good judgement as he had then still been able to muster in his anger – had found their way to their own great good place; even on the morning that threatens their greatest danger, with the risk of

---

47 Gruenter, p. 6: 'Das Verdikt "nicht schuldig" ist nur einem aller Vernunft Beraubten glaubwürdig.'

discovery by the King's hunting party, they are still drawing joy from that sustained idyll with its tirelessly welcoming birdsong, its refreshing spring, its gentle winds and its blossoming plain.[48] The joy that fills their outer and inner senses, so much in contrast to that disabling, dispiriting dreariness that increasingly fills Marke's inner and outer being, is the power that tempers their fear. And just as Isolde had contrived to dominate her fear on the occasion of the ordeal (and Tristan, too, had been able to play his part), so now the lovers, their wits made more skilfully and constructively contriving by the joy that fills their hearts, are enabled to hit upon the device with the sword between them, deceptive only to the self-deceiving, that is going to avert danger and allay suspicion. But of course Love has also to lend her gilding hand.

The truth of Gottfried's poem – 'die Wahrheit dieser Dichtung', to quote Wolfgang Mohr again – '[läuft] eben auf die Spannung [heraus]': Love is not being demonized or (in another view) sanctified as some form of metaphysical Absolute, nor is Society being criticized to its moral destruction[49] (let alone being subverted to its actual destruction). But of course the very social persons of these two lovers are at such odds with their society and its institutions, which is in its turn also at such odds with a demanding Love; and that Love is so victoriously strong in the pursuit of her claims, and so skilled alike in the arts of warfare or the chase as in the devices of the law, or yet again in the crafts of painting and gilding, needful to that pursuit.

Such a tension, such a dilemma calls for a dialectic; and in trying to formulate afresh a moral and especially cognitive problem that is central to that dialectic, and to find in a particular quality of discretion a subsuming principle that can accommodate the polar terms of that dialectic, I am conscious that scores of questions still throng in, and countless suggestive comparisons, too.

Not to mention contrasts, as, for example, with Hartmann's Enite, who first with her sighs and her words betrays – and then under peremptory but inescapable pressure from her husband, lord and king gives more formal expression to – a worry that is in her heart, and who then in her wholly admirable way not only copes with the storm of obloquy and degradation that her husband unchains, but also works to lift him out of the opprobrium into which the trajectory of his course is taking him more

---

[48] F. C. Tubach, 'The "Locus Amoenus" in the *Tristan* of Gottfried von Straßburg', *Neophilologus*, 43 (1959), 37–42; Rainer Gruenter, 'Das *wunnecliche tal*', *Euphorion*, 55 (1961), 341–404.

[49] Wolfgang Mohr, review of Friedrich Heer, *Die Tragödie des heiligen Reiches* (Stuttgart: Kohlhammer, 1952) in *Euphorion*, 51 (1957), 78–92 (p. 90) (arguing also with Gottfried Weber and Helmut de Boor).

and more deeply: in her labour of thus raising him up again out of this hurtful and harmful state, she uses every art and wile of which she is capable, not least the occasional protective untruth. But that, and other comparisons and a host of other questions, are other stories and other issues, and must be reserved for other occasions.

Medieval German Dwarfs:
A Footnote to Gottfried's Melot

SIDNEY M. JOHNSON

Although Gottfried's Melot plays a relatively minor role in the story of Tristan and Isolde, he immediately calls to mind many other dwarfs in medieval literature and raises questions about their roles in literature and society. It will not be necessary, nor possible within the limits of this paper to treat the subject of dwarfs exhaustively – this has already been done for dwarfs in German heroic literature[1] – but perhaps certain aspects of dwarfs can be described through typical cases, and these may suffice to put little Melot into a broader context. We shall attempt to see the dwarf figures in the various Tristan versions – Eilhart, Béroul, Brother Robert or Thomas, and Gottfried – within a kind of rough typology of medieval dwarfs and note their relationship to one another and to the dwarf tradition in general.

Dwarfs have always held a fascination for many normal-sized people, whether it be the appeal of the very small, the bizarre or the very ugly or deformed. As curiosities they were intriguing even in ancient times, and there are records of interest in dwarfs in many places. In Egypt they are frequently seen as watchers of clothing or workers in gold. Although such people may well have been crippled or deformed Egyptians, true pygmies were imported from central Africa to perform as dancers in religious ceremonies or to serve as entertainers. Pharaohs kept dwarfs at court for entertainment and probably also because of their resemblance to the Egyptian deity Bes (sometimes also Ptah), who is frequently depicted with the large head, the pot-belly and short legs characteristic of dwarfs.[2] Although there are apparently no records of dwarfs at court among the

---

[1] August Lütjens, *Der Zwerg in der deutschen Heldendichtung des Mittelalters*, Germanistische Abhandlungen, 38 (Breslau, 1911).
[2] C. J. S. Thompson, *The Mystery and Lore of Monsters* (New York, reprinted 1968), p. 186; Edward J. Wood, *Giants and Dwarfs* (London, 1868, reprinted 1977), pp. 253–54; H. Breasted, *Geschichte Ägyptens* (Berlin, 1911), p. 350; E. Tietze-Conrat, *Dwarfs and Jesters in Art* (London, 1957), p. 9.

Greeks, they were certainly not unknown there. The Greeks believed in the existence of a whole race of dwarfs or pygmies who lived near Oceanus, in India and/or in Egypt.[3] Every year the pygmies were compelled to struggle against cranes which attempted to destroy their fields sown with grain. Armed with arrows and riding on goats, they would ride to the sea each spring in order to destroy the eggs and the young cranes. The Cercopes, whom Hercules caught after they had stolen his weapons, were gnome-like creatures, small jesters whom he subsequently freed because of their cleverness.[4] Such pygmies, although known in the scholarly literature of the Middle Ages, seem to have had little impact on vernacular narrative literature, except as curiosities of foreign lands among other exotic creatures.[5]

Dwarfs were especially popular in Rome in imperial times. Emperors and nobles alike kept dwarfs for entertainment. In fact, the demand for dwarfs was so great that a real trade existed in them, and to help satisfy the demand for such exotic creatures, attempts were made to create dwarfs artificially by binding the limbs of children or by confining children to small cages or chests. The emperor Augustus was especially fond of dwarfs and had them collected from all lands. He kept them to talk to and played games with them. One of them, a certain Lucius, was scarcely two feet tall and weighed only seventeen pounds, but he appeared in a show and had a very strong voice. Augustus had a statue made of him. Marcus Antonius also had a dwarf, named Sisyphus, of approximately the same size, who was reportedly very intelligent. Augustus's niece, Julia, kept two dwarfs not more than 2 feet 4 inches in height in her suite. One was a man named Conopus, the other a woman named Andromeda. Domitian was able to gather many dwarfs around him, formed them into troops of gladiators and had them actually fight one another. Tiberius had a dwarf who ate at the table with him and was influential in political matters. It

3   Friedrich Nick, *Die Hofnarren, Lustigmacher, Possenreißer und Volksnarren älterer und neuerer Zeiten; ihre Spässe, komischen Einfälle, lustigen Streiche und Schwänke,* 2 vols (Stuttgart, 1861), I, 582; Thompson, p.185; Wood, p. 237. These accounts are based on Homer, *Illiad* 3.6–7, Aristotle, *Hist. Animalium*, III.12, Herodotus, II.32; IV.43 and especially Pliny the Elder, *Nat. Hist.* 4.70 and 88; 7.26. See also R. Henning, 'Der kulturhistorische Hintergrund der Geschichte vom Kampf zwischen Pygmäen und Kranichen', Rheinisches Museum für Philologie, 81 (1932), 20–24.
4   See article 'Zwerge' by K. Schauenburg in *Lexikon der antiken Welt* (Zürich and Stuttgart, 1965), p. 3347; Wood, p. 237.
5   e.g. Isidor of Seville, *Etymol.*, XI.iii.7 and 26; *Liber monstrorum*, 11.7; Honorius of Autun, *De imagine mundi*, I.11 (de India). See also *Herzog Ernst B*, 4896–5012; Heinrich von Neustadt, *Apollonius von Tyrland*, 10962–975; *Straßburger Alexander*, 6061–69. For medieval views on the origins of dwarfs, see Roy A. Wisbey, 'Die Darstellung des Häßlichen im Hoch- und Spätmittelalter', in *Deutsche Literatur des späten Mittelalters, Hamburger Colloquium 1973*, edited by Wolfgang Harms and L. Peter Johnson (Berlin, 1974), p. 25.

was not uncommon to find dwarfs in the salons of aristocratic Roman ladies, running about naked, dressed only in gold and jewelry. The fashion of keeping dwarfs lasted until the time of the emperor Alexander Severus (third century A.D.), who expelled the dwarfs from his court.[6]

Turning to Germanic dwarfs, we have to leave 'historical' sources and resort to literary sources that were written down at a much later date. However, many of these sources reflect what must have been very old ideas about dwarfs. In contrast to Roman dwarfs who formed, as we have seen, an element in Roman society, Germanic dwarfs are mythological figures with special attributes. According to old Saxon tradition, four dwarfs supported the celestial dome created by Odin. They were also seen as having unusual magical powers, supernatural intelligence and foresight. They lived in secret places, usually underground, and were considered to be the owners of buried or hidden treasure. They were expert goldsmiths and incomparable blacksmiths. Indeed, the weapons of the gods and the jewelry of the goddesses were their creation. Far from being handsome, they were almost always deformed, hunchbacked or twisted, with large heads, pale faces, and long beards. They are not usually found in the company of normal human beings, but at most have contact with men of heroic proportions, who frequently defeat them or force them to give up their wealth. Occasionally, especially in later literary sources, they take on courtly attributes while still retaining their supernatural powers.[7]

We have, therefore, two distinct traditions involving dwarfs. The one places the dwarf in a social position at court and derives from the practices of antiquity. The other has its background in mythology and attributes to the dwarf supernatural powers which separate him from ordinary human beings. The task then is to follow up the first tradition, if possible, through the social history of the Middle Ages and then to look at dwarfs in literature, specifically German dwarfs and their French counterparts, if they have any, and to see how they relate to Gottfried's Melot. We shall confine ourselves primarily to dwarfs in works of the eleventh, twelfth, and thirteenth centuries, thereby encompassing Gottfried's *Tristan*.

It seems very likely that the custom of keeping dwarfs at court or in the households of noble families did not die out with the fall of the Roman

---

6 Nick, pp. 590–94; Wood, pp. 255–56; Thompson, p.187. These accounts are based on Pliny the Elder, *Nat. Hist.* 7.16; Statius, 1.6.57; Pliny the Younger, *Epist.* 9.17; Pseudo-Longinus, *De sublimitate* 44.5 and other sources.
7 See article 'Zwerg' by E. Mogk in Hoops, *Reallexikon der germanischen Altertumskunde*, 5 vols (Strassburg, 1911–1919), 5, 597–98. See also J. Grimm, *Deutsche Mythologie*, fourth edition by E. H. Meyer, 3 vols (Berlin, 1875–78), I, 369–91, 465 and 467.

empire.[8] Unfortunately, there are few historical records to substantiate this. Most scholars writing about dwarfs are content to draw on literary sources as evidence of dwarfs at court. Actual historical evidence is very sparse until the fifteenth and sixteenth centuries when the presence of dwarfs at court is amply attested in written reports, in painting, and in other art forms. It is interesting to note that the practice was continued well into the nineteenth century in western Europe and particularly in Russia in the eighteenth and nineteenth centuries. There are a large number of dwarfs recorded by name and with fairly complete descriptions. In more recent times dwarfs have, of course, become a standard feature in circuses and as statuettes in domestic gardens.

But returning to the Middle Ages, we find reference to the fact that William, Duke of Normandy, had dwarfs as part of his retinue and that it was customary at that time to employ dwarfs as pages or valets, to hold the bridle of the king's horse in state processions.[9] In a very interesting letter from Meinhard to Bishop Gunther of Bamberg dating from the beginning of 1064, we learn that Gunther kept a monster, probably a dwarf, named Askericus, of whom he was very fond.[10] Apparently he had promised Askericus to King Henry IV, who was at that time 13 years of age, but had delayed sending him, whereupon the king had become quite displeased. Meinhard laments the fact that the king and the bishop were in conflict over such a creature. In the Chronicle of Johannes Oxenedes in the year 1249, there is reference to a dwarf named Johannis, who was 18 years old and scarcely three feet tall, whom the queen kept in her company.[11] In the household accounts of Mahaut, Countess of Artois and Burgundy and niece of Louis IX, there is mention of several dwarfs maintained at various times at court.[12] One, a Sicilian dwarf named Calo Jean, was a servant of the Countess's father and was given a pension after his master's death in 1302. The dwarfs were apparently great favorites of the Countess and may well have been important in the entertainment at court. Then, much later, in 1432, there is a notation in the Gemeine Kämmerei-Rechnung der Stadt Braunschweig: 'Item enen halven gulden des lantgreven van Hessen dwerghe.'[13] This is admittedly not much historical evidence to go on, but taken together with the literary evidence, it seems

8   Thompson, pp.188–241; Wood, pp. 256–446.
9   Wood, p. 257.
10   MGH, Briefe der deutschen Kaiserzeit, 5, 226, Meinhard letter 28; Carl Erdmann, 'Fabulae curiales', ZDA, 73 (1936), 91.
11   A. Schultz, Das Höfische Leben zur Zeit der Minnesinger, 2 vols, second edition (Leipzig, 1889), 1, 207, note 4; also cited by G. Schoepperle Loomis, Tristan and Isolt, second edition (New York, 1963), p. 246.
12   Jules-Marie Richard, Mahaut, Comtesse d'Artois et de Bourgogne (Paris, 1887), pp.111–12; cited also by Lütjens, p. 5, esp. note 1; and G. Schoepperle Loomis, p. 246.
13   Schiller-Lübben, Mittelniederdeutsches Wörterbuch, I, 614.

reasonable to assume that there were indeed dwarfs at the courts of royalty and the nobility during the period in which we are interested and that the dwarf of courtly literature may reflect to a certain extent the social situation of the time. This does not mean that the impetus for including a dwarf or an encounter with a dwarf in a narrative came from real situations at court. The figure of the dwarf came with the material for the tale and goes back to whatever sources there are for the traditional stories whether they come from folklore or from heroic narrative. Nevertheless, the presence of dwarfs at court could possibly have had some effect on the ultimate representation of dwarfs in literature.

For dwarfs at court we need go no further than to Hartmann von Aue.[14] In *Erec*, the dwarf Maliclisier, accompanying a knight and his lady, brutally and insolently lashes out with his scourge, striking first one of the Queen's ladies and then the unarmed Erec, who is unable to retaliate and must withdraw in disgrace (52–108). Erec later insists on punishment for the dwarf, threatens to have his hand cut off but settles for having him flogged by two men with stout rods so that his back bled and the marks could be seen for twelve weeks thereafter (1021–77). He then sends the knight, the lady, and the dwarf to King Artus. Although Maliclisier is a minor character, he is the catalyst that initiates the action. He has very little profile. Insolence is his chief characteristic, and that is something he seems to have derived from his master, the arrogant Îdêrs fil Niut. This is important to remember, since dwarfs frequently reflect the characteristics of their masters.

Maliclisier is not the only dwarf in *Erec*. At the wedding of Erec and Enite we find among the guests King Bîlêî and his brother Brîans from the

14 Here and in subsequent references to other works the following editions were used: Hartmann von Aue, *Erec*, edited by Albert Leitzmann, Altdeutsche Textbibliothek, 39, (Halle, 1939); *Iwein*, edited by G. F. Benecke and K. Lachmann, seventh edition revised by Ludwig Wolff, 2 vols (Berlin, 1968), I, Text; Wolfram von Eschenbach, *Willehalm*, edited by Karl Lachmann, sixth edition (Berlin and Leipzig, 1926, reprinted Berlin, 1960); *Ruodlieb*, edited by Fritz Peter Knapp, Universal-Bibliothek, 9846, (Stuttgart, 1977); *Das Nibelungenlied*, edited by Karl Bartsch, thirteenth edition revised by Helmut de Boor, Deutsche Klassiker des Mittelalters (Wiesbaden, 1956, sixteenth printing, 1961); *Ortnit*, in *Ortnit und die Wolfdietriche*, edited by Arthur Amelung and Oskar Jänicke, 2 vols, Deutsches Heldenbuch, Dritter Teil (Dublin and Zurich, 1968, reprint of 1871 edition), I; *Laurin A*, in *Laurin und der kleine Rosengarten*, edited by Georg Holz (Halle, 1897), pp.1–50; Wirnt von Gravenberg, *Wigalois, der Ritter mit dem Rade*, edited by J. M. N. Kapteyn, Rheinische Beiträge und Hülfsbücher zur germanischen Philologie und Volkskunde, 9 (Bonn, 1926); Eilhart's *Tristrant*, in *Eilhart von Oberge*, edited by Franz Lichtenstein, Quellen und Forschungen zur Sprach- und Culturgeschichte der germanischen Völker, 19 (Strassburg, 1877); Béroul's *Tristran*, in *The Romance of Tristran by Beroul*, edited by A. Ewert, 2 vols (Oxford, 1939, reprinted 1971), I; *Tristrams saga ok Ísöndar*, in *The Saga of Tristram and Ísönd*, translated and with an introduction by Paul Schach (Lincoln, Nebraska, and London, 1973); Gottfried von Straßburg, *Tristan und Isold*, edited by Friedrich Ranke (Berlin and Frankfurt a. M., 1949).

land Antipodes (2086–113). Bîlêî is described as 'der getwerge künec', shorter than any other dwarf, while his brother is a span and a half taller than anyone else. Bîlêî is praised for making up in 'muot' what he lacks in size. He has great wealth and has brought with him two kings, Grigoras and Glecidolân, also dwarfs, or at least 'herren über getwerge lant' (2109ff). They play their cameo roles at the wedding and are promptly forgotten, but we should note that Bîlêî and his fellow dwarfs represent the idea of a kingdom or race of dwarfs that we saw in sources from antiquity.

It is difficult to decide whether Guivreiz le pitîz, King of Îrlant, is really a dwarf (4282–317). Hartmann describes him as 'vil nâ getwerges genôz', but his arms and legs are very large, and his breast is powerful and sturdy. He is an excellent knight, despite his size, and plays a considerable role in Erec, losing to Erec at their first encounter, then defeating Erec the second time they meet. Guivreiz is extremely generous in his care for the wounded Erec. His two sisters also provide Enite with a fabulous horse and saddle and Guivreiz accompanies Erec to his final test at Joie de la curt and ultimately back to King Artus. If Guivreiz is indeed a dwarf king, then we have another example of a royal dwarf of extensive power and wealth with all the necessary courtly attributes.

At the opposite end of the courtly scale from Guivreiz is another dwarf in Erec (7395–425). He has no name and is described only as a wild dwarf. It is his horse that Guivreiz finds tied to the branch of a tree in front of a cave in a mountain, and which is eventually given to Enite. The dwarf is distressed and outraged to find his horse gone and offers Guivreiz three thousand gold marks for its return, but Guivreiz turns the offer down, keeps the horse and leaves the wild dwarf lamenting. This dwarf plays no role except to be part of the story of Enite's fabulous horse, but the idea of a 'wild dwarf' occurs repeatedly in medieval German literature. One need only think of Wolfram's reference to 'den wilden getwergen' when he describes the difficult mountainous path on which Willehalm rides to escape the heathen at the end of Willehalm, Book I (57, 24–25). The wild dwarfs would have had trouble to climb where his horse took him.

We should mention one more dwarf before leaving Hartmann. That is the nameless dwarf who accompanies the giant Harpîn in Iwein (4924–926) and drives his captives along with a scourge. This is the only mention of the dwarf. He simply drops from sight after Iwein kills Harpîn. Here again, as in Erec, the dwarf exhibits the same characteristics as his master in the cruelty with which he treats the prisoners.

Dwarfs living in caves have a lengthy tradition. One of the first literary occurrences in the German-speaking area is in Ruodlieb. In the last section (XVIII) Ruodlieb has apparently just defeated a dwarf in front of his cave. The dwarf is in a fit of rage at having been captured, but he finally falls exhausted and begs Ruodlieb to spare him. He offers to tell Ruodlieb the future if he will free him. He will show Ruodlieb the treasure of two kings, Immunch and his son Hartunch, and the dwarf predicts that Ruodlieb will kill them and win the hand of the daughter, Heriburg, who will inherit the whole kingdom. The dwarf goes on to say that this will not happen without a lot of blood being shed, unless Ruodlieb frees him. Ruodlieb does not want to hurt the dwarf, but he does not quite trust him. At this, the dwarf replies that dwarfs are not like men, who are always treacherous. Dwarfs are to be trusted. They are always truthful, avoid foods that cause illness, and therefore live to a very old age. To convince Ruodlieb to trust him, the dwarf offers his wife as hostage. She falls at Ruodlieb's feet and begs him to free her husband after he has done everything he had promised. Unfortunately, we are left to speculate on the outcome, because the fragment breaks off at this point. However, it is interesting to note here that the motif of a dwarf living in a cave is enlarged. The dwarf has the power to foretell the future, and beyond that, the dwarf and his wife are presented as noble creatures.

Among the best known dwarfs is Alberich in the *Nibelungenlied*. Hagen tells how Siegfried gained possession of the Nibelungen treasure and put Alberich in charge of it after having first won the *tarnkappe* from him (87–99). Later Siegfried must fight with Alberich again when Alberich does not recognize him upon Siegfried's return to the land of the Nibelungs (493–502). Here Alberich is called 'ein wildez getwerc'. He has a beard and is armed with a knout made of gold with seven metal spiked spheres attached by thongs or possibly chains. He wears a helmet and chain mail, is very strong, and smashes Siegfried's shield to pieces with his knout before Siegfried is able to subdue him. Alberich has fulfilled his task of protecting the treasure faithfully, and he even yields it ultimately to the Burgundians because it is Kriemhild's rightful dowry (1117–24). Alberich is associated with supernatural powers, first by his possession of the *tarnkappe*, then by his control of the treasure, in which incidentally there is a magic golden wand (1124). As a wild dwarf he lives in a mountainous region, yet he is related to the dwarf Maliclisier in *Erec* and the unnamed dwarf accompanying the giant Harpîn in *Iwein* in that he uses a scourge or knout.

The dwarf Alberich in *Ortnit* is another example of 'ein wildez twerc' (118). He is invisible to all save the possessor of a gold ring with a magic jewel (143). Although small in stature he has the strength of twelve men (106). He promises Ortnit a magnificent suit of armor, that he has made himself, and a special sword named Rose (111–116). He is a king like Ortnit, but his realm is underground and three times as extensive as Ortnit's (128–29). As things turn out, Alberich is actually Ortnit's father, or perhaps more correctly, surrogate father, who provided a male heir for the kingdom when it appeared that Ortnit's father and mother were unable to have a child of their own (169–73). Alberich eventually helps

Ortnit in his quest for a bride, the daughter of the heathen King of Jerusalem (13–15). The success of the mission is made possible in part by Alberich, who, being invisible, is able to assist in numerous ways. Although he calls himself 'ein wildez twerc', Alberich in *Ortnit* is a far cry from the Alberich in the *Nibelungenlied* or other nameless wild dwarfs. He is no dwarf with a long beard. Ortnit thinks that he is a child when he first sees him, and much is made of his rich clothing. The fact that he rules a subterranean realm places him in a courtly world of his own. Yet he has the traditional attributes of great hidden wealth, the magic power to be invisible, and the ability to manufacture armor and weapons. His advice to Ortnit is very important. As we have seen, it is essential to the success of Ortnit's search for a bride, and when he disregards the advice of his father and falls asleep, Ortnit is ultimately devoured by the dragon he was seeking to kill (555–75).

In speaking of dwarf kings, however, we should not forget Laurin. In *Laurin A* he is described as scarcely three span tall, yet he has cut off hand and foot of many a man who was three times taller than he (55–60). All wild lands serve him, and all dwarfs are subservient to him (62–65). He lives inside a mountain very lavishly amidst gold and jewels with many dwarfs both male and female (825–40, 977–1053). Outside on a meadow is his rose garden, in which the roses are decorated with gold braid and with gold and jewels (101–07). The entire garden is surrounded by a silken thread (69–70; cf. 147). Like Alberich, Laurin can make himself invisible by putting on his *helkeppelîn* (481–85), and he has a magic belt that gives him the strength of twelve men (533–36). Dietrich and his men devastate the lovely rose garden, whereupon Laurin appears and fights with the intruders only to be defeated finally by Dietrich, who hurls him to the ground thereby breaking his belt and reducing his strength (543–56). But Laurin had earlier carried off Dietleib's sister, Künhilt, using his *helkeppelîn* (731–60). Eventually Laurin invites Dietrich and his men to his realm inside the mountain. After some hesitation the men go inside, where they are greeted with unimaginable splendor and entertained by music, singing and knightly games by the noble dwarfs living there (957–1053). Despite the luxury, Künhilt really wants to escape because the dwarfs are not Christians (1087–1102) and confides this to her brother, Dietleib. Laurin, however, locks Dietleib in a room, drugs his four companions, and imprisons them in a dungeon (1183–1200). Dietleib is released by his sister, and, with the aid of a magic ring that makes it possible for him to see the dwarfs despite their *helkeppelîn*, frees the four other prisoners, returns their armor, and starts fighting with the dwarfs. With the help of a magic belt and other magic rings the five heroes are able to defeat all the dwarfs and the five giants that are called in to help. Ultimately all the dwarfs and giants are slaughtered, save Laurin, who is taken to Bern to perform as an entertainer (1574), a role which may well have been typical for dwarfs at court in the Middle Ages.

Although he lives in a mountain, Laurin is by no means 'ein wildez getwerc'. He is not a Christian, but he is a powerful ruler over a kingdom of dwarfs with immense wealth. Life within his mountain and on the plain before it is very pleasant, with anything one might wish. But Laurin is treacherous and uses his magic powers to his own advantage, and he can be overcome only by the heroic efforts of Dietrich and his heroes, aided by a little magic of their own. Here again we have the motifs of immense wealth, of dwelling in a cave, a kingdom of dwarfs, magic powers, confrontation with heroes, and the added motif of evil treachery.

In *Wigalois* by Wirnt von Gravenberg there is mention of several dwarfs. The first one is the most interesting to us because it presents a dwarf in his function as entertainer. A maiden comes to King Artus's court riding a white horse. Standing behind her on the horse with his hands on her shoulders is a dwarf. As they approach the hall, the dwarf begins to sing:

> ein liet sô wünniclîche
> daz si alle gelîche
> ir selber vergâzen
> die in dem sale sâzen.   (1728–32)

The maiden requests aid for her lady, and Artus allows young Wigalois to undertake the adventure. Wigalois, the maiden, and the dwarf set forth, and after several tests of Wigalois's courage and knightly skill, another dwarf joins them (2574–644, 3255–62). As they travel on, one of the dwarfs tells stories about who his master was, how he had sent him there, and how things were in Îrlant, thereby providing entertainment to help pass the time (3287–96). Later, Wigalois is to receive armor that had been stolen by a woman from a dwarf, who lived in a mountain and who had worked on it for thirty years. It was as light as a shirt, but no weapon could break or pierce it (6066–90). Eventually, Wigalois also fights Karriôz, a knight of Glois, who has long arms and short legs 'nach der getwerge sit' (6591), and defeats him after a long fight. Karriôz appears to be another Guivreiz-figure.

There are, of course, many more dwarfs that could be mentioned, and our selective survey has covered works only from the end of the eleventh century to the second half of the thirteenth, but it has enabled us to determine some of the characteristics of medieval German dwarfs, and these are quite varied. One thing, however, stands out, and that is the fact that the dwarfs in Arthurian literature, with few exceptions, are part of the court, or travel with knights and ladies of a court. They lack the special, magical powers of those dwarfs that have a more traditional, folkloristic, or even mythological background, although reference is made to these, too. Dwarfs at court are the retainers and the entertainers in normal courtly life, whereas the others are exotic creatures with immense powers and are usually associated with wealth and weapons. Interestingly enough, it seems that there is a gradual transference of courtly qualities to the dwarfs whose origins go far back into mythology, so that they too begin to take on courtly characteristics.

Let us turn now to the dwarfs in the various *Tristan* versions.[15] In Eilhart's *Tristrant* the dwarf is named Aquitain (3931) and, as in the other versions, is allied with the jealous barons who, led by Antrêt, conspire to bring about Tristrant's fall from favor. Aquitain is not a member of the court, living rather somewhere apart. He has the power to see in the stars all that has been and all that is to be (3390–97). The dwarf's helper, Satanâs, shows the barons where Aquitain is, and the devilish dwarf tells them that Isalde is holding Tristrant in her arms (3408–17). Brought before the king, Aquitain suggests the plan for the hunting expedition which would give Tristrant and Isalde the opportunity to meet secretly in the absence of the King (3426–37). Marke agrees to the plan and accordingly returns with the dwarf to observe the lovers' meeting from the vantage point of a linden tree in the garden. Eilhart obviously condemns Aquitain by calling him a 'vâlant' (3406) and by suggesting that the devil, Satanâs, must have helped him up into the tree (3480–88). When Tristrant and Isalde foil the dwarf's plot, Marke becomes incensed and would like to kill the dwarf, but Aquitain falls from the tree and flees (3614–19).

In the other episode with Aquitain, Tînas, the lord high steward, finds the dwarf in a thicket in the woods on a mountain while hunting and brings him back to court, promising to restore him to Marke's favor (3774–88). This time the dwarf's plan to entrap Tristrant and Isalde by strewing flour on the floor between the beds succeeds, when Aquitain, who had been hiding under Marke's bed, sounds the alarm. Tristrant, having bloodied the bed when his old wound burst open, tries to leap back to his own bed but can not quite make it, stepping once on the floor and leaving his footprint in the flour (3821–51).

In Béroul the dwarf is named Frocin. Marc, hiding in the tree alone, becomes very angry at the dwarf for making him believe untruths about Tristran and Yseut. He threatens to have Frocin hung or burned and also has in mind to put him to the sword for having him believe an outright lie (264–94). Frocin is described as a hunchback, who knows the paths of the stars and observes the seven planets. He can foretell the events of a child's life at birth. He knows that Marc is threatening him, and he flushes and swells with anger. He turns black, then pale with rage and soon flees to

---

15 Compare A. H. Krappe, 'Der Zwerg im Tristan', *Romanische Forschungen*, 45 (1931), 95–99.

Wales (320–336). However, he is summoned back later upon the advice of the three wicked barons and with his plan to entrap Tristran and Yseut offers to let Marc kill him, if he does not provide proof positive of their guilt. In Béroul, the dwarf does not hide under the bed. He leaves the room with Marc, but Tristran has seen him strewing the flour on the floor. The outcome is the same, with some minor variations (635–843).

Béroul adds one episode that ends with the death of the dwarf. While Tristran and Yseut are banished to the forest, the dwarf gets drunk and reveals to the barons that he knows the king's secret. He tells the barons that he will lead them to a hawthorn bush, under which there is a hollow place, and he will speak to them from the hollow. They have to make the hollow place larger because the dwarf has a large head. He is pushed inside up to the shoulders and tells the secret that he had sworn not to reveal: Marc has horse's ears. The king blames his condition on the dwarf and decapitates him (1306–50).

If the dwarfs in Eilhart and Béroul are not, strictly speaking, members of King Marke's court but are brought to the court by the jealous barons, Brother Robert's dwarf in the *Tristrams saga* (and very likely the dwarf in the version of Thomas) is quite at home there. In fact, he either sleeps in the royal chambers or very close by, because Markis tells him to ac-company him to matins when he rises in the dark of night in the scene where Tristram leaps from his bed to Ísönd's in order to avoid stepping on the fíour that the dwarf had strewn on the floor (Chapter 55). In the preceding episode (Ch. 54), the dwarf comes upon Tristram, who is cut-ting chips from a twig as a signal to Ísönd, and says that Ísönd wants to see him in the place where she had met him last. The dwarf mentions also that evil men envy him (the dwarf) and if he delays there, will denounce him to the king as the instigator of all the wickedness that goes on be-tween Ísönd and Tristram. Although Tristram does not tell the dwarf anything of importance, it is obvious that he had been trying to trap Tristram into revealing his plans to meet Ísönd by attempting to ingratiate himself. King Markis later climbs the tree to spy on Tristram and Ísönd at the dwarf's suggestion, but apparently the dwarf is not present.

In another later episode (Ch. 67), after the return from the Cave of Lovers, Markis and the dwarf come to a garden where Tristram and the queen had been embracing. Now, however, they are just sleeping. The king tells the dwarf – who in the matching fragment of Thomas had led him to the orchard – to wait there while he goes to fetch some of his barons as witnesses. What happens to the dwarf at this point is not clear either here or in Thomas. Tristram and Ísönd wake up, realize that the king has seen them together and decide to part. The evil dwarf, as he is frequently called by the narrator, simply drops from sight.

Two differences between Brother Robert's version and those discussed earlier should be noted. The dwarf is very definitely a part of the court. He does not live apart. He is still evil and hostile to Tristram and Ísönd, but he does not have the power to foretell the future that the dwarfs in Eilhart and Béroul possessed. In this respect he lacks some of the colorfulness of his counterparts – he is even lacking a name – but he does have a sort of courtly polish that is missing in the others.

We have returned to our point of departure: Melot petit von Aquitan, whom Gottfried introduces as a dwarf at court (14240), and who, it was alleged, had the ability to read about secret matters in the stars at night. But Melot never demonstrates that ability, and Gottfried quickly goes on to say that he will tell only what he finds in the true story: Melot was knowledgeable, artful and eloquent (14246–249). He had access to the king and to the queen's chambers and was recruited by Marjodo, to spy on Tristan and the queen. He used lies and deceit night and day and laid his traps for the lovers until he soon found out that they were indeed in love and accordingly informed King Marke (14261–273).

When Marke is away hunting, Tristan and Isot meet eight times secretly under the olive tree in the garden before Melot notices their assignations. However, 'daz vertane getwerc,/ des valandes antwerc' (14511–512), as Gottfried calls him, is unable to recognize Isot clearly, and he resorts to a ruse to try to get Tristan to reveal that it was indeed the queen whom he had met secretly. Tristan immediately sees through Melot's simulated friendship and tells him to leave. But Melot persuades the king to return secretly from the hunt and, concealed in the branches of an olive tree, to wait for the lovers. Of course, the shadows of Marke and Melot reveal their presence, and Melot's plan is foiled. Marke, now convinced of Isot's innocence after hearing the conversation, curses Melot for having deceived him and for having slandered his wife (14916–941).

Melot's last appearance is his attempt to incriminate Tristan and Isot by strewing flour on the floor (15117–266). Here Gottfried follows Brother Robert, or, if you will, Thomas, in practically every detail of the action, so that it is unnecessary to examine it closely. It tells us nothing more about Melot.

Looking back now on the dwarfs we considered outside of the *Tristan* poems and comparing them to the *Tristan* dwarfs, we can see certain elements not present in the latter. Most obvious is the fact that among the *Tristan* dwarfs we find no royal dwarfs, no Bîlêîs, no Guivreizes, no Alberichs (Ortnit's father), no Laurins. The *Tristan* dwarfs are not masters of great wealth or treasure, they possess no superhuman strength, they have no caps that make them invisible, nor do they make weapons. In short, they do not have the traditional folkloristic qualities of most of the other dwarfs, nor are they associated with the idea of a race or kingdom of dwarfs. But there are still traces of such traditions. The dwarfs in Eilhart, Béroul and, possibly, Gottfried are certainly no strangers to occult powers. They have knowledge of the future from the stars and are at least related directly to the dwarf in *Ruodlieb* in that respect and perhaps indirectly to the others. Eilhart's Aquitain is connected to the wild dwarfs in that he lives apart from court society. He is found in a thicket in the woods on a mountain, although that is admittedly not an underground realm or even a treasure room as in the *Nibelungenlied*. Frocin in Béroul's version is a hunchback, and this would seem to relate him to the wild dwarfs, or at least the more traditional dwarfs of folklore. But he is still called the King's dwarf, and that connects him directly to the court, although he does have to be sought out and later flees to Wales. Perhaps there is even a trace of the underground realm of dwarfs when Frocin is pushed into the hollow under the hawthorn bush. He also falls into a rage in his frustration like the dwarf in *Ruodlieb* and the wild dwarf from whom Guivreiz got the horse for Enite in *Erec*.

All the *Tristan* dwarfs have at least one thing in common: their association with the court. In this respect they are quite similar to the dwarfs in *Erec*, *Iwein* and *Wigalois*, the Arthurian romances we have treated. They are part of the court scene, functioning as retainers, but they can hardly be called entertainers as in *Wigalois*. They reflect the qualities of their masters, as in Hartmann, or at least those with whom they are most closely associated, King Marke himself, or the jealous barons. However, none of the *Tristan* dwarfs uses a scourge or knout like other Arthurian dwarfs or Alberich in the *Nibelungenlied*. Another characteristic they share, either expressly stated or implied, is a relationship with the devil or at least an association with evil, and they use their cleverness, deceit and evil intent to function at court.

Melot petit von Aquitan is truly a court dwarf. With his access to King Marke and to the royal chambers, he was probably a chamberlain of some sort, as dwarfs may well have been at some medieval courts. He fits well into the court to which he is attached. It is a court full of jealousy, intrigue and suspicion, and he is able to play on these traits to his advantage. He is an essential part of court intrigue, and his role as intriguer is developed somewhat more than it is in Gottfried's source. There is just a vestige of his literary heritage in the fact that he is 'said' to be able to read the secrets of the stars, but Gottfried passes over that lightly. It could be just dismissive of Eilhart or a generous nod on Gottfried's part to dwarf tradition (it is not in his source), and he involves Melot, not as an entertainer, but as a courtier, a talented and evil participant in the intrigues and jealousies of King Marke's court, reflecting, perhaps, the activities of some of his counterparts in real life.

Wounds and Healings:
Aspects of Salvation and Tragic Love
In Gottfried's Tristan*

PETRUS W. TAX

Gottfried's *Tristan* is peculiar in the sense that the love story proper, the amatory life and death of Tristan and Isolde, seems to begin only over 11,000 lines after the prologue.[1] Even if we discount the introductory story of Tristan's parents, it takes still almost 10,000 lines before we reach the episode of the love-potion, the actual beginning of the love story. In the past, several attempts have been made to point to all kinds of devices with which Gottfried appears to be bridging the gap – anticipations, *Motivreim*, preludes, prefigurations of a typological or non-typological nature, etc.[2] Without perhaps being able to say yet that the whole story is devoted to the theme of love, we certainly can maintain that images of love in a number of variations shape the work.

For the depiction and characterization of love Gottfried uses metaphors from several areas; one thinks specifically of the images of music, the

---

* In order to make the notes briefer and more readable I have listed the primary and secondary literature in a bibliography at the end of this contribution; thus I can normally refer to a short title or an author's (editor's) name only, but where necessary I use a short addition for clarification.

[1] This has been observed by scholars, but not questioned too much; for instance, Ruth Kunzer says only: 'The second part of the narrative mainly concerns the love story of the hero and heroine. In fact, the entire first part of the epic may be regarded as an extended prelude to the story of Tristan and Isolde as lovers' (p. 141). Still, from the point of view of composition and structure, the pre-amatory exposition would seem much too long and thus the whole narrative unbalanced, unless the prelude itself is basically amatory. It appears more and more that this is the case, and this paper attempts to further highlight more specifically Isolde's role in establishing and 'saving', perhaps even 'salvaging' love, before the love-story proper starts.

[2] e.g., Heinz Stolte, passim, Ann Snow, John Anson, Lucy Collings, Rolf Keuchen; see now in particular Franziska Wessel's *opus maximum*, passim (best accessible via her *Stichwortregister*, p. 645, s. v. 'Typologie').

hunt, birds and other animals, and also of wounds and healings.[3] In this area of vulnerability and curability many observations have been made by previous scholarship, but it seems to be possible to come up with some clearer patterns and a tighter overall interpretation. Unfortunately, it is not feasible in this paper to discuss the many cases of wounds in *Tristan* that are deadly – Morgan's, Morold's, Urgan's for instance.[4]

Metaphors of wounding and healing appear in several scenes in Gottfried's *Tristan*, most prominently in the episode of the first sexual fulfillment of the couple itself, also in the similar, prefigurative situation of Tristan's parents, then in the healing process of Tantris-Tristan at the Irish court after Tristan has been mortally wounded by Morold's poisoned sword. Before I return to this latter episode, I would like briefly to address an extension of the wounding/healing metaphor: the relationship between healing, wholeness, and salvation or redemption, or, to use the German wordplay, that between *Heilung, heil*, and *Heil*. I refer specifically to the often-observed phenomenon in Gottfried's work that women in love evidence a more emotional and spiritual depth than men, and even a kind of spiritual healing power. It suffices to mention Isolde, not only in the scene at the end when Tristan flees, but also in the Petitcreiu episode.

---

3 For recent studies in the area of *Bildlichkeit* in general see now especially the books by F. Wessel and Siegrun Kraschewski-Stolz; for the imagery of wounds and healings in particular Margit Sinka's dissertation (which I directed), the relevant parts of Hans Rolf's book, and Wessel, passim, esp. her section 'Minne als Krankheit und Ärztin', pp. 488–97. Some of Sinka's and Wessel's observations point in the direction of my own analysis, but the thrust of my approach is different from theirs and, as far as I have been able to ascertain, from other previous scholarship.

Several traditions of wound imagery can be distinguished: the classical-literary, especially Ovid, the Bible, classical, Germanic and medieval medicinal lore, etc. – see now especially Rüdiger Schnell's comprehensive investigations; cf. also the imagery of wounds and healing in Boethius' *Consolation of Philosophy*, and the role of the glosses, the commentaries, and particularly biblical exegesis (see the prologue of Hartmann's *Gregorius*). It is likely that a learned man such as Gottfried von Strassburg had access to several traditions, but in a mixed and merged form, a stream, from which his artistic genius would take what it could use. Unfortunately, Lambertus Okken in his recent commentary on Gottfried's *Tristan* has nothing of interest to say about wounds and healings; one of the appendices to his work, 'HEILKUNDE' (vol. 2, pp. 343–60, by H. M. Zijlstra-Zweens), remains purely factual.

4 Cf. M. Sinka, pp.106–116, and H. Rolf, esp. pp. 249–289. Some time ago I tried to interpret at least Urgan's wounds and death as love-allegorical, whereby Urgan himself appears, at this juncture in the narrative, as Tristan's alter ego (see Tax, 'Urgan'), but, ironically, the article was so badly treated by a *Setzteufel* or *-teufelin* that it – having never been proofread – is almost unreadable. F. Wessel read it nevertheless and admiringly questions its allegorical message in her *Exkurs* V, pp. 250–262, by taking my question mark seriously. But her own re-interpretation of Tristan's combats overlooks several important aspects and is not the last word either; I am preparing an article on all of Tristan's personal combats as 'allegories of love' in Gottfried's *Tristan*.

Ingrid Hahn summarizes this feature well: 'Isolde, so können wir vorsichtig sagen, übt in Gottfrieds Dichtung Heilsfunktionen aus'.[5]

Back to Tantris-Tristan. As we learn at the end of the Morold episode, Tristan's poisoned wound can only be healed by Morold's sister, the queen of Ireland. Since Morold's statement to this effect occurs during the fight on the little island, only Tristan knows that his deadly wound is, in fact, curable and by whom it can be cured. Ever prudent, Tristan hides the fact that Morold has wounded him from Morold's Irish retinue so as not to be found out and thus jeopardize his chances of being healed by Morold's sister.

Naturally, Tristan undertakes the voyage to Ireland in order to be cured by Queen Isolde. But is he healed by her?

A careful reading of the text shows that Gottfried, as so often, modifies the story considerably. Although the older Isolde recognizes the poisoned and deadly wound and promises to cure it, what she actually does looks only like a beginning: she makes Tantris approachable by somehow doing away with the stench of his wound:

> umb miner vrouwen arzatlist
> und umbe ir siechen genist
> wil ich iu kurzliche sagen:
> si half im inner zweinzec tagen
> daz man in allenthalben leit
> und nieman durch die wunden meit,
> der anders bi im wolte sin.   (7955–61)[6]

From here on, so it seems, young Isolde takes over. She is in the limelight all the time, is taught by Tantris, *gebezzeret* by him in the arts, especially of course in music, and trained in what Gottfried calls *moraliteit*. She publicly demonstrates what she has learned:

---

5   I. Hahn, p.118, at the end of a section in which she interprets Tristan's 'Ungedanken' and the couple's final separation.
6   Gottfried's *Tristan* is quoted from the edition by Friedrich Ranke. – In all previous scholarship it is stated that 'courtly' Gottfried polemicizes with Thomas's version and/or with Wolfram's presentation of Amfortas's wound; cf. Rüdiger Krohn's *Stellenkommentar*, pp. 91–92. Indeed, Thomas must have been quite explicit at this point, for the *Saga* gives many 'realistic' details of the healing procedures and Brother Robert is not likely to have added them to his source – cf. Paul Schach's translation, pp. 45–47. The connection with Wolfram is bound up with the unresolved question of chronological priority. The narrator's subsequent refusal to tell all the details of the medical cure would seem to be the more justified if he cannot really 'show and tell' it realistically because the healing process is primarily a spiritual one and on an interpersonal level that is higher than and different from natural medicine, however sophisticated, as administered by Queen Isolde.

Sus hæte sich diu schœne Isot
von Tristandes lere
gebezzeret sere.
si was suoze gemuot,
ir site und ir gebærde guot;
si kunde schœniu hantspil,
schœner behendekeite vil:
brieve und schanzune tihten,
ir getihte schone slihten,
si kunde schriben unde lesen.   (8132–41)

Tristan's training of Isolt and his cure are linked by rhyme:

nu was ouch Tristan genesen
ganz unde geheilet garwe,
daz ime lich unde varwe
wider luteren begunde.   (8142–45)

It is possible to interpret the situation and its results in different ways. Perhaps one has to assume that the healing powers of the older Isolde work also through her daughter. In fact, such a 'cooperation' might be seen in a wider context: I would suggest that the opposition between the role of the females and that of the male here is significant. Tristan receives his wound from Morold's poisoned sword. One may assume that the poison has a symbolic function. At any rate, Tristan's wound, coming from Morold, is a 'male' wound and, being a thigh wound, signifies some aspect of sexual love. The antidote to the 'male' wound is a 'female' cure: two women are needed to heal it, and they heal it completely. There is a striking parallel here with Erec's cure, especially in Hartmann's *Erec*,[7] and however different Tristan's 'male' wound may be from Erec's, I have no

---

[7]   There is a striking parallel with the stages of Erec's healing in Hartmann's work. Overall, the cure of the wound in his side is exclusively attempted by females. But the first phase of the process, administered by Queen Ginover with the help of Famurgan's *phlaster*, turns out to be less than successful (5129–52 and 5710–38), whereas the second stage, Erec's complete healing, is achieved by King Guivreiz's two sisters and by Enite herself (7188–236), but still with the help of Famurgan's salve (7225–31); see M. Sinka, pp. 30–40. In addition, the names of the two sisters, Filledamur and Genteflur (7786–7; they occur only in Hartmann's work), suggest an allegorical message. Since the concept of *antidotum* pervades medieval medicine, one wonders whether in such heterosexual love stories as Erec's and Tristan's the cure by several females, a 'liehte vrouwine schar' (so *Tristan*, 9345), does not indicate a basic male flaw in the hero which he cannot 'handle' himself. Even if this is so in principle, one should be aware that such flaws are likely to differ according to the character of the male protagonist; wounds as well as healings themselves are personal.

doubt that Gottfried here connects his story with Hartmann's, perhaps trying to outdo him.

But it is unwise to pretend to know more about the healing powers of the older Isolde than the narrator tells us. In line with Margit Sinka's interpretation,[8] I rather believe that Gottfried *changes* the configuration drastically so that Tristan's pre-amatory involvement with young Isolde causes the second and more positive stage of his healing process to be fully successful. The healing of Tantris-Tristan by young Isolde has its counterpart in the way young Isolde is raised by Tantris-Tristan to his own artistic level of perfection. Young Isolde is now well prepared to understand and help Tristan, not only on the artistic level, but particularly in her later function as healer. It seems to me, therefore, that Gottfried here, in the first phase of the Tantris-Tristan sequence, creates another prefiguration of later events on the amatory level; this scene thus becomes full of dramatic irony.

Such an interpretation can be strengthened and reinforced by a closer look at the second Tantris scene, in which Tantris is discovered in the bath by young Isolde. Tantris has been found by young Isolde, Isolde the Queen, and Brangaene (three females!) after his fight with the dragon, another male figure. When they find him in the pool he is not wounded in a literal sense, but has been overcome by the poisonous fumes of the dragon's tongue. Apparently, Tristan still carries the sword with which he had killed Morold (as well as the dragon, and cut out the latter's tongue), and which lacks the piece that stuck in Morold's skull.

Just before the bath scene proper the narrator connects Tantris' present state with his situation at the end of the first stage: both Isoldes had taken good care of him:

> ir beider vliz was alle wege
> mit süezer bedæhtekeit
> niuwan an diu dinc geleit,
> diu sin helfe solten wesen.

---

[8] I tend to agree with M. Sinka's statement: 'Neither Famurgan's salve (in Hartmann's *Erec*) nor Queen Isolde's medication can heal the respective heroes. Tristan is simply made presentable to others. Queen Isolde mitigates the terrible nature of his wound and thereby paves the way for the young Isolde's entrance. The actual cure will result from Tristan's tutoring of Isolde' (p.112); cf. also F. Wessel, pp. 329 and 346 about Isolde's 'purifying' effect on Tristan in this scene: '(Young Isolde,) die ihn, anders als bei Eilhart, nicht ärztlich geheilt hat, deren Einwirkung auf Tristans Zustand vielmehr, der Metapher des Läuterns entsprechend, einen innermenschlichen Bereich einschließt . . .' (p. 346). It is strange that Gerhard Schindele in his otherwise perceptive book reads Gottfried's narrative at this point as if it were still Eilhart's: 'Die Mutter heilt Tristan noch vor dem Bad . . .' (p. 51).

> ouch was er iezuo wol genesen,
> lieht an dem libe und schone var.   (9986–91)

One notices that the rhyme with *genesen* and the light imagery that illustrated Tantris' recovery are repeated here. It is young Isolde who discovers that Tantris is identical with Tristan, her uncle's killer, and she
does this via the damaged sword.

From a narrative point of view, the fact that Isolde turns her attention
to the knightly equipment of the *spilman* Tantris is not too well motivated,
but the language the narrator uses is certainly erotically suggestive:

> und enweiz niht, wie si des gezam,
> daz si daz swert ze handen nam,
> als juncvrouwen unde kint
> gelustic unde gelengic sint [9]
> und weizgot ouch genuoge man.   (10065–69)

Isolde studies the sword[10] for a long time and intensely, the thought
strikes her that the missing piece is in her possession, and:

> si brahte in unde saztin dar:
> nu vuogete diu lucke
> und daz vertane stucke
> und waren alse einbære,[11]

---

[9]   cf. the description of Marke's newly aroused sexual desire for Isolde at the end of
the love grotto episode:
> in gelangete unde geluste,
> daz er si gerne kuste.   (17591–92)
The feature of voyeurism is common to both scenes and connects them on a thematic level. Clearly, the narrator suggests love and sex in both episodes.
[10]   The somewhat surprising use here of the word *gebreste* in 10072 and 10077 – according to Melvin Valk's *Word-Index* a hapax legomenon in Gottfried's work – for the
splinter rather than for the gap in the sword – emphasizes more than other words that
something is missing and carries overtones of a bodily, perhaps also moral nature
('flaw').
[11]   On the purely narrative level Tristan later uses his sword to kill Urgan and also to
deceive Marke in the famous scene in the love grotto. He uses it, too, in his combats
toward the end of the work. Since nobody, not even Marke, apparently, notices the
'repaired' spot, the sword must at least look whole. Gottfried certainly knew that a
once damaged sword could not be restored by normal means (cf. the *als ob* in 10084).
Still, I believe that poetic truth requires it to be whole again, and it is evident that it
functions as such in the rest of the story. It is significant that, *if* Gottfried had finished
the story according to Thomas's version, Tristan would have received a second, equally
poisonous wound which causes his death. In Thomas's story Tristran receives this
wound by defending his namesake, Tristran the Dwarf, who himself is killed in the
fight; see Hatto's *Tristan* translation, pp. 338–41. For a love-allegorical interpretation of
this scene see the end of my article on Urgan, pp. 51–52. If Tristan and his fate seem to

als ob ez ein dinc wære,
als ouch gewesen waren
innerhalp zwein jaren. (10080–86)

Isolde makes Tantris' sword whole again, or rather, it is Isolde who makes Tristan's sword whole again. There is much narrative and dramatic irony in this scene, but I can safely leave it to the reader to think through and perhaps enjoy the many implications that Tristan's restored sword may have.[12] Suffice it for me to say in the context of my argument that Isolde, so to speak, 'heals' Tristan's sword, and that the key terms *einbaere* and *ein dinc* anticipate on the one hand the narrator's immediate reaction to the effect of the love-potion on the couple:

si waren beide einbære
an liebe unde an leide
und halen sich doch beide, (11730–32)

and on the other, Isolde's famous phrase in her last words to Tristan at the end:

nu gat her und küsset mich:
Tristan und Isot, ir und ich,
wir zwei sin iemer beide
ein dinc ane underscheide. (18351–54)

Again, therefore, young Isolde, unwillingly and unwittingly, prefigures her own later 'healing' actions in the realm of love. It is, I think, of some significance that the sword- 'wound' was of Tristan's own, 'male' making; again a female, but this time only one female – she will soon become his companion in love – restores it.

The next step is the linguistic discovery by Isolde that Tantris is identical with Tristan. Tristan had changed his name when he came to Ireland for the first time in order to disguise his identity. The fact that it is young

---

be reflected in the casualties and 'adventures' of his sword, its essential irreparability (*gebreste*) neatly symbolizes Tristan's imperfection, also as a lover. And if the dragon also and in an allegorical sense stands for *amour-passion* (cf. Anson, p. 603), the fact that Tristan (or rather Tantris) kills it with his at this point still 'imperfect' or 'incomplete' sword may very well prefigure the outcome of his personal struggle with love: the phenomenon of passionate love is mastered, also by him, but at the price of a diminished *integritas* on his part.

12 According to M. Valk's *Word-Index* the word *einbaere* occurs seven times in *Tristan*: 2393, 5246, 6609, 10083, 10984, 11730, 16965, also twice as *einbaereliche* in 913 and 10190. It always – except in the scene of Tristan's sword – signifies that two normally *different* (heterogeneous) things or persons become, or appear as, one. In all cases, the narrator appears to perceive two things as one and wants the reader to do the same.

Isolde who turns Tantris back into Tristan and restores Tristan's real name is significant in itself and another aspect of Isolde making Tristan whole again. But there is more.

After Tristan's birth the narrator drives home the etymology of Tristan's name, deriving it from *triste* (1. 2003), perhaps also from *an*, a variant for *on*, *homme*:[13]

> er [Tristan] was reht alse er hiez ein man
> und hiez reht alse er was: Tristan. (2021–22)

No doubt, Tristan's birth and his later life are essentially *triste*. Perhaps we should not forget this etymology at this point. In order to stay out of trouble, Tristan has cut up his name and rejoined it in such a manner that the etymology was not recognizable any longer; in fact, the name Tantris is quite nonsensical. It is Tristan who has destroyed the etymology of his own 'sad' name – whether wittingly or not – whereas Isolde (no doubt unwittingly) restores it. Tantris becomes Tristan again, the real name of the male protagonist was lost but is found again. Soon Tristan will be united with Isolde in love. Young Isolde, therefore, not only makes Tristan's sword (by the way, originally a gift from Marke) whole again, but also his real name, the symbol of his destiny.[14]

Somewhat later, Isolde explains her discovery to her mother:

> 'sich, muoter' sprach diu tohter do
> 'wie wunderlichen ich bevant,
> daz er Tristan was genant:
> do ich des swertes zende kam,

13 Brother Robert probably translated Thomas quite literally here. Having stated that the child is named Tristram because of the many sorrows surrounding its birth, he continues: 'For in this tongue *trist* means *sorrow* and *hum* means *man*. And the reason his name was changed is that *Tristram* sounds nicer than *Tristhum*' (Schach, p.19). It is likely that in and around Strassburg one would pronounce French *(h)on* as *an* – cf. Gottfried's use of *van* instead of normal MHG *von*. The wordplay *Trist-an* = *Trist-(h)on* may very well have been intended by Gottfried, too; cf. Hertz' learned note, pp. 499–501. And considering the fact that Isolde as a woman is so much more in tune with unconditional love – especially toward the end – than Tristan, one may perhaps infer that Gottfried wished to show in Tristan's life and death a typically 'manly' destiny.
14 My 'precise' interpretation – the clean reversal of the parts of the names Tris-tan / Tan-tris – is based on Gottfried's own precision. In the other versions, the disguised form Tantris is stable, but it does not constitute a pure reversal of the hero's name: almost always Tristrant in Eilhart (see the index in Lichtenstein's edition, pp. 470–71), Tristran (Tristrans, Tristram, Tristans) in Thomas's fragments (see the index in Wind's edition, p. 235), Tristran (Tristrans, Tristranz) in Béroul (see the index in Muret's edition, p. 157). One may assume that Gottfried 'created' the precise form Tristan (especially without the second *r*) also in order to keep the etymological derivation from *trist(e)* present.

die namen ich ze handen nam
Tantris unde Tristan;
nu ich si triben began,
nu beduhte mich an in zwein,
si hæten eteswaz in ein.' (10598–606)

She then explicates her whole linguistic analysis to her. The Queen reacts
as follows:

diu muoter segenete sich:
'got' sprach si 'der gesegene mich![15]
von wannen kam dir ie der sin?' (10623–25)

We know where Isolde's sophistication comes from. Tantris, as Tristan in
disguise, has taught her. We are coming full-circle here: *she* un-disguises
Tantris with the same *sin* he had taught her, thus – not without some
measure of narrative irony – restoring his identity with the help of his
own intellectual weapons. Thus a pattern is set that will be used consciously and consistently time and again after the couple fall in love: I
mean their virtuoso plays with words by means of which they are able to
mislead Marke and the court and avoid discovery and disaster.

It seems that a similar but much deeper rational faculty inspires Isolde
at the end to rise above the situation when she expresses her confidence,
based on their mutual love, that she and Tristan will remain one and
undivided in separation,

'stæte unz an den tot,
niwan ein Tristan und ein Isot'. (18357–58)

This points ahead to Tristan's love affair with Isolde Whitehand. It is not
without significance that there is another identity problem here: whereas
Isolde had turned Tantris back into Tristan – two names for one person –
Tristan has to struggle with different aspects of 'Isolde', one name for (at
least) two persons. More importantly, Isolde's tendency is to restore and
unite, Tristan's to divide and dissolve. On the whole, one can maintain
that the Tristan figure is a tragic hero and lover. His predominant character trait, his intellectuality, leads him often, and particularly when confronted with irrational love, into predicaments into which he does not
want, or is not prepared, to get. On the basis of his 'personality', his
character in the modern sense, his downfall at the end (whether it would
have led to the consummation of the marriage with Isolde Whitehand or
not) is well motivated so that his tragic end is consistent and quite un-

---

[15] There might be some narrative irony here in Queen Isolde's *segenen*, 'making the
sign of the cross' over herself, and then in her asking God to bless her (*gesegenen*) – with
the same 'sign' of the 'cross'?!

avoidable. But Isolde's case is very different: her death is a mere accident, assuming that Gottfried would have followed Thomas or Eilhart, but more to the point, her much more accurate and deeper assessment of the spiritual dimension of their mutual love[16] makes her see her partner's flaws in a sharp light so that she recognizes the dangers for him and still can assure herself that their love will emerge stronger, stronger, in fact, than death.[17] In other words, from Isolde's vantage point as Gottfried develops it, this love is not tragic, however near-tragic it may be; loving Isolde anticipates her partner's struggles with aspects of their love, is able to resolve the dilemma for herself and might even stretch out her helping and 'healing' hand to troubled Tristan.[18]

BIBLIOGRAPHY

Primary Literature and Translations

Béroul, *Le roman de Tristan, Poème du xiie siècle*, ed. by Ernest Muret (Paris, fourth edition, 1957)

Eilhart von Oberge, *Tristrant*, ed. by Franz Lichtenstein (Strassburg and London, 1877)

Gottfried von Strassburg, *Tristan und Isold*, ed. by Friedrich Ranke (Berlin, 1930, reprint, 1949)

Gottfried von Strassburg, *Tristan. Translated entire for the first time. With the surviving fragments of the 'Tristran' of Thomas, newly translated*. With an introduction by A. T. Hatto (Harmondsworth, 1960)

Hartmann von Aue, *Erec*, ed. by Albert Leitzmann, Altdeutsche Textbibliothek, 39 (Tübingen, second edition, 1957)

Tristan und Isolde von Gottfried von Strassburg. Neu bearbeitet von Wilhelm Hertz. Fünfte Auflage. Mit einem Nachtrag von Wolfgang Golther (Stuttgart, 1907)

---

[16] About Isolde as the more profound lover see now F. Wessel, passim, esp. pp. 444–53 and 564–66; this feature had been pointed out before, e.g. by I. Hahn, pp.112–118, Jackson, pp.113–14, Batts, p. 70, Tax, *Wort*, pp.116, 154–56, 175–77, or Tax, 'Urgan', pp. 46–47. But already Dante places Tristan, not Isolde, among the lovers who burn in his *Inferno* (Book V), next to Paris and Helen of Troy.

[17] That true love such as that between Tristan and Isolde transcends life and death is most clearly expressed in Gottfried's two 4-line stanzas with the *brot: tot* rhymes at the end of his prologue, 233–40.

[18] cf. Isolde's words at the end, when Tristan sails away:

> mit swelher not ich sin enber,
> mir ist doch lieber vil, daz er
> gesundes libes von mir si,
> dan er mir also wære bi,
> daz ich mich des versæhe,
> daz im schade bi mir geschæhe. (18583–88)

The Saga of Tristram and Ísönd, translated with an introduction by Paul Schach (Lincoln, Nebraska, 1973)
Les fragments du Roman de Tristan, poème du xiie siècle par Thomas, ed. with commentary by Bartina H. Wind (Leiden, 1950)

Secondary Literature

Anson, John S., 'The Hunt of Love: Gottfried von Strassburg's *Tristan* as Tragedy', *Speculum*, 45 (1970), 594–607

Batts, Michael S., *Gottfried von Strassburg* (New York, 1971)

Collings, Lucy G., 'Structural Prefiguration in Gottfried's *Tristan*', *JEGP*, 72 (1973), 378–389

Hahn, Ingrid, *Raum und Landschaft in Gottfrieds 'Tristan': Ein Beitrag zur Werkdeutung* (Munich, 1963)

Jackson, W. T. H., *The Anatomy of Love: The 'Tristan' of Gottfried von Strassburg* (New York, 1971)

Keuchen, Rolf, *Typologische Strukturen im 'Tristan': Ein Beitrag zur Erzähltechnik Gottfrieds von Strassburg*, Diss. (Cologne, 1975)

Kraschewski-Stolz, Siegrun, *Studien zu Form und Funktion der Bildlichkeit im 'Tristan' Gottfrieds von Strassburg* (Göppingen, 1983)

Krohn, Rüdiger, *Gottfried von Strassburg, 'Tristan'*, vol. 3: *Kommentar, Nachwort und Register* (Stuttgart, 1980)

Kunzer, Ruth Goldschmidt, *The 'Tristan' of Gottfried von Strassburg: An Ironic Perspective* (Berkeley, California, 1973)

Okken, Lambertus, *Kommentar zum Tristan-Roman Gottfrieds von Strassburg*, 2 vols (Amsterdam, 1984–85)

Ranke, Friedrich, *Tristan und Isold* (Munich, 1925)

Rolf, Hans, *Der Tod in mittelhochdeutschen Dichtungen* (Munich, 1974)

Schindele, Gerhard, *Tristan: Metamorphose und Tradition* (Stuttgart, 1971)

Schnell, Rüdiger, *Causa amoris: Liebeskonzeption und Liebesdarstellung in der mittelalterlichen Literatur* (Berne, 1985)

Sinka, Margit M., *Wound Imagery in the Medieval German Epic: Structural Significance of Wounds*, Diss. (Chapel Hill, North Carolina, 1974)

Snow, Ann, 'Wilt, wilde, wildenaere: A Study in the Interpretation of Gottfried's *Tristan*', *Euphorion*, 62 (1968), 365–377

Stolte, Heinz, *Eilhart und Gottfried. Studie über Motivreim und Aufbaustil* (Halle, 1941)

Tax, Petrus W., *Wort, Sinnbild, Zahl im Tristanroman. Studien zum Denken und Werten Gottfrieds von Strassburg* (Berlin, second edition, 1971)

Tax, Petrus W., 'Tristans Kampf mit Urgan in Gottfrieds Werk: Eine Psychomachie der Liebe?', *Michigan Germanic Studies*, 3 (1977), 44–53

Valk, Melvin E., *Word-Index to Gottfried's 'Tristan'* (Madison, Wisconsin, 1958)

Wessel, Franziska, *Probleme der Metaphorik und die Minnemetaphorik in Gottfrieds von Strassburg 'Tristan und Isolde'* (Munich, 1984)

The Love-Potion as a Poetic Symbol in Gottfried's Tristan

AUGUST CLOSS

In Gottfried's *Tristan* the love-potion and the grotto of love are of central significance. My endeavour in this symposium volume is to re-interpret the artistic meaning of the love-potion scene alone. It is the key to Gottfried's great work and it is essentially symbolic in character. He endows *minne* with an almost religious but not absolute value. A poetic genius, and theologically highly trained, Gottfried is the first German medieval author to direct his invocation not to the Christian deity but to another transcendental power – to Apollo and the Nine Muses (4869). At the ordeal with the *iudicium ferri candentis* Isolt depends for her protection upon 'gotes hövescheit' (15556.) Gottfried distances himself from morbid superstitions and rituals with the comment:

> daz der vil tugenthafte Krist
> wintschaffen alse ein ermel ist.   (15739–40)[1]

In his abundant goodness Christ himself is fickle ('wetterwendisch') as a windblown sleeve. There is an unmistakably inordinate tone in this passage. As to Ordo: in his inaugural lecture, Bernard Willson deals discerningly with the concept of divine ordo as *mensura, numerus, pondus,* and with Gottfried's unorthodox concept of God. Everything is measured – numbered – weighed according to the heavenly order of things, as presented in the apocryphal wisdom of Solomon; therefore, man's disorderly self-will (*superbia*) and the passion of love are in opposition to that ordo. However, Isolt prays to the 'courtly' divinity, and Gottfried's stand-

---

[1]   The *Tristan* quotations are from the edition by Reinhold Bechstein and from my own annotated selection with introduction and glossary: *Tristan und Îsolt. A poem by Gottfried von Strassburg,* Blackwell's German Texts (Oxford, 1944, reprinted ²1947, ⁵1974). All translations from Middle High German into English are my own unless otherwise indicated. Thomas is quoted from J. Bédier, *Le Roman de Tristan par Thomas. Poème du XIIe siècle* (Paris, 1902–05). Also cited: J. Bédier, *Le Roman de Tristan et Iseut.* Traduit et restauré . . . Preface by Gaston Paris, 347th ed. (Paris, 1900).

ards are those of the order of the 'noble hearts' who live in 'ein ander werlt'.[2]

In the Prologue to his *Tristan* Gottfried devotes his whole being to this other world, i.e. the world of the noble hearts – 'fins cuers leals'. Anything lying outside this totally dedicated life is meaningless. It is a world of extremes, of 'verderben oder genesen' (66), an existence of demonic rapture in which the dear and the sad, heart's delight and mournful death live together. Yet such love is immortal: 'ir süezer name der lebet iedoch' (223). Here is the relevant passage from the Prologue:

> ein ander werlt die meine ich,
> diu sament in einem herzen treit
> ir süeze sûr, ir liebez leit,
> ir herzeliep, ir senede nôt,
> ir liebez leben, ir leiden tôt,
> ir lieben tôt, ir leidez leben:
> dèm lebene sî mîn leben ergeben,
> dèr werlt wil ich gewerldet wesen,
> mit ir verderben oder genesen . . .   (58–66)

(I mean another world,/which unites in one heart/the sweet bitterness, the dear sadness,/the heart's delight, the pain of yearning,/its beloved life, its mournful death,/its beloved death, its mournful life:/to *this* life may my life be dedicated,/to *this* world I want to belong,/to perish or be saved with it . . .)

The originality of language and vision in this passage introduces us into Gottfried's 'ander werlt'. Nothing in it is purely imitative. Gottfried shows particular originality in the treatment of the love-potion scene. In his source (Thomas's *Tristan*), the love-drink is the *cause* of love. In Gottfried it is neither the excuse nor the reason for love, but a poetic symbol. My claim (as I hope to prove through Gottfried's own text) is: Liebestrank oder nicht – the climax in Gottfried's *Tristan* is inescapable. The author, moreover, speaks from his own experience:

> ich weiz ez wârez alse den tôt
> und erkenne ez bî der selben nôt . . .   (Prologue, 119–20)

and

> Diz weiz ich wol, wan ich was dâ.   (Cave of Lovers, 17104)

Thomas denies such personal experience:

---

[2]   H.B. Willson, 'Love and Order in the Medieval German Courtly Epic', Inaugural Lecture, University of Leicester (Leicester, 1973).

Pur essemple l'ai issi fait
E pur l'estorie embelir,
Que as amanz deive plaisir,
E que par lieus poissent trover
Chose u se puissent recorder ... (3136ff)

and

Ne la raison dire ne sai,
Por ce que esprové ne l'ai.
La parole mettrai avant,
Le jugement facent amant ... (1086–89)

At the end of the Prologue, Gottfried, in a characteristically liturgical tone, evokes a metaphor with mystical associations: 'ir leben, ir tôt sint unser brôt' (236). The analogy to the *Sermons on the Song of Songs* by the Cistercian Dr Mellifluus, St Bernard (1090–1153), is undeniable. However, the love between Tristan and Isolt is not a Christian love: it is of a different 'ordo' in which marriage is unthinkable, and yet in which Tristan and Isolt remain ultimately faithful to each other. Gottfried's unique power of imagination and of psychological insight into human feelings and passions presents us with the secret of a gradually awakening *unconscious* love *long before* the 'Liebestrank', and in a progressive heightening he leads us to a culmination which has the finality of a Greek tragedy.

The key to the understanding of the lovers' fatality lies in the text itself. There is no serene 'unio mystica', but (as the Prologue tells us) Minne brings sweetness as well as pain. The 'gotinne Minne' (Venus) acts already in the Riwalîn-Blancheflûr episode as the 'gewaltærinne' ('Gewalt-haberin'). In *Tristan* Minne is the 'verwerrærinne' ('Verwirrerin'); the 'strickærinne' ('Ver- und Bestrickerin'), an 'ensnarer'. Minne is the way-layer of all hearts, huntress and persecutor, conquering the citadel of the heart, 'erbevogetîn', the Lady of the Manor.

Love is presented as a daemonic force which has already taken possession of Tristan's parents, Riwalîn and Blancheflûr, but without the introduction of a love-potion. However, their love cannot convincingly be compared with that of Tristan and Isolt. The 'Minnetrank' (11682ff and 12491ff) and the preceding scenes lead *gradually* to an *inescapable* fate. This, as the text will show, strongly suggests that the love-potion is but a symbol of what has happened between the two lovers a *long time before* the magic potion is accidentally presented.

I am not alone in claiming this interpretation as the only true reading of Gottfried's text: a number of scholars have already made similar suggestions. Julius Schwietering for example evoked in his 'Deutsche Dichtung des Mittelalters' (1942) the 'leiblich-seelische' union of the two lovers: 'Das Erwachen der Liebe längst vor dem Zaubertrank ... die Schuldlosigkeit der Liebenden aus der Perspektive des Dichters' (pp. 185–86). In his comprehensive study, 'Gottfrieds von Strassburg 'Tristan' und die Krise des hochmittelalterlichen Weltbildes um 1200', 2 vols (Stuttgart, 1953), Gottfried Weber also stresses the symbolic character of the love-potion: ' . . . der symbolische Zaubertrank, der keineswegs die längst unbewußt vorhandene Liebe der Seelen [my italics], wohl aber den unwiderstehlichen Zwang der Begierde und der Sinnesekstase auslöst . . . ' (I, 125).

We find a kindred view, although not so forcefully expressed, already in Friedrich Ranke's Tristan und Isold (1925). For him, too, the love-potion scene is a fundamentally symbolic act. He maintains that the love-scene was probably invented by the anonymous author of the first (now lost) unified Tristan-Romance. Thomas's version, as reflected in the Tristrams saga, describes how King Mark, unlike Isolt, drinks some of the remaining potion in the wedding-night. Thus Tristan and King Mark are forever bound to Isolt. Above all, in contrast to Gottfried, Thomas presents the 'Zaubertrank' scene traditionally, i.e. the fatal love-passion is in Thomas's version simply initiated and exclusively motivated by the magic potion, cf. Bédier's modern French version of this scene: a little serving maid 'présenta [le vin/le hanap] à sa maîtresse. Elle but à longs traits, puis le tendit à Tristan, qui le vida'. The only acceptable, psychological interpretation is provided by Gottfried who, as Ranke emphasized, thought of Tristan formally offering the love-cup first to Isolt, before he drinks – a significant change in the lovers' relationship. No Tristan-poet thought of this before Gottfried. Moreover, Gottfried was able to reveal his hero's inner feelings: 'Es konnte sich . . . hier nur noch darum handeln, die Vorgänge im Innern seines Helden in einzelnen Szenen herauszustellen . . . er kennt . . . im Grunde keine andre Moral als das Gesetz der Liebe' (Ranke, Tristan und Isold, p. 198). A careful reading of Gottfried's text will confirm that the accident of the love-potion – an event of mere chance – cannot be interpreted as the one and only reason and instrument of the lovers' fatality. To dismiss categorically the symbolic character of the love-potion scene cannot be justified. But before I refer to different interpretations, one more point needs mentioning here, to ensure that there is no misunderstanding of Gottfried's text.

There is, of course, not the faintest suggestion of a Wagnerian 'Todeslust' in Tristan's bold words about ecstasy and death in response to Brangaene's warning that the draught will be the death of both lovers: 'der ist iuwer beider tôt' (12493). Tristan wants 'dirre tôt', i.e. carnal rapture, which he longs to experience again and again, thus wooing a loving death:

> 'sô wolt ich gerne werben
> umb' ein êweclîchez sterben.'   (12505–06)

'Dirre tôt', death in loving ecstasy, is contrasted with 'jener tôt', actual human death:

'ez hât mir sanfte vergeben. ('it has poisoned me tenderly')
i'ne weiz, wie jener werden sol.' (12500–1)

The lovers' bodily and mental suffering and yearning are as if woven into
one heart and *one* soul:

si wâren beide under in zwein
mit übele und mit guote al ein. (14341–42)

This deadly conflict between loyalty and passion, yearning and anguish,
is already the theme in the Prologue.

Before presenting my own reading of the relevant passages in Gottfried
I turn briefly to the main aspects of two views in which the symbolic
interpretation of the 'Liebestrank' is plainly, even fervently rejected. Both
authors differ in their arguments, but they are of one mind as to the
function of the potion. Both authors – as I see it – lead us away from
Gottfried's text. In each case I shall offer considered reasons (supported
by the text) for my claim that Gottfried's love-potion is *symbolic* and can
only have a *symbolic* meaning.

Gottfried's *Tristan* – one of the greatest creative works in German and
in world literature – has suffered from an overlay of critical artifices. My
only concern, again, is to establish the true nature and function of the
love-potion scene.

In his article 'Minnetrank und Minne',[3] P.F. Ganz considers the
'Liebestrank' as *the* 'causa causans': 'der Zufall wird zum Instrument des
Schicksals' (p. 66). The potion is not seen as a symbol of what psychologically has been going on between Tristan and Isolt. But is there no trace of
affection or *unconscious love* to be discovered in the relationship between
them both *long before* the love-potion scene? Not even when Isolt finds out
who the minstrel Tantris really is? And is Gottfried's own text not in
conflict with Ganz's ingenious artifice according to which Minne, in her
many rôles and masks, endowed with an absolute *transcendental* power,
actively guides, shapes and decides the fate of Tristan and Isolt. Minne is
the 'erbevogetîn', the decoyer, enticer, ensnarer, the mistress of the chase,
and above all the guardian as well as the controller of the already mysteriously *preconditioned* characters of the lovers. Such a concept of the rôle of
Minne, generating and moulding the unalterable, predetermined destiny
of Tristan and Isolt would make void all creative originality on the part of
Gottfried and invalidate his subtle psychological characterization of their
awakening, unconscious love leading to their ultimate fatality. The essen-

---

3 'Minnetrank und Minne. Zu *Tristan*, Z.11707f', in *Formen mittelalterlicher Literatur:
Siegfried Beyschlag zu seinem 65. Geburtstag*, edited by Otmar Werner and Bernd
Naumann, Göppinger Arbeiten zur Germanistik, 25 (Göppingen, 1970).

tially antithetic world of 'les fins cuers leals': *süeze sûr, liep/leit, wunne/senede nôt* (which, as we pointed out earlier, is re-echoed in Gottfried's vision of 'ein ander werlt') is also a central theme in *The Plaint of Nature*: the *De planctu Naturae* by the philosopher, theologian and (finally) Cistercian monk Alanus de Insulis (Alan of Lille, *c.*1116–1202), a work cited by P.F. Ganz[3] with reference to U. Stöckle (Ulm, 1915), and earlier – with lesser emphasis – by Gustav Ehrismann in his literary history. Ehrismann points to the importance of Alanus's *Planctus* because it mirrors the ethical centre in Gottfried's work: 'den ethischen Kern des *Tristan*' (2.2, 1, p. 326 note).

The question is: does Gottfried, like Alanus, see in Nature the 'Dei auctoris vicaria', and does her 'subvicaria' (Venus) guarantee Nature's order? So far no serious claim for a wider influence of the *Planctus* on Gottfried's *Tristan* has been established. Ganz's image of the absolute function of Minne, mysteriously shaping, directing the nature as well as the destiny of the lovers in *Tristan* is, no doubt, tempting, but it cannot be superimposed upon Gottfried's text which reveals to the reader another, no less exciting scenario. According to Ganz's interpretation, Minne, the 'erbevogetîn', whose power is supreme, 'hat die *natiure* der beiden Liebenden geschaffen, und beide gehören ihr an, bevor sie sich kennen lernen' (p. 70). Such a supposition of an *a priori* predisposition, a fixed tendency of the characters, and an *a priori* situation in which the fate of Tristan and Isolt is *supernaturally* guided by Minne, would, as has been pointed out, reduce Gottfried's mastery of psychological motivation (in which he excels) to empty gestures. Moreover, Gottfried's text unfolds before us with irrevocable force the lovers' *gradually growing, unconscious* passion of love. But according to Ganz's view, '*des trankes craft*' is the *one* and *only* cause, 'die reale Ursache des zu Geschehenden' – 'Die Wirkung des Trankes wird durch nichts vorweggenommen' (p. 65). Thus, *chance*, in conjunction with *natiure*, becomes fate or, as Ganz emphatically puts it: 'Der Trank bleibt die causa causans' (p. 66).

In the Introduction to his translation of Gottfried's *Tristan*,[4] A.T. Hatto presents problems and ambiguities of the work. He admits that Tristan and Isolt 'are certainly occupied with each other in some way prior to drinking the potion'. Alas, he soon retracts and adds, surprisingly, that 'it would be very modern and therefore very profound of Gottfried to have them unconsciously in love'. Against this it should be stated that Gottfried is indeed profound and, as a creative writer, in advance of his time. In his penetrating study: 'The *Renovatio Amoris* in Gottfried's Tristan', R.A. Wisbey, whilst not underestimating the influence on

---

[4]   A.T. Hatto, Gottfried von Strassburg, *Tristan. Translated entire for the first time. With the surviving fragments of the 'Tristran' of Thomas, newly translated. With an introduction*, Penguin Classics (Harmondsworth, Middlesex, 1960)

Gottfried of the medieval rhetoric of passion, unreservedly pays tribute to Gottfried's imaginative power and 'supreme understanding of the psychology of love'.[5]

In contrast to Thomas, as already indicated, Gottfried personally experienced and had insight into the psychology of passionate love: 'ich weiz ez wârez alse den tôt/und erkenne ez bî der selben nôt' (119–20; cf. 108–18). The author builds up the story of the lovers in a psychologically irresistible progression: see e.g. Isolt's remark: 'ein lîp alsô gebære/ . . . der solte guot und êre hân' (10031–33), which reflects her admiration for Tristan's shapely proportions and noble demeanour, and her inquisitiveness about his birth and social status. The interpretation of such statements, even in a medieval text, should not be ruled out as smacking of modern psychology!

Hatto is sure that it was a philtre which made the lovers fall in love: 'Love had come because Tristan and Isolde had chanced to drink a magic draught together' (pp. 22–23) . . . 'it was a philtre which made his lovers fall in love' (p. 28). Yet he also acknowledges Gottfried's 'deep understanding of human motives' (p. 22), and he even applies the term 'symbolic' to the use of the love-potion, while at the same time insisting on the conventional view that it was 'causa causans'. He writes (p. 29): 'It would be fair to say that although Gottfried employs the love-philtre symbolically (how could it fail to symbolize fatal passion?), this does not preclude it from being the cause of Tristan and Isolde's love'. This acceptance of the word 'symbolic' is very different from what is meant in the present essay by the symbolic character of the love-potion. The potion is not just a visible sign for the 'cause' or onset of love; but Gottfried with imaginative insight suggests to us the gradual awakening of unconscious love long before the actual 'Liebestrank' is offered. Moreover, Hatto strangely compares the fatal passion of the lovers with that of Tristan's parents, Riwalîn and Blancheflûr. In spite of the obvious differences of character and circumstance, he even finds here a parallel and a clue to the situation of Tristan and Isolt and comes to the bewildering conclusion (pp. 28–29): 'There were no hints of unconscious love in Rivalin before Blancheflor sighed at him; so that this parallel alone is enough to suggest that there was no unconscious love between Tristan and Isolde . . . any change in Isolde's character must be attributed to the potion'. The claim of a compelling parallel between the love of Tristan's parents and Tristan and Isolt, and also the categorical insistence that in *both* cases 'there was no unconscious love' involved (p. 29), are unjustified. Gottfried's artistic subtlety is illustrated already long *before*, and also particularly just before, the love-potion scene in Isolt's *long-drawn-out* laments (11574ff) and agitated

---

5   In *London German Studies I*, edited by C.V. Bock, Publications of the Institute of Germanic Studies, University of London, 26 (London, 1980), pp. 1–66 (p. 61, note 112).

tirades against Tristan: he killed her uncle Morolt, the protector of Ireland
. . . he discomfited and brought shame on the 'truhsæze', the seneschal,
marriage with whom would have been preferable to the fate of being sold
to the King of Cornwall. It is a sign of Gottfried's supreme human insight
– truly a master stroke of psychological characterization – that Isolt's
outbursts of hatred under the mask of mockery in reality betray a deeper
sorrow than she can express. Her vehement words of grief are psychologically persuasive and act as 'inverted' remonstrances which are human, in
fact very human expostulations, and not 'too modern'. Isolt does, above
all, not argue like the 'verschmähte Geliebte' in Wagner's opera:

> 'Ungeminnt
> den hehrsten Mann
> stets mir nah zu sehen!'

Isolt's outbursts of fury in Gottfried's *Tristan* are not Wagnerian; they are
not even in the mood of the violent passage in Thomas (cf. Bédier, p. 51):

> . . . lui le ravisseur, lui le meurtrier du Morholt . . . 'Chétive!' disait-
> elle, 'maudite soit la mer qui me porte! Mieux aimerais-je mourir sur
> la terre où je suis née que vivre là-bas! . . .'

Although Bédier did not intend to modernize Thomas, it must be ad-
mitted that there does prevail a somewhat Wagnerian tone in these words
of Isolt. But I remain, as indicated, within my special theme and therefore
avoid the temptation to refer to twentieth-century variations and problems, such as those encountered in Thomas Mann's *Leiden und Größe
Richard Wagners* (1933), Frank Martin's oratorio *Le vin herbé* (1938–41),
Rosemary Sutcliff's *Tristan and Iseult* (1971), or Hannah Closs's *Tristan*
(1941, German translation 1984).

In addition to arguments already offered and often overlooked, e.g.
Isolt's grief under the cloak of resentment, I now turn to a few more
concrete proofs of my proposition, thus following the example of revered
scholars like Robert Priebsch, Wolfgang Stammler and others, whose first
and main principle of research was, in all questions of presentation and
interpretation, to return to the original and to anchor all findings safely in
the text.

Gottfried's art, no doubt, poses a particularly knotty problem. The chief
difficulty, I believe, is caused by the fact that the medieval poet is expected to be consistent, e.g., in our case, in the traditional use of the love-
potion theme. But in his *Tristan* Gottfried does not treat the 'Liebestrank'
as the reason and excuse for the love of Tristan and Isolt, as his predecessors did. He builds up before us the *crescendo* of the lovers' passion,
feelings and action with the force of an overwhelming conviction. It
seems quite inconceivable to me that the love between Tristan and Isolt

(in Gottfried) which reveals elemental human emotion and destructive forces with gradually increasing intensity, could be engendered by anything so *clumsy* as an *accidental* event. (Alas: 'und ist ir doch niht vil gewesen,/die von im rehte haben gelesen').

To sum up, I shall briefly stress some relevant stages by which Gottfried builds up the relationship between the two lovers *step by step* to its ultimate, unavoidable culmination.

In the episode of the 'Bridal Quest' there is Tristan's ecstatic praise of Isolt's ravishing beauty, which surpasses that of Helena and Leda (8257ff):

> 'Îsôt . . . daz ist ein maget,
> daz al diu werlt von schœne saget,
> deist allez hie wider alse ein wint.'   (8257–59)

This excessive and hymnic utterance is a youthful extravagance: hardly more than 'Jugendschwärmerei', and unproblematic. Tristan was too interested in knightly exploits for feelings of love to become 'Schicksal' to him yet.

In the scene 'Notch in the Blade' (9996ff) Isolt looks at Tristan and scans him with unusual interest:

> nu nam Îsôt sîn dicke war
> und marcte in ûz der mâze
> an lîbe und an gelâze;
> sî blicte im dicke tougen
> an die hende und under ougen.   (9996–10000)

Here already Gottfried moves a step forward in the psychological development of the story. Soon afterwards Isolt confirms her presentiment of Tristan's noble birth. Her inquisitiveness is more than curiosity about his origin. Her angry outburst after the discovery of the splinter from the sword stretches over several pages. It is a moving expression of personal grief and fury; 'die zwô widerwarte ('foes'), . . . zorn unde wîpheit' (10262–64) fight in her heart. She knows now that Tantris/Tristan is a nobleman, yet the object of her heightened interest proves to have killed her uncle. In these scenes, and later, on the boat, in the long lament under the mask of resentment, Gottfried demonstrates his artistic mastery and suggestive power without having to explain the obvious.

In a unique way he succeeds in motivating a growing, unconscious affection between the two lovers. Surprisingly, many interpreters have overlooked the significance of a remarkable fact: once Isolt's mother takes control of the situation, Isolt immediately talks excitedly about how she discovered that Tantris was Tristan, and all this without ever reviling him or impugning his honour:

Hie mite giengen die vrouwen dan
in ir heinlîche sunder
und ahteten hier under
sîn gelücke und sîne linge
an iegelîchem dinge.
ir iegelîchiu seite
von sîner wîsheite . . .   (10594–600)

(Then the ladies went/into their private closet/and reflected on/his luck and his success/in everything./Each of them spoke/of his ingenuity . . .)

Later, on the ship ('The Love-potion Scene'), Tristan tries to console Isolt, who again starts to fret and express resentment. She thinks of her friends and her country. It is a scene of ominous tension. Here again we encounter Isolt's already quoted, prolonged grief under the disguise of derision. She calls Tristan 'ein harte müelîch man' ('a tiresome fellow'). After all, she has had to leave her parents, a daunting future lies ahead, and Tristan is responsible for what she sees as her misfortune. The crucial point is reached when both sit down and speak for the first time about matters which concern them *alone*:

und alse er zuo ir nider gesaz,
und redeten diz unde daz
von ir beider dingen,
er bat im trinken bringen . . .   (11667–70)

('and when he sat down beside her,/and they discussed matters/which concerned them both,/he asked for a drink . . .')

Love-drink or not – the climax was bound to come. It is difficult to understand that anyone rereading this text can deny that there was unconscious love long *before they accidentally drank* the love-potion. The two lovers had already experienced much together. Now they had sat down and talked about things which affected them *both alone*. Only *one* conclusion seems acceptable: it was *not* at all the fortuitousness of the love-potion offered . . . but the very occurrence of the incident that Tristan and Isolt chose to sit down together, to talk and to drink, which is of utmost significance and symbolic importance here. To put it succinctly: nicht *was* sie tranken, sondern *daß* sie tranken – that is what is in question. As mentioned already, there is a significant change in the lovers' relationship. Gottfried is the first Tristan-poet who makes Tristan offer the cup to Isolt before he himself drinks. As to Isolt's own decision: not *what* Isolt drank, but *that* she drank and then *gave* Tristan to drink . . . that is the most decisive point here.

Nothing but the inevitable *could* happen, and after Isolt had drunk reluctantly: 'ungerne und über lanc' (11687), she did not put the cup down but handed it back to Tristan: 'und gap do Tristand' '. She herself acted as the cup-bearer and presented the drink to Tristan. Thus, of her own free will, she had actually abandoned her opposition. It was the final surrender of her resistance. The fact that the pair do not give in at once, but that their fate dawns on them slowly, makes it all the more natural. Thus reality and symbol converge closely and uncannily.

The conclusion is irrefutable. There is a sense of total inevitability, of irresistible climax and a finality which reveals Gottfried's rare power of psychological penetration and poetic imagination in an essentially symbolic presentation of the love-potion.

Senen *and* triuwe:
Gottfried's unfinished Tristan

H.B. WILLSON

The prologue to Gottfried's *Tristan* highlights two closely related aspects of human behaviour. They are *senen* and *triuwe*. The poet characterises his hero and heroine as *edele senedære* who displayed *reine sene* (126–27) and the story of their love as a *senemære* (168) which he hopes will give some comfort to other *senedære* when *they* are afflicted with *seneder schade, senedez leit* or *senediu not* (83ff).[1] As for *triuwe*, it is the one and only virtue specifically mentioned in the prologue. Gottfried sees it not merely as the bond between the lovers, but also between them and those who listen to or read their story. The *inneclichiu triuwe* of Tristan and Isolt, he says, is sweet and ever new (219–20) and *ir triuwe, ir triuwen reinekeit* (231) is the bread of all noble hearts. He describes the story he is going to tell as one of *reiniu triuwe*: 'wan swa man hœret oder list,/daz von so reinen triuwen ist,/da liebent dem getriuwen man/triuwe und ander tugende van' (177ff).

In the story itself, as one might therefore expect, there are frequent indications of the paramount importance of this ethical ideal of *triuwe*, particularly *triuwe* between lovers. In one of his digressions on *minne*, for instance, Gottfried defines true and perfect love as *triuwe, diu von herzen gat* and *triuwe under vriunden* (12336 and 12346). It is an ideal which we false lovers (*wir valschen minnære*: 12311) utterly fail to realise. When they are in the Minnegrotte the only nourishment said to be required by *die getriuwen senedære* Tristan and Isolt is *diu reine triuwe* (16830); *triuwe*, in fact, as this coupling of the two ideas suggests, is inseparable from *senen*. They are interdependent and complementary: the longing of a *senedære* and a *senedærin* for each other is the result of their mutual and reciprocal *triuwe*. As true, as opposed to false, lovers they remain faithful to each other throughout all vicissitudes, at least in theory.

---

[1] All *Tristan* references are quoted from the latest edition of the Ranke text, ed. R. Krohn (Stuttgart, 1980), but with signs of length omitted, for uniformity with the rest of this volume.

This close association of both *senen* and *triuwe* with Tristan and Isolt in Gottfried's prologue can have no other purpose but to make clear beyond all doubt that these ethical ideals (for *senen* must also be considered as one such) are fundamental to the poet's vision of his protagonists. As *ge-triuwiu senedære* they are exemplary, meant to set an example to other noble hearts like themselves and inspire emulation. Their 'exemplariness' consists in the fact that they are designed by the poet to embody and demonstrate above all else *sene* and *triuwe* in all their quintessential *reine-keit*. They are to show their nobility of heart in its fullest measure. That is the undeniable implication of the prologue.[2]

Nevertheless, it may reasonably be questioned whether the conduct of the hero and heroine towards each other in the story which follows, or at least that of Tristan towards Isolt, really is exemplary, whether their *triuwe* is *reine*, and whether they really are *senedære*, displaying *reine sene* in the fullest, most exemplary sense of the word as Gottfried wishes it to be understood and as he uses it himself in his prologue. It is true that at Marke's court they have to put up with a certain amount of inconveni-ence, even distress on occasion, for they are frequently under surveillance and at considerable personal risk. Traps are set for them, Isolt is forced to submit to the ordeal and they are temporarily separated when Tristan goes away to Swales, where he acquires Petitcreiu. During this separation the lovers yearn for each other and Isolt suffers *senede swære* (15903), showing her compassionate *triuwe* to Tristan by breaking the bell off the little dog. It is then said of her: 'diu getriuwe stæte senedærin, / diu hæte ir vröude unde ir leben/sene unde Tristande ergeben' (16400–02). But does all this add up to very much in terms of real suffering, of *herzeleit*, as it might be called?[3] The lovers are, after all, together at the same court most of the time and can see each other often and even enjoy their love, thanks to Brangaene and *list*, until Tristan goes into exile. At Marke's court they suffer a great deal of frustration, there is always tension, and for Isolt the ordeal is a terrible experience, but it is debatable whether most of what they suffer can be called *senen*, which must surely be understood as an intense longing, or languishing, for each other. It may also be questioned whether the degree of *triuwe* they are required to show towards each other at Marke's court is particularly high. As long as they are together there, indeed, they hardly seem to be *senedære* in the full sense of the word

---

2   Ruth G. Kunzer (*The Tristan of Gottfried von Strassburg. An ironic perspective* (Los Angeles/London, 1973), p. 192) believes that the prologue cannot be seen as program-matic, since 'the exposition of the Tristan *minne* in the narrative' is 'in ironic contrast to the expectations raised by the narrator in the prologue . . . '. Disagreement with this view is the whole premise of the following paper.

3   Elsewhere Gottfried clearly brackets *herzeleit* with *ungeschiht,/diu hin in daz herze siht* (13080–82), implying that this is the highest degree of sorrow conceivable.

as implied in the prologue. All in all, they seem to derive as much *liep von liebe* as *von liebe leit* (cf. 204–05), if not more. There isn't a great deal of languishing. Moreover, the actual designation *senedære (-in)* is never used of either of them while they are together at Marke's court, though, as I have quoted, it is applied once to Isolt while Tristan is away in Swales and once to both of them in the Minnegrotte. By contrast, a part of their stay together in Cornwall, admittedly of short duration, is referred to as a *wunschleben* (15043).

But when Tristan goes away for good, leaving Isolt behind as Marke's wife, the situation of the lovers changes dramatically. For the first time since drinking the potion they really are separated, apparently with little hope of ever being re-united. It is therefore most appropriate and significant that, just before Tristan leaves, Isolt should give him a ring, with the accompanying words 'und nemet hie diz vingerlin:/daz lat ein urkünde sin/der triuwen unde der minne' (18307–09). The ring is a symbol and token of true love, of what might be called the 'alternative marriage', in which the lovers are joined together by a 'covenant', which is the nearest English equivalent to the word used by Thomas, namely *covenance* (Wind, Sneyd I fragment, 407).[4] From this time on *triuwe* becomes, so to speak, of the essence: it is all a question of fidelity, of loyalty, of keeping the covenant. That Isolt is married to Marke in a 'conventional' marriage cannot be helped, but her love belongs exclusively to Tristan, with whom she drank the potion.

During the last episode of Gottfried's poem, however, which we may call the White Hands episode, Tristan's *triuwe* to the first Isolt is severely tested by the beauty of Isolt II. His relationship with the latter, in fact, is widely held to constitute *untriuwe* to Isolt I, particularly as he refers to himself as *ich ungetriuwer* (19142) and *ich triuweloser* (19154). It cannot be denied, either, that on more than one occasion the idea of being unfaithful to Isolt I crosses his mind. In his *zwivelnot* (19352) he sometimes does not know which Isolt to love, because they both have the same name. The poet has to admit that Isolt II caused Tristan to 'waver in his love' ('an siner liebe wanken', 19248). But this wavering in his love for Isolt I cannot under any circumstances be equated with *untriuwe*, no matter what Tristan himself may think of his conduct. The ultimate criterion of *untriuwe* in such a context must surely be willing sexual relations with another person, and there is absolutely no evidence of any such relations between Tristan and Isolt II at any time during the White Hands episode. On one occasion, to be sure, personified *stæte* does find it necessary to remind Tristan urgently of the *triuwe* Isolt I has always shown to *him*, a warning which effectively banishes for the time being all thoughts of

---

4 Quotations from the original text of Thomas de Bretagne are taken from the edition of B.H. Wind (Leiden, 1950).

untriuwe: 'so was aber diu stæte da:/"nein", sprach si, "herre Tristan,/sich dine triuwe an Isot an,/gedenke genote/der getriuwen Isote,/diu nie vuoz von dir getrat" ' (19256–61). Here Gottfried is patently enjoying himself with rhetorical word-play on *triuwe, stæte, wanken* and *zwivel*, just as Wolfram von Eschenbach does in his *Parzival* prologue,[5] but his meaning is not thereby obscured: in spite of his temporary *wanken* Tristan does not become *ungetriuwe*. The two terms *wanken* and *untriuwe* are by no means synonymous, and *wanken* and *triuwe* are not exact antitheses. It is from these subtle differences of nuance that the word-play derives its force. If there had been any sexual relations between Tristan and Isolt II that would indeed have been a clear breach of *triuwe* to Isolt I, and it would then have been too late for *stæte* to remind Tristan of the need to preserve his *triuwe* to the latter. Although Kaedin urges his sister to make herself as engaging to Tristan as she can *mit rede* (19099), he is careful to say that she must not *do* anything without consulting him and their father first! Elaine C. Tennant comments: 'The scene [scil. of Tristan's wavering in his love for Isolt I] does not contradict or mitigate the love Gottfried describes in his prologue. It shows it rather in its unabated intensity . . . . The potion does not preclude the sort of doubt Tristan experiences: it is responsible for it, for this is one of the specific varieties of anguish which love produces . . . '.[6]

At the very end of the White Hands episode, however, Tristan begins to wonder whether Isolt I really cares about *him* any more. Why is she not making strenuous efforts to find and contact him? He then conceives the idea that, if Ovid is right, a way of easing his *senen* for the love of Isolt I might be with another *trutschaft* (19433). After all, as he sees it, Isolt I is enjoying the pleasures of love with her partner Marke, while he, Tristan, has to forgo them for her sake. The *triuwe* and *minne* he has for his lady, Isolt I, is getting him nowhere (19468ff). Shortly after this Gottfried's poem breaks off, but in the version of Thomas, which Gottfried praises very highly in his prologue and which he claims to be using as his source,[7] Tristran does actually turn to another *trutschaft*, to use Gottfried's word, and marries Ysolt II. If Gottfried had gone on much further it seems eminently reasonable to suppose that *his* hero would also have married Isolt II, since the situation could scarcely have developed in any other way, and in any case the German poet expressly tells us in the prologue that he is going to follow Thomas's version of the story. Under normal

---

[5]   For a discussion of this word-play and its importance see the author's 'Wolframs *bîspel*. Zur Interpretation des ersten Teils des Parzivalprologs', *Wolfram-Jahrbuch* 1955, 28–51.
[6]   'The principle of authority in Gottfried's concept of narrative writing', *Euphorion*, 76 (1982), 222–59 (p. 222).
[7]   *Tristan*, 150ff.

circumstances, to be sure, such a marriage of the hero to Isolt II would certainly have meant *untriuwe* to Isolt I, ring or no ring, as it would have led naturally to willing sexual relations with his new wife, the marriage itself having been voluntarily entered into. But Thomas makes it quite clear that the circumstances are far from being normal and natural, because when he catches sight of the ring Ysolt I had given him Tristran is reminded of his covenant with her, so that he cannot possibly bring himself to consummate the marriage to Ysolt II. Yet, because he *has* married her he feels it is his duty to lie in her bed with her, but even in her very arms Tristran suppresses his natural instincts and refrains from intercourse, making the excuse that he has a 'bodily infirmity' which incapacitates him (Hatto, pp. 308–10).[8] Never does he deprive Ysolt II of her virginity. Even though he is in the closest possible physical contact with her every night he always manages to conquer the 'loveless lust in his mind' with the aid of his true love for Ysolt I and to avoid intercourse (Hatto, p. 309). Although Nature wants satisfaction, 'la raison se tient a Ysolt', which of course means Ysolt I (Wind, Sneyd I fragment, 596). Tristran himself sees this struggle as penance for what *he* regards as his betrayal of Ysolt I by marrying Ysolt II, but for Thomas Tristran clearly remained faithful to Ysolt I throughout, since his true love for her always emerges victorious in this conflict with the purely carnal desire, in other words the lust, he feels for his wife. What matters is not that Tristran has a strong desire to have intercourse with Ysolt II – he undoubtedly has – but that his reason, that is, his love for Ysolt I, never allows him to satisfy it.[9]

If the emphasis on the exemplary *triuwe* of the lovers in Gottfried's prologue means anything at all, and is not pure irony, it can hardly be doubted that he would have continued the story along the same lines. Both this and the fact that he goes out of his way in the prologue to praise the version of Thomas above all others would seem to indicate that he would have followed the *rihte* (156) of the Anglo-Norman poet right to the end of the story, as is the view of Friedrich Maurer,[10] Petrus Tax[11] and, more recently, Elaine Tennant.[12] In the part he did complete, as Arthur Hatto says, 'Gottfried kept closely to his [scil. Thomas's] narrative despite subtle changes'.[13] If he had gone on to the end there would doubtless have

---

8   A.T. Hatto's English translation of Gottfried's poem and Thomas's fragments (Penguin Classics, revised and reprinted, Harmondsworth, 1986) is used when quoting Thomas, except when the original French is referred to (see note 4, above).
9   In the 'bold water episode' (cf. Hatto, pp. 319–20) Isolt II makes it abundantly and graphically clear that she has never had intercourse with her husband Tristran.
10   *Leid. Studien zur Bedeutungs- und Problemgeschichte besonders in den grossen Epen der staufischen Zeit* (Berne/Munich, 1951), pp. 234ff.
11   *Wort, Sinnbild, Zahl im Tristanroman* (Berlin, 1961), pp. 169ff.
12   ibid., p. 222.
13   p. 358.

been further 'subtle changes', with perhaps some *amplificatio* and / or *abbreviatio*, but this would almost certainly not have affected the fundamentals of the tale, and since one of those fundamentals, perhaps the most fundamental fundamental of all, is the relationship between the protagonists, it seems highly likely that Gottfried would have attached the same importance as Thomas clearly does to the fact that Tristran never had intercourse with Ysolt II, or indeed with any woman other than Ysolt I. He would therefore have deemed Tristan's *triuwe*, his loyalty to and his true love for, the latter to have remained intact throughout the story, *his* story, if he had completed it, based upon the story which Thomas *had* completed and which Gottfried must have had in his mind as a complete and integrated whole while he was composing his own poem. There is no sexual intercourse between Tristran and Ysolt II in Thomas and none in Gottfried, as far as his story actually goes, and there never would have been any however far he might have gone. If there had been any he could not have claimed in his prologue that Tristan was going to be an exemplar of *triuwe*, which he does, even though he could have said it of Isolt I. Neither could he have claimed with any degree of veracity that he was following the *rihte* of Thomas, which he also does.

As is well known, the surviving fragments of Thomas, of whose nonexistence Constance Bouchard utterly fails to convince me,[14] begin at almost the exact point at which Gottfried breaks off, thus providing a very convenient 'conclusion' to the story left unfinished by the German poet. There is an undeniable continuity from the one to the other. In particular, the suffering of the lovers, their longing for each other, already very marked in Gottfried's episode of the White Hands, despite Tristan's occasional *wanken*, is both sustained and intensified in Thomas. Their mutual fidelity emerges ever more strongly as the story proceeds. Tristran, for his part, longs for Ysolt I throughout the concluding part of the story, and although he does occasionally get to visit her and enjoy her love, for most of the time he is forced to adore a life-like substitute, namely the image he has had made and placed with that of Brangvein in the Hall of Statues. The statue of Ysolt I significantly depicts her holding in her hand the ring she gave him, which, as we know from Gottfried, is a token of *triuwe*. Inscribed on it are the very words she spoke to him as they parted, and when he looks at it it reminds him of their covenant, just as the real ring reminded him of their covenant on his wedding night (Hatto, p. 316). Tristran is said to suffer double pain and double grief because of his love for Ysolt I. Whatever he may wish, he is married to Ysolt II and cannot

---

[14] 'The possible non-existence of Thomas, author of *Tristan and Isolde*', *Modern Philology*, 79 (1981–2), pp. 66ff.

legally desert her, but he cannot and will not love her (Hatto, p. 317). Paradoxically, Tristran's 'wavering' in his love for Ysolt I ceases as soon as he is married to Ysolt II.

Likewise, Isolt/Ysolt faithfully keeps *her* covenant with Tristan/Tristran throughout Gottfried's poem and Thomas's fragments, in spite of the hero's fears that she may have taken another lover and in spite of her being married to Mark. With Isolt I there is never even any *wanken*, either in Gottfried or in Thomas, of the kind to which Tristan is subject in Gottfried, and indeed in Thomas right up to his marriage. She rejects out of hand the advances of the handsome but cowardly Cariado. Thomas draws special attention to her desire to share Tristran's sorrow when he leaves after the reconciliation with Brangvein: 'Having seen Tristran languishing, she wishes to share in his sorrow. Just as she has shared love with Tristran, who has languished for her, so she desires to share the sorrow and hardship' (Hatto, p. 336). A little later she is said to don a leather corslet over her bare flesh and to wear it there night and day, except when she lies with her lord. Thomas comments: 'A more loyal lady was never seen' (Hatto, p. 336). As we saw, Isolt I's compassionate love for Tristan is given special prominence in the Petitcreiu episode in Gottfried when she breaks the bell off the dog in her desire to 'suffer with' Tristan. Her *triuwe* is therefore never in doubt, although, like that of Tristran, it is only in Thomas that it assumes its most exemplary form. As the wife of Mark, of course, Isolt/Ysolt I has normal marital relations with the latter throughout, a fact which causes Tristan/Tristran considerable distress, but for Thomas, and also for Gottfried, as far as he went, this does not detract from her *triuwe*. Because Mark is her lord she has no choice but to let him do as he wishes, but, as Tristran himself concedes, her sexual relations with Mark are completely against her will and are therefore 'conduct contrary to love' ('ovre ki est contre amur': Wind, Sneyd I fragment, 161).

The high point and culmination of Thomas's poem, the peak of its emotional intensity, is undoubtedly the description of the events leading up to the deaths of the lovers and of those deaths themselves. Then the bond of fidelity which unites them, or, to use Gottfried's key MHG words, their *senen* and *triuwe*, is most powerfully expressed. The events are brought about by the poisoned wound suffered by Tristran in his combat on behalf of Dwarf Tristran. Because he has remained true to Ysolt I Tristran is able to send Caerdin to her with the ring to ask her to come and heal him. He assures Caerdin that his wife is still a virgin and that he has never loved any woman but Isolt I and therefore asks him to 'bid the Queen *by her loyalty* ('sur sa fei': Wind, Douce fragment, 125) to come to me in this my need' (Hatto, p. 344). The subsequent death of Tristran, to which Gottfried refers early on in *his* poem as 'alles todes übergenoz,/aller triure ein galle' (2016–17), is of course the direct result of Ysolt

II's desire to punish him for that very loyalty to Ysolt I which constitutes infidelity to her, his lawful wedded wife. If he had been a proper husband to Ysolt II she would never have been so vindictive and deliberately lied to him about the colour of the sails, nor would Ysolt I have come to him. When the latter finally arrives in Brittany after a most hazardous and frustrating voyage to find Tristran dead of longing for her, she 'willingly rendered up her spirit', as Thomas describes it, 'pur la dolur de sun ami' (Wind, Sneyd II fragment, 815). He continues: 'Tristran died of his longing, Ysolt because she could not come in time. Tristran died for his love, fair Ysolt because of tender pity' (Hatto, p. 353).

This extremely powerful ending to Thomas's poem, culminating in the deaths of the lovers, must be seen in conjunction with the particular emphasis placed on those deaths by Gottfried in his prologue, where he significantly links them with the exemplary *triuwe* to which frequent reference has been made in this paper. Gottfried says, for instance, that their deaths will *den triuwe gernden triuwe geben* (226). Their death will live and be new for evermore to us, the living (228–29). He also says: 'wir lesen ir leben, wir lesen ir tot,/und ist uns daz süeze alse brot' (235–36), clearly referring to the story as a whole, as he has read it in Thomas, who tells of the lovers' deaths as well as of their lives. Gottfried's own poem, however, does not tell of the deaths of the lovers; there we only *lesen ir leben* (and not all of that), whereas in Thomas we also *lesen ir tot*. But these crucial words in Gottfried's prologue, *wir lesen ir tot*, leave no room for doubt that if he had completed his poem Gottfried would also have described the deaths of the lovers. What is more, there is absolutely no reason to think that that description would have been dissimilar to the treatment by Thomas. Unquestionably, their deaths would have shown in Gottfried's ending, as they emphatically do in that of Thomas, the full extent and depth of their *triuwe* to each other and of their *senen* for each other. By their deaths they would have been confirmed as *senedære* in the full meaning of Gottfried's very expressive word. The potential 'exemplariness' of the lovers, which is unmistakably indicated in the prologue, would have been fully realised in Gottfried's ending, in complete accordance with the ending of Thomas. Gottfried would have shown how Tristan and Isolt, like other exemplary lovers before them, were *von sene verdorben* (cf. 17186) and how their true love for each other and their deaths were indissolubly linked as cause and effect. If he had not intended to do this Gottfried would not have been able, in his prologue, to attach such anticipatory importance to their deaths as a source of *triuwe* for others. Elaine Tennant remarks: '. . . the final scenes of Gottfried's fragmentary *Tristan* mark the beginning of what would probably have been the poet's major development of the lovers' anguish, of their *liebez leit*, their *senede not*, and eventually also of their *leiden tot*, all of which have been foretold in the prologue. This would doubtless have been a depiction of *Minnekrankheit* unparalleled in MHG literature.'[15]

Unfortunately, however, Gottfried never got far enough to show, in his poem, just how *getriuwe* these *senedære* could be to each other and what a shining example they could be to other *senedære*. There is, let's face it, not quite enough in Gottfried, as far as he goes, to set an example to other lovers and inspire emulation, which is hardly surprising, since Gottfried did not follow the story through to its climax and culmination. If he had, the exemplary *triuwe* of the lovers he foretells in his prologue would have been revealed in all its essential purity and nobility of heart. Because this is so, Gottfried's prologue, indeed his whole poem, or rather his half- or three-quarters poem, only makes complete sense if we also take into account the ending as found in Thomas. This is not to place a label of inadequacy on Gottfried von Strassburg, who proves beyond all doubt in the part of the story he did complete that he was a much greater poet than Thomas; it is merely an acknowledgement of the fact that the poem is not finished, probably because of Gottfried's untimely death. That the poet died before he could finish it is by far the most likely explanation of the fragmentary character of his *Tristan*.[16] It was, unfortunately for Germanists, Thomas, not Gottfried, who began *and* finished that version, depicting at the end the sequence of events highlighting the fidelity of the lovers to each other as never before. But we may be absolutely certain that if Gottfried had reached *his* conclusion *he* would also have depicted those same events, and with much greater poetic effect than Thomas had done before him. The emotional impact of his poem would then have been infinitely more powerful than it is already. His concept of the noble heart, ultimately prepared to die for love, would have been greatly enhanced and enriched.

Nevertheless, that having been said, and as things really are, Gottfried's *Tristan* remains a torso; it has a beginning and a middle but no ending. It is not an integrated whole because it was never finished. The poem in itself does not fully execute the conception outlined in the prologue. This lack of a vital part of the tale, its conclusion, is undoubtedly a serious obstacle to the full understanding and appreciation of Gottfried's poem, but, as I have suggested, the obstacle can be overcome, if only to a limited extent, by reference to Thomas – *faute de mieux*. Gottfried's *Tristan* can become a *whole* poem, as it were, if we add to the part he actually

---

[15] ibid., pp. 252–53.
[16] In the first lines of their 'continuations' of Gottfried's *Tristan* both Ulrich von Türheim and Heinrich von Freiberg also express the opinion that Gottfried died before he could finish the poem. B. Mergell's belief that *Tristan is* complete is quite unacceptable (*Tristan und Isolde. Ursprung und Entwicklung der Tristansage des Mittelalters*, Mainz 1949, p. 177).

wrote the surviving fragments of Thomas, supplemented on occasion, of course, by Brother Robert *et al*. This is what is very properly and most usefully done, in translation, by Arthur Hatto. We simply cannot ignore Thomas when dealing with Gottfried, even though so little of the former's work is extant. We cannot do justice to Gottfried if we attempt to appreciate or interpret his incomplete work on its own, that is, in isolation from its 'continuation' and 'conclusion' as found in Thomas. Only when we take the two together, Gottfried and Thomas, can we get a larger view, if only dimly, giving, so to speak, an extra dimension to our consideration of Gottfried's own, *partial*, treatment of the story. If we do not bring the two together, even hypothetically, as I have tried to do, there is a grave risk of misinterpreting that treatment.

Living in the Presence of the Past:
Exemplary Perspectives in Gottfried's Tristan[1]

ROY WISBEY

In his reminiscences of war-time Amsterdam, which bear the precisely descriptive as well as evocative title of *Untergetaucht unter Freunden*, Claus Victor Bock relates how his mentor Wolfgang Frommel had annotated and interleaved his edition of Stefan George's *Der Stern des Bundes* with observations of his own, linked with quotations from German Classical and Romantic authors, but also with other fruits of his wide yet eclectic reading. This ranged from Eastern sages, Greek antiquity (Heraclitus, Plutarch, Plato) and the Bible, through the mystical exegete Philo of Alexandria and the neoplatonist Dionysius the Pseudo-Areopagite to Fathers of the Church (St Augustine, Gregory the Great), to Joachim of Fiore and the German mystics Tauler, Meister Eckhart, Jacob Boehme. With some notable exceptions, similar tastes are evident in his choice among more recent authors, although this cannot occupy us here. For Frommel, this reading, however much re-interpreted, was clearly inseparable from the view of life he embodied: 'Wie alle Humanisten zitierte er gerne – und mit viel Geschick. Zitate waren ihm Glieder einer goldenen Kette. Sie verbürgten ein hohes, die Zeiten überspielendes Gespräch der Geister. Deshalb war Zitieren die ihm liebste Form der Beweisführung. Er rief aus der Vergangenheit seine Zeugen auf'.[2]

Deprived of their modern context, these words might pass at first sight as a comment upon Gottfried. Judgements derived by one means and another from the literary canon, together with the storehouse of traditional wisdom represented by proverbs and *sententiae*, accompany, inter-

---

1 'Der Hang der Menschen, sich in ihrem Denken und Handeln an den Erfahrungen der Vergangenheit zu orientieren, [scheint] unausrottbar fortzuexistieren' – M. Fuhrmann, 'Das Exemplum in der antiken Rhetorik', in *Geschichte – Ereignis und Erzählung*, edited by R. Koselleck and W. -D. Stempel, Poetik und Hermeneutik, 5 (Munich, 1973), p. 449.
2 C. V. Bock, *Untergetaucht unter Freunden. Ein Bericht. Amsterdam 1942–1945* (Castrum Peregrini: Amsterdam, 1985), pp. 76–77.

pret and validate events in *Tristan*, as in the lapidary comment on the fortunes and misfortunes of war at the very beginning of the work:

> hie mite so gant urliuge hin;
> verliesen unde gewinnen
> daz treit die criege hinnen.   (368–70)

Gottfried was no doubt prompted to this utterance by a reference in Thomas, his source, to the vicissitudes experienced by Kanelengres (Riwalin) during his campaigns, a reference preserved by the *Tristrams saga* in the form: 'Sometimes he too lost some of his men, as can often befall in battle'.[3] Accordingly, Gottfried first records the losses sustained by Riwalin ('ouch nam er dicke schaden dar an: /er galt mit manegem biderben man,/ ... Morgan .../ ... tet in dicke schadehaft', 361–65), then, like the *saga*, generalizes from the particular: 'wan zurliuge und ze ritter- schaft/hœret verlust unde gewin' (366–67). Finally, Gottfried elevates both the particular and the generalization dependent upon it to perma- nent validity in the memorable reformulation already cited (368–70). In so doing he rises above the events recorded (and above Thomas?), arriving at the detached objectivity of a *sententia* to rival Latin encapsulations of the harsh realities of war – see Virgil's *scelerata insania belli, Aeneid,* vii.461 – as in the dictum: 'Belli nemo fore victor valet absque cruore'.[4]

No less in the grip of forces ultimately beyond their control, Tristan and Isot seek to conceal their relationship from the court and from Marke as strenuously and as effectively 'so si diu blinde liebe lie,/diu mit in beiden umbe gie' (16453–54). In describing how the lovers are betrayed by their loving glances, the involuntary reflex of their feelings, Gottfried chooses to call into play the authority of proverbial truth, invoking an inherited consensus about shared patterns of human behaviour:

> er hæte vil war, der da sprach:
> swie mans hüetende si,
> si sint doch gerne ein ander bi,
> daz ouge bi dem herzen,
> der vinger bi dem smerzen.   (16472–76)

---

[3]   *The Saga of Tristram and Ísönd.* Translated with an introduction by P. Schach (Lincoln, Nebraska, 1973), p. 3. For the original (*Tristrams saga ok Ísondar*) see the edition with German translation by E. Kölbing in *Die nordische und die englische Version der Tristan-Sage,* pt.I (Heilbronn, 1878), here p. 5, 25–26. For Thomas see *Les Fragments du roman de Tristan,* edited by Bartina H. Wind (Geneva and Paris, 1960).

[4]   *Proverbia sententiaeque latinitatis medii aevi,* collected and edited by H. Walther, pt.I, no. 1976, in *Carmina medii aevi posterioris Latina,* II, 1 (Göttingen, 1963). Virgil is quoted in the edition, with English translation, by H. R. Fairclough, The Loeb Classical Library, 2 vols (London and Cambridge, Mass., 1965–66).

Among the Greek (Plutarch), Latin, French and German occurrences of the proverb concerned – one of them introduced with the words 'C'om dist ueraiement' – is an instance in the *Roman d'Eneas*, where Lavinia asserts, without identifying the adage: 'Li oilz est sanpres a l'amor / et la main est a la dolor' (9885–86).[5] Since the behaviour of Eneas does not at first appear to conform to this accepted pattern of experience, Lavinia concludes, erroneously and prematurely, that her love is not reciprocated. Gottfried, on the other hand, states explicitly that Tristan and Isot (unconsciously) behave exactly according to the proverbial norm, thereby arousing the suspicion of the court: 'als taten die gelieben ie' (16483). In both works, the use of this proverb contributes to a much wider view of passionate love as an affliction, as a painful condition which – unless remedied – brings suffering and even death. Such proverbial utterances – and much the same is true of *sententiae* and *exempla* – carry conviction since they are distilled from the experience of generations. Against this background, the destiny of individual figures in the works unfolds before a chorus of witnesses from the past. In their turn, the events narrated augment the stock of positive and negative models, whether intended for emulation, or serving as a timely warning for those who – like Gottfried's characters, his audience and his readers – are still shaping their lives in the fluidity of the present, themselves about to become the subject of comment by generations yet to come.[6]

There is evidence in Gottfried's Riwalin and Blanscheflur episode which suggests that tragic stories of love (*senemære*) have been a formative influence upon Marke's sister. Later in *Tristan*, Marke's receptive ear for songs about ill-fated lovers is one aspect of his vulnerability. It is upon the King's own request for an encore that Tristan, newly arrived at the court, sings, not unspecified lays as in the *saga*, but a further 'seneclichen leich . . ./ de la curtoise Tispe / von der alten Babilone' (3615–17; 'about Noble Thisbe of Old Babylon'). Subsequently, Gandin wins Isot from Marke by

---

5 See Lambertus Okken, *Kommentar zum Tristan-Roman Gottfrieds von Strassburg*, 2 vols (Amsterdam, 1984–85), I, pp. 557–58 and II, p. 75. Both the French instances cited will be found in S. Singer, *Sprichwörter des Mittelalters*, 3 vols (Berne, 1944–47), I, pp. 57–58. *Eneas* is quoted in the edition by J. -J . Salverda de Grave, 2 vols, CFMA (Paris, 1973 and 1968).

6 See H. Dörrie, *Der heroische Brief. Bestandsaufnahme, Geschichte, Kritik einer humanistisch-barocken Literaturgattung* (Berlin, 1968), pp. 341–42 ('Die exemplarische Bedeutung der ovidischen Frauengestalten'). Dörrie maintains that the sufferings of the Ovidian heroines provide the Middle Ages with norms of human behaviour. They are always cited with the aim 'ein bestimmtes Verhalten zu empfehlen oder vor bestimmtem Verhalten zu warnen'. See too K. Stierle, 'Geschichte als Exemplum – Exemplum als Geschichte', in *Geschichte – Ereignis und Erzählung* (above, note 1), pp. 347–75: the *exemplum* offers orientation by placing situations and decisions in a moral relation to each other. In corresponding circumstances, therefore, 'läßt sich der Ausgang des Exemplums begreifen als Vorgriff auf den Ausgang der eigenen Situation' (p. 357).

exploiting this same weakness, only to show himself equally prone to it in losing her to Tristan through the same ruse. In the *saga*, Tristan performs for Gandin 'sweet songs', and finally a 'lay of love, especially sweet to hear'. This lay, selected by Tristan, 'was long and had a rather sad ending'. In Gottfried's *Tristan*, Gandin specifically asks for 'den leich von Didone' (13347) as Tristan's second offering.[7] In the 'cave of lovers' episode, of course, Tristan and Isot are shown to be intimately conversant with the sad fates of various heroines of antiquity, including Dido:

> [si] triben ir senemære
> von den, die vor ir jaren
> von sene verdorben waren.   (17184–86)

Significantly, it is not only to intuition that Blanscheflur owes the realization that she is the victim of a passionate love, manifesting itself as a malady, inducing confusion of the senses, uncertainty, melancholy, and disorientation of the reason. She recognizes the tell-tale signs, not least the sudden readiness to abandon the rules of propriety, her unaccustomed willingness to expose herself to risks which hitherto would have been unacceptable:

> min tumber meisterloser muot . . .
> er wil und wil joch al ze vil,
> des er niht wellen solte,
> ob er bedenken wolte,
> waz vuoge wære und ere.   (1045; 1048–51)

She is enabled to interpret her situation by acquaintance with tales of passionate love as *dulce malum*, that is by vicarious experience of the past:

> '. . . swaz ich allen minen lip
> umb rehte minnendiu wip
> und umbe liebe han vernomen,
> daz ist mir in min herze komen:
> der süeze herzesmerze,
> der vil manic edele herze
> quelt mit süezem smerzen,
> der liget in minem herzen.'   (1069–76)

More can be gathered about Blanscheflur's *éducation sentimentale* from the later passage in which she learns that Riwalin is about to depart, on

---

7   *Tristrams saga*, chapter 50; Schach, p. 79; Kölbing, p. 62, 25 and 34–36, translation p. 162. W. Hoffa, *ZDA*, 52 (1910), 339–50 (p. 340), already concludes that it is Gottfried who makes the request specific.

hearing of the great force Morgan had mustered against his country. In the *Tristrams saga*, and presumably in Thomas, she assigns herself to the category of those women who have loved unwisely (Kölbing, p. 13,29: 'ósynju vildi þik elska'; Schach, p. 16).

The characters of the 'romans d'antiquité' illustrate the fact that passion involves great danger. Even when a woman is embarking upon a potentially legitimate relationship, she is likely to be aware that only the future will show whether her self-abandonment is to result in a legitimate, long-term union. What guarantee can she have in advance that her senses are not leading her into a transient entanglement which will make of her yet another *exemplum*, parallel to the Ovidian tales of women who loved and lost, and who ended their lives in despair?

In the French *Eneas*, Lavinia, like Dido before her, also recognises that she has been assailed by the *furor* (8207, *la rage*) of passion. With good cause she fears that this *amor stultus* will be the death of her (8170, cf. 8254ff). In the event, her situation turns out favourably, not least because she has the courage to declare her love to Eneas, despite her fears that he might consider her forward and inconstant (8366ff).[8] In a passage of the *Tristrams saga*, which presumably goes back to Thomas, Blensinbil (Blanscheflur) has similar scruples, scruples which – like Lavinia – she successfully overcomes (Kölbing, 10,22ff; Schach, p. 10):

> 'for he would immediately discover my folly and lack of foresight, and would think at once that I was accustomed to such fickle love affairs and would swiftly and shamefully reject me'.

Gottfried makes no direct use of this passage, which is also closely paralleled in Isalde's love monologue in Eilhart's *Tristrant* (2580ff).[9] For the moment, as we are told, following the consummation of her love and the conception of Tristan, Blanscheflur lives totally in the present: 'son sach si doch niht anders an / wan liebe liebe und lieben man' (1345–46), just as Riwalin has been characterized earlier as living with complete disregard for the future: 'wan lebete und lebete und lebete et dar' (304). Yet the youthful, headstrong career of Riwalin was doomed to a premature end (305ff), precisely because he did not heed the lessons of history (275ff), and Blanscheflur's happiness with him was thus destined to be short-lived:

8   See also Veldeke's *Eneide*, edited by G. Schieb and Th. Frings, 10409ff.
9   Edited by F. Lichtenstein (Strassburg and London, 1877). The section concerned is not among the preserved early fragments of the work, being found only in the fifteenth-century manuscripts *H* and *D*, see Eilhart von Oberg, *'Tristrant'. Synoptischer Druck der ergänzten Fragmente mit der gesamten Parallelüberlieferung*, edited by Hadumod Bußmann, Altdeutsche Textbibliothek, 70 (Tübingen, 1969). However, the very parallels adduced above tend to confirm a twelfth-century context for the passage.

> Doch werte daz unlange;
> wan in ir anevange,
> dos allerbeste lebeten
> und in dem wunsche swebeten,
> do kamen Riwaline boten.   (1373–77)

Here we are back at the point where Blanscheflur interprets her situation like one of the heroines of the Ovidian *exempla*, seeing herself as the victim of a blandishing but irrational, deceptive and inconstant passion (*furor, amor stultus*). In the formulation of Isidor, that prime repository of ancient wisdom, partly echoing the commentary on the *Aeneid* by Servius: 'nihil amantibus levius, nihil mutabilius invenitur . . . stultus est et inrationabilis amor'.[10] In Blanscheflur's anguished words:

> minne, al der werlde unsælekeit,
> so kurziu vröude als an dir ist,
> so rehte unstæte so du bist,
> waz minnet al diu werlt an dir? . . .
> din gespenstigiu trügeheit,
> diu in so valscher süeze swebet,
> diu triuget allez, daz der lebet:
> daz ist an mir wol worden schin.   (1400–03; 1410–13)

The crucial last line of this passage shows that Blanscheflur is consciously experiencing her own fate as *demonstratio*, as an *exemplum*, illustrating the way in which passion lures and deceives with false and unstable sweetness. This lament, *clagemære*, as Gottfried calls it, has no exact equivalent in the *saga*. It reads – is designed to read – like the lament of a Phyllis (cited in *Tristan*, Villise von Traze, 17189, cf. *Heroides*, II.27: 'Dic mihi, quid feci, nisi non sapienter amavi?'),[11] or of a Dido (*Tristan*, 17196, cf.13346f; *Heroides*, VII) with whom Blanscheflur shares the plight (VII.133) of expecting the child of the lover she now regards as faithless. Recalling her surrender to Aeneas in the cave, Dido too sees herself as having been deceived: 'I had heard a voice; I thought it was a cry of the nymphs – [it was] the Eumenides sounding the signal for my doom!' (*Heroides*, VII.95–

---

10 *Etymologiae*, edited by W. M. Lindsay (Oxford 1911; reprint 1966), VIII.11.80. See R. A. Wisbey, 'The *Renovatio Amoris* in Gottfried's *Tristan*', in *London German Studies*, 1, edited by C. V. Bock, Publications of the Institute of Germanic Studies, 26 (London, 1980), pp. 1–66 (p. 15 and note 73).

11 Ovid, I, *Heroides* and *Amores*, edited with a translation by G. Showerman, second edition revised by G. P. Goold, The Loeb Classical Library (Cambridge, Mass. and London, 1977). On *Heroides*, II.27, see P. Ganz, 'Tristan, Isolde und Ovid. Zu Gottfrieds *Tristan* Z. 17182ff', in *Mediævalia litteraria*. Festschrift for H. de Boor, edited by Ursula Hennig and H. Kolb (Munich, 1971), pp. 397–412 (p. 399 and note 5).

96 ... nymphas ululasse putavi – /Eumenides fati signa dedere mei!). At this moment Blanscheflur's understanding of her own predicament seems to confirm the misogynous comment in the *saga*, doubtless originating from Thomas, about the general infatuation of the women and girls with Riwalin (Kanelangres), who excelled all others in knighthood, and about the dangers of *amor furiosus* (Kölbing, p.8, 10–18; Schach, p.7):

> All of them desired his love, even though they had never seen him before and did not even know from what country or family he came or what his name was. Yet they inclined their hearts and minds towards him, for that is the way of women. They prefer the fulfilment of their desires rather than moderation, and often desire what they cannot obtain while they reject and neglect that which is theirs to have and to hold. Thus it was with Dido, who was so ardently in love that she burned herself to death when her dearest, who had come from a distant land, deserted her.
>
> Thus, misfortune has befallen many who willingly abandoned themselves to such great sorrow.

In reality, of course, Gottfried's Riwalin is no Aeneas. Blanscheflur has misinterpreted her situation; she has fallen victim to the plausible, but here misleading parallels suggested to her by the voices of the past. Her error becomes apparent in the very first line after she has assumed herself to have been deserted, when her 'trutgeselle Riwalin' enters 'mit weinendem herzen' (1418–20). As soon as he understands Blanscheflur's situation, his response leaves nothing to be desired:

> leit unde liep, übel unde guot,
> und allez daz, daz iu geschiht,
> da von enscheide ich mich niht. (1524–26)

Of the three causes of suffering (*leit*), which Blanscheflur regards as *tœdic* and *unwendic* (1465), two can be resolved by Riwalin's *triuwe* towards her. The ruin precipitated by *amor stultus* can be averted by *leal amur* (1362). Blanscheflur, unbeknown to herself, *is* to become an *exemplum*, but as a tragic variant of the Penelope figure. Her unwavering loyalty to her husband finds expression in her early death, which, like that of Riwalin, has long been forecast (1338; 311ff).

Such stories (*senemære*) 'von den, die wilent waren / vor manegen hundert jaren' (12323–24; 'of those who lived once upon a time, many hundreds of years ago')[12] move Gottfried's audience or readers in part through the (in the last instance) unflinching commitment of the lovers to

---

[12] This rendering is from the English translation by A. T. Hatto (Harmondsworth, 1960; reprinted 1976), p. 203. Where, occasionally elsewhere, changes have been intro-

mutual loyalty (*triuwe*) and steadfast constancy (*stæte*). This should suffice to give Riwalin and Blanscheflur a similar status to that accorded primarily to Tristan and Isolt as *exempla* justifying commemoration:

> von den diz senemære seit,
> und hæten die durch liebe leit,
> durch herzewunne senedez clagen
> in einem herzen niht getragen,
> son wære ir name und ir geschiht
> so manegem edelen herzen niht
> ze sælden noch ze liebe komen.   (211–17)

It is important to recall, however, that the word *exemplary*, like Fortuna herself, is of ambiguous aspect. In considering Blanscheflur's piteous end, Gottfried guides the audience in drawing the necessary conclusions from her fate:

> ir jamer unde ir ungemach
> beclage ein ieclich sælec man;
> und swer von wibe ie muot gewan
> oder iemer wil gewinnen,
> der trahte in sinen sinnen,
> wie lihte misselinge
> an sus getanem dinge
> guoten liuten uf erstat . . .   (1774–81)

In the final words of this passage, the message inherent in the *exemplum* constituted by the events the audience has just witnessed, is expressed in the form of a *sententia*. By means of the *sententia*, conversely, the events are validated as an *exemplum*. Clearly, 'exemplary', in this context, does not imply that these lovers, despite their mutual love and tragic death, are an absolute model, intended for imitation in every respect. A twelfth-century *accessus*, introducing the reader to Ovid's *Heroides*, speaks of the 'misfortunes which proceed from foolish (i.e. passionate) and illicit love'.[13] Here Gottfried shares common ground with Ovid, although a detailed comparison would show how far Blanscheflur's death outdoes that of Dido, quite apart from its intended prefiguration of Isolde's eventual end.[14]

---

duced into Hatto's text in order to bring out specific formulations in the original, this is indicated by the use of square brackets.

13 See Wisbey, '*Renovatio Amoris*', pp. 11–12 and note 58: 'visis . . . infortuniis vel incommoditatibus quae ex illicito et stulto amore proveniunt . . .'.

14 *Inter alia* see F. P. Knapp, *Der Selbstmord in der abendländischen Epik des Hochmittelalters* (Heidelberg, 1979), p. 247. Isolde's death was to have provided the climax of Gottfried's work: 'Eine Vorahnung vermittelt Blanscheflurs Tod'.

Nevertheless, the abiding impression of the tale of Tristan's parents is that of a love dogged by misfortune (*misselinge*), the *misfall* of the *saga*, the *infortunium* of the heroines of Ovid.

Similar terms are encountered everywhere in tales of passionate excess. The well-known prologue to *Romeo and Juliet* anticipates the action of the play, which rests upon the *furor* of both parents and children alike:[15]

> From forth the fatal loins of these two foes
> A pair of star-cross'd lovers take their life;
> Whose misadventur'd piteous overthrows
> Doth with their death bury their parents' strife.
> The fearful passage of their death-mark'd love,
> And the continuance of their parents' rage,
> Which, but their children's end, nought could
>   remove,
> Is now the two hours' traffic of our stage. . .

The words of this prologue could supply most elements needed for an acceptable summary of Ovid's tale of Pyramus and Thisbe (*Metamorphoses*, IV.55–166),[16] that underlies both the *leich* with which Tristan had diverted King Marke and the unintentionally humorous 'play within a play' in *A Midsummer Night's Dream*. This play entertains Theseus, ruler of Athens, his consort Hippolyta, and their guests, following the multiple nuptials, but it also constitutes a reminder to all present, and to the audience, of the folly, blindess and mortal dangers provoked by the irrationality of love, as exemplified not least by the preceding action. This irrationality at one point prompts even the less than well-educated weaver Bottom – *alias* Pyramus – to a prosaic *sententia*: 'to say the truth, reason and love keep little company together now-a-days' (III.1.131–32).[17]

---

15 The Shakespeare edition used is that by P. Alexander, *The Complete Works* (London and Glasgow, 1951; reprint). See also the edition of *A Midsummer Night's Dream* (with Introduction) by S. Wells, New Penguin Shakespeare, 2 (Harmondsworth, 1967).

16 Ovid, III, *Metamorphoses*, translated by F. J. Miller, third edition, revised by G. P. Goold, The Loeb Classical Library (Cambridge, Mass. and London, 1977), I, pp. 182–90.

17 Puck's magic, worked in the dark confusion of the thicket, has left Bottom metamorphosed. His head is, in appearance, temporarily that of an ass. Oberon's 'love potion' causes Titania (a name itself probably derived from the *Metamorphoses*, cf. S. Wells, above, p. 15) nevertheless to fall in love with Bottom, against all reason ('madly dote', II.1.171). The episode illustrates the traditional view of love as folly, see the quotation from Isidor above. The same point is made, derivatively, by Helena earlier in the play:
> Love looks not with the eyes, but with the mind;
> And therefore is wing'd Cupid painted blind.
> Nor hath Love's mind of any judgment taste;
> Wings and no eyes figure unheedy haste;
> And therefore is Love said to be a child,
> Because in choice he is so oft beguil'd. (I.1. 234–39).

The harmonious conclusion of this comedy sees all three pairs of lovers joined in wedlock, rather than united in death like Pyramus and Thisbe. The wayward supernatural beings who but recently have wreaked such havoc in nature, now themselves participate in the general concord. The Pyramus 'entertainment' here takes the place of an *epithalamium*, the farcical misadventure of its ending transcended in a blessing on the legitimate marriage bed:

> And the issue there create
> Ever shall be fortunate.
> So shall all the couples three
> Ever true in loving be;
> And the blots of Nature's hand
> Shall not in their issue stand. . .   (V.1.394–99)

That *Romeo and Juliet*, the Pyramus story itself – and *Tristan* – do not end on such a note is not merely a question of genre. To some extent, chance, as well as the temperament and circumstances of the protagonists, determines whether the outcome in a particular instance will be tragic. The potential for tragedy is abundantly present even in *A Midsummer Night's Dream* and, apart from the intervention of supernatural agencies which eventually prove benevolent, the positive ending owes much to the self-mastery of wise Theseus. In *Romeo and Juliet* the Prince recognizes the perils of *disordinatio*, but, after intervening decisively at the start, has little control over subsequent events. His banishment of Romeo brings about the tragic dénouement, with which, finally, he can only confront the warring families.[18] King Marke in Gottfried's *Tristan* becomes a weak king, ruled by his own passions. Thus reduced to ineffectuality, he is incapable of directing others. Pyramus and Thisbe lack all mature guidance, since – as in *Romeo and Juliet*, where the wiser counsels of Friar Lawrence, like those of Brangaene in *Tristan*, are rejected – the parents offer nothing but prohibitions. In all these works – and, in many of its scenes, *A Midsummer Night's Dream* is no exception – passion overwhelms the reason, ruling out moderation and, with it, discrimination between positive and negative models, concentrating the gaze of the lovers wholly upon the present moment to the exclusion of cautionary perspectives gained from wisdom and experience, shutting out the warning voices of the past. This community of message explains Goethe's assertion that 'Romeo und Julie ist

18   Where be these enemies? Capulet, Montague,
See what a scourge is laid upon your hate,
That heaven finds means to kill your joys with love!
(V.3. 290–92).

eben das Sujet von Pyramus und Thisbe', quite apart from the question of actual influence of the latter upon the former.[19]

The Tristan story undergoes the same influence. It has been pointed out that Ovid's tragic tale prefigures the eventual union in death of Gottfried's lovers.[20] It also contains important elements of the situation of Tristan and Isolt in life:[21] their mutual, passionate and forbidden love (*Metamorphoses*, IV.62: 'ex aequo captis ardebant mentibus ambo'; IV.61:'vetuere patres'), their need to circumvent *huote* (IV.85: 'fallere custodes') in order to meet by night, and to communicate their loving words (IV.70: *blanditiae*) in secret by whispers and meaningful signs (IV.63: 'nutu signisque loquuntur'), as well as the fact that concealment only strengthened the fire of their love (IV.64: 'quoque magis tegitur, tectus magis aestuat ignis'). This latter passage is particularly reminiscent of the scene in which close surveillance drives Tristan and Isot to seek the disastrous meeting which leads to their final separation:

> al zehant do daz geschach,
> daz in ir wunne und ir gemach
> so mit der huote vor bespart
> so mit verbote benomen wart,
> do was in ande und ange:
> der gespenstige gelange
> der tet in allererste we,
> we unde maneges wirs dan e.   (17833–40)

This episode shows Gottfried's lovers acting out an Ovidian mode, like that exemplified by Pyramus and Thisbe. Driven by their passion to behave in a way which is destructive of their best interests, they fall away from the highest achievement of their own past, namely the harmony and balance of their union in the grotto. Throwing caution to the winds in the midst of society, they now incur the penalty of extreme *herzeleit* (16439), in the form of parting and eventual death. In terms of their life together, and

---

[19] See F. Schmitt-von Mühlenfels, '*Pyramus und Thisbe*'. *Rezeptionstypen eines Ovidischen Stoffes in Literatur, Kunst und Musik*, Studien zum Fortwirken der Antike, 6 (Heidelberg, 1972), p. 141 and note 66. See also chapter 3,1: 'Der Triumph der dämonisierten Liebe', pp. 66–84.

[20] See R. Krohn, Gottfried von Strassburg, *Tristan*, vol.III, *Kommentar* (Stuttgart, 1980), p. 50 and Okken, *Kommentar*, I, p. 199. The latter's note 529 refers to Ganz, 'Tristan, Isolde und Ovid', p. 405 and note 30. Ganz cites in this context Nicola Zingarelli, 'Tristano e Isotta', in *Scritti di varia letteratura* (Milan, 1935), pp. 117–18. Cf. also Knapp, *Der Selbstmord*, p. 257: behind the 'Schmerzestod' of Isolde '[bleibt] gleichwohl das Schlußtableau der antiken Erzählung von Pyramus und Thisbe erkennbar'.

[21] Okken, *Kommentar*, II, p. 26, note 529, refers in this context to the parallels cited by Marcella Delpino, 'Elementi celtici ed elementi classici nel *Tristan* di Thomas', *Archivum Romanicum*, 23 (1939), 312–336 (pp. 330–31).

268 GOTTFRIED VON STRASSBURG AND THE MEDIEVAL TRISTAN LEGEND

of Gottfried's relationship to Ovid, this scene is in counterpoint to that later episode in which Tristan presents one of the saddest spectacles in the whole work. Following the enforced parting from Isot, he is obliged, although initially against his will, to descend into living in accordance with the precepts of Ovid in the *Remedia Amoris*,[22] travelling in foreign lands and seeking martial exploits (*Rem.*, 153–54) as 'trost ze siner triure' (18417):

> nu gedahter, solte im disiu not
> iemer uf der erden
> so tragebære werden,
> daz er ir möhte genesen,
> daz müese an ritterschefte wesen. (18438–42)

In Tristan's encounter with Isolde Weißhand his resort to the Ovidian remedies becomes more blatant. Moreover, it is undertaken exactly in the spirit of Ovid, namely in order to assuage the sufferings of love, and to seek relief from them, a doctrine which Gottfried had flatly contradicted in his prologue, since this suffering is the fire in which the sensibilities of true lovers are refined into an acceptance of love's polarities:

> diz leit ist liebes alse vol,
> daz übel daz tuot so herzewol,
> daz es kein edele herze enbirt,
> sit ez hie von geherzet wirt. (115–18)

Ovid is concerned to prevent desperate lovers making an end to their unhappy lives, as many of the characters in his stories do: 'He who, unless he give o'er, will die of hapless love, – let him give o'er' (*Rem.*, 21: 'Qui, nisi desierit, misero periturus amore est, / Desinat . . .'). He counsels the willing acceptance of pain, but in the form of remedies by which to regain health, i.e. freedom from obsessive love (226 '. . . ut valeas, multa dolenda feres'). Gottfried echoes the 'siquis amat' of Ovid (13), but the message is radically changed into an affirmation of suffering:

> swer innecliche liebe hat,
> doch ez im we von herzen tuo,
> daz herze stet doch ie dar zuo. (108–10)

---

[22] Ovid, II, *The Art of Love, and Other Poems*, with an English translation by J. H. Mozley, The Loeb Classical Library (London and Cambridge, Mass., 1969). Okken, *Kommentar*, I, pp. 649ff, quotes relevant passages from the *Remedia*, with reference (p. 652 and note) to G. Meissburger (1954), p. 15.

Far from achieving this in his separation from Isot, Tristan accepts the Ovidian model, seeking, in a denial of his name and identity (2003ff), to become 'ein triureloser Tristan' (19464). Ovid warns that 'until you un-learn your love, you must craftily deceive yourself' (*Rem.*, 211f: 'donec dediscis amare, / Ipse tibi furtim decipiendus eris'). If we leave out the notion of conscious craft, this is almost a summary of events at Arundel. Ovid warns in the same passage: 'you will weep, and the name of your deserted mistress will haunt your mind' (*Rem.*, 215: 'Flebis, et occurret desertae nomen amicae'). Preoccupation with the name Isolt is, of course, a key motif in the episode of Isolde Weißhand, e.g. 19000ff. In dwelling on imagined offences of Isot (19484ff), Tristan is once more following Ovid's recommended practice:'It helped me to harp continually on my mistress' faults' (*Rem.*, 315: 'Profuit adsidue vitiis insistere amicae'). Above all, as is well known, Tristan, towards the end of Gottfried's fragment, actually paraphrases that passage of Ovid's *Remedia* (441ff) in which he advocates pursuing two loves, or even more, at one time: 'Alterius vires subtrahit alter amor' (444: 'one passion saps the other's force. Great rivers are diminished by much channelling . . .'):

> sol mir daz uf der erden
> iemer gesenftet werden,
> daz muoz mit vremedem liebe wesen.
> ich han doch dicke daz gelesen
> und weiz wol, daz ein trutschaft
> benimet der andern ir craft. (19429–34)

With this specific appeal to the authority of the past,[23] Tristan is clearly seeking 'unmuoze . . .,/ diu reiner liebe missezeme' (95–96) and abandon-ing the elevation of Gottfried's conception of love. One may seek mitiga-tion only in the thought that, if Gottfried had followed Thomas in the sequel, he would have shown how love for the first Isolt renders the consummation of Tristan's unworthy intention impossible, and that on his deathbed it is his first love which totally dominates Tristan's mind. In this way, Tristan, as in Thomas, would perhaps have proved, from Ovid's

---

[23] Here too, Okken, *Kommentar*, I, pp. 669–72 supplies the matching passages from the *Remedia*, basing himself on Meissburger, p. 7, Hoffa (1910), pp. 345–46 and G. -D. Peschel, *Prolog-Programm und Fragment-Schluß in Gotfrits Tristanroman*, Erlanger Stu-dien, 9 (Erlangen, 1976), pp. 191–95. One may agree with Hoffa (who gives priority to Heinzel) that the specific allusion to Ovid here is lacking in Thomas, but Fragment Sneyd begins just after this point in Gottfried's text, while the formulation in the *saga* does not allow final certainty about Thomas, see Schach, p. 107: '[Tristram] could come to no other decision than that he wished to try to find some pleasure to counter the love which he had so long endured with grief and anxiety and sorrow and distress. For he desired to discover if new love and delight might enable him to forget Ísönd. . .'.

point of view, one of those hopeless cases who, having been nearly cured, relapsed into love (*Rem.*, 611: 'Reccidit'); in Gottfried's terms he would have regained both the name of true lover and his own identity, confirming and yet overcoming Ovid once more in the bitterness of his death, which was to be greater than that of any before or after him, an end:

> daz alles todes übergenoz
> und aller triure ein galle was.   (2016–17)

The prologue is thus only one of the several passages in the work where Gottfried confronts the Ovidian position, subsumes it, polemicizes against it, and in the last instance rises above it. This creative tension can be seen at work if we concentrate briefly on differences rather than parallels between the story of Tristan and Isot and that of Pyramus and Thisbe. The love between the latter two figures is mutual and their commitment to each other is absolute. However, their relationship is never to be consummated. They escape from constraining surveillance to a tryst under a tree, close to a cool spring, but this spring is located by a tomb, it is sought out in darkness, and the lovers are united there only in suicide. The scene includes a cavern, but Thisbe alone enters it, fleeing from the lion in fear of her life. Tristan's masterly harping and singing of the relevant *leich* may foreshadow the intended death of Gottfried's lovers, but, in retrospect, it suggests above all the many ways in which his Cave of Lovers scene overcomes not only the shared experience of Pyramus and Thisbe, but of the deserted or unrequited Ovidian heroines of antiquity who are commemorated there.[24]

Even in this place of their greatest happiness, Tristan and Isot, for once left to choose freely for themselves appropriate forms of activity, elect to live in the presence of the past (see p. 260 above). Outside the Cave of Lovers they tell the stories of the Ovidian exemplars, mourning and lamenting their 'misadventur'd piteous overthrows':

> si beredeten unde besageten,
> si betrureten unde beclageten,
> daz Villise von Traze,

---

[24] F. Ohly, 'Bemerkungen eines Philologen zur Memoria', in *Memoria. Der geschichtliche Zeugniswert des liturgischen Gedenkens im Mittelalter*, edited by K. Schmid and J. Wollasch, Münstersche Mittelalter-Schriften, 48 (Munich, 1984), pp. 9–68, devotes a passage (pp. 49–52) to Gottfried's acceptance in the prologue of *Tristan* of 'das Amt des Dichters, ein Gedächtnis zu verwalten oder neu zu stiften'. As Ohly himself puts it: 'Soll die Menschheit nicht wie Sisyphos das von ihren Großen einmal Empfangene als Vergebliches immer neu verlieren, ... bedarf sie des Gedächtnisses zur Bewahrung des ihr in der Zeit je zugefallenen Gewinns an Möglichkeit des Menschseins oder Selbst- und Weltverstehen'.

> daz der armen Canaze
> in der minnen namen geschach;
> daz Biblise ir herze brach
> durch ir bruoder minne;
> daz ez der küniginne
> von Tire und von Sidone,
> der seneden Didone
> durch sene so jæmerliche ergie.
> mit solhen mæren warens ie
> unmüezic eteswenne.   (17187–199)

The women Gottfried names, with one arguable exception, died, like Pyramus and Thisbe and Romeo and Juliet, by their own hands.[25] Unlike Thisbe, Juliet and Isolt, they represent women abandoned by their lovers, victims of incestuous love, or love not reciprocated. What they all have in common is the demonstration of the excesses to which women have been driven by the *amoris intemperantia* – to which in the ancient and widespread medieval view the fairer sex is more prone by nature – after male indifference or heartlessness has reduced them to despair. One will hardly be tempted to assume that these examples, two of which involve the death of a love-child as well as of its mother, are laid before us here for straightforward *imitatio*. Nor is it appropriate to speak of the morbid fondness of (Gottfried's) two lovers for sad stories of doom-laden, mortal passion, prefiguring their own fate.[26] Tristan and Isolde's feeling of solidarity with and pity for these Ovidian heroines is to be explained by an acute awareness that they share their hazardous mode of life with those lovers in the past to whom an excess of passion brought ruin, those 'die vor ir jaren / von sene verdorben waren', 17185–86. It is, after all, to such stories that they owe their emotional apprenticeship. Even in the ambience of the Cave of Lovers, in fact, Tristan and Isot do not forget the lesson of the classical *exempla*, that love as *furor* (frenzy) and *misselinge* (misadventure, disaster), illicit love and ruin, are twin sisters.

As scholarship has long since recognised, however, Gottfried has given events in the Cave of Lovers episode a pronounced typological dimension.[27] In other words, the union of Tristan and Isot, lived out within the

---

25 Byblis wept herself to death in a frenzy of grief, *Metamorphoses*, IX.655ff. Knapp, *Der Selbstmord*, p. 258, shows that she too could be seen as having killed herself.
26 Krohn, III (*Kommentar*), p. 169, with reference to U. Ernst, 'Gottfried von Straßburg in komparatistischer Sicht. Form und Funktion der Allegorese im Tristanepos', *Euphorion*, 70 (1976), pp. 48–50.
27 For the notion that components of the 'romans d'antiquité' can stand to the courtly romance like Old Testament to New Testament, i.e. in the relationship of prefigurative type to superior, fulfilling antitype, see J. Schwietering, 'Typologisches in mittelalterlicher Dichtung', first published 1925, reprinted in J. S. , *Philologische Schriften*, edited by

272 GOTTFRIED VON STRASSBURG AND THE MEDIEVAL TRISTAN LEGEND

seclusion of the grotto under circumstances of quasi-legitimacy after their banishment from Marke's court, manifests something approaching the full potential of human love, an achievement which Gottfried sees as only partially foreshadowed by the lovers of antiquity. His deliberate intention of transcending the ill-starred victims of passion in the canon of Ovid is signalled not least by the fact that their stories are retold and their fates lamented *outside* the Cave. When the moment comes to forget these tales of the past, Tristan and Isot move into the interior of the grotto for their own distinctive fulfilment (17200ff).[28] There, the physical is granted its due, then (*danne*, 17205) the lovers cause their music-making to fill the

F. Ohly and M. Wehrli (Munich, 1969), pp. 269–81. The concept of extrabiblical typology was developed and applied by Ohly in *Sage und Legende in der Kaiserchronik. Untersuchungen über Quellen und Aufbau der Dichtung*, Forschungen zur deutschen Sprache und Dichtung, 10 (Münster, 1940; reprinted Darmstadt, 1968). See also Ohly's collected *Schriften zur mittelalterlichen Bedeutungsforschung* (Darmstadt, 1977), pp. 312–400, and his essay 'Typologische Figuren aus Natur und Mythus', in *Formen und Funktionen der Allegorie. Symposion Wolfenbüttel 1978*, edited by W. Haug (Stuttgart, 1979), pp. 126–66, with a critique of previous research (note 1, p. 144).

Apart from J. Schwietering, e.g. 'Gottfrieds *Tristan*', *Philologische Schriften*, pp. 426–437 (English version in *Germanic Review*, 29 (1954), 5–17) and F. Ohly, *ADA*, 68 (1955/56), 123 and see note 28 below, those who at an early stage adopted a typological approach to aspects of Gottfried's *Tristan* included H. G. Nauen, 'Die Bedeutung von Religion und Theologie im *Tristan* Gottfrieds von Straßburg' (inaugural dissertation, University of Marburg, 1947), p. 58; G. Weber, *Gottfrieds von Straßburg 'Tristan' und die Krise des hochmittelalterlichen Weltbildes um 1200*, 2 vols (Stuttgart, 1953), I, pp. 292–93 and II, pp. 88–89; P. W. Tax, *Wort, Sinnbild, Zahl im Tristanroman. Studien zum Denken und Werten Gottfrieds von Straßburg*, Philologische Studien und Quellen, 8 (Berlin, 1961), pp. 122–125 (Cave of Lovers). Ingrid Hahn in her review of the latter, *ADA*, 75 (1964), 171–78 recognizes the historical perspective provided by the heroines of antiquity, but describes them, with Isolde and Tristan, as 'Heilige der Göttin Minne' (p. 173). Although Hahn questions the presence of typology here (unlike in her *Raum und Landschaft in Gottfrieds 'Tristan'*, Medium Aevum, 3 (Munich, 1963), p. 131), she accepts that antiquity and the Ovidian view of love are seen as only 'bei aller empfundenen Ahnherrenschaft Vorform, Präfiguration', a prefiguration to be fulfilled by Tristan and Isolde. The lovers embody 'das neue Evangelium der Minne', which the audience is intended to perpetuate. For the present writer's differing view on this point, see below. That Gottfried's intentions *are* typological is now widely accepted, cf. for instance J. Rathofer, 'Der "wunderbare Hirsch" der Minnegrotte', *ZDA*, 95 (1966), 27–42 (reprinted in A. Wolf, *Gottfried von Straßburg* (Darmstadt, 1973), here pp. 372–75); H. Kolb, *Der ware Elicon*, *DVLG*, 41 (1967), 1–26; A. Wolf, '*diu wâre wirtinne – der wâre Elicôn*. Zur Frage des typologischen Denkens in volkssprachlicher Dichtung des Hochmittelalters', *Amsterdamer Beiträge zur älteren Germanistik*, 6 (1974), 93–131; U. Ernst (1976; see note 26 above), pp.37–38; Wisbey, '*Renovatio Amoris*', especially pp. 37–39; T. Tomasek, *Die Utopie im 'Tristan' Gottfrieds von Straßburg*, Hermaea, 49 (Tübingen, 1985), p. 185; Franziska Wessel, *Probleme der Metaphorik* (1984), see above, p. 223, note 2.

[28] See Dörrie, *Der heroische Brief* (1968), p. 351 and his note 25. The observation is already in Tax, *Wort, Sinnbild, Zahl* (1961), p. 124, note 37, and incipiently, if without reference to the tragic heroines, in Hahn, *Raum und Landschaft* (1963), p. 131, note 107. But I owe the insight to an oral statement by F. Ohly, *c.* 1955, cf. his mention in *ADA*, 68

grotto with sweet harmony. The songs they sing are 'leiche unde noten der minne' (17211: 'songs and melodies of love'). Their content is not revealed to us, but the manner of their delivery, 'senelichen unde suoze' (17207, cf. 17217), is reminiscent of Tristan's earlier performance of the 'senelichen leich' of 'Tispe', to his own accompaniment with the harp (3614ff). Whatever the exact matter commemorated or invoked in the grotto, the distinctive feature of the narrative at this point is that, for the first time in the work, the beguiling sweetness of the lovers' singing and playing to the harp, previously offered to the court separately by one or the other of them (cf. 3584ff and 8064ff) now expresses the physical and spiritual attunement of the lovers to each other.[29] The intermingling and interlacing harmony of voice and accompaniment, the effortless, chiastic reversal of musical roles, mirroring the 'Tristan Isolt, Isolt Tristan' of the prologue (130), does not deny in its wistful yearning the precariousness of the human situation they share with lovers of the past, but rises above it in the celebration of their mutual love.

A cavern had been the scene of the union between Dido and Aeneas (*Aeneid*, IV.160–68) during a violent storm and, as we have seen, the refuge of Thisbe in her nocturnal flight from the savage lion. The ancient model of love as passion, with associations of suffering, tragedy and death, is borne out in both these cases. In the *Aeneid*, the narrator comments as follows on the consummation of the love between Dido and the exiled Aeneas: 'ille dies primus leti primusque malorum / causa fuit' (IV.169–70; 'That day was the first day of death, that first the cause of woe'). In Eilhart (and in Béroul) Tristrant and Isalde are outlaws in the wilderness and lead a life of hardship and deprivation there. Even in Thomas, the lovers suffer fluctuations of climate.[30] In Gottfried too, the lovers undergo banishment (see above), but their life in the richly allegorized cave and its paradisiacal environs, culminating in their supreme experience of a mutual and fulfilled love, characterized – in this episode – by felicity, harmony and concord, is unambiguously designed to surpass the predecessors of Tristan and Isot, just as Gottfried aims in his work to outdo his literary forerunners from Virgil and Ovid to Thomas.

Thus Gottfried's cave is said to have been 'hewn into the wild mountain in heathen times, before Corynaeus' day' (the name is drawn from *Aeneid*, IX.571 and XII.298 and taken up by Geoffrey of Monmouth), when 'giants ruled there' (Hatto, p. 261): 'daz selbe hol was wilent e / under der heidenischen e / vor Corineis jaren,/ do risen da herren waren,/ gehouwen

---

(1955/56), p. 123 (in Wolf, *G.v.Str.*, p. 188) of a study on the 'Minnegrotte' which he read to the 'Germanistenverband' Frankfurt at that time.

29 Krohn, III (*Kommentar*), p. 169.

30 *Tristrams saga*, Chapter 64; Kölbing, p. 79, 31–32; Schach, p. 101.

in den wilden berc' (16689–93). Gottfried enriches this artefact with meaning (*meine*) through his extensive moralization of its architectural features and of its surroundings (16923–17099). Here, techniques derived from scriptural exegesis are used to show how the literal, structural fabric of the grotto, that has survived intact from the pre-Christian era, can be transfigured by the recognition of a spiritual dimension which was always potentially present, but, hitherto, was at best only partially realized. In the same way, the purposes of carnal intimacy for which the giants had created the grotto ('heinliche ... han'; 'mit minnen umbe gan', 16695–96), dedicating it in effect to the sensual Venus, *Venus vulgaria/voluptaria*, are transcended there in the union between Tristan and Isot, in which the physical is uplifted into that spiritual concord associated with 'mundana musica' and the cosmic harmony.[31] Gottfried expresses this overcoming of the earlier history of the grotto in charged words like *bewæret* (17228), indicating typological fulfilment of the tales of old in the present:

> swaz aber von der fossiure
> von alter aventiure
> vor hin ie was bemæret,
> daz wart an in bewæret.   (17225–28)

Now, for the first time, the grotto is fully dedicated to the activities of *Venus legitima*, the true mistress ('diu ware wirtinne') of the Cave of Love. These surpass all that had occurred there in years gone by:

> diu ware wirtinne
> diu hæte sich dar inne
> alrerste an ir spil verlan:
> swaz e dar inne ie wart getan
> von kurzewile oder von spil,
> dazn lief niht ze disem zil ...   (17229–34)

(Only now had the cave's true mistress given herself to her sport in earnest. Whatever [love play] or pastimes had been pursued in this grotto before, they did not equal this . . .', Hatto, p. 267.)

These lines would provide an optimistic conclusion to this essay, if the work ended at this point. In reality, of course, the events of the Cave of Lovers scene take place in seclusion, remote from society, after Marke has sent the lovers away together (16603–04). This allows Gottfried to avert his gaze for a time from the illicit nature of their relationship, and from the consequences which flow from that inescapable fact. With the return of Tristan and Isot to court they re-enter the realm of the ill-fated *exempla*

---

[31]   Wisbey, *Renovatio Amoris*, pp. 38–39.

which their stay in the grotto had allowed them to overcome, if – and we may take this as a luminous comment on the human condition – only fleetingly, and in episodic fashion. Events now drive them swiftly towards parting, towards a resumption of the Ovidian mode in which passion (and its remedies) replaces fulfilment and harmony. Eventually, this course leads them – as was Gottfried's obvious intention (cf. 2013ff) – to the bitterness of that traditional death which makes of them a tragic *exemplum* in their own right (211ff).

Before the parting scene, however, where the action of his work begins to decline into the familiar pattern of misadventure and suffering, Gottfried reinforces the positive message of the grotto episode by a digression, in which he points to the possibility that a woman can overcome the *intemperantia* which is her legacy from the past, indeed from Eve herself. Such an achievement allows her to commit her life to reason and moderation, so that the rose flowers from the nettle-root of fallen nature ('der nezzelen ursprinc / der roset ob der erden', 17984–85).[32] *Misselinge* and *infortunium* have no access to the living paradise of union with a woman who has achieved this non-Ovidian metamorphosis. 'In such a paradise', Gottfried asserts, 'the man on whom Fortune smiles might find his heart's [felicity] and see his eyes' delight' (Hatto, p. 279):

> da möhte ein sæliger man
> sines herzen sælde vinden an
> und siner ougen wunne sehen. (18091–93)

Gottfried proceeds to relativize the validity of his two lovers as absolute models: 'In what would he be worse off than Tristan and Isolde? If only he would take my word for it, he would not need to exchange his life for Tristan's':

> waz wære ouch dem iht wirs geschehen
> dan Tristande und Isolde?
> der mirs gevolgen wolde,
> ern dörfte niht sin leben geben
> umb keines Tristandes leben ... (18094–98)

Such a woman will free her beloved from sufferings of the heart 'as no Isolde ever freed her Tristan better':

> so wol so nie dekein Isot
> dekeinen ir Tristanden baz. (18108–09)

---

[32] See Wisbey, ibid., pp. 41–42, and note 145; also the contribution by Janet Wharton in this volume, pp. 143–54.

Gottfried concludes the *excursus* with a terse *sententia*-like condensation of his views:

> und han ez ouch binamen vür daz:
> der suohte, alse er solde,
> ez lebeten noch Isolde,
> an den man ez gar vünde,
> daz man gesuochen künde.   (18110–14)

('And I firmly believe that, were one to seek as one ought, there would still be living Isoldes in whom one would find [completely] whatever one [might] seek', Hatto, p. 279)

In the word *gar* ('wholly', 'completely'), Gottfried has again planted a typological signal indicating how the past can be fulfilled in the present. In the Cave of Lovers episode, Tristan and Isot commemorated the suffering through love of the heroines of antiquity, then moved on to the high flights of their own experience inside the grotto. Here, at the distressing moment in his story when the lovers will bring disaster upon themselves through unbridled desire, Gottfried encourages the audience to go beyond Tristan and Isot and the tragic outcome of their *senemære*, to view them with admiration and compassion for their commitment to love, but to regard them ultimately as only a partial model. Gottfried points to the superior attractions of a love likewise committed to loyalty and constancy, while based on moderation and restraint. Tristan and Isot must be left behind as the audience moves to occupy a thornless inner paradise (or *claustrum*) of the heart, from which passionate excess and thus frenzied misadventure have been banished. In the last instance, Gottfried sees his masterpiece as a cautionary tale. Yet for him there is no conceivable alternative to living in the presence of the past, with its memorable greatness, its joy and its grief, since the only worthy gesture of solidarity with those 'die wilent waren / vor manegen hundert jaren' is to surpass them in the present:

> 'Sollen nicht endlich uns diese ältesten Schmerzen
> fruchtbarer werden?'[33]

---

[33] Rainer Maria Rilke, *Duineser Elegien*: Die Erste Elegie, *Sämtliche Werke*, edited by E. Zinn, vol.I (Wiesbaden, 1955), p. 687.

Index

Gottfried's *Tristan* is not included in the index since this work forms the central focus of the volume and all but one of the contributions refer to it. Similarly, the figures of the Tristan story are not indexed directly as an excessive number of references would result. However, figures which are the subject of individual analysis are listed under *character portrayal*. Medieval men and women are indexed under their Christian names. Considerations of space have prevented the inclusion of scholar names.

dwarfs xiii
    Germanic 211–13
    in classical antiquity 210–11
    in MHG literature 213–18
    in Tristan narratives 218–21

Eckermann, Johann Peter 104
Eckhart, Meister 257
Eddic Nibelungen tradition 156–60
    passim, 164
Edward I, king of England 43
Edward III, king of England 49n, 51n
Edward, the Black Prince 49n, 50
Eichendorff, Joseph von 93
Eilhart von Oberg, *Tristrant* 6n, 47,
    52, 54n, 57, 59n, 61, 68, 123, 136n,
    160, 161, 169, 209, 218–21, 227n,
    230n, 232, 261, 273
Eleanor of Aquitaine, queen of France
    and England 114
Eneas 33, 56n, 60, 78–79, 259, 261
Engelbert von Admont, *De regimine
    principum* 105
Englynion y Beddau 24
Enite 128, 206–07, 226n
ere see honour
Erec 58, 62, 213, 214, 226
ethics, classical 77–82
Etzel 156n, 160, 166
Eumenides 262, 263
Eve 11, 12n, 13, 14, 15, 139, 143–45,
    275
exempla 257, 259, 261–64, 271, 274–75
    see also Ci nous dit, proverbs, *senten-
    tiae*

Fall of Man 8, 13
    in secular and religious art 10–14,
    16
    in Gottfried's *Tristan* 14–15, 139,
    143–53
    see also Adam, Eve
Faust 102, 103
fidelity 247–56, 263–64
Finn 22
Fitzstephen, William, *Vita Sancti
    Thomae* 36–39
Fortuna 264
Frederick I, Barbarossa, emperor 50
Frederick II, emperor 68, 140
Freidank, *Bescheidenheit* 199

frescoes
    Iwein at Rodenegg Castle 5–6, Figs
    6–7
    Meliadus at St Floret (Auvergne) 9
    other references 12n, 13n, 15–16
Freud, Sigmund 125
Frollo 51, 58–59
Fulgentius, *Super Thebaiden* 85–86
furor see passion

Gawain (Gwalchmai) 24, 56n, 59, 62
*Gemeine Kämmerei-Rechnung der Stadt
    Braunschweig* 212
Geoffrey of Monmouth, *Historia Regum
    Britanniae* 26n, 51, 56, 58, 59, 62, 63,
    64, 273
George, Stefan, *Der Stern des Bundes*
    257
Geraint 25
Gervinus, Georg Gottfried 93n, 94,
    104
Gesta episcoporum Halberstadensium 34
giants, combat against 60–63
Ginover 226n
Giraldus Cambrensis, *De principis in-
    structione* 106
Glecidolân 214
God 60, 80, 186, 187, 189, 235
    courtesy of 190–94, 198, 199
Goethe, Johann Wolfgang von 266
    Faust xii, 95, 102–04
    Torquato Tasso 93
Goliath 60
Grainne 22
grammar (Trivium) 69–71, 84–85, 86–
    88
Gregory I, the Great, Pope 257
Gretchen 102, 103
Grigoras 214
Guivreiz le pitîz 214, 217, 220
Gunther (Gunnarr) 157–66 *passim*
Gunther, bishop of Bamberg 212

Hagen 160, 161
Harpîn and his dwarf 60n, 214, 215
Hartmann von Aue xii, 57, 74, 115
    Arme Heinrich, Der 127
    Erec 47, 58n, 62, 128, 139–40, 152n,
    206–07, 213–14, 220–21, 226–27
    Gregorius 224n
    Iwein 60n, 128, 214, 221
Hebbel, Friedrich 95